GunDigest® PRESENTS

AR-15

SETUP, MAINTENANCE AND REPAIR

BY PATRICK SWEENEY

Copyright © 2021 Caribou Media Group, LLC

All rights reserved. No portion of this publication may be reproduced or transmitted in any form or by any means, electronic or mechanical, including photocopy, recording, or any information storage and retrieval system, without permission in writing from the publisher, except by a reviewer who may quote brief passages in a critical article or review to be printed in a magazine or newspaper, or electronically transmitted on radio, television, or the Internet.

Published by

Gun Digest® Books, an imprint of Caribou Media Group, LLC
Gun Digest Media
5600 W. Grande Market Drive, Suite 100
Appleton, WI 54913
gundigest.com

To order books or other products call 920.471.4522 ext. 104
or visit us online at **gundigeststore.com**

DISCLAIMER: Any and all loading data found in this book or previous editions is to be taken as reference material only. The publishers, editors, authors, contributors, and their entities bear no responsibility for the use by others of the data included in this book or the editions that came before it.

WARNING: For any modern firearm, it is essential that you adhere to the loading recommendations put forth in the reloading manuals of today's components manufacturers, as well as to the owners manual of the maker of your individual firearm (some of today's firearms are so specialized that they will chamber and function reliably only within a very narrow set of criteria in a given caliber range). The potential for things to go wrong is exacerbated in guns long out of production, those chambering obsolete cartridges, and those using cartridges containing black powder or cordite. As a separate caution, you must never fire any cartridge in any gun just because it looks similar to, or has a similar designation to, the cartridge the gun is chambered for. This can be extremely dangerous. Almost is not good enough, so if you are at all uncertain about the proper cartridge, have a competent gunsmith check the bullet diameter and case dimensions and firearms chamber and headspace.

ISBN-13: 978-1-951115-47-0

By Patrick Sweeney
All photos by author except where noted.
Cover design by Gene Coo
Design by Jon Stein
Edited by Corey Graff

Printed in the United States of America

10 9 8 7 6 5 4 3 2 1

Introduction

As difficult as it may seem, there are many owners and shooters new to the AR-15 who are not planning on a campaign of building a dozen different ARs, each with a perfectly matched set of options, parts, features and goodies.

So, if you are simply looking for info on which AR-15 to buy, how to keep yours running, how to debug it if it acts cranky, or you need to set right some minor error that the factory or builder didn't tend to, this is the book for you. If you pay attention, your AR-15 will be reliable, accurate, properly sighted-in, and all the parts and accessories on it will stay tightly attached. Plus, for those who just have to have it, this will have detailed assembly instructions, with the assumption that you have somehow acquired a box 'o parts and want to turn them into a working AR-15.

Or you started with a vanilla-plain AR-15 and realize that you need, want or simply must have something better. You may want to swap out parts, or upgrade to better parts or replace worn ones. We'll also cover the "which is the higher quality part?" or why you might want A over B or X over Z type of questions.

In the modern world, it seems that asking, "And just how do you know that to be true?" is an impolite question. Ask a politician that question, and they'll hem and haw and evade answering until security hustles you outta there. Ask someone in non-elected authority, and you risk having the entire bureaucracy turned against you. In some instances, prudence demands you not ask. Which is a shame. But here, you can ask. In many cases, the answer is simple; because I tested it and learned from expending ammo.

Or I was standing next to the guy who figured it out when the lightbulb went on.

Also, from time to time, a slight amount of political leaning will creep into the book. The people who do not know much or misuse their knowledge are not limited to new owners. Some people don't like the AR, and not just because they think other rifles are better. So, to ensure you're up to speed on terms and their use in this subject, I'll tell you precisely where people from "the other side' are trying to misinform.

So, let's get to it.

Dedication

The old hands know the drill. To the new readers, this book is dedicated to Felicia and the present member of the poodle pack: Ajax. And to the future promise, and historical freedom, of America.

Table of Contents

Introduction 3
Dedication 4
Chapter 1 – AR-15 Basics 6
Chapter 2 – Tools, Essential and Extra ... 22
Chapter 3 – Testing the AR-15 42
Chapter 4 – Uppers 52
Chapter 5 – Barrels and Choices 78
Chapter 6 – Barrel Fitting 114
Chapter 7 – Barrel Cleaning 130
Chapter 8 – Bolts and Carriers 136
Chapter 9 – Front Sights and Gas Blocks ... 174
Chapter 10 – Sights 182
Chapter 11 – Lowers 198
Chapter 12 – Stocks, Springs and Buffers ... 224
Chapter 13 – Triggers 240
Chapter 14 – AR-15 or M16? 252
Chapter 15 – Finishes 260
Chapter 16 – Torque and Tech Data 270
Chapter 17 – Magazines 278
Chapter 18 – Handguards 288
Chapter 19 – Pistols, Braces and SBRs ... 300
Chapter 20 – Ammunition and Muzzle Devices ... 310
Chapter 21 – Build Sequence 316

■ The military sees the rifle or carbine as a tool among many tools. This Marine has an M4, but added to it are an M203 grenade launcher, a Trijicon ACOG, an infra-red laser targeting and illuminating module, a sight for the M203 and backup iron sights. Everything but a cup holder and a kitchen sink.

1

AR-15 Basics

"**The world** is changed. I feel it in the water. I feel it in the earth." So said Galadriel in *The Lord of The Rings*. The firearms world has changed and has been changing. When I started this journey, the firearms world was still one of walnut and blued steel. Old hands almost spat on the ground when you muttered the word "plastic." Now, a highly-polished blued-steel firearm is seen as quaint or collectible, to be stored away while it increases in value.

The gun universe is now one of Melonite and Tenifer. Black oxide and Parkerizing. Various polymers, nylon, plastic and carbon fiber, are reinforced with fiberglass or molded-in structures like rebar in concrete. All overcoated with Cerakote, "rattle-can camo" paint jobs, and in some instances stickered like a NASCAR vehicle or driver's jacket.

At one time, shooters laminated trajectory cards, taped notes on the inside of gun cases or used felt-tip pens to make cryptic notes on a sling. Ballistic data is available from various apps, smartphones, and even chips built into the optics themselves.

The job used to be to blaze a path, learn new things, discover the unknown. Now, it seems like the job is just keeping up.

The world is full of new shooters, new gun owners. The most recent gun-buying surge (one might even call it a frenzy, impulse or panic) has seen millions of first-time gun owners entering the fold. And a lot of previous shooters who hadn't owned an AR-15 bought one.

So, now what?

You learn. You learn parts, methods, skills, history. You learn the background, you learn technical details, you learn that the world, while new and ever-changing, can be a fun, profitable and enjoyable place. You learn security. What you will learn here is how to set up, maintain and repair your AR-15. There are plenty of places — websites, books, magazine articles — where you can learn the AR-15's history and the progress that got us to where we are now. In fact, I have written a lot of them. But here, we are going to focus on the nuts and bolts (not figuratively, the AR-15 doesn't have

A pair of retro AR-15s. Top, a clone of a late-model M16A1, with fixed sight but black anodizing. Bottom, an early XM-177, with medium-gray anodizing, and the shortie "moderator," which did more to make the gun run than it did to quiet it down.

any nuts or bolts, at least not the basic design) of making it work, making it the way you want it to be and fixing it if something goes wrong.

In places where I must clarify why we are doing things, or to ensure you are fully informed when deciding on parts or setup, I will give you a brief background or history. I will (because I can't help myself) also be giving you my viewpoint on things. Fair warning: my perspective comes from decades of experience with the AR-15 and related firearms. It won't be a rehashed point of view found in an online forum or website someplace. It came from having worked on and used the AR-15. A lot.

A little bit of a roadmap now: The AR-15 is an inter-related set of systems. It is difficult to thoroughly discuss one part of it (the barrel would be one example) without also discussing how it is attached, how it works and what makes it work or not work. So, the barrel is pressed into the upper and held on using a big nut called the barrel nut. The barrel has a bolt that locks into the rear of the chamber (yes, I know I just said there aren't any nuts and bolts on the AR-15; again, this isn't your typical nut and bolt, as we'll see later in more detail). The barrel has a gas system of one kind or another that works the action when you shoot. The barrel gets hot, so there must be a handguard, something to keep your hands off the hot steel. So, this one part, we find, has four related systems that you should keep in mind when working on or with barrels. And we haven't even touched on flash hiders or suppressors yet.

Each of those systems relates to other systems. As a result, you will find that the various chapters will have some overlap, just because we can't avoid

it. I will keep them as separate as I can, but they will overlap. Also, there is the matter of assembly. Some readers want a straightforward "Build an AR-15 from a box of parts" laundry list. That method works fine if you are building from parts kits. But it isn't useful if you have an assembled AR-15, one that happens to have a problem. A Step A, Step B assembly workflow doesn't help you diagnose a problem. It also doesn't help much if you want to upgrade or change things. So, first, I go over each step, and at the end, I give you the rundown of the assembly sequence, so you can build from a box o'parts if you wish.

There's also a question that many new AR-15 owners ask themselves: did I buy the right one? If you visit online forums or go to the local gun club and practice, you will find that there will be AR-15 snobs. Unless you happen to luck into buying something they consider "appropriate" or "good enough," you will be treated to disappointed looks, even condescension, over your purchase. "Hobby guns" is one descriptor you might encounter. The thing is, the supposed "experts" can't even agree amongst themselves which AR-15 makers are good enough and which aren't. I am reminded of the old joke: Ask ten economists for their opinion on a given matter, and you get: ten, no, wait, eleven, answers. Ask ten AR-15 self-proclaimed experts on a list of "Tier One" manufacturers, and the lists will be all over the map. They might mostly agree on four or five names. Then they would argue over the next five and make a list of twelve "Top makers" and

On top is a custom build, a clone of the Mk 12 Mod 0. Bottom, an M4gery that has been built to be a quad-rail carbine, ca. 2005 in service.

another half-dozen "four out of ten mavens agree" makers who might make the list.

The thing is, the AR-15 can be what you want it to be. This is America, you get to choose, and you get to upgrade, or not, as you see fit.

And in the end, practice matters more than the brand name. Let's say your local mavens can agree that "Brand X" is the best. I'll bet that it also is one of the most expensive. So, you've just spent your gun budget on the rifle and have no money left over for magazines, ammunition, optics or other essentials. In the long run, you would be better off spending a thousand dollars less (and that is easily done) on a rifle "Not Brand X" and putting the rest of the money into ammo, magazines and practice. You

> **Know and Follow the Firearm Safety Rules!**
> 1. Treat every gun as if it is loaded.
> 2. Always point the gun in a safe direction.
> 3. Always keep your finger off the trigger until ready to shoot.
> 4. Be sure of your target and what's beyond.

can make the Not Brand X rifle half a step behind the Brand X rifle, and you get to do the work yourself. There's pride in that. Plus, having done the work, you are more familiar with your rifle, and there's security in that.

Now, no amount of work is going to make a poor barrel perform like a top-notch one, but here's your first bit of historical background: previous rifle-buying periods have driven the poor barrel makers out of business. *If you are a new shooter, even if you are a reasonably good one, even the cheapest barrel is more accurate than you are.*

There is another historical and technical term that you must know right from the beginning: *mil-spec*. As in military specifications. As with zealots

CHAPTER 1 – AR-15 BASICS **11**

who insist on "the best" or nothing, some people worship at the altar of mil-spec. What is mil-spec? That's simple: it's a detailed list of the materials, processes and dimensions that a given product must conform to. There is, however, a saying in the military that is probably more universal than it wishes to admit: "The minimum becomes the maximum." Mil-spec is as good as it needs to be, and no more. The reason for this is two-fold. One is, the spec is fixed. The best example here is the bolt (which we'll go into in detail about later). A mil-spec bolt must be made of a specific type and brand of steel. Are there better steels? Probably, since the kind the military wants (Carpenter 158) was developed when Dwight Eisenhower was president. A lot has changed since then. But no bolt maker supplying the military can use those better steels and keep the contract. Second, cost. Better steels cost more. The winner of the bid is the one who quotes the least cost. If they raise the cost, the extra expense comes out of the manufacturer's profit. They can't pass it on, no matter how much better it makes the product. So, mil-spec is guaranteed quality, but not necessarily the *best quality*.

But to some, it is mil-spec or bust. Ignore them. Many products have been improved since then, and if you want to use one, do it. The results of your decisions will be tabulated on the range in terms of reliability and accuracy.

My format for each chapter will be the same. I will first explain what the part or system is that we are discussing. Then, what variants may be available, selecting proper ones, and avoiding low-value parts. Next, I'll walk you through how to assemble it as a new-in-the-wrap-

> **"The thing is, the AR-15 can be what you want it to be. This is America, you get to choose, and you get to upgrade, or not, as you see fit. And in the end, practice matters more than the brand name."**

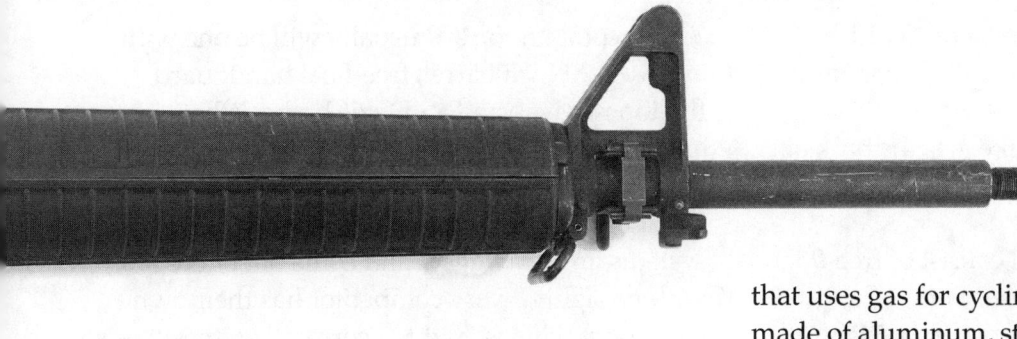

■ Here, we have a pair of extremes. The top is an A2 clone, which also serves as an NRA competition rifle, and (bottom) an SBR — a piston SBR at that.

per product, as well as suggesting similar parts that will work with it. After that, it will be how to remove the old parts and replace worn-out or better products. And finally, the extreme cases, where you've gotten yourself into a situation, or you bought a rifle that had been mishandled or abused by a previous owner and needs some serious TLC to work correctly.

So, we're off to learn a system. The AR-15 system. We'll assemble, we'll tear down and replace, we'll upgrade, and through it all, we'll stay safe.

What is An AR-15?

Simply put, the AR-15 is the smaller, caliber 5.56x45mm NATO/.223 Rem. rifle derived from the larger AR-10 (caliber 7.62x51mm NATO/.308 Win.), which Eugene Stoner designed in 1956. The AR-15 was scaled down and put into its pretty much final form by Jim Sullivan, working with Stoner. The AR-15 is a lightweight rifle or carbine that uses gas for cycling the mechanism and is made of aluminum, steel and plastic.

Since the AR-15's initial development, gun makers have morphed it into a variety of versions, and here we'll go over, in thumbnail, the different ones. That way, new shooters can get up to speed on what the more experienced are saying, and those who are beginners but not totally new to the scene can be sure they are up on the jargon.

M4gery

An "M4gery" is a carbine that looks like an M4 carbine (the select-fire version the U.S. military fields). Instead of the 14.5-inch barrel, it will have a 16-inch barrel. Also, it features a machined recess around the barrel for mounting an M203 grenade launcher. It will have a fixed front sight and a flat-top upper receiver. It will sport a tele-stock, usually the bare-bones M4 style, not an improved version. The handguards will be plastic, mostly with aluminum heat shields inside, but the low-cost versions will be just plastic. As a base model with easy-to-produce and easy-to-build-up inventory, it is attractive to manufacturers. As a base on which to build something "better," it is appealing to shooters.

■ The arm brace, used to stabilize the AR pistol, has been wildly popular, with estimates from 3 to 10 million sold.

It is called an M4gery, a *portmanteau* word, a combination of the model designation "M4" and "forgery," hence M4gery.

This variant, or something like it, is the bulk of the production and the market of AR-15s at the moment.

Manufacturer upgrades will consist of free-float or railed handguards (sometimes both) or upgraded polymer handguards like those from Magpul.

Retro

Retro refers to ARs built to earlier standards or patterns. The hard-core retro builders will think almost exclusively about the M16A1-pattern rifles with triangular handguards — or the XM-177 carbines, which are short and light even by AR standards. The term can also include M16A2-pattern rifles. Over time, "retro" will (if it hasn't already) encompass M16A3 and A4 rifles and the Knights handguard models issued by the USMC early in the Iraq war.

3-Gun Competition

This term is a wide-open description, but a 3-Gun competition AR usually will be one with an 18- or 20-inch barrel, free-float handguard, flat-top receiver, and a muzzle brake. What sights and other components it has will be determined by which Division the competitor has entered. Competition guns commonly have mid-length gas systems, match triggers and come out of the box with no sights. Every competitor has their own idea about what is "right," "correct," or "best" — so the makers don't even bother to add sights or other components.

NRA High Power

An NRA High Power AR-15 is also varied according to the Division entered and could be a basic M4 clone or a rifle that would be a useful Designated Marksman Rifle (DMR). The two main differences are using iron sights or a magnifying optic of no more than 4X magnification power. The weight limits of an NRA High Power rifle are generous, so it is not uncommon for a Service rifle (one that fits within the description of a current-issue M16) to have added lead weights and tip the scales at over 15 pounds.

SBR

SBR is a legal term and is the acronym for Short-Barreled Rifle. To own one, you must first live in a state that allows them under state law. Then, apply to the ATF to build one and pay the $200 tax. Once all the paperwork is approved, then and only then may you build or buy one. There is no such thing as a "standard" SBR since they require so much extra work. The proud owners either buy precisely what they want or build it to their exacting standards.

AR Pistol

An AR pistol is an AR-15 without a stock on the buffer tube. The buffer tube may be bare, it may have an arm brace (state and federal law permitting), and as a pistol, it can have a barrel shorter than the legal limit for rifles, so under 16 inches.

Everything Else

The AR-15 has been called "Barbie for Men" — everything can be customized, rebuilt, modified or experimented with. If your gun club has an active 3-Gun or 2-Gun program, or some serious experimenters, you could see just about anything.

■ Once you have built your AR, or upgraded it, and painted it, and tested it, it is yours, and unlike anyone else's.

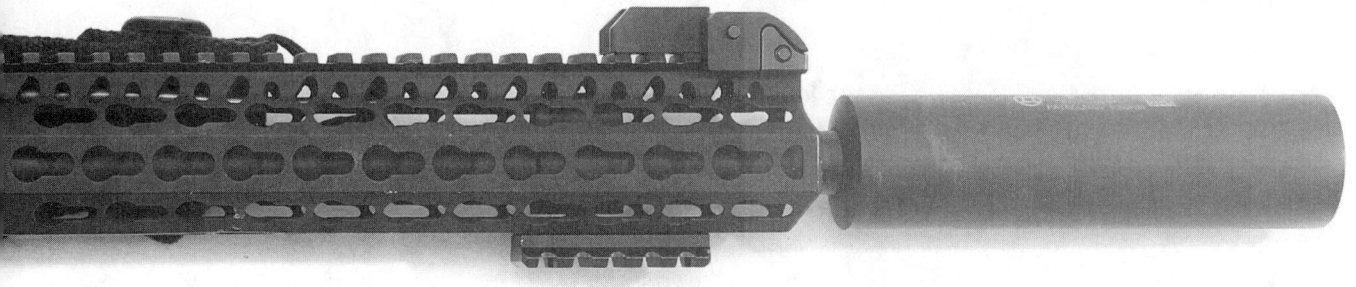

■ The AR-15 pistol, here with an arm brace (assuming the regulations haven't been changed to preclude them) and on the other end, a Gemtech suppressor.

CHAPTER 1 – AR-15 BASICS **15**

AR-15 Parts Identification

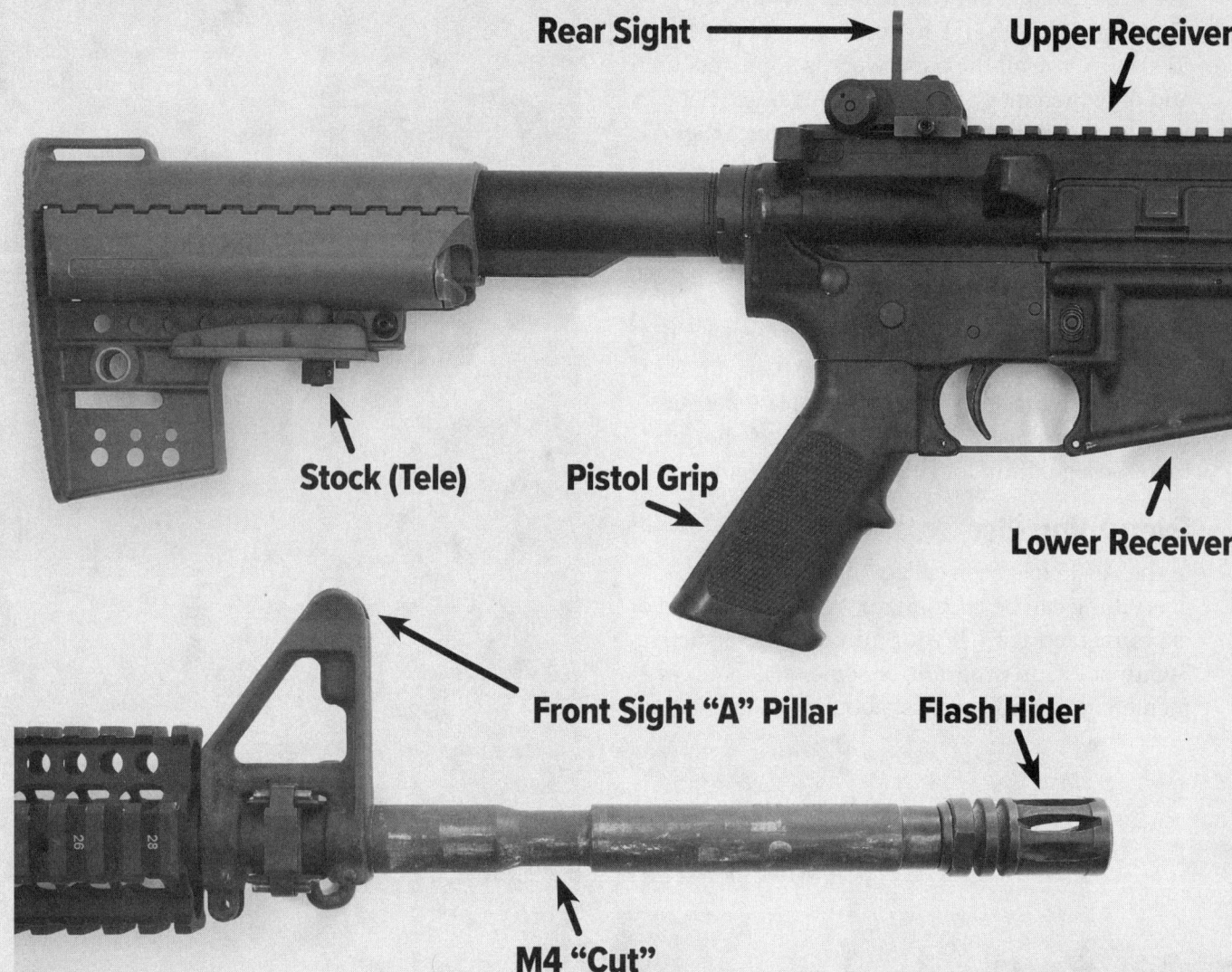

In this book, we'll be discussing, dissecting, repairing, upgrading or otherwise cleaning and maintaining the AR-15. Let's start with an overview, kick the tires, slam the doors and peek under the hood. We'll begin with an assembled AR-15 and take a quick look around before we delve into the particulars.

At the front, we have the flash hider. Now, some ARs won't have a flash hider, nor even the threads by which you'd screw one on. Too bad for you. The flash hider sits on the front end of the barrel, which you will see poking out of the handguards. The barrel is secured to the upper receiver, on which you may or may not have a rear sight. Behind the upper (as it's called), attached to the lower receiver, is the stock, also known as the buttstock.

Looping around and heading underneath to the lower receiver (or "lower"), we have the pistol grip. Note that in some locales (pretty much the same ones that won't permit a flash hider), you can't legally have a pistol grip on your AR-15 or any other rifle for that matter. As clever people do, designers have found ways in those jurisdictions to make an AR-15 legal by installing a device in this location that does not fit the legal definition of a "pistol grip" and still allows you to use it as a firearm.

Let's get back to the front end of the rifle and look at a vanilla-plain AR-15, known as an "M4gery." (A non-select-fire, aka not a machine gun, a clone of the M4 issued in the military, with a 16-inch barrel.) Behind the flash hider, there is a groove in the barrel. This groove is the mounting location for the

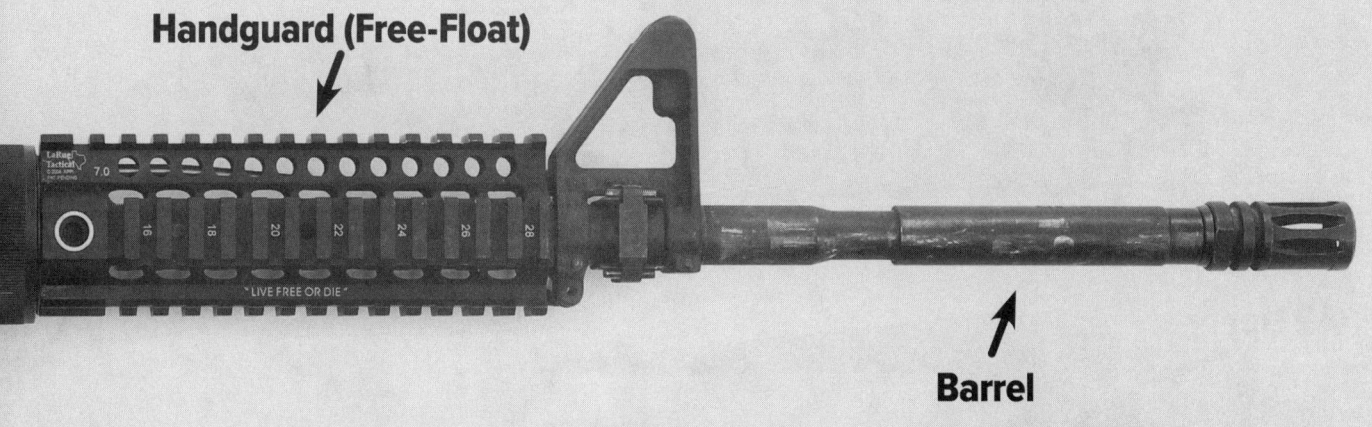

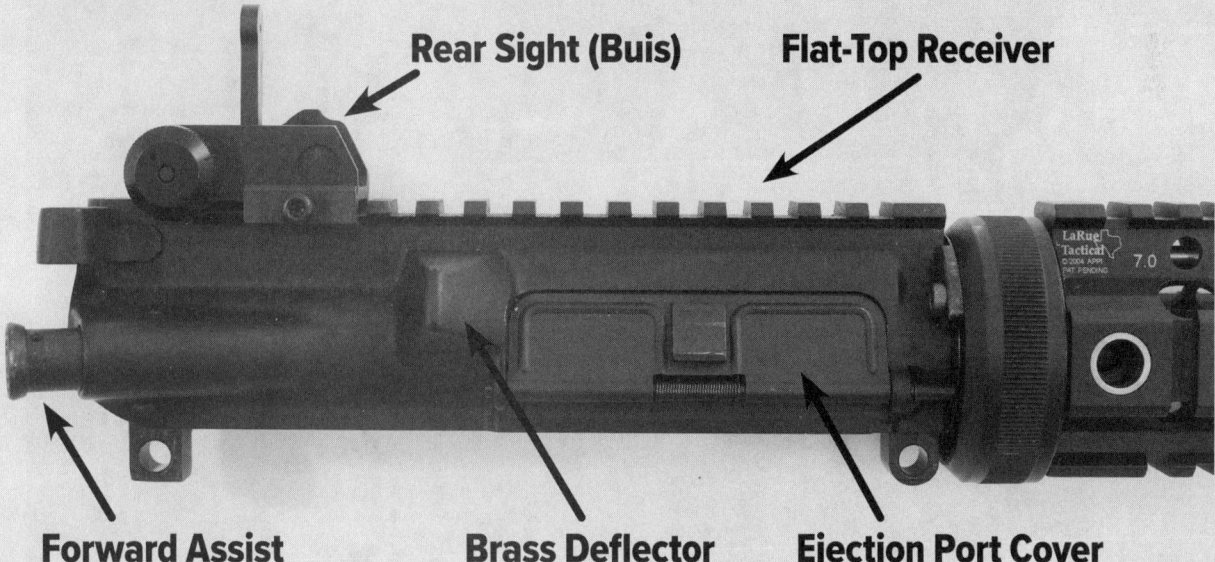

M203 grenade launcher. Can you buy an M203? Yes. It is, however, the same as a machine gun under Federal law and requires a Transfer Tax application, a tax payment of $200, and a long wait.

Why is the barrel groove there? Because it is easier for the barrel maker to keep it, and some customers insist on having it.

Behind that is the front sight "A" pillar, which is also the gas block. The front sight is at the top of the "A" pillar. You screw it up and down to adjust the bullet impact point and zero the rifle. Behind the "A" pillar, you will find the handguards.

The barrel and the handguards are attached to the upper receiver. The upper receiver is the place you will find rear iron sights if the receiver has them, or where you would mount iron sights on a flat-top. Also, you can mount a red-dot sight on the flat-top, a magnifying optic or some combination of these. On the right side, the upper receiver has the ejection port cover or dust cover door. This door is spring-loaded and snaps closed but is forced open when the bolt cycles. It stays open until you press it closed again.

There will be a brass deflector on most of the upper receivers you will see, also known as the ejector pyramid or ejector lump. The ejected brass bounces off this angled surface and keeps the hot brass from being ejected back at you. Or, in the case of left-handed shooters, into your face. Behind the ejector pyramid is the forward assist, a device you will seldom use. In fact, using it imprudently can cause a malfunction (I go into more

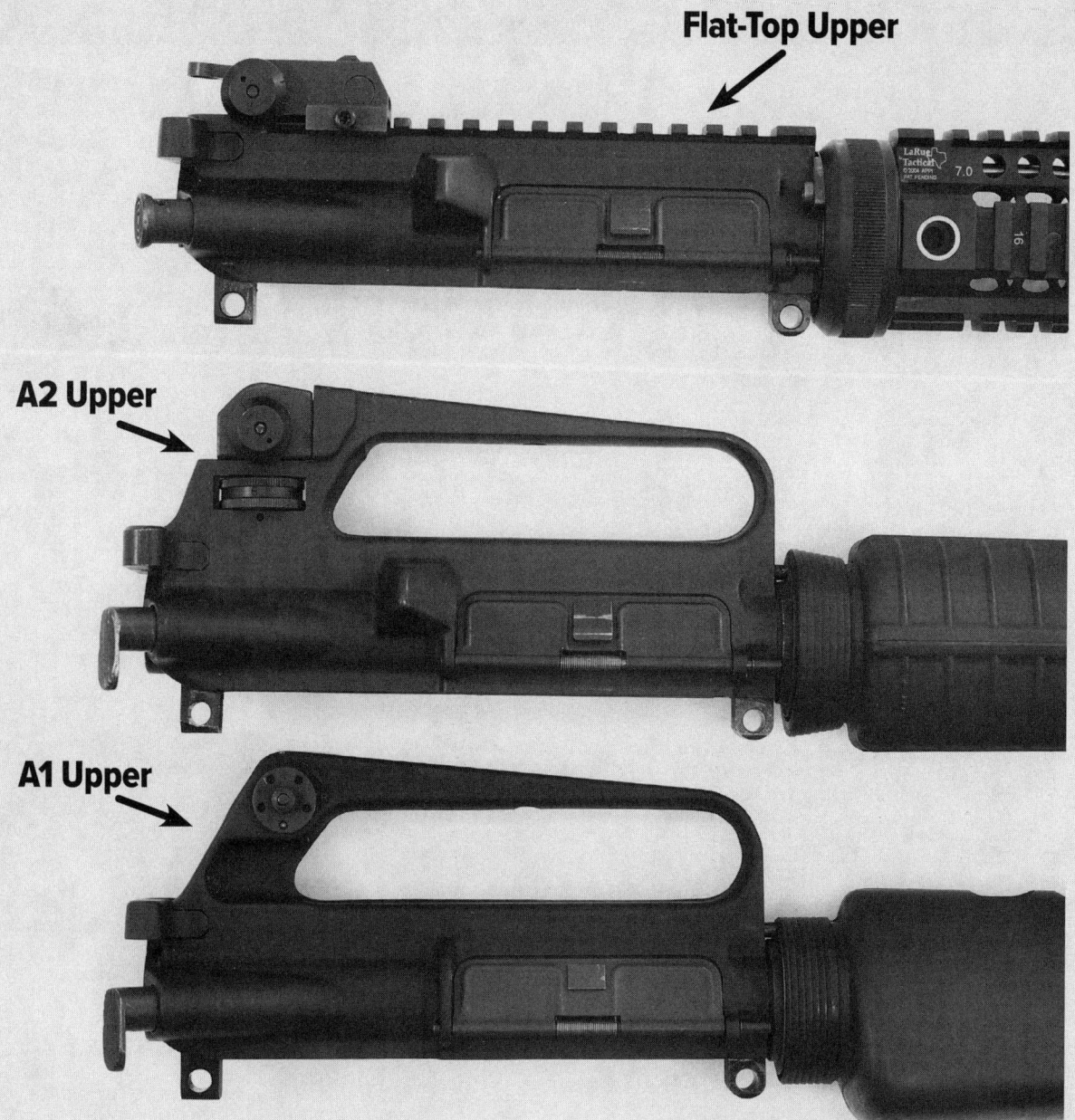

Flat-Top Upper

A2 Upper

A1 Upper

depth later in the book about when and how to use the forward assist). A simple rule: in almost all cases where you might be tempted to use the forward assist: *don't*.

Upper receivers can be found in one of three general categories. The original A1 has an iron rear sight that cannot be adjusted with your bare hands. You need a tool, as the cruel joke of "Use a bullet tip to change the rear sight" usually ends with a marred bullet tip, brass scrapings on your upper and frustration. The A2 has a rear sight that you hand-adjust and is meant for target and long-range iron-sight shooting. Both have a loop on top of the upper receiver, termed the carry handle, but here's a hot tip: no one carries an AR-15 that way. Back in the 1950s, when the AR-15 was designed, it was assumed that the future of rifles would involve such a carry handle. If you see someone carrying an AR-15 that way today, they are even newer than you are, however new you might be. Don't be that guy.

The latest and most common design is the flat-top, with a grooved rail on top meant as a mounting location for sights or optics.

Let's pop back out near the muzzle for a moment and study one of the operational parts of the AR-15. If you were to remove the handguards or slide the free-float handguard back slightly (if you could), you'd see the gas tube. This tube transports

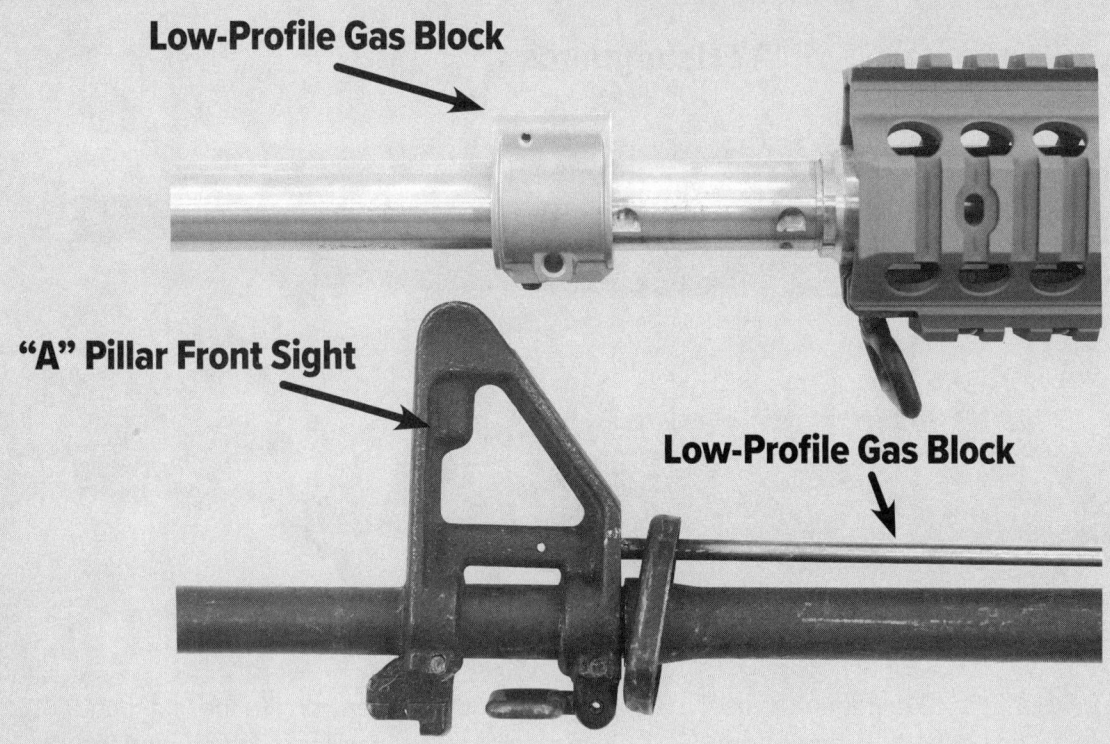

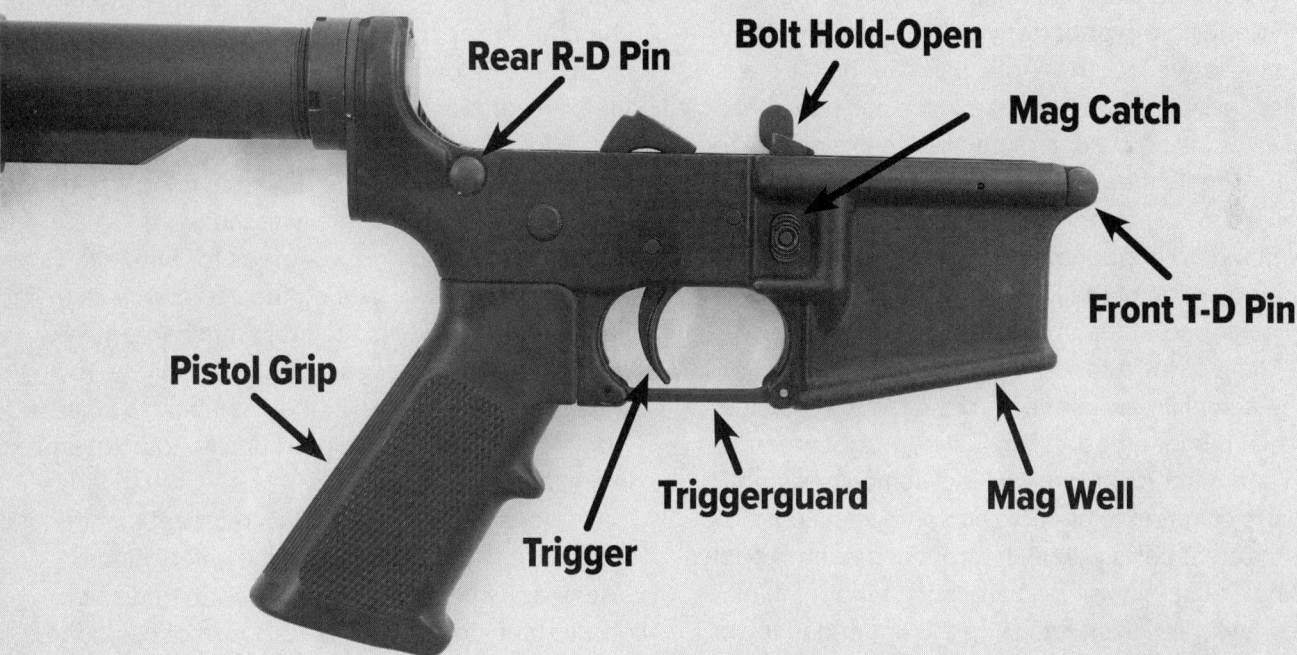

the gas, bled from the bore on each shot, back to the upper receiver. That gas drives the semi-automatic action of the system. The "A" pillar front sight holds the gas block on most rifles, but the gas block is smaller on many of the newest ones. Since it doesn't require a front sight (the front sight can be mounted on the free-float handguard), the gas block can fit under the handguard, known as a low-profile gas block.

If you have handguards of the traditional type, you will have one of two types: The A1 will be triangular. A1 handguards are a left and a right, and you need a pair. If you break a left one, you must get a left-side replacement and vice-versa for the right.

CHAPTER 1 — AR-15 BASICS   **19**

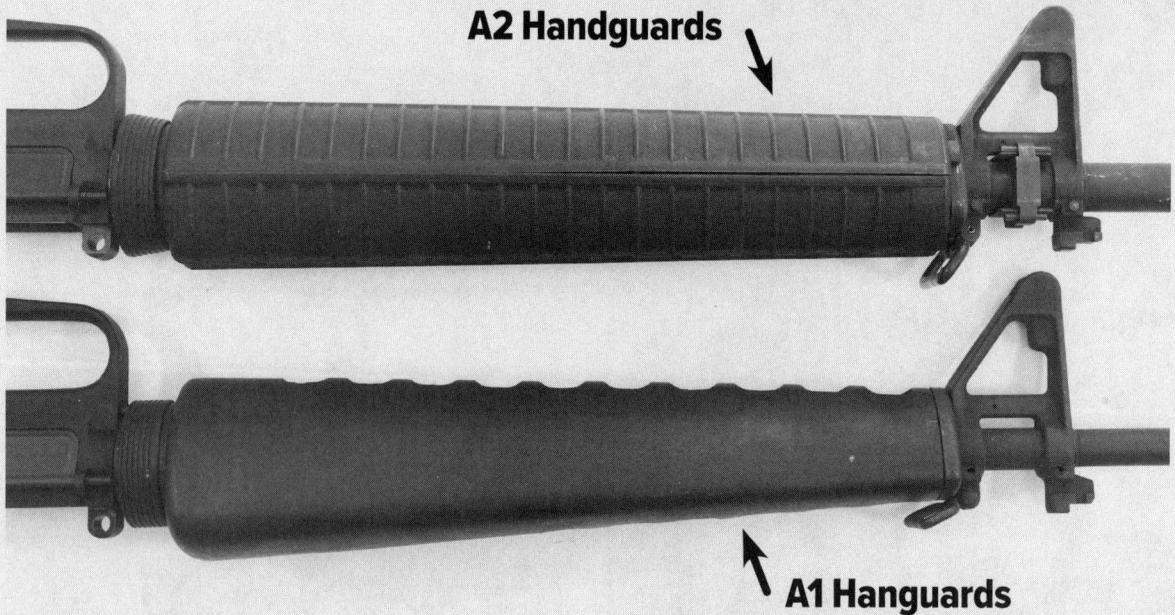

A2 Handguards

A1 Hanguards

A1s only come in one length. A2 handguards are identical and are installed on the top and bottom. If you break one (not easy, the A2 upgrade used an improved plastic formulation), you simply get another, no top or bottom matching required. A2s come in two lengths — rifle and carbine. There is also the A2 M4 handguard, which has two heat shields inside instead of one like the A1 or A2. You can identify the A2 M4 by its oval shape, how it's taller top-to-bottom than the regular A2.

Standard handguards are held in place by the spring action of the Delta ring, the spring-loaded circular part at the front of the upper receiver.

Moving down to the lower receiver, which is the actual firearm under Federal law and has the serial number (uppers are just parts, not firearms in and of themselves), we have some consistent parts common to all ARs and some variations. The consistent parts will be the front and rear takedown pins. These pins slide in and out (to the right) of the lower receiver, attaching the upper and lower together. The lower has the magazine well — the opening for the feeding device — and behind it the magazine catch. This button releases the magazine when pressed. Below the magazine catch is the triggerguard, which keeps the trigger from catching on inadvertent objects. On a standard AR-15, the triggerguard is hinged, and you can lower and pivot it down to the pistol grip.

On the left side of the lower, you will find the bolt hold-open button. When you fire the last round, the magazine follower will rise and engage the bolt hold-open. It locks the bolt to the rear, letting you know the rifle is empty. That makes it easier to chamber the next round after you have inserted a fresh mag. Below that is the trigger, and behind it is the pistol grip. In between the bolt hold-open and the pistol grip is the Safety/Selector.

The safety prevents the rifle from firing when the arrow is pointed horizontally at the word "Safe." Rotating the selector 90 degrees to "Fire" allows you to fire the rifle. Rotating the selector back to Safe at any time locks the firing mechanism and precludes firing. (It does not, however, remove any cartridge that might be in the chamber, so while it won't fire, it is still considered unsafe to point a rifle in an unsafe direction.)

It is worth pointing out at this moment that the AR-15 does not have a magazine safety. Some pistols do. Some jurisdictions view them as beneficial safety tools. The AR-15 does not have one, it has never had one, and as far as I know, no one has ever seriously considered inventing or installing one. It is up to you, the user, to keep the AR-15 always pointed in a safe direction.

The lower receiver's rear is the stock's mounting location. There are three types of hardware: the tele-stock, a telescoping stock that allows you to adjust the length of pull to fit your size and permit more compact storage; the fixed stock, which is

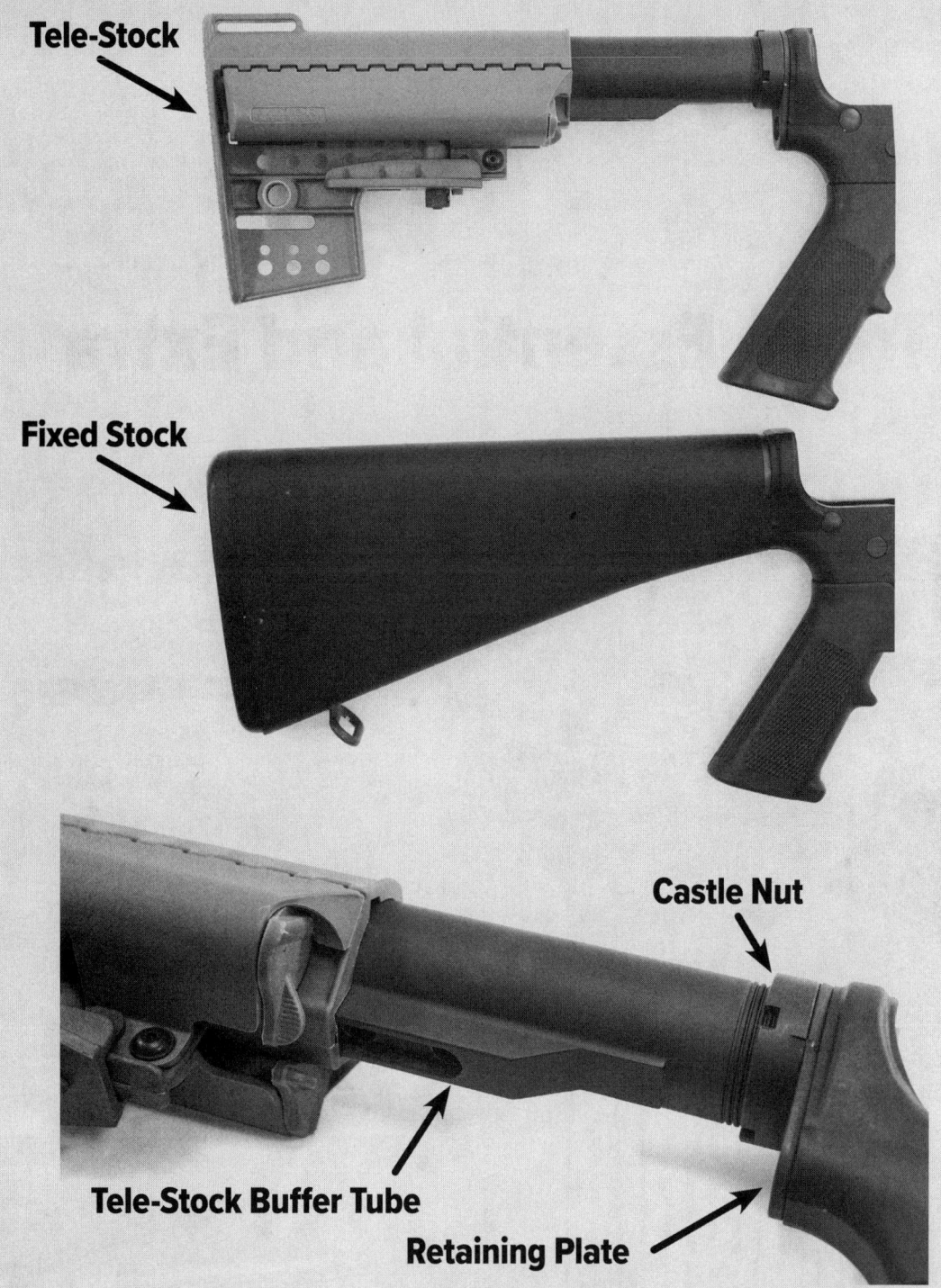

just what it says, fixed in length; and the arm brace, which is not meant as a stock to shoulder, but as a brace to shoot the AR-15 unshouldered like a pistol. All stock types have a buffer tube with the buffer weight and spring inside. You'll identify the tele-stock buffer tube by the rib on the bottom, which keeps the stock aligned and contains the locating sockets for length adjustments. You can't swap stocks willy-nilly. A tele-stock requires its own buffer tube, and the fixed stock a different tube. For assembly, the tele-stock uses a castle nut to lock the tube in place and the retaining plate to keep the lower internals in position, specifically the rear takedown pin spring and plunger.

So, when you are at your local gun shop (aka LGS, in online or email acronym-speak), those are the parts you will be looking at.

2
Tools, Essential and Extra

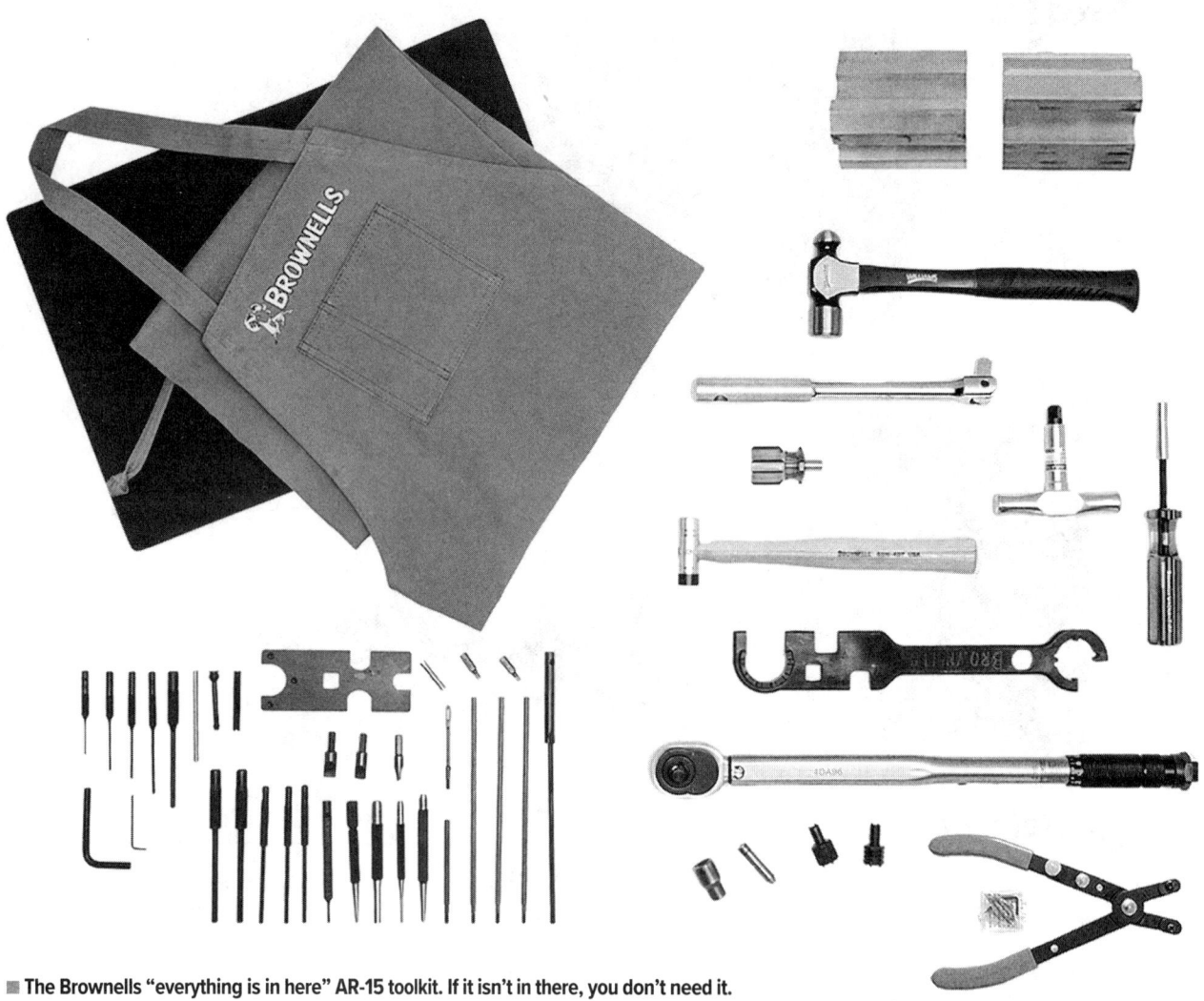

■ The Brownells "everything is in here" AR-15 toolkit. If it isn't in there, you don't need it.

What tools do you need to work on an AR-15? That depends. If all you are ever going to do is keep yours running, perhaps install some optics, a light, a sling, and keep it clean, then a cleaning kit and a literal handful of hardware-store-standard tools will do the job.

If you perform the firearms equivalent of open-heart surgery, you'll need pretty much every tool made for the AR-15. If that's your goal, you can make life easy, if expensive, by simply going to Brownells and ordering its GEN II AR-15 Armorers Kit. If you get the Standard or the Premium, it will

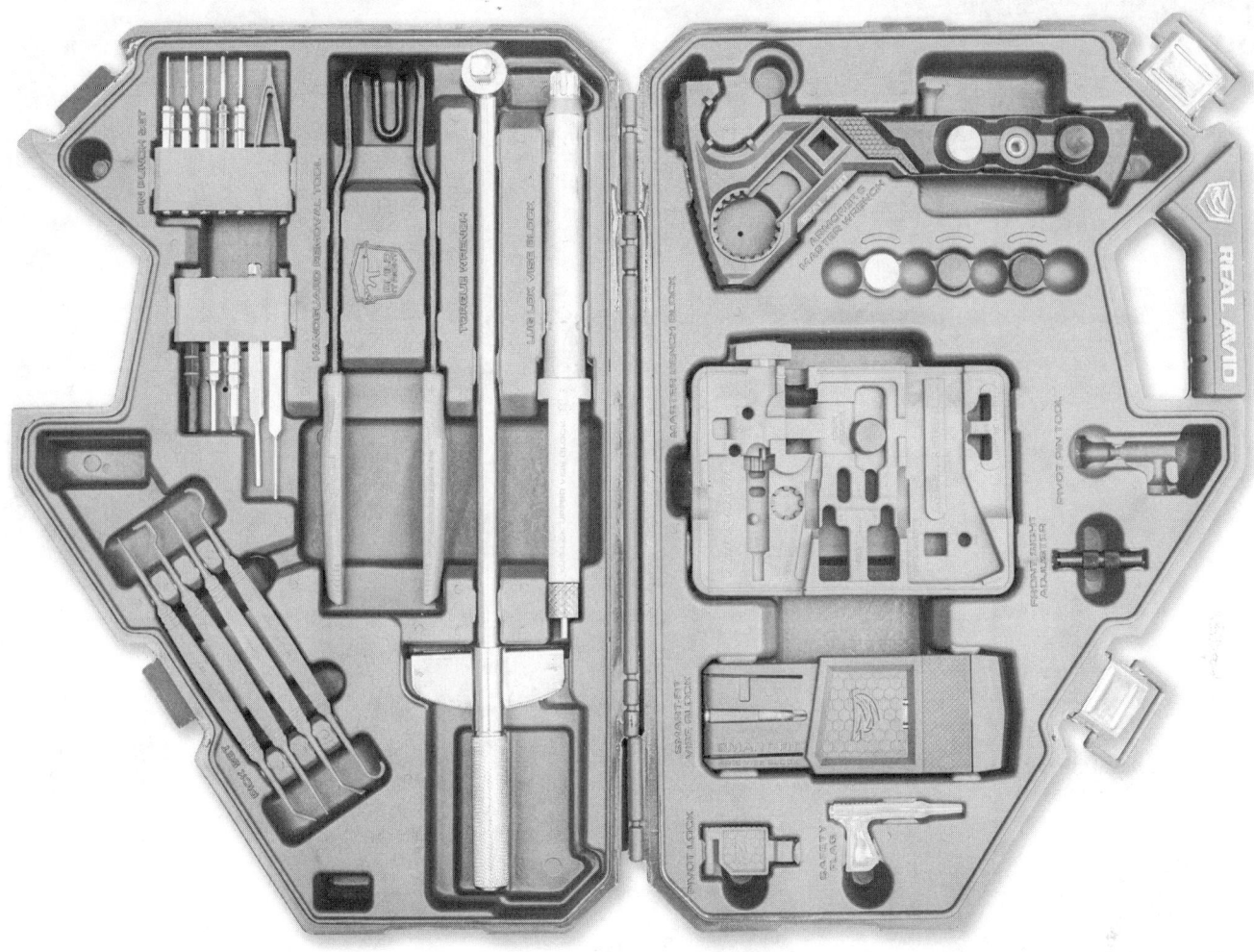

■ Inside the Real Avid Kit, all the tools are laid out and held in place.

set you back some $1,770 to $2,130. They come in Pelican cases with fitted drawers. If there's a task to be performed on the AR-15, there's a tool in there to do it.

I love the Brownells folks like they are family, but that's not something I'm going to spring for (I already have all the tools I'll need).

A less expensive kit, and one that will include many, if not every tool you'll need, is the Real Avid Master AR-15 Armorer's Kit.

Since we aren't going to spring a couple of mortgage payments on a maintenance kit, let's work our way up the ladder of tools, from basic to involved.

Tool selection and assembly break out into three categories: Cleaning, inspecting and building.

■ The Wilson Combat upper receiver scrubbing tool.

CHAPTER 2 – TOOLS, ESSENTIAL AND EXTRA   23

■ This upper was in the category of "clean enough." Clearly not, since one pass cleaned this much gunk out.

Getting Started

You need a cleaning kit. We'll cover the tools, and their uses as well, for cleaning. I'll list here and describe the inspection and building tools, but I will cover how to use them in the relevant chapters for that tool involved.

Chamber and Bore Cleaning

You can accomplish chamber and bore cleaning using the flat USGI pouch with a segmented rod. It can be the Otis Cleaning Kit that comes in a zippered round pouch, about the size of a pinch can for your tobacco products. (Those who use them, the rest of us will think, "Thick hockey puck.") Or a Hoppes Boresnake. These will all clean the bore. You need

■ The Wilson cleaner comes with its own scrubbing pads.

powder and copper solvents, patches and shop cloths to clean up. The shop cloths are about the only thing you can get at the local big-box hardware store, as well as a few screwdrivers.

You'll need a chamber brush with a "T" handle rod. The chamber brush is a copper brush the size and shape of the chamber, with a stainless steel bristle collar, which scours the chamber and throat and the locking lugs of the barrel extension. You need a T-handle rod because it takes some torque to rotate the rod once it is fully inserted, and you won't be able to do that with just the bare rod as a handle.

You'll have to clean the bolt and carrier, and in extreme (or thorough) instances, you'll have to clean the inside of the upper and the buffer tube interior.

Bolt and Carrier Cleaning

Bolts and carriers get extremely dirty when you shoot your AR-15. The bolts can get powder residue baked on from the heat of shooting. You'll need a selection of scrapers that can scour the baked-on powder residue from the bolt and out of the tunnel in the carrier in which the bolt rides. You can get a combo hand tool such as the Real Avid Gun Tool AMP, or Gun Tool Core, both of which have a selection of appropriately sized scrapers and other tools. Or you can go with a CAT M4 tool, which scrapes the bolt tail, the carrier tunnel, and the firing pin where the gunk collects. Otis makes the BONE tool,

■ The Otis Cleaning Kit is great for use in the field when you need to clean something right now. But save it for the field, and get a real rod set for work in the shop.

■ You will go through solvents and lube at a fast clip. One-ounce bottles of anything are a waste unless you are just sampling or testing.

■ Lots of patches. You will be cleaning bores, swabbing out the internals and disposing of grubby patches. Get a lot of them, they are not expensive.

which does the same thing. That so many companies make a special tool for such a mundane task should give you a clue about how important it is to keep that area clean.

Just an aside, and not to jump to the bolt maintenance section, do not use a brush to clean the burned-on carbon from the bolt tail. The plastic ones won't have any effect, and the steel ones risk flicking a gas ring out of the bolt, which will be a problem later when you shoot.

■ The Real Avid Chamber Cleaning Tool offers several bonuses: it not only lets you rotate the chamber brush, but it has special felt pads to scrub the locking lug recesses. And it comes with an upper prop to keep the halves apart. You can even store everything in the handle!

■ When you scrub the chamber, insert the steel bristles all the way into the locking lugs. (This barrel is not in a receiver for clarity.)

■ Here you see the chamber brush and the Real Avid Locking Lug Scrubbers.

The carrier bore needs scouring or scraping, but the exterior just needs to be hosed and scrubbed and wiped. The gas key? Clean the outside, leave the interior alone.

General Interior and Exterior Cleaning

The inside of the receivers can get very crudded up. In fact, you can build up so much powder residue and scale that cleaning it becomes a problem later. The usual solution is to invest in several cans of aerosol cleaning solution and some plastic brushes. As environmentally unfriendly as it sounds, the standard method is to retire to the gun club parking lot, separate the upper and lowers and remove the internals from each. Then, spray the interior liberally, brush and drain. The solvents, powder residue, oils, etc., all go into the gravel of the parking lot to reside there with the drips of motor oil from the cars. The only other method is to use up most of a roll of paper towels, spraying and wiping, spraying and wiping, and then stuffing the towels into the club's dumpster. (Oh, did you know that Dumpster was a registered trademark? Not all metal bins for garbage are dumpsters. Trademarked back in 1935, the company has since let the trademark expire.)

Getting the interiors of the uppers and lowers clean enough for a white-glove inspection is going

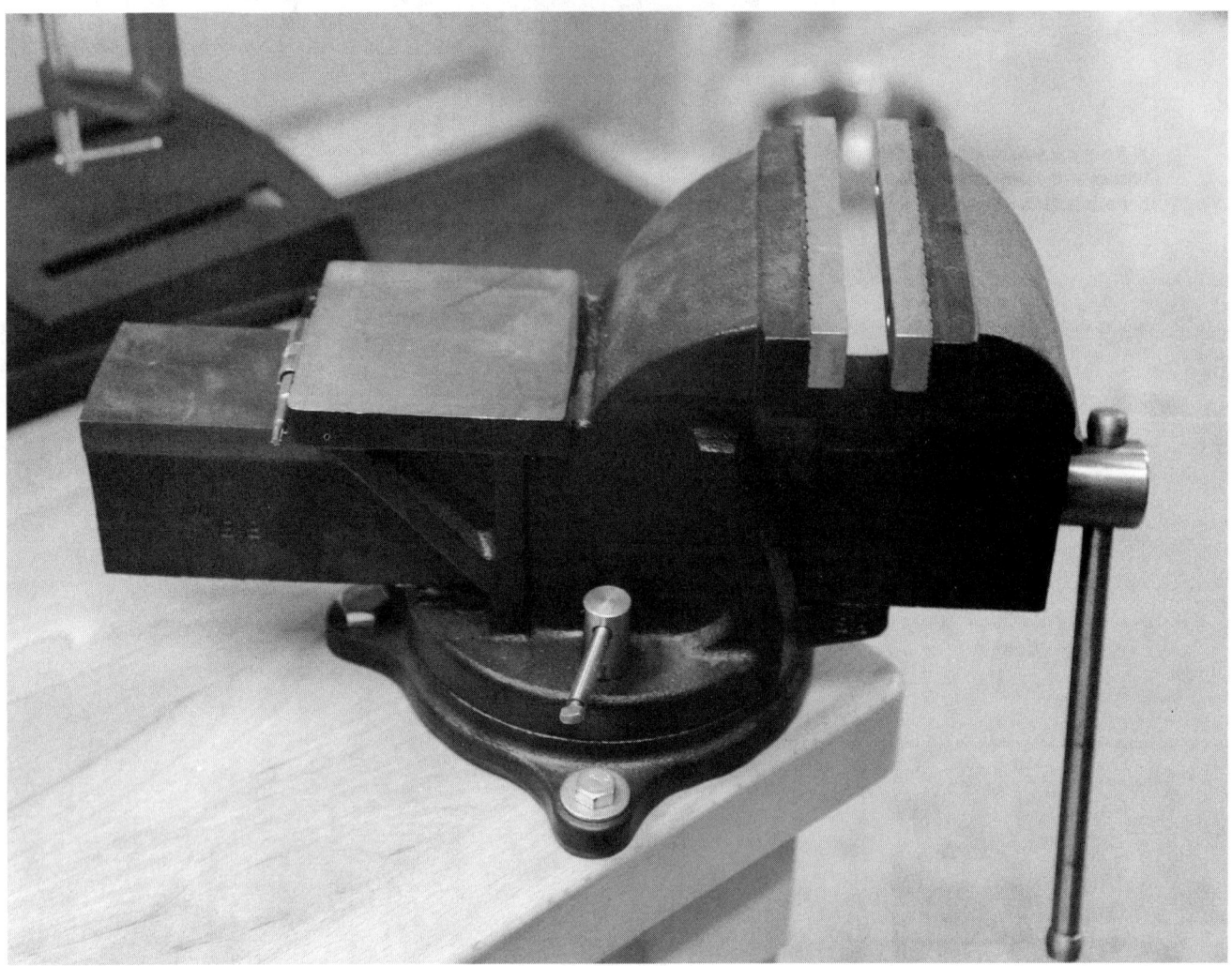

■ A solid bench vise is an excellent thing to have. Be careful, though, as you can crush some parts of the AR-15 if you are too enthusiastic. But a bench vise is your best third hand.

to end up with you looking like you just got off a shift at the coal mine. You will not be alone if you only clean these areas on your AR-15 enough to ensure proper function.

Wilson Combat makes a special interior cleaner with diameters to fit the AR-15 and AR-10 for scouring the receiver's interior. It comes with its own special-sized pad for scrubbing, but I suspect a clever AR-15 owner can come up with suitable replacements.

Basic Hand Tools

You will need screwdrivers of various sizes and types to keep the threaded fasteners tight on your rifle. Screwdrivers come in two types, four if you consider the socket-head screws as needing screwdrivers. They are: blade, Phillips, Allen and Torx.

Before we begin, a quick primer on techno-speak: cam-out. A mechanical tightener is designed to work one of two ways: it is made to cam out; or, it is not made to cam out. If it is made to cam out, once you reach a certain level of effort, it will force its way out of the attachment point.

Blade screwdrivers are just that — the flat blade. The typical household and hardware screwdrivers are made to cam out. Once you get to the max effort it is designed to work up to, the angle flats of the blade will force it out of the slot. Firearms screwdrivers are "hollow ground," which means the flats are not angled. A firearms screwdriver will not cam out. This is both good and bad. It is good in that you can put maximum effort into it and torque a screw tight. It is bad in that if you reach the limits of the screw head, it will bend the slot walls and mangle the slot as it forces its way out. Or the blade will break. Good for us; most fasteners on AR-15s don't require a blade screwdriver. And those like the pistol grip don't need anything close to the force needed to mangle the slot or break the blade.

Phillips screwdrivers are the ones with the "X" slots in the screw head. They were designed to cam out. Few Phillips screwdrivers are made that are the equivalent to being hollow-ground. Trying to tighten a Phillips screw past its torque limit is a colossal waste of time, and I usually swap Phillips out if it is in any way possible. I just don't need the hassle.

Allen head screws are the ones with the hexagonal hole in the top. The Allen wrench is a screwdriver, not a wrench, but that's what it got called in the beginning, so we're stuck with it. Allen screws are not cam design, but the typical Allen screw (and wrench) is steel so soft that you can easily bend it. It is common to see small Allen-screw fasteners on firearms, with the hexagonal hole washed out and mangled. Do not apply too much torque to an Allen-head fastener; it is another waste of time.

Now, finally, we are up to modern fasteners. The Torx screwdriver is the one with the star-head shape, and the screw has a six-point-star shaped recess on top. Torx screws and screwdrivers are designed not-cam, and you can achieve some high torque levels with them. The ones I have worked with have all been made of good steel (no *Chine-*

■ Many of the tools you will need, such as Allen wrenches, Torx wrenches, screwdrivers and punches, can be bought at the local hardware store. They won't have the specialized ones; sets like this don't have to come from a mil-spec AR-15 parts provider.

■ One fantastic tool in the excellent Real Avid Toolkit is the pin holder. It even locks tight to hold the pin for driving.

CHAPTER 2 – TOOLS, ESSENTIAL AND EXTRA ■ 29

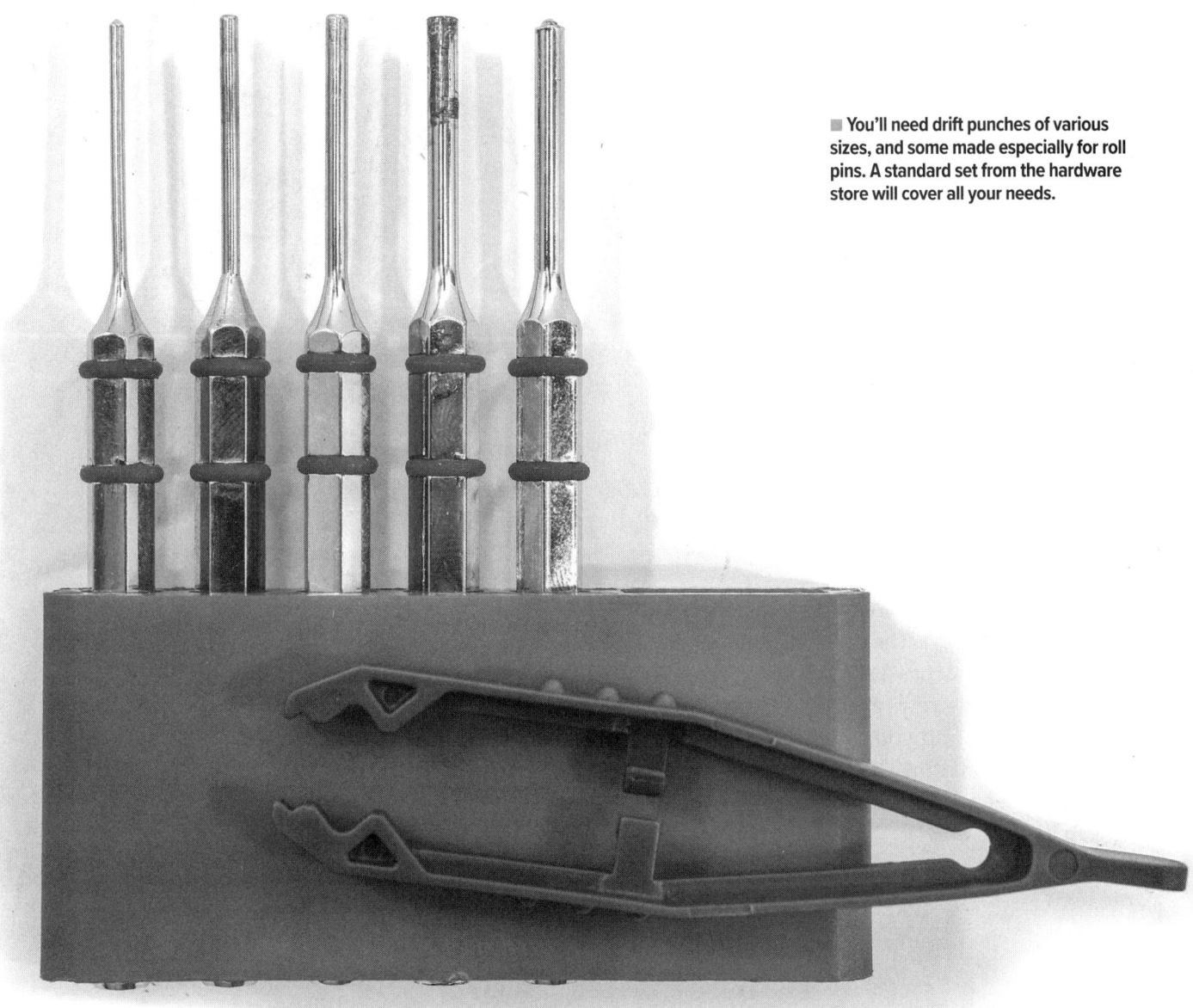

You'll need drift punches of various sizes, and some made especially for roll pins. A standard set from the hardware store will cover all your needs.

sium here, so far), and you can tighten them more than you probably should.

Punches

Punches come in three types for our needs. There are taper punches, which you use to get a pin started. Then there are the straight punches, which you use to do the final hit to make a pin flush. And then there are plastic or brass punches, so you can move recalcitrant things like pistol sights without marring them by hitting them with a steel punch. There is a specialty punch, called a roll-pin punch, one that has a small hemispherical nub on the tip. This is meant to rest in the hollow center of the roll pin and move it without damaging it. If you are careful, you can drift a roll pin with a regular punch and not damage the pin. And, the roll pin punch has to be the exact and correct size for the pin you are moving, or else it will damage the pin anyway. You will find that most of the people working on AR-15s started their careers using roll-pin punches. When they lost or broke them, they just used regular punches and did not mangle the roll pins. Risky business, but it works just fine, at least, until it doesn't.

Wrenches

If you move to high-end scope mounts and other items, you will need open-end or box-end wrenches. The industry is rapidly standardizing on half-inch for the size of these, so a stop at the local hardware store (if you have one) will make that easy. Any will do.

■ Midwest Industries makes an excellent multi-use barrel wrench that is also many other tools.

Power Tools

A few power tools will come in handy if you will be doing full-build and custom mods to your AR-15. A bench grinder with one wheel replaced with a wire wheel can grind metal or polish rusted parts. A belt sander is even more rarely needed, but if you do, nothing else lets you quickly sand something with a straight edge. (You can't do that with a bench grinder.) A drill press helps you get holes drilled in the right location, straight and prepped for tapping. But ARs don't need that work much these days. Even fewer need millwork since we can buy flat-top uppers and don't have to make our own.

A lathe can be useful, but that is a significant investment for an occasional flash hider, muzzle brake or other mods. A cheap one is no use, and a useful one will set you back a couple of grand. And if you go that route, you'll need elbow room, electricity and tooling.

Fixtures

You need a way to hold the rifle while you work on it. The basic one is generally called a cleaning cradle, and this is the kind where you have a tabletop setup, and the rifle rests on the toe of the buttstock and the handguard in a cradle arrangement. While these work and can be helpful for some tasks, the AR-15's peculiarities make them less valuable than other rifle designs. For instance, it is challenging to clean the bore on an AR-15 in a regular cleaning cradle because you need the rear of the upper receiver open

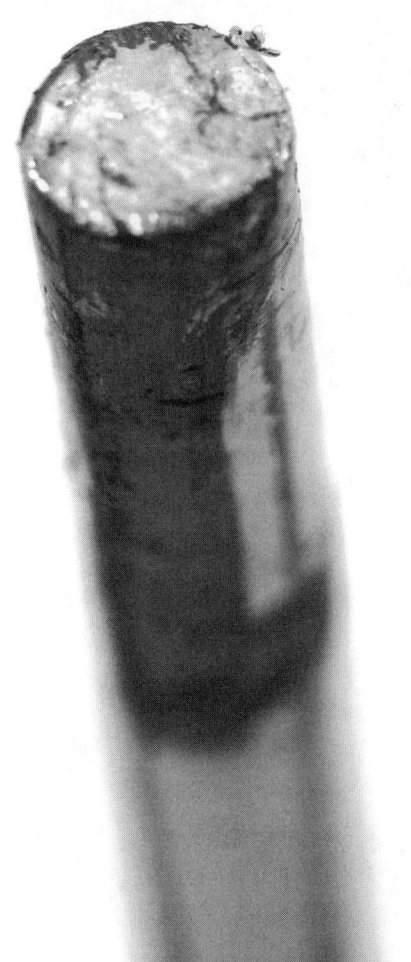

■ It is obvious which is for the roll pin. The right-hand one has the central bump to keep it in place on the roll pin end.

CHAPTER 2 – TOOLS, ESSENTIAL AND EXTRA ■ **31**

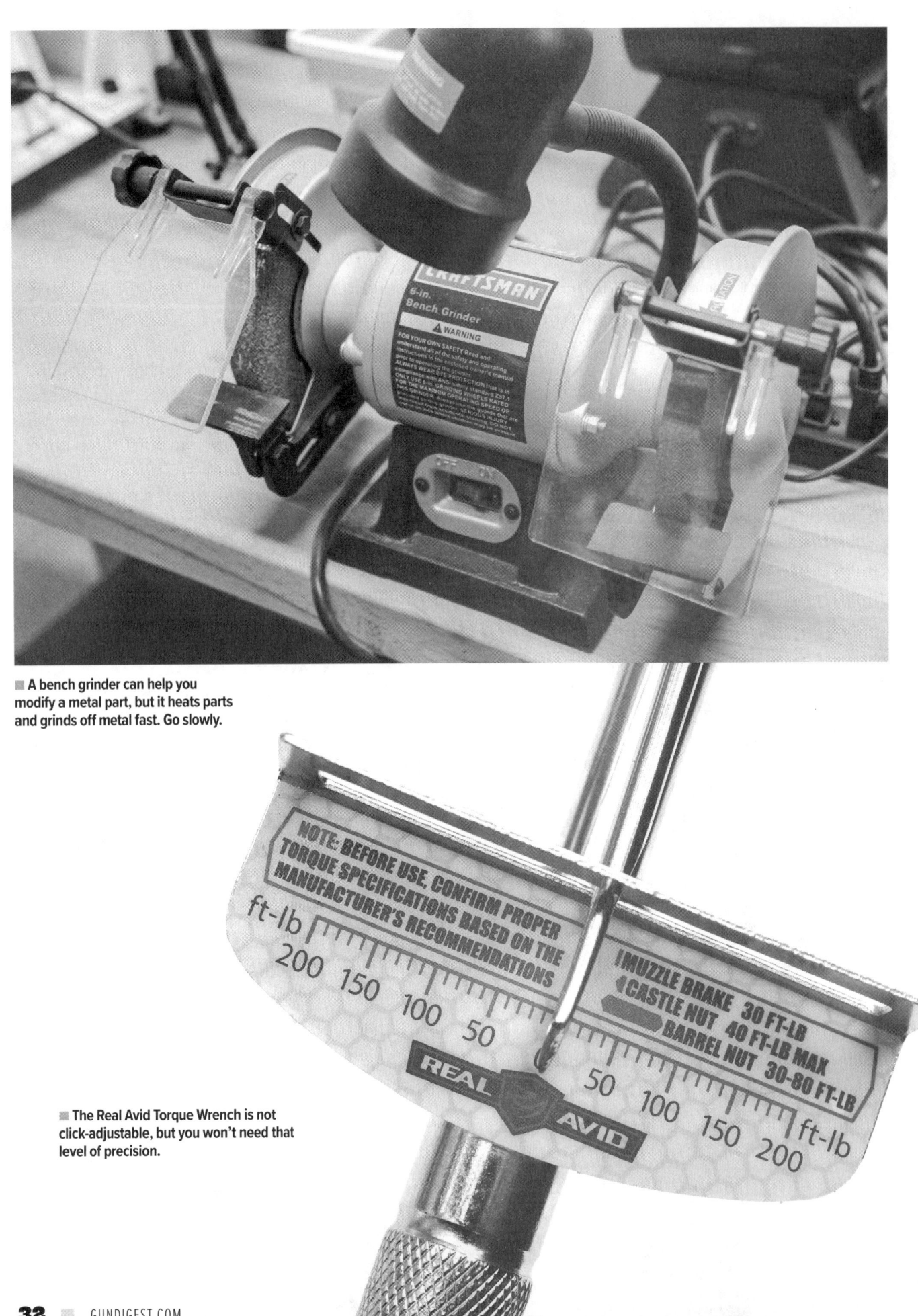

■ A bench grinder can help you modify a metal part, but it heats parts and grinds off metal fast. Go slowly.

■ The Real Avid Torque Wrench is not click-adjustable, but you won't need that level of precision.

■ The belt sander is specialized. It can replace a bench grinder, and it works better to keep the ground spot flat. But mostly, it is for sharpening knives, again with a soft touch and gentle pressure.

and the bolt/carrier out to properly run the rod down the bore.

So, to hold the upper and lower, you need separate tools, and you do this with the upper and lower separated. Or you can use a special prop to hold the upper open but angled, still attached to the lower.

To hold the lower, you need the magazine block. This is simply a plastic block shaped like a magazine. (In the old days, I saw a few machined from aluminum, but that was deemed overkill even then.) You slip the block into the mag well of the lower and then clamp the block where it protrudes from the lower, in your bench vise.

A brief aside: I'm assuming that you have a solid bench and a good vise attached to it for the purposes of our discussion. If you do not, you need to re-consider a career of wrenching on your AR-15. We will be discussing tasks that simply cannot be done while holding the parts in your bare hands.

For the upper — and this will be the only use you will have for them — you will need the angled aluminum barrel blocks. If you have regular, plastic handguards, you take the handguards off and carefully clamp the barrel in your vise using the blocks. You can then work on sights, clean the bore or do other tasks. You do not use the aluminum blocks when changing barrels. There are far better tools for that now.

If you have free-float handguards that cannot be readily removed, you will need the upper receiver clamping fixture. This fixture is a glass-reinforced pair of blocks that nestle around your upper receiver. In your vise, you slide the blocks on and clamp the blocks with the upper squeezed between them. They were initially made to do barrel swaps, and you can still use them for that, but we have a better tool for barrel work, and the clamp blocks work great to clean bores. They are obviously of no use for sight work, but that leads us to the better barrel tool: the reaction rod.

The reaction rod came about through tool evolution. The aluminum barrel blocks couldn't clamp barrels tightly enough to handle the torque needed for barrel changes. Users hated having to take optics, sights and other extras off uppers to secure them. The reaction rod is a steel or aluminum rod that slides into the upper receiver, with lugs or teeth that engage the locking lugs of the barrel extension. To use one, you clamp the rod in your vise. You then slide the upper onto it and wriggle it until the teeth on the rod engage the locking lugs of the extension. It prevents your barrel and receiver from rotating when you apply torque. You can also use it to work on sights, optics and other upper gear, with one realization: nothing keeps the upper from moving forward off the rod. If you bump it in that direction, it will move, and it could slide off. So, take care when doing sight work.

Also, since the reaction rod is in the upper and engages the locking lugs, there's no way to use it to hold the upper for bore cleaning.

Two Main Tasks

The two main details that shooters may attend to are dealing with stock issues or stock swaps and barrel changes. Those tasks require some extra tools. First, stocks come as either fixed or telestocks, the latter being adjustable in length. Some hideous modifications are needed in some states,

■ If you have two bench grinders, you can replace the grinding wheels with wire wheels and do some aggressive cleaning like in this well-equipped shop.

■ It isn't often you'll need a drill press, but it is helpful for many other tasks besides working on AR-15s. And, if you need to enlarge a hole, then a sharp drill bit lets you do that.

CHAPTER 2 – TOOLS, ESSENTIAL AND EXTRA   **35**

■ The 2Unique Barrel Nut Wrench is one of the best to be had if you are using a standard barrel nut. With nine posts to grab lugs, you will have to work hard to make it slip off.

where pistol grips are banned, and the tele-stocks are considered evil. However, they (and arm braces) attach to the receiver the same way the other stocks do. So, if you know how to attach, replace, swap or tighten the two types, you can handle the Kaliforniastan "stocks" or the AR-15 pistol arm braces.

Let's look more closely at fixed stocks. The fixed stocks attach to the buffer tube using a special screw, the top screw of the buttstock buttplate. This screw has a hole drilled through it to drain water, and the threads have a thread-locking compound to resist vibration. All you need is a blade screwdriver to loosen or tighten it. The buffer tube it slides over (see Stock Chapter for details) is tightened to the receiver by the flats on the end of the tube. All you need for that is a crescent wrench.

The tele-stocks are more involved. They have a buttstock portion that slides back and forth and is locked in each setting by the spring-loaded latch on the bottom. Installing or removing the slider does not require tools, just moderately good hand strength.

■ The Real Avid Lower Fixture keeps the lower in place. You clamp the fixture in a vise, then slide the lower onto it. This is just for assembling internals, not installing the buffer tube.

However, the buffer tube is clamped on with the "castle" nut threaded around it. To tighten the nut, you need a special wrench — no other will do. Luckily, that wrench is not expensive; you can get one for $10-$20 at the low end. The tele-stock castle nut must also be secured in its location by staking the steel plate it tightens up to. That calls for a spring-loaded center punch, another not-expensive hardware tool. Barrels are another matter.

Barrel Swap

Swapping barrels calls for some way to hold the receiver in place while you unscrew the barrel nut. You need either the clamshell plastic clamps fixture (to clamp the receiver in the vise) or the reaction rod (to slide the receiver over). You will need a barrel nut wrench, and here the first piece of advice I can give you is simple: avoid the mil-spec "wrench." That thing is a small-ish steel plate with three teeth poking up out of the plate. It has a square hole for the torque wrench and slots on the sides for the flash hider and other items.

The military wrench is adequate for a small percentage of the barrel swaps ever done. Of the rest, it is an invitation to hurt yourself and damage your rifle. The military wrench cannot handle torque limits past the low end. If you must apply more than a modest amount of force, the wrench pegs will slip out of the teeth of the barrel nut, rounding the edges of both pegs and teeth, and probably cause you to slip and gouge your hand. Or hurl the wrench to the floor, along with your attached torque wrench. Despite some people claiming that it is the "proper tool," save yourself the hassle and skip it.

■ The Reaction Rod slides into the upper receiver and holds the barrel in place by its locking lugs.

■ Note the splines on the Reaction Rod that mate with the locking lugs in the barrel extension.

■ To remove the ejector from an AR-15 bolt, it is highly suggested that you invest in this tool. The ejector disassembly fixture is made by Young Engineering. It is possible to remove the ejector without one, but it is well worth the money to buy this tool.

■ The M-Guns MOACKS. To properly stake the gas key on your carrier, you must have this or one of the various versions Ned Christensen makes.

I haven't tried them all, and this is only a partial list, but I have had good luck with 2Unique, Midwest Industries, a wrench that DPMS once offered, and the Real Avid wrench built into the Armorers hammer.

If you are going to swap barrels, you'll also have to deal with the gas tube. Now, if you have shot a barrel enough to have worn it out, you have also likely put enough rounds on the gas tube that you should replace both at the same time. If you don't care about saving the old one, you can simply use a hacksaw to chop the old gas tube, junk the parts and proceed. You will still need a new gas tube, roll pin, and punches to install the roll pin. You may or may not feel the need for a gas tube alignment gauge, but many gas tubes have been installed without that gauge.

If you use the same USGI plastic handguards, you'll want to take the delta ring assembly apart to install on the new barrel. That calls for reverse pliers, a typical hardware store tool.

The installation requires some thorough cleaning, but you've got the cleaning supplies. You can Loctite or epoxy the new barrel into the upper (there are two sides to that decision, which we'll go into in the barrel swap chapter), so you may or may not need those.

You'll also want to remove the handguards, the

flash hider, any lights, lasers or other gear mounted on the upper. But those all call for regular tools you'll already have by this time in the book.

Things you may be told you need but probably won't: headspace gauges and erosion gauges. If you buy a new bolt with your new barrel (prudent, bolts do not have an infinite life, unlike carriers, which do), it will be appropriately headspaced by the suppliers. Erosion gauges are used to measure service life left in a barrel. They are handy when rifles are issued to end-users who really aren't all that invested in any particular one. The only way for military or LE armorers to tell if a barrel still has "life" left in it is to poke an erosion gauge into the chamber end. If it goes too deep, the barrel has too much wear on it, and it will get a new barrel.

> "Things you may be told you need but probably won't: headspace gauges and erosion gauges. If you buy a new bolt with your new barrel (prudent, bolts do not have an infinite life, unlike carriers, which do), it will be appropriately headspaced by the suppliers."

Note that your rifle won't be handed to just anyone to shoot however much they shoot it. You'll have a reasonably good idea of how much ammo yours has shot because you fired it. For most shooters, somewhere between 5,000 and 10,000 rounds will be a barrel's service life. Some barrels will last longer. Some shooters won't notice a drop-off in accuracy until 10,000 rounds, simply because they haven't the skills yet, or haven't heated their barrel toasty in multiple practice sessions. Others will notice and will want to replace a barrel sooner.

Keep good track of your ammo consumption (not difficult, given the cost) and start looking for a new barrel before yours is used up.

■ You can install barrels and other parts by feel, but a torque wrench lets you learn that "feel" that much sooner.

■ In the old days, we tried to change barrels by clamping the barrels in aluminum blocks. It is a pitiful method and one to avoid. Get proper tools.

CHAPTER 2 – TOOLS, ESSENTIAL AND EXTRA ■ 39

■ The Real Avid parts kit includes the Multi-Use Hammer.

■ The Real Avid Hammer is also a castle nut wrench.

■ The hammer is also a barrel nut wrench with multi splines.

■ And it has ten pegs for locking securely into the notches on the barrel nut collar.

Advanced and Special Tools

One particular tool is for those who will insist on keeping the USGI plastic handguards. Most new rifles these days come with one or another free-float handguard, but there are still many plastic handguards on rifles. They are held using the delta ring on the front edge of the receiver (back end of the handguards), which can be tough to remove. So much so that the Army TM showing disassembly illustrates the process, with two pairs of hands involved. That's fine if you are part of a team. But an individual doesn't have three hands. (Not even Chernobyl tour guides have three hands. Yet.) So, several companies make a special wrench to make it easy. Real Avid (you'll be seeing that brand name a lot, along with Brownells, get used to it) makes one and includes it in its Master Armorers Kit.

Another specialty tool is the Brownells sight block. You use it to remove (or install) the tapered

■ If you are going to do any front sight or gas block work, you must have the Brownells sight pin block. One side lets you take the pins out, the other put them in. And it is clearly marked.

pins on a barrel's "A" frame sight assembly. Without it, the task is annoying and risks damaging or at least marring the sight or barrel. With it, the job is simple and easy. If you need it, it is the best $40 you'll ever spend. You can still use it as a backer block for other pin removal or installation if you don't. ■

■ This 2Unique barrel nut wrench looks like the USGI one but is far superior. The GI one has three pegs, the 2Unique nine. People have hurt themselves when the GI one slipped.

CHAPTER 2 – TOOLS, ESSENTIAL AND EXTRA

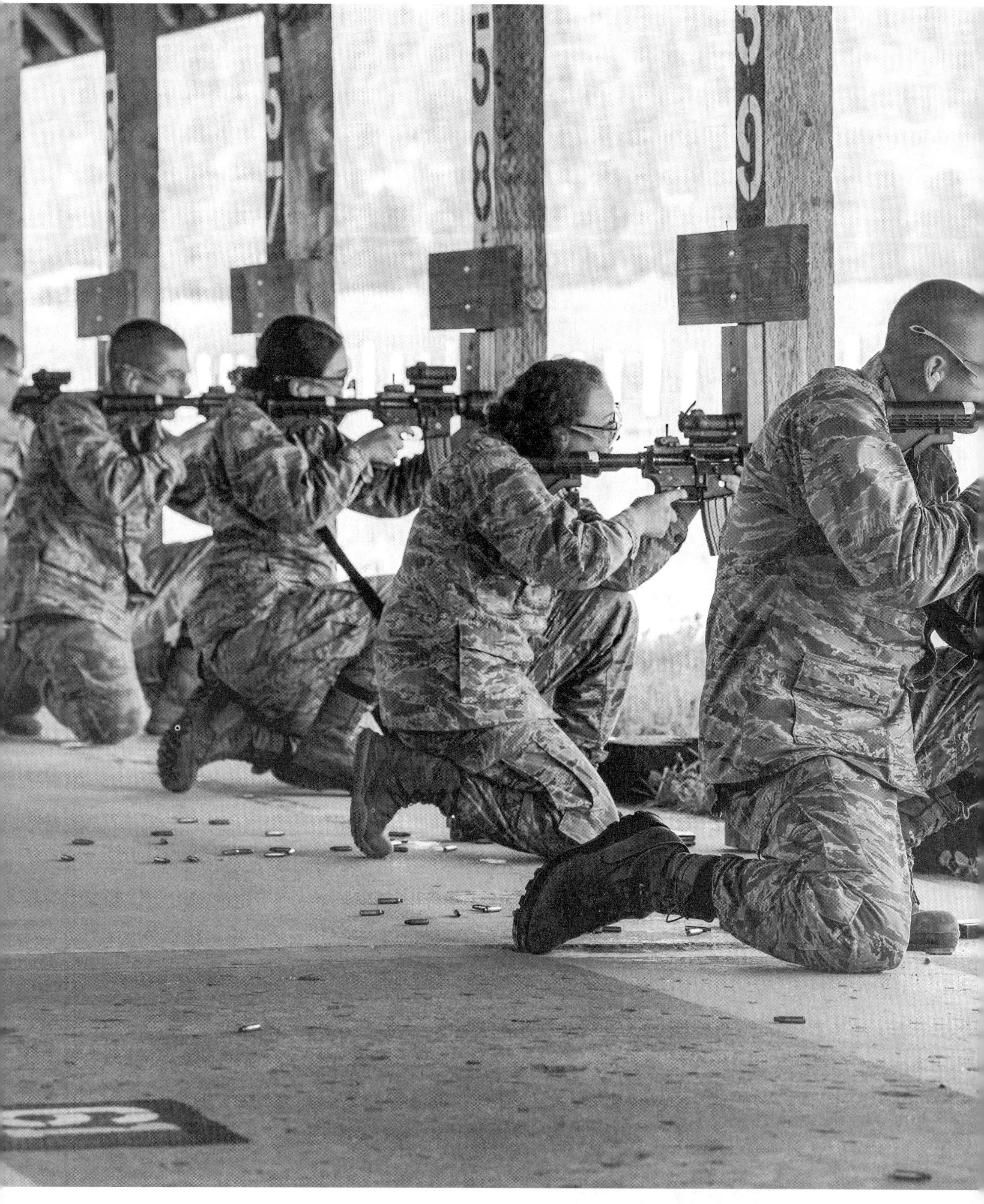

3

Testing the AR-15

We will have the testing part of the book upfront for a simple reason: many new AR owners didn't buy a parts kit and didn't build it themselves. They purchased a rifle ready-to-go. (Well, maybe they had to buy sights or a scope, but you get the idea.) And they want to know if it is a good and proper rifle and if it works the way they expect it to.

So, we'll cover testing now and come back later with a laser focus on specific parts of the AR-15 when we do the work to build, upgrade or replace parts.

You can do testing before or after the actual purchase process in three phases: visual inspection, mechanical check and range function. Oh, and a brief aside: gun shops might be a bit leery of letting you do all the visual and mechanical checks. Having a customer taking a rifle apart on the counter isn't the happiest moment in the life of a retail guy at the gun shop. So, there may be things they won't let you do. At a gun show, it apparently is common to have everything locked with zip ties, so nothing functions. You're going to get a visual inspection and not a thorough one at that. Then again, you are probably buying an AR-15 "new in the box," and if there's a problem, you have the manufacturer's warranty to cover you.

■ Many ranges are organized at this level. You will have to keep track of your magazines and won't have the freedom to just stroll down and check your targets when you want to. Testing the function and zero of a new AR-15 can eat up most of a day.

■ When you remove your extractor and find it has a blue buffer and no O-ring, it might be alright. But if you have any problems in test firing, install an O-ring or D-Fender.

You can probably go right to the firing line and perform the function tests at the gun club, assuming you have the ammo with you to do so.

Life isn't always a clean checklist.

Visual Inspection

The visual inspection is just what it says. You look at everything and make sure that all is as it should be. We'll assume you're at a gun shop, or a gun show, or the gun club, and someone has offered you an AR-15 for sale. What do you look at, and what do you look for? The first step is what I call the "tire tracks and hammer marks" look. Are there scratches, gouges, dings, dents, cracks or other signs of abuse or hard use? Mis-matched paint or different types of finish? Such issues won't matter much in and of themselves. Receivers that have had the high spots worn white simply mean it got a lot of rubbing and abrasion, but if the upper and lower are still tight to each other, that probably isn't a big deal. (Except cosmetically, of course.)

We'll start with a basic A2 or M4 clone, with plastic handguards and looking very much like a USGI rifle or carbine.

■ This photo illustrates why you either dry-fire with the bolt in place or position your thumb in front of the hammer. The thin wall of the bolt stop slot will get bent if you let the hammer slam into it.

Open the action and make sure it is unloaded. Close the bolt. Close the dust cover. Both should snap into place. Check the fit of the upper to the lower. Wobbling isn't a sign of unreliability, but it can be aggravating. If you can live with the wobble, let it go. Otherwise, pass. Does it have sights? Are they tight, or do they wobble? Peer over the action's top and look at the front sight pillar. Is it vertical? A tilted front sight A-pillar is a bad sign, pass. Check the sight for tightness. Again, if loose, pass on it. Look at the front sight post. The plate in which the post sits should be flush with the top deck of the sight pillar. If the sight is visibly unlevel, then look at the sight pillar. Is there an "F" in the casting? Look at the front face of the upper receiver. There should be (if it is an M4 flat-top) a stamped "M4" above the gas tube hole. A zeroed

■ If the carrier doesn't stand on its own weight, the gas rings are worn and need to be replaced.

■ The castle nut on a carbine must be staked if you expect it to stay tight.

■ Colt doesn't mark it with a very large letter, but this is an H buffer, and this carbine works well with it. Use the heaviest buffer your carbine works reliably with.

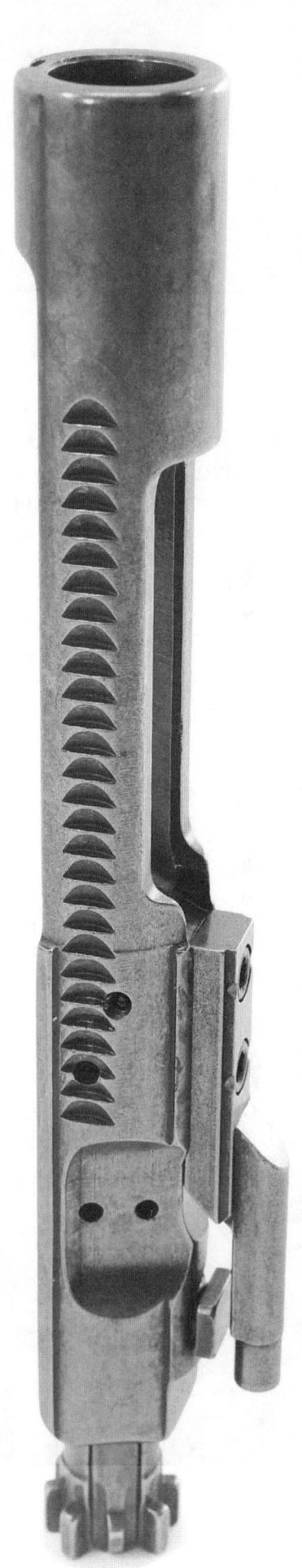

CHAPTER 3 – TESTING THE AR-15

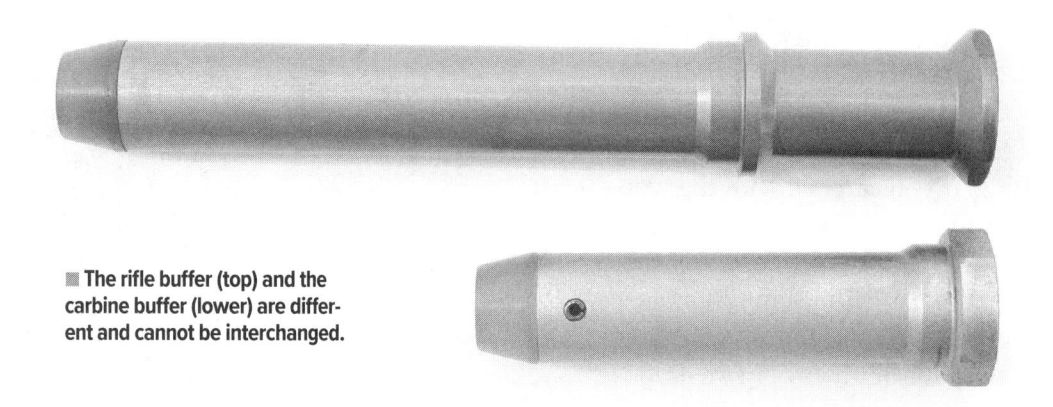

The rifle buffer (top) and the carbine buffer (lower) are different and cannot be interchanged.

rifle with the front sight perched too high is a sign of an improper barrel/receiver match. Unless you like "project" guns, pass on it.

Are the handguards tight? Are they aligned? Cockeyed handguards indicate that the barrel nut isn't correctly aligned, which can lead to many other problems. Is the stock tight? If it has a tele-stock, is it vertical, and does the slider slide smoothly fore and aft?

Push the rear takedown pin out, hinge it open, and extract the bolt and carrier and the charging handle. (You can separate the two halves at this point if you wish.) Set the carrier and handle down. Look down the bore. Unless you have exceptional eyesight, you won't be able to see more than "Is there daylight down the bore?" but you need to see that much.

Look at the inside of the upper receiver: If clean, there should not be any visible wear, bright lines, marks or other signs of tools being jammed in and worked around.

Inspect the bolt and carrier. The bolt lugs should be clean and whole, with no chips or cracks. The face should not have more than a test-fire ring of

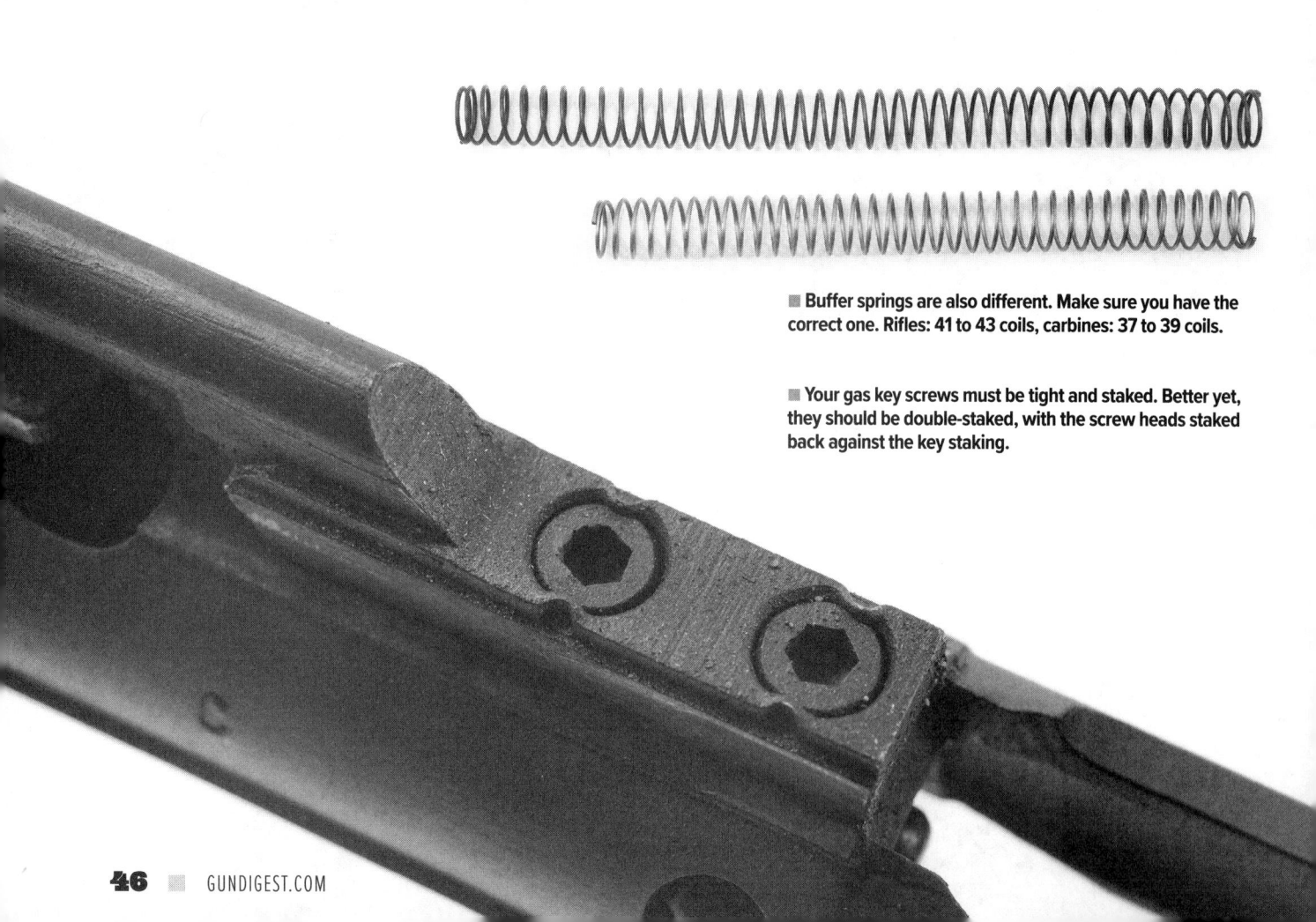

■ *Buffer springs are also different. Make sure you have the correct one. Rifles: 41 to 43 coils, carbines: 37 to 39 coils.*

■ *Your gas key screws must be tight and staked. Better yet, they should be double-staked, with the screw heads staked back against the key staking.*

■ For actual testing and trajectory verification, you need to know bullet velocity. For that, there's nothing like a chronograph, and the Labradar shines here.

brass or primer sealant around the firing pin hole. Look at the gas key. It should have the screws held in by stakings, where metal has been peened over the hole to keep the screws in place. If you see any cracks, chips or missing metal, pass. You can fix a gas key needing staking, but it might call for some bargaining. Pull the bolt to full extension, and then stand the bolt/carrier assembly on its face. If the weight of the carrier causes the assembly to close down, then the gas rings are either missing or worn. That, too, is cause for negotiations, but it also indicates either a poor assembly job or excessive shooting.

Look at the inside of the lower. It probably has a plain trigger set installed, so look at the spring on the hammer. The crossbar of the hammer spring should be tight against the back of the hammer, with the struts parallel to the hammer. The hammer spring legs need to be on top of the trigger pin outside the trigger spring hoops.

Look at the buffer assembly. The buffer retainer should be sticking up enough to block the buffer, and not by using just the tip of the retainer.

Check the tightness of the pistol grip and the stock. You can quickly tighten both, but looseness here is a sign something might be amiss. If it has a tele-stock, look at the castle nut. It should be assembled with the large notches to the rear. The small ones (on the front held in place by the retaining plate) should be staked. Missing stakings here is yet another sign of poor assembly. Flip the lower over and eyeball the alignment of the telestock with the receiver. A tipped telestock assembly on

> "Check the tightness of the pistol grip and the stock. You can quickly tighten both, but looseness here is a sign something might be amiss."

top of all the others is the final clue that this was assembled by a hack, and you should either pass or get a great bargain on it — it is going to be a project to clean up the missing elements.

Last visual check, but also the first of the function checks. Insert an unloaded magazine into the mag well. It should slide in smoothly, and the bolt hold-open should rise when the magazine follower presses it. When you press the magazine button,

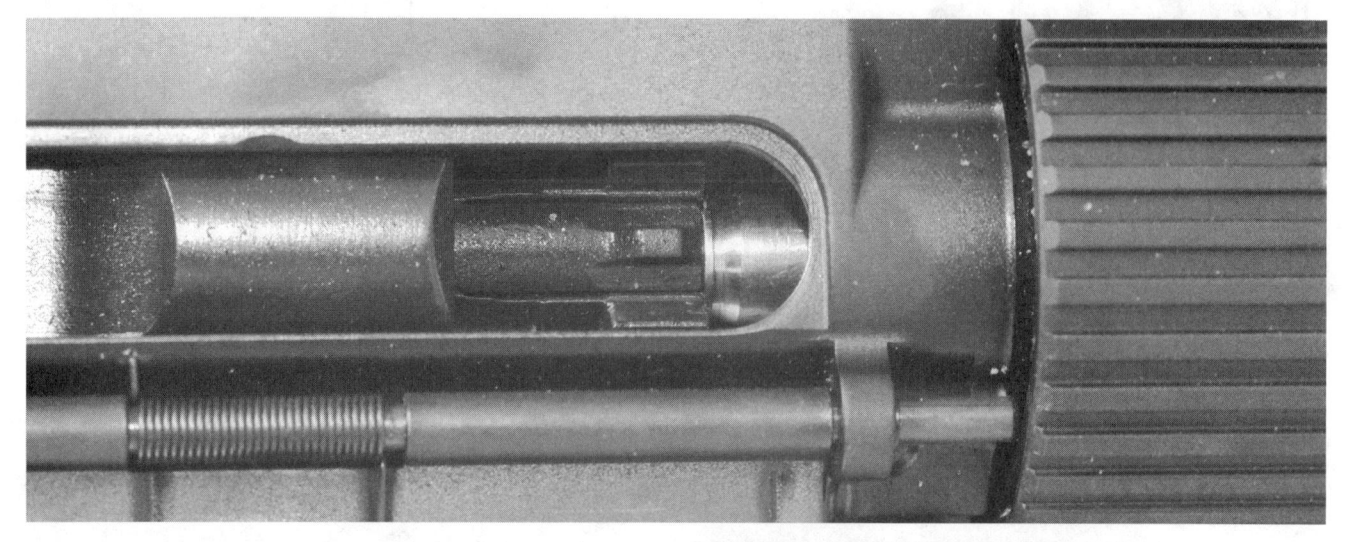

■ This round absolutely won't go into the chamber. There's no point in trying to pound it in. Remove it and find out why the problem happened.

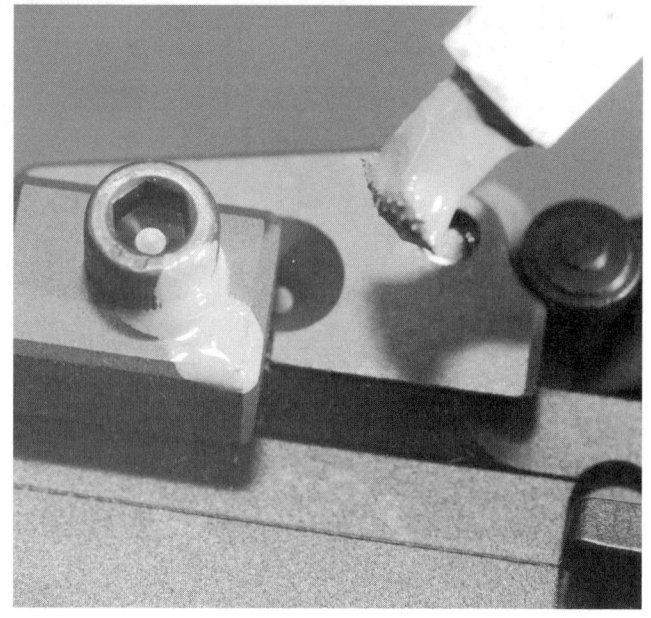

■ You should paint and mark every bolt or screw that can loosen. That way, you can tell if they have come loose.

does the magazine fall out of its own weight? So far, so good.

Reassemble the Rifle

This is where the gun shop or the gun show proprietor might start getting a bit fussy. If they don't let you check things, get a written warranty on function.

Look at the magazine catch button. The center screw should be flush with the ridged surface of the button. If not, more ham-handed assembly.

Try moving the selector from Safe to Fire. It should move with some force but smoothly and click into each position. If it is an ambidextrous setup, both levers should work properly. Move the selector to Safe. Press the trigger, up to about 10 pounds of pressure. Let go, and then push the selector to Fire. *The hammer should not fall.* If it does, hand it back, you are done here. Press the trigger and hear the hammer fall. Keep holding the trigger back, and then work the action. Once the bolt is closed, slowly ease the trigger forward. You should hear a click as the disconnector hands the hammer off to the trigger. If you hear a *thunk* — the hammer falling onto the firing pin — you have a disconnector problem, and that will require gunsmithing. If the disconnector doesn't let go of the hammer at all, that is a different problem, but one that you can readily correct.

Insert an empty magazine. Pull the charging handle back; the bolt should lock open. Remove the magazine, and the bolt should stay open. Close the bolt.

Test Fire

To test fire, you'll need at least one 30-round magazine and 40 to 50 rounds. Don't panic; you won't be firing them all. Load the magazine with five rounds. Carefully shoot a group at 25 yards. What

> "This is where the gun shop or the gun show proprietor might start getting a bit fussy. If they don't let you check things, get a written warranty on function."

■ The Ballisticker on this AR-15 gives the shooter known drops to distances for a better chance of a first-shot hit.

■ Once your parts are correctly located (after you've tested them, obviously), then use paint and a small brush or a paint pen, and mark their locations. If this screw loosens, you will be able to tell.

you are looking for is simple: the group should be centered left-to-right and an inch or a bit more below the point of aim. (How much depends on the zero range intended by the builder or owner.) The empties should have been tossed in a similar direction and distance. Some people get wound up about making a rifle eject to an exact, specified angle and distance. If it is consistent, you are good. Much too far forward or to the rear, there may be problems you'll have to tend to. But if the empties are between two o'clock and five o'clock (assuming your firing direction is Noon), then you are good.

The bolt must have locked open when you fired the last round. Failure here may be a magazine problem, so you want to do this test with a mag of known reliability. If the magazine is not worn and of known reliability, failing to lock open is a problem.

Now, load the magazine to its full 30-round capacity. Close the bolt, and insert the magazine. In some circles, magazines are supposed to be "down-loaded," that is, loaded with only 28 rounds, so there is always compression room when inserting a magazine. What you are testing here is: is there compression room? Ideally, you should be able to seat the magazine, albeit with more force than if it was down-loaded, but you should be able to seat it. If you must hammer the magazine hard, or it simply isn't possible to seat it, then the dimensions of the lower, upper, mag catch carrier and magazine all stack against you. If you can live with that, since you always down-load your magazines anyway, then this is fine. If it has to seat a fully loaded 30-round mag, then this isn't the rifle for you.

Pull the charging handle back and let go. The bolt should strip the top round from the magazine and chamber it. If it doesn't, the action spring is tired, or the extractor has too much tension, or the rifle is just so new it hasn't yet been broken in.

Fire another five-round group. Here, you check that the rifle doesn't cycle so quickly that a fully loaded magazine can't lift the full cartridge stack enough to feed.

You're Done

If it passes all these tests, then you are at one of two points: you have successfully built or modified your rifle — or you have tested a rifle new to you, and the only thing left is to wrangle on the price.

Now let's look at things your rifle must have to be genuinely ready for a training class or real-world self-defense.

New or old, plain-Jane or hi-zoot, no-name or fancy name, any rifle I take to a class or have in the rack to be depended on, has the following items checked or tested, or done to it:

Staked

The gas key and castle nut are inspected, and if not staked, then re-fit and staked.

Ring

The extractor gets checked, and it has the internal buffer, black, and an external O-ring or D-Fender. These are things the gun shop or gun show won't let you check, though your buddy at the gun club might. But they are also easy enough to fix on your own once you get the rifle home.

Leade

Again, leade is something the shop or show won't let you check, but it's also a detail that's easy to fix.

Buffer

I make sure my AR-15s have the proper buffer and the heaviest ones that run reliably in a carbine with a tele-stock.

■ The military uses the "SPORTS" acronym to solve problems in the field. It stands for, Slap on the bottom of the magazine; Pull the charging handle to the rear; Observe the chamber for an ejection of the round; Release the charging handle; Tap the forward assist; Squeeze the trigger again. But at the range, not under pressure, it is better to figure out why the problem happened and solve it at the source.

Christiansen doesn't make them for every combination (I'm not sure that is even possible), but you can come close. I mean, if the chart says you'll get a 2.5-inch drop at 200 yards, and in testing your rifle, it produces a 2.4- or 2.75-inch drop, does it really matter?

The point is to know, close enough, how much you might have to account for, should you need to be reaching out that far. Yes, you could use a marking pen or tape a range card, but the Ballisticker is more elegant.

SPORTS

The military uses an acronym: SPORTS. This means Slap on the bottom of the magazine. Pull the charging handle to the rear and Observe the chamber for an ejection of the round. Release the charging handle. Tap the forward assist and Squeeze the trigger again.

As a system of getting a rifle running again in a combat situation, it works OK. In a defensive situation, the same applies. But, at the gun club or a competition, you may not have to do all that automatically.

We can dispense with the slap part of it if, while inserting a magazine, you push it in until it clicks and then tug it to try to remove it. If it stays, it stays; no slapping is needed later. You will want to see if something comes out when you work the charging handle, but you need to take extra action if nothing does.

If nothing comes out, then lock the bolt back. Remove the magazine. Stick your fingers up into the magazine well and dislodge any wedged rounds. Re-insert the magazine, hit the bolt release and get back to shooting.

You never need the forward assist, except in one very particular situation: If you are chamber-checking your rifle to check for a round in the chamber, you ease the bolt back. You look and feel and then close the bolt. You might want to press the forward assist, then and only then, to ensure the bolt has fully closed on the round. Usually, it closes with the full force of the buffer spring and weight. Lacking that, it might not fully close, and the forward assist solves that issue.

In no other situation do you need the forward assist, and using it enthusiastically will usually get you into trouble. ■

Paint

Anything that is bolted on, or needs to be secure and not move, gets a dab of paint as a location marker. If the paint bridge across the parts is broken or not lined up, something has changed and needs to be checked before taking it to a class or using it for a competition or duty/defense.

Zeroed

The rifle will be zeroed, and the front sight and any optics will have their locations painted to indicate that they are zeroed.

And an Extra

I also have added a Ballisticker to some of my rifles. The Ballisticker is an adhesive-backed ballistics chart made by Ned Christiansen of M-Guns (m-guns.com). It shows the trajectory of a given load, so I know that (if I should need it) the drop of that rifle at 200 yards is X inches, for example.

4 Uppers

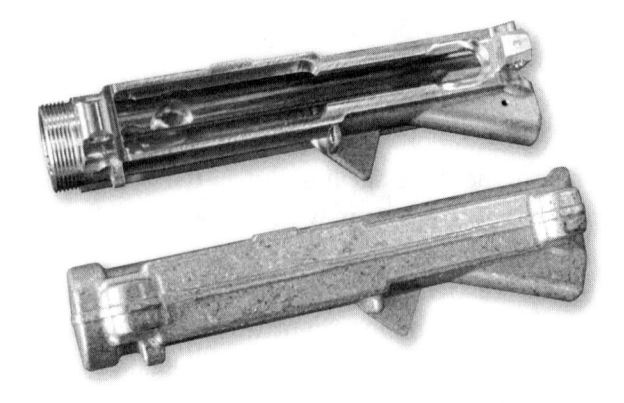

■ The upper comes from a forging (or a billet) and gets machined, like the bottom. You can see the line down the bottom of the forged lower, blanked out of the platter.

A famous line that all students learning Latin are expected to know goes: "All Gaul is divided into three parts." This was said by Julius Caesar and provides several lessons in Latin grammar and sentence structure. I don't know what Jules would make of the AR-15, but uppers are made of aluminum and are also divided into three parts — or types — if you will. They are A1, A2 and flat-top. You might not have seen either of the A1 or A2 if you are a recent AR-15 shopper. Almost everything AR these days is produced with a flat-top upper, also known as the A3/A4 upper in some circles. But you may want something different, or you may be offered something different. There is also the subject of "retro" builds. That's where someone builds a rifle like the ones made in 1968. So, here's the breakdown:

■ The various military branches have carry handles that bolt onto the flat-top M4 uppers because they bought a lot of them "back in the day," and they still work.

CHAPTER 4 — UPPERS

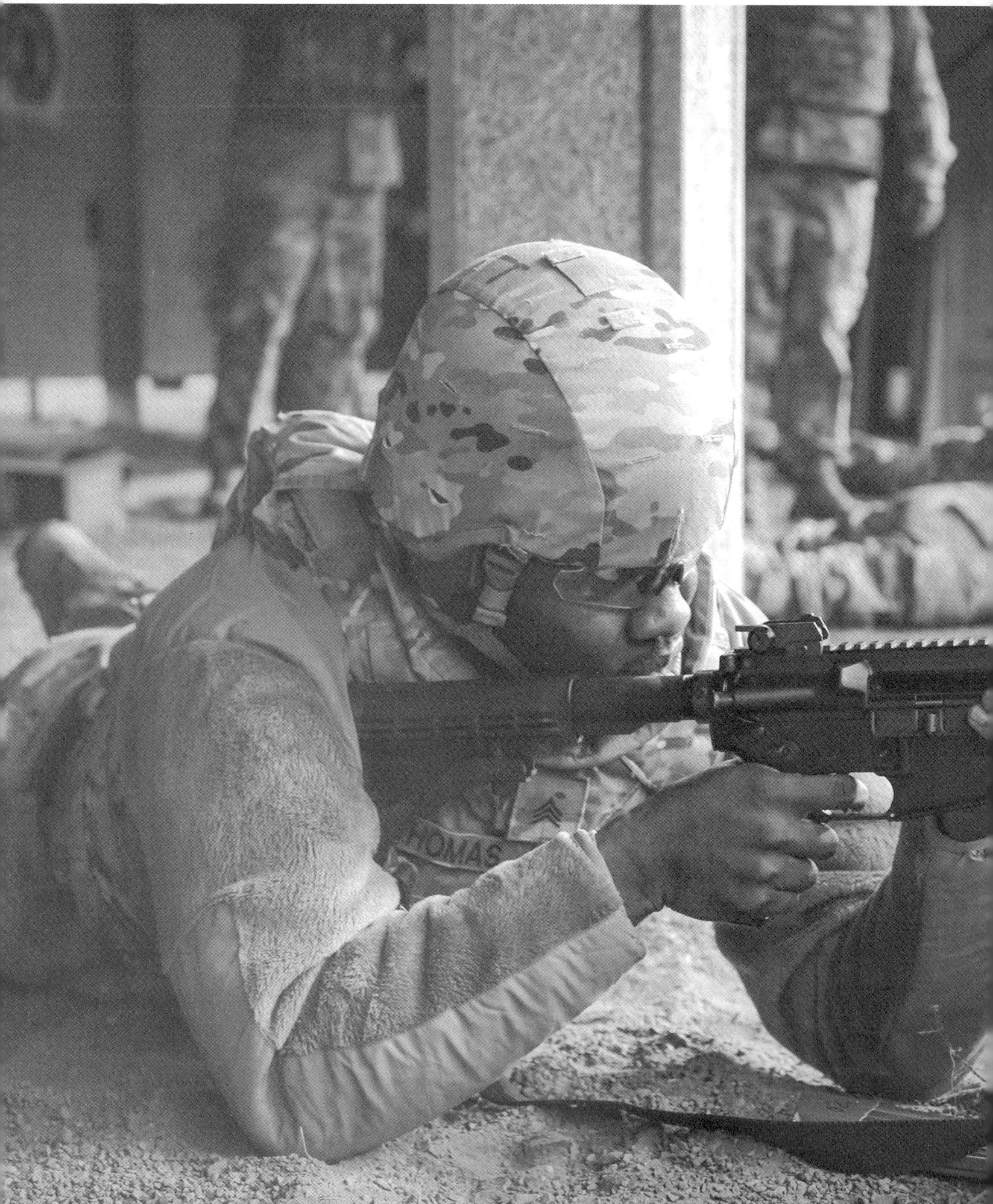
HOMAS

■ The flat-top upper makes it easy to mount optics, but the government still uses iron sights. Iron sights don't use batteries that can go dead.

A1

The A1 is the original, fixed-handle upper with the two-position flip-set rear sight, also known as a "Vietnam" upper. An A1 upper may or may not have a forward assist (FA) button, and those lacking them are known as "slickside" uppers. The A1 upper will lack a pyramid on the right side, which is a brass deflector. The deflector keeps brass from hitting left-handed shooters when they are shooting left-handed. Just to complicate things, when we adopted the A2, the Canadians kept the A1 upper but had the ejector block added to the forging. So, if you see "C7" in an upper or rifle description, you know that's what combo it is.

The retro builders will obsess over the "fence" around the magazine release button on the lower. The raised rib also contains the spring and plunger for the front takedown pin retainer, which we'll cover in the chapter on lowers. But just be aware that an A1 upper, to be correctly "retro," must go on one or another style of A1 lower.

A2

The A2 is the upper that came about in the 1980s when the idea was to make a more accurate and capable long-range rifle. "Accuracy" was defined as target-range-suitable and range-adjustable, not just a fixed-sight combat weapon. The A2 has a large, blocky rear sight, and the sight has adjustments built-in, hand-adjustable for range and windage. All A2 uppers have a forward assist button and the ejector pyramid. The A2 is not seen much these days, as the whole idea of shooting with iron sights has been relegated to "emergency" status, something you do when your "real" sighting system — red-dot or other optics — have gone and broken on you.

Flat-top

With the flat-top, the carry handle (which was seldom used to carry the rifle) is essentially machined off, replaced with a slotted rail for mounting sights and optics. The manufacturers used a new forging mold. Instead of forging the aluminum billet into an A1 or A2 form, the mold hammers the upper into a near-cylindrical shape with a slotted rail on top. Flat-tops also have both the forward assist and the ejector pyramid.

In the old days, to make an AR-15 more amena-

■ The flat-top was a development by Colt that allowed the easy mounting of optics. Flat-tops are now standard.

ble to optics, we had to cut off the carry handle and secure a rail to the top of the receiver. This alteration involved screws and epoxy, as the aluminum used to make the AR-15 is unhappy being welded. Plus, the receiver walls are so thin that it would

> "Now, flat-top uppers are not just common; they are pretty much the standard. And they don't cost much even in the current craze, an upper going for $60-$70 when they are in stock."

take a skilled welder to weld a rail on and not warp things. We were all cheap, we used epoxy, and a lot of it, mixed with black dye.

Now, flat-top uppers are not just common; they are pretty much the standard. And they don't cost much even in the current craze, an upper going for $60-$70 when they are in stock. People want uppers, so as soon as a supply comes in, whoever is selling fills backorders, and then the rest evaporates quickly.

Aluminum

What is aluminum? And why do we use it?

Aluminum is the third-most abundant element on the planet. (And in case you were wondering, the first and second are oxygen and silicon.) Why, then, is it not everywhere? Why can't you just haul chunks of aluminum (aside from the discarded soft-drink cans you find) out of the dirt in your backyard? The answer: Because it is so reactive, it has been bound into mineral combinations with other elements. And the reaction creates a bond so strong that it is nearly impossible for different reactions to free it. Basically, in nature, aluminum oxidizing and reacting to form various minerals is a one-way street. Aluminum is found in over 250 minerals; the primary ore-bearing type is known as Bauxite.

Soft, durable, lightweight and malleable, aluminum has a lot of uses in modern society. However, it takes a modern society to produce it in any significant amounts. Bauxite holds aluminum in its bosom so closely that it takes a considerable effort to separate the metal from the ore. What about steel? With steel, you heat up the ore, blow air or oxygen through it, and skim off the slag to make iron from ore. Then pour off the iron.

Compared to aluminum, you could train your pet retriever to make steel. The various processes (and there are many) use combinations of the big three — heat, electricity, chemical reactions. Depending on the method used, the price of making aluminum just in electricity alone can be more than a quarter of the finished cost. So ferocious was the cost of aluminum production that Napoleon III was rumored to have an aluminum dinner set for himself and left the platinum, gold and silver dinnerware for his guests. As a result, it was pretty easy to tell where you were in the pecking order of the Second Empire court. Platinum? You're good. Gold? Need to work on your skills. Silver? Keep an eye over your shoulder because unless your courtier skills got a significant upgrade, you were gone with the next batch of aggressive social-climbing arrivals. As amusing as the tale is, no one really knows for sure, but it gives you an idea of how fabulously expensive it was to make metallic aluminum before the 20th century.

Aluminum, in its pure metallic state, is not useable as a metal to build things with. It is too soft and too easily corroded. In a manner of speaking, we alloy steel to improve its mechanical properties. We alloy aluminum to enhance its mechanical properties and keep it from corroding so quickly it won't stand up to use.

A brief aside to give you an idea of how much metals can differ in this regard. Aluminum will corrode and disintegrate if you aren't careful. In fact, the alloy used in the AR-15 was changed early on when manufacturers found that the peculiar combination of perspiration and a humid jungle environment caused it to basically melt away. Steel corrodes, but it stands up to a lot of abuse before it gives way. Titanium, on the opposite end, corrodes not at all in the way we think. Oh, the surface oxidizes, but the oxide created is an impenetrable "skin," and the corrosion cannot proceed further. In fact, titanium oxidizes so quickly it is difficult to produce a surface of titanium that isn't oxidized to Ti-oxide color.

As with steel, we can alloy aluminum with many other metals and elements. The two we will be most familiar with here are 6061 (aka "aircraft aluminum") and 7075. But there are many others. I recently found out about 5083, an alloy with a lot more manganese — magnesium and a good dollop of chromium in it. Used in shipbuilding and some applications of naval aircraft, it welds like a dream and has excellent corrosion resistance. It isn't heat-treatable, but it doesn't lose its strength when welded.

But we should spend our time looking at the common ones in the AR-verse.

■ The "M4" marking on the front face of this flat-top upper means it is machined for M4 feed ramps.

■ The two iron-sight AR-15 uppers. In front, the original A1. In the rear, the A2, or the "new" one, from the mid-1980s.

6061 Aluminum

6061 is indeed an aircraft alloy or was the most prevalent one back when aircraft manufacture shifted from wood-and-wire to aluminum. It is alloyed with magnesium and silicon, and it is a precipitation-hardening alloy. While it welds nicely, it loses tensile strength at the area of the weld. So, a basic alloy, un-heat-treated, would be a 6061, while something that has been heat-treated would be 6061-T6. (The "T6" reflecting the heat-treatment process.)

If you took a part that was formed and heat-treated, then welded on it, the areas around the weld would lose the strength added by the heat treatment. In the location of the weld, the joined parts would be soft. That's a drawback, but only if you view the world solely through welding goggles.

6061 was developed in the mid-1930s and used in aircraft production. For some of you, the light bulb just went on. "Rivets." Yep, that's why aircraft then (and many now) have such a profusion of rivets. If you were to weld the skin of the aircraft fuselage to the ribcage or spars, you'd lose tensile strength at the welds. But, if you drill holes through the plates, then rivet them on, you don't lose strength.

If you're willing to put up with the loss of tensile strength or are willing to heat treat after you weld, 6061 welds like there's no tomorrow. It is also very amenable to extrusion. OK, a quick up-to-speed on extrusions.

If you take a hot and malleable (but not molten) piece of metal, and you shove it through a shaped die, the metal flows thorough, yes, just like a tube of toothpaste. You can extrude a bar and then machine it to whatever final shape you need. A neat trick in extrusion is to extrude a plate, then,

ALUMINUM ALLOY CONSTITUENTS, BY PERCENTAGE

ALUMINUM	SILICON	MANGANESE	COPPER	CHROMIUM	ZINC
6061	.6	1.0	.25	.20	—
7075	—	2.5	1.6	.23	5.6

in multiple operations, curve the plate until it is a pipe, and then allow the heated parts to re-join. Doing that just saved you a whole lot of time and cutter work, instead of boring out a bar to make a tube. 6061 extrudes nicely, which is why your free-float handguard will be made of 6061-T6.

7075 Aluminum

The alloy you are more likely to have heard of is 7075, specifically 7075-T6. Again, the "T6" part of it is the heat-treatment process given the aluminum alloy. 7075 is an aluminum alloy with a big helping of zinc. The total composition is zinc, 5.6 to 6 percent; magnesium, 2 to 2.5 percent; and copper, 1.2 to 1.6 percent, with trace amounts of iron, silicon, titanium, manganese, chromium and others. Some trace amounts are there simply because it isn't worth the effort to eliminate them from the aluminum-bearing ore, and others are brought in from the various scrap sources. Recycled metals can't all be treated like steel scrap. There is no Bessemer process for recycled aluminum, whereby you can "blow" out the alloying ingredients as slag and produce pure aluminum.

In tensile strength, 7075-T6 rivals that of mild steel. With a tensile strength of around 75,000 PSI, it's used in many applications where the engineer ensures stresses will be under that ceiling. If you need more, you must jump up to steel and take the weight hit. Such is life.

■ This upper is a billet cut example, as you can tell by the flat panels on the upper. In a forging, they would be curved.

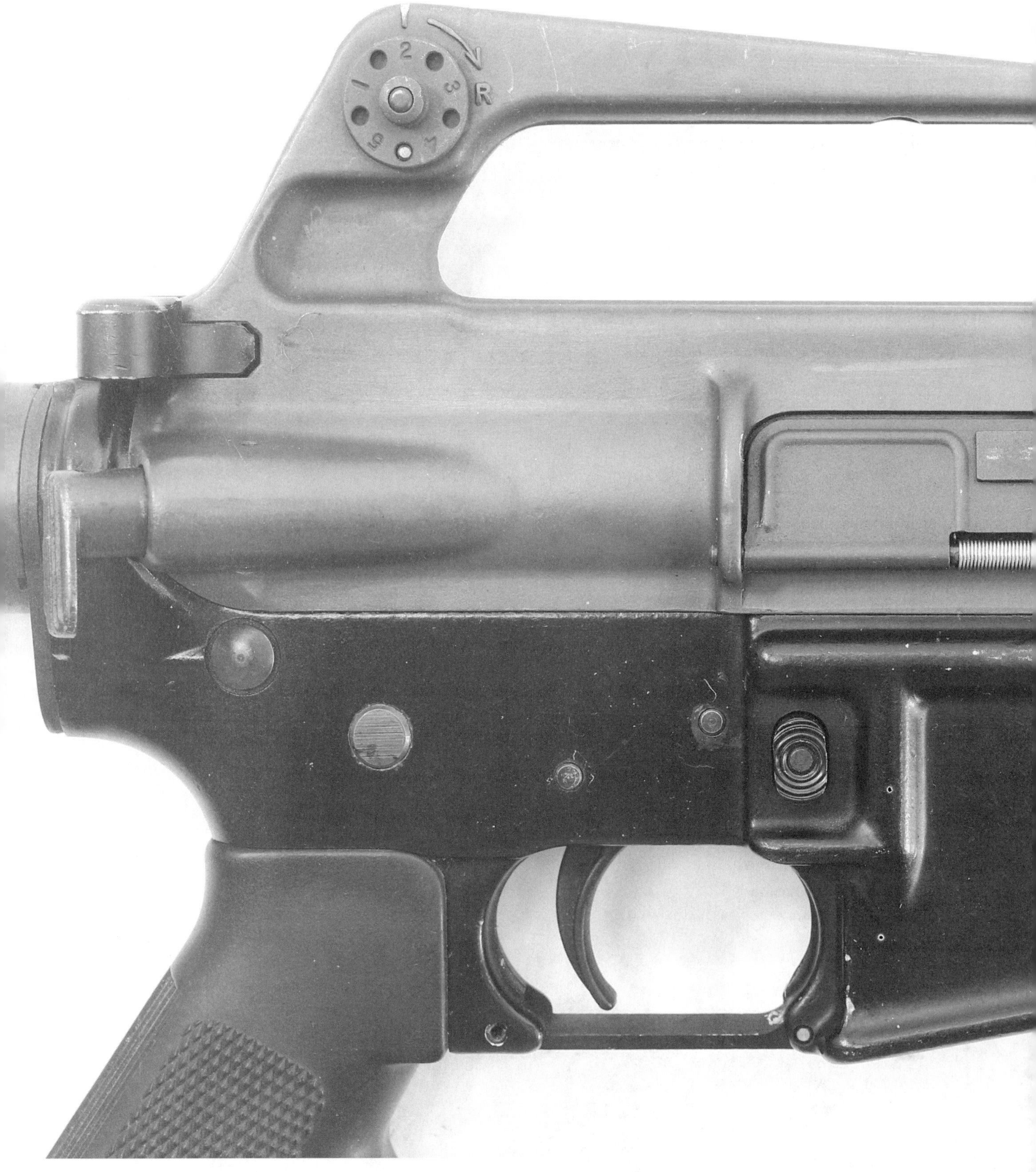
1
2
3
4
5
R

■ The original anodizing was given a light grey, and a medium gray (as pictured) before the military settled on black. On top is a medium gray, which was an M16A1. The lower is a 1980s flat black anodizing.

To make uppers and lowers of aluminum and do it properly, the manufacturer must do two things: forge the parts and heat treat them. So, let's go right into the life history of the upper you are holding in your hands. (I won't ask how you're reading this and holding an upper, but the imagination is capable of many things. Just look at the budget Congress puts out each year.)

The upper arrives at the forge shop in truck-length bars, each 4 to 6 inches in diameter. It comes as 7075-0 alloy, with the proper amounts of each metal in it, but no actual heat treating. All it has is inadvertent heat treatment caused by the bar-making process. In some instances, the mill will heat-soak the bars to relieve stress and remove (anneal) any unintentional heat treatment from heating aluminum and squeezing it out as bars.

The forge shop will cut the bars to length. The specific diameter is something handled in the customer's order and done by the mill. The lengths are cut by the forge shop because not all parts need the same sizes. The cut sections are then wheeled to the forge floor. There, a furnace feeds one or more forges. The furnace operator heats each bar to the correct temperature (for aluminum, it isn't all that high a temp) and then yanks them out when they are done, in turn, and feeds them to the forge. At the forge, the forge operator places the heated blank into the dies and trips the forge switch. The upper half slams down onto the lower half (each half has the 3-D mirror image of the part machined into its face), and the part is shaped. Depending on the machine, the alloy used, and the part, the forge may come down once or several times.

That part, now called a "platter," is hauled to a different furnace. There, it is heat soaked for the heat treatment. For the T6 treatment, this involves first heating it up to just under 850 degrees Fahrenheit. It will sit there for a few hours (depending on the part, the job specs, and the furnace operators' experience) and then it is shuffled off to a different furnace.

The parts will sit for a full day "aging" at 250 degrees Fahrenheit in the second furnace. Then they are allowed to cool. At this point, your upper looks like an upper trapped in an aluminum pancake. The bin of platters is crated up and shipped off to the machine shop.

The first step (if the forge shop didn't already do it) is to use a cookie-cutter-like machine to cut the upper out of the disk of the platter. This is known as "blanking" and, if done well, produces no scrapped parts and a quick production rate. If poorly done, it makes scrapped platters, slows production and costs the machine shop money. Then, an indexed surface is carefully cut onto the blanked upper. This is what the CNC tombstone will clamp onto to hold the parts while they are machined.

The CNC machine (computer numerical controlled) will whir away for minutes or hours and finally be done. The operator removes the completed uppers, replaces them with new blanks and closes the doors.

From here, the uppers get boxed up and sent off to the anodizing shop. Like forging, anodizing is a specialized operation, and it is almost unheard of for an AR manufacturer to both machine parts and anodize them. As you'll read later, anodizing involves vats of chemicals, with electricity pumped into them. This is not a home-shop operation, not something you do in-between your "real" workdays.

Once the parts return, they are inspected, graded and assembled into rifles (if the machine shop is also the rifle manufacturer) or shipped off to the assembler. The specialized work of CNC machining requires a significant capital investment, and to pay it off calls for constant production. It isn't unusual for a manufacturer who machines uppers and lowers to use them both in their own assembly and sell excess production to other assemblers.

So, you may have ABC Corp, an AR manufacturer, also making uppers that it sells to DEF Co., which also assembles rifles and sells uppers to GHI Industries, a wholesaler that sells to stores that sell you your bare upper.

That is pretty much the way a modern, industrial economy works, and firearms are no different. (Now, your current-generation iPhone didn't get built that way because Apple controls the entire chain. But your non-Apple phone may well have been made that way. Apple is rare in this respect, as most industries do not have that level of vertical integration.)

Machining

Back to the uppers. The forged parts are machined to final dimensions. The exterior surfaces

■ When mounting a scope, it is customary and prudent to use a cantilever mount, so you won't have the mount on two parts, upper and handguard.

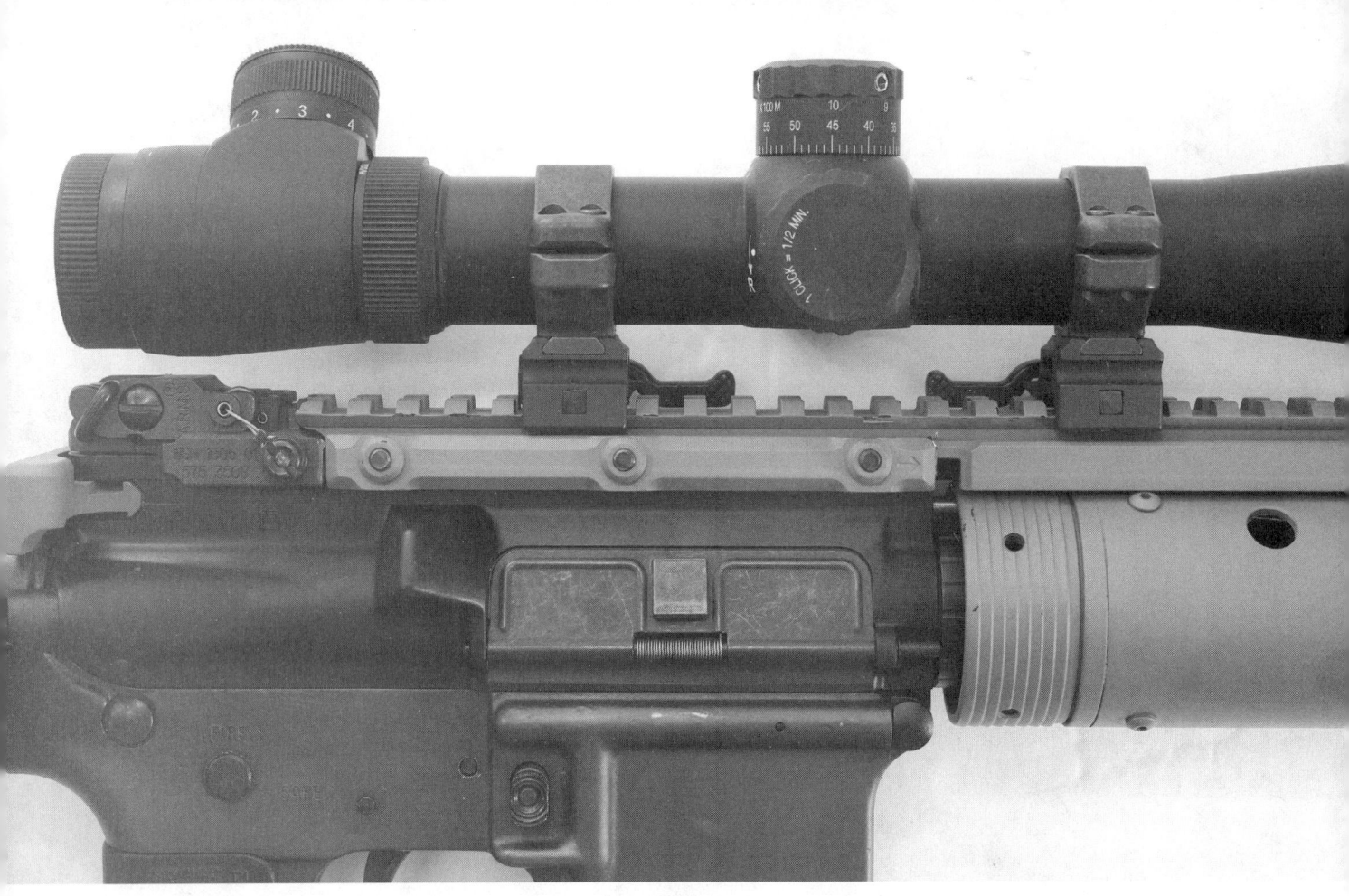

■ Primary Research got around the too-short upper rail problem by using an extra rail that bridges both and rigidly aligns the two and keeps them that way. No scope torquing here.

are left mostly untouched. The rail slots on the flat-top and the assembly lugs will be machined, but the rest of the exterior is left as-is. The interior is bored out, the barrel nut threads cut, and the ejection port machined into the side, along with a few other details. The exterior is as it came out from the forge and anodizing processes.

Billet

The advent of CNC machining caused another type of upper (and lower) to come about: the billet receiver. Here, a pre-hardened rectangular block of aluminum is machined until there is nothing left but the receiver. Billet receivers can be readily distinguished from forged once you see a few, mainly by the lack of the forged receivers' pebbly surface texture and stylistic details.

Billet uppers may or may not have the forward assist, the ejector pyramid, or other features. Since they do not depend on a forging mold for shape, but each is cut from blocks, they can be whatever the machinist or customer wants them to be.

The advantage of a billet receiver for the manufacturer is adaptability. The blocks that go in are all the same. What comes out depends on the programming fed into the CNC machining station. A maker who builds on forgings must work with forgings. If they want something different, they have to pay for a new set of forging dies (these can cost as much as a luxury SUV) and wait for the forge shop to produce forged receivers in their production schedule. So, an upper shop making flat-tops that receives an order for a batch of A2 uppers has to buy A2-proper forgings from the forge shop — they cannot make them from the flat-top forgings. Ditto A1s. If they make them from billets, they can switch easily.

A CNC station can make a different upper from each clamped-in billet in the "tombstone" fixture inside the machine.

Upper Markings

Your upper will give you a clue as to who made it. If it is forged, the forging company will leave its mark on it. The various marks (a square, a keyhole, a stylized cardinal, etc.) indicate who forged it. Forging companies usually don't machine. The forgings go to a machining company, and then it might get more markings. Colt will sometimes put a "C" on the upper, sometimes not. Companies like Bravo mark an upper "Bravo" or "BCM" so you know who made it. Many companies are proud of their product. Others are just happy to get the product and be able to sell it. Once a forging leaves the forge, it could be machined by anyone with a CNC machine tool. Many small job shops do that kind of work, and a wholesaler might have half a dozen they call on for product.

You could fill a room with nothing but upper receivers that have all the variations of forge marks, machining company marks, trademarks, etc. I don't know why you'd amass such a collection, but it is possible.

One marking to look for is found on flat-top uppers: This is an "M4" stamped on the front face of the upper, above the gas tube hole. It means the receiver has been machined to accept a barrel with M4 feed ramps. As we'll cover in the chapter on barrels, you need the correct combination of upper and barrel for the feed ramps.

Anodizing

Aluminum is a soft metal. The upper and lower receivers of your AR-15, made of 7075-T6, require surface treatment. This treatment is a strong aluminum alloy with good corrosion-resistance properties. But it is soft. So, the parts (and all

> "One marking to look for is found on flat-top uppers: An "M4" stamped on the front face of the upper, above the gas tube hole. It means the receiver has been machined to accept a barrel with M4 feed ramps."

other aluminum products you will be dealing with) are given an electrochemical process known as anodizing. Anodizing creates a tough surface on the aluminum. As with so many industrial processes, there are various types or levels. The top level is Type III Hard Anodizing. This level provides the strongest and thickest protective surface. However, Type III has one failing: color. Anodizing does not have color. The anodized surface has the same aluminum color it started with — you need to dye it to make it something other than "aluminum." Type III will only take black, no different colors. If you want some other color, you'll need to "settle" for Type II, which is not

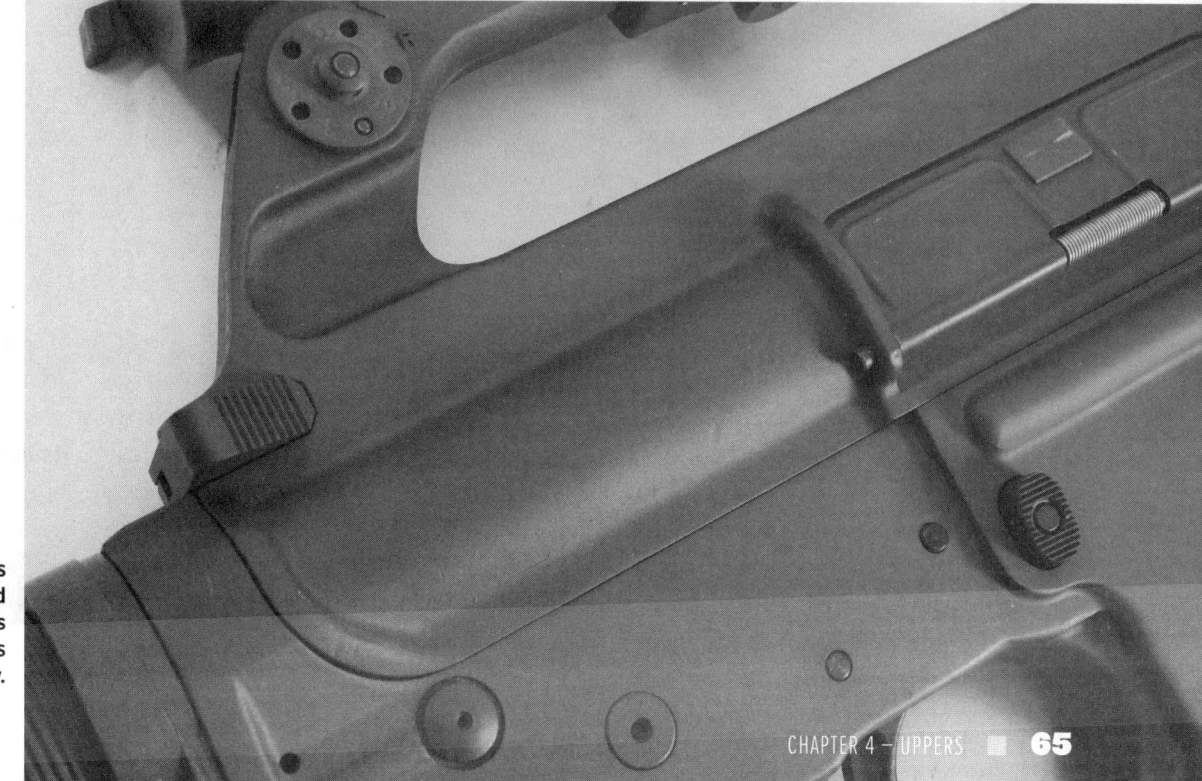

■ The very first AR-15s did not have the forward assist. The Air Force was OK with it; the Army was not. The Army got its way.

■ A simple set of shim pieces under the forward assist housing will keep the upper in place while you start the roll pin.

quite as hard or deep. Bright-colored aluminum parts of 7075-T6 for the AR-15 are typically Type II, which is not a problem for almost all users. You are highly unlikely to need the extra strength of Type III anodizing, even in a rifle you plan on using for defense.

The way to make your rifle something other than black and still have the Type III anodizing strength is to coat it with Cerakote or spray paint. A point to take note of: if you are planning on having your AR painted or coated, do that last. Do it after you have assembled and tested it, and ensure that you won't make changes or do follow-up adjustments or rebuilds. Otherwise, you risk having a rifle that is partly coated and partly uncoated, or with various scrapes, gouges, buffed-off areas where the coating had to come off — or replacement parts that don't match.

Which Upper Do You Need?

All uppers work. The upper receiver performs four tasks: it attaches to the lower receiver to create a complete rifle. It holds the barrel. It retains and guides the bolt/carrier assembly as those parts cycle back and forth when you fire. It contains the charging handle. As long as it properly does all these things, any upper design will serve. If, however, you wish to mount a scope, red-dot or magnifying optic on your rifle, you will need the flat-top. If you plan on doing precision iron-sighted competition work, you will need the A2, and depending on your skill level, the sight system may need to be rebuilt or upgraded. If you are not interested in optics and don't need an adjustable rear sight system, the A1 or C7 will serve you well.

The default upper today is the flat-top. With it, you can have all of the above. You can mount optics if you wish. You can mount optics and have an emergency-use set of iron sights as well, called a Back-Up Iron Sight, or BUIS. Those usually fold down and out of the way, but not all do. You can bolt on a durable, adjustable, or fixed sight and

With the forward assist boss supported, start the roll pin.

■ Once you line up the forward assist parts and press them into the spring, you can tap the roll pin down to capture them. Last step: use a roll-pin punch to make the pin flush.

combine it with a folding or fixed front sight. That adaptability has caused all currently built rifles and the majority of bare uppers to be flat-tops.

Working with Flat-tops

OK, let's start with a bare flat-top upper. You've just unwrapped it from the box; what do you do? Turn it over in your hands and inspect the exterior closely. Look for nicks, dings, scratches, etc. If you bought a new, unused upper, and it shows use or alteration, now is the time to send it back. A mark from handling or having been in a bin with a hundred other uppers might not be sufficient cause for a return. After all, you will likely mar it more than that on the first day of hard practice. If any of the anodizing has been filed, scuffed, or worn down to the bare metal, for sure, send it back.

Next, check how well it fits on your lower. Press

your lower's takedown pins to the open position. Place the upper on the lower and check the fit of the lines and edges. Now, press the front pin across to hold the upper in place. Does the upper freely pivot up and down on the front pin? Good. If not, there's something wrong. You don't know if it is the upper or lower at this point, so don't jump to any conclusions. In decades of AR work, I've only run into one upper that wouldn't pivot. It turns out that it was so out of spec in every dimension that it wasn't salvageable. Yours will most likely pivot.

Now, hinge it down to close it, and press the rear takedown pin across. This step is the crucial part. While every maker of uppers and lowers works hard to keep tolerances within spec, they do not all have access to the blueprints. They adjust their machine cutter paths over time from customers' feedback to ensure their uppers fit across all lowers. The ideal fit is with the rear pin pressing across with just a hint of resistance. But once across, the upper and lower fit snugly with no wobble. A bad

> *"... instead of buying your new upper from someone online, go to a gun shop. Yes, it will cost you more. But if you are polite and ask nicely, they will let you check the fit of their uppers on your lower ..."*

fit is one where the two, once closed up, wobble on the pressed-closed pins. Worse yet is a fit where you have to pound the rear pin across to make it fit. On the first issue, you will always be annoyed at your wobbly fitting AR. On the second, sooner or later, you're going to get too heavy-handed in punching the pin open and bust part of the receiver. Or, you'll mar the receiver with the punch pin you have to use to get the pin started.

■ The spring is easy. If the short leg is up, the long leg is down, and both legs flush to the receiver, you're good. If any of those are not the case, it is wrong.

CHAPTER 4 – UPPERS ■ 69

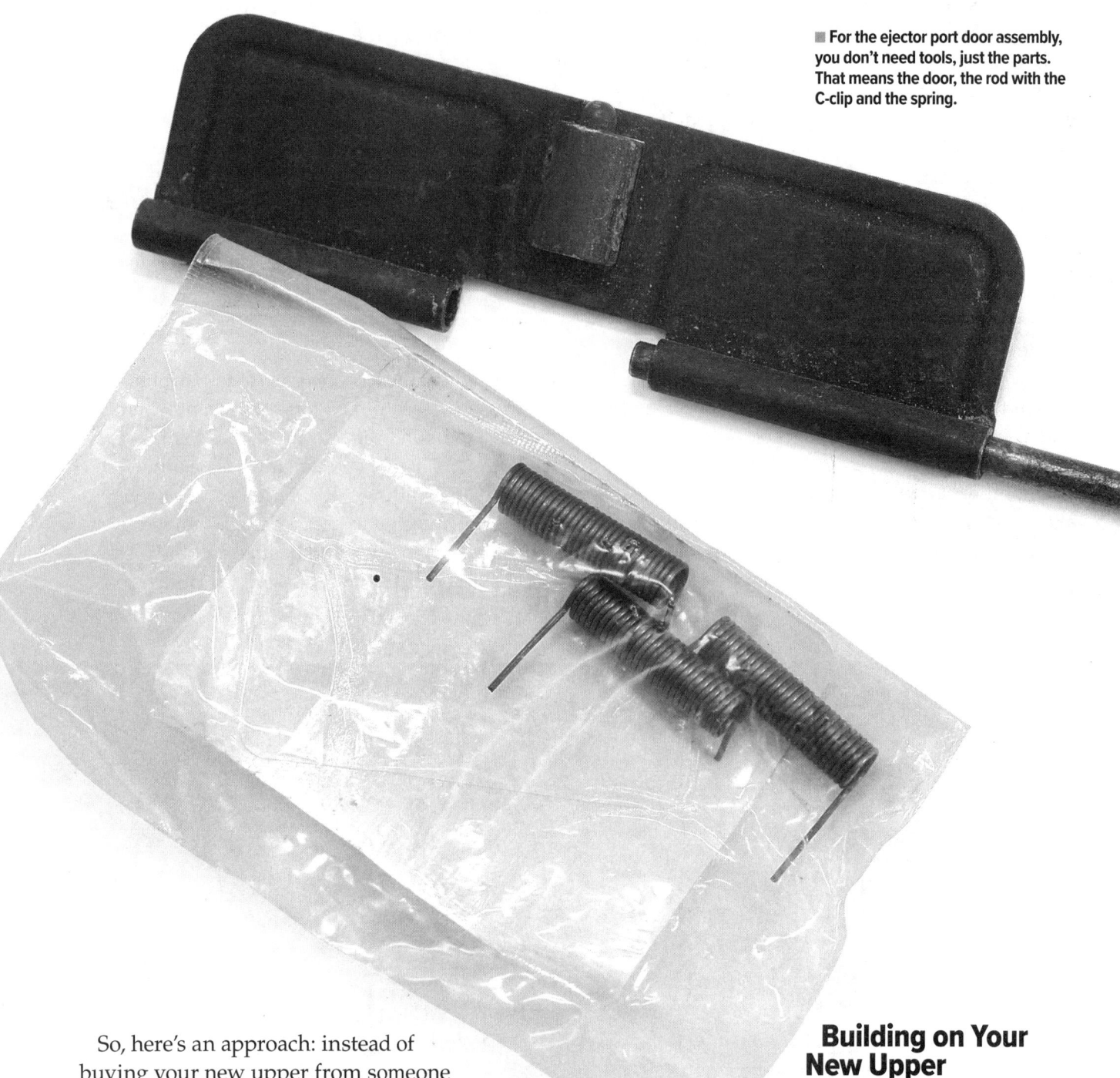

■ For the ejector port door assembly, you don't need tools, just the parts. That means the door, the rod with the C-clip and the spring.

So, here's an approach: instead of buying your new upper from someone online, go to a gun shop. Yes, it will cost you more. But if you are polite and ask nicely, they will let you check the fit of their uppers on your lower, and once you find the perfect fit (I'm not going to use the goldilocks analogy), you plunk down your card and pay for it. Will it cost more than an online purchase? Maybe, even if you add shipping and handling to the "discount" price that the online seller teased you with. If it costs a bit more, that's the price of making sure your local gun shop stays in business and can be there to provide that and other services to you.

Building on Your New Upper

Unless you bought an upper that is complete, you have a couple of tasks ahead of you. You'll need to install the forward assist and dust cover. The forward assist is easy to install or change, even when the upper is assembled into a complete upper, with the barrel, handguards, etc. The dust cover, or ejection port cover, is an extreme pain in the neck to install or swap if the barrel and handguards are already in place. So, you should do both now, not later.

Forward Assist Install

The forward assist is the spring-loaded plunger on the right side of the receiver. You use it, rarely, to make sure the bolt is fully closed.

OK, a brief aside here: more people get themselves in trouble with the forward assist than it seems possible. Let's say you are loading your rifle. You insert a magazine, grab the charging handle and cycle it, or hit the bolt stop to close the bolt, but it won't fully close. What to do? Do not slam onto the forward assist. I repeat: DO NOT.

There is some serious problem here. Your rifle is trying to tell you something. So "listen." The most likely causes include: Your rifle is so grubby it doesn't have space in the chamber for the cartridge. Or there is some debris in there. Or the round you just tried to chamber is so bent, dinged, creased, corroded or out-of-round that it doesn't want to go in. Or it is the wrong cartridge. Remove the magazine and work the charging handle to remove the round. Find out why it wouldn't go in. If it means cleaning your rifle, then clean it. If the ammo is defective, find out why, and if any others in that batch are also messed up. We're straying a bit far from gunsmithing into operational habits, but it is essential to know this.

What if you simply pound on the forward assist until it closes? That could mean that the fouled chamber has a very tight round in it. This will increase pressures, and that adds wear.

It could lead to your not being able to pound the forward assist enough, and the bolt still won't close, and now you've really wedged things tight. Getting it open may require tools.

The worst-case? The cartridge you tried to chamber that wouldn't go is a .300 Blackout in your 5.56 chamber. By pounding the forward assist, you got the bolt closed. When you pull the trigger, you will be trying to shove a .308-inch bullet down a .224-inch barrel. That will break your rifle. The bolt, carrier, barrel, handguard, optics, and charging handle will all be broken. The lower might sustain some damage but be salvageable. *Might.* You probably won't be injured, but there are no guarantees.

Do Not Slam the FA.

Back to the installation.

The forward assist is three parts, the FA itself, a preassembled contraption consisting of two parts and a spring assembly. (They are never shipped un-assembled.) There's the return spring and the retaining pin. You'll need a way to hold your upper, a hammer and drift punch, a small pair of needle-nose pliers, and the forward assist parts.

Using your vise, you can clamp the upper in an upper fixture, but you still need a way to brace it. You'll be hammering the upper off-center, and the upper holders use cross pins through the assembly lugs. That isn't good for them. So, if you use the vise fixture to hold the upper, put solid bracing underneath the FA housing lump. I simply stand it up on a flat bench surface, put a brace under the FA lump, and then get to work. This isn't sledgehammer work, just tapping in a pin.

Take the needle-nose pliers or the Real Avid pin tweezers and pick up the roll pin that holds the FA in place. Place the end of the pin into the hole on the FA lump and tap the end just enough to get it started. Once in place, you can let go of the pliers and put them down. Pick up the FA itself and its spring. Notice the flat on the FA assembly? That's the clearance flat for the roll pin. Align the FA, so the clearance flat corresponds with the roll pin location. Slide the FA spring onto the assembly and press the unit into the upper. (A sandbag or the end of the bench at the wall is one way to keep the upper in place.) Hold it there.

Now you can hold the upper in place, and the FA in it, with one hand and use the hammer to tap the roll pin down to capture the forward assist. You won't have to keep it compressed once the roll pin goes far enough into the housing to capture the forward assist. You can now tap the roll pin down flush with the hammer — or use the hammer and the drift punch. At the end, use a roll pin punch to tap the pin flush with the housing. That's it, you are done.

The ejection port cover doesn't require a hammer but does require some dexterity.

Ejection Port Cover

The cover is three parts — the cover assembly itself, the pivot rod, and the round spring with two legs that power the cover. For this procedure, you most definitely want to be using the upper fixture in your vise to hold things in place. I've done it free-

■ The C-clip on the ejector port door goes to the front. That's why you put it on before you install the barrel or handguards. It won't stay if you install it from behind (the C-clip won't keep it from falling out), and putting the C-clip on after you assemble the door is an arduous task.

hand, but it was always a scary thing, with springs threatening to hurl themselves across the room and hide under immovable furniture.

Keep two orientations in mind when you do this: The cover goes on with the spring-loaded plunger (that's the rectangular housing *thingy*) up and to the inside when it is hinged closed. And the spring goes with the short leg pointing up and the long leg on what will be the inside of the cover flap.

Hold the cover in your left hand up between the two bosses with the hinge pinhole. Take the pivot rod and, with the C-clip on the end towards the muzzle, insert the rod through the front boss and into the front part of the cover.

When this is all together, the C-clip will prevent the rod from falling out the back, and the handguard assembly (of whatever kind you use) will keep it from leaving out the front.

With the rod holding the ejector cover in place, pick up the spring. Slide the rod a bit deeper into the cover until it pokes out into the gap in the cover, and slip the spring over it, with the long leg of the spring pointing down, along the ejection port cover, and bearing against the ejection port cover.

The next step is kind of like the kid's game of patting your head while rubbing your stomach. Take the back end of the spring with the short leg, and give it a full rotation tensioning it towards the edge of the ejection port until the leg is again ready to lay down against the exterior of the receiver. Hold it in alignment with the rod, and push the rod through the spring. When the rod gets to the end of the spring, it will not be in alignment with the cover, and you'll have to press things to make them line up. Once you get the rod into the second half of the cover slot, it will try to push the cover out of alignment with the rear boss and its hole. So, keep pushing the door to maintain alignment, and press the end of the rod through the boss.

If you do this correctly, the cover will now be spring-powered to flip open. If not, it won't; you'll have to take it apart and start over.

Upper Sights

Those with flat-top uppers will be (if you install sights) bolting on a folding or fixed rear sight, and it will come assembled. The others?

A1 Sights — The Original Style

The A1 sight is adjustable for windage and has

■ The A1 rear sight is adjustable for windage only, but the adjustment requires great effort as it is meant to be an "adjustable" fixed sight.

an "L"-shaped sight aperture post that you can rotate from short-range (unmarked) to long-range (marked with an "L") for distance adjustments. The difference is achieved by the sight aperture manufacturer drilling the two aperture holes at different distances from the windage screw. The long-range aperture is slightly higher (measured from the windage screw) than the short-range sight. By placing the aperture higher, the designers force the shooter to lower the rifle's rear (relative to the front sight) and thus achieve a higher arc or trajectory to the bullet. The difference matters for military use where targets may be engaged hundreds of yards removed. In defense, a long shot is likely to be across a small parking lot.

For those who insist on iron sights only on rifles, the A1 is preferred, as it has fewer parts and is less likely to be misadjusted after you've zeroed the rifle. To assemble from a bare receiver, place the sight spring in the recess in the upper receiver. Press the sight aperture down on the spring and enter the sight screw from the left side. (Orient the sight so that the stamped L is visible to the shooter when the long-range aperture is up.) Rotate the screw to capture the sight body and continue rotating it until it enters the right-hand wing of the carry handle. Press the screw across and keep the sight aperture body off the right-hand wing. Turn the sight screw until the sight is centered between the carrying handle ears.

Lay the receiver on the left side. Oil the sight plate spring hole, insert the spring and the detent ball. Turn the screw, so the hole through it is parallel to the axis of the bore. Press the plate down on the end of the screw. Note the plate's retaining pin hole location. Adjust the screw so the hole in the plate (when pressed down over one of the detent holes) lines up with the hole through the screw. Use your 1/8-inch punch as a slave pin to hold the plate to the screw while pressing down on the plunger. The best direction to insert is from the muzzle. That gives you room to work on the sight from the rear, where there are no receiver parts in the way.

Hold the sight retaining pin with needle-nose pliers, and tap the pin to start it in. Once it is in place and stays on its own, set aside the needle-nose pliers and use a drift punch and hammer to drive the pin flush to the plate. In so doing, you'll knock the slave 1/8-inch punch from the sight.

Once you've assembled the sight, check the rotation of the assembly. Turning the plate should make the rear sight move left or right across the rear of the carry handle.

To replace or change a rear sight, drift out the roll pin, remove the plate and detent, and turn the screw to release the old sight. Then assemble as if from a bare receiver.

A2 Sights

The A2 sight came about primarily due to the Marine Corps' need for marksmanship. The A1 sights, while entirely adequate for close-range use (in a military context, "close range" can be out to 300 meters), was a crude tool for longer-range applications. As the Corps routinely fired to 500 meters for qualification, it needed a better iron sight. (The changes were made in the early 1980s when the suggestion of optics would have been literally laughed down.)

It is not only click-adjustable for windage but also for elevation as well. While the basic zero is done (as with the A1) using the front sight, you make all range corrections with the rear sight once you've established the zero.

The sight assembly of the A2 is like that of the A1. It uses a windage screw and retaining plate, with spring and plunger in detents on the retaining plate. Where it differs is in the plate and aperture body. The plate is finger-adjustable for windage. Unlike the A1, where you need to use a bullet tip or tool to unlock and rotate the plate,

■ The A2 sight has a knob on the side to adjust windage, and it is easy to do. In fact, it's so easy that, once you get yours sighted-in, you should paint it to make sure no one messes with it.

you can move the A2 windage knob with your fingers. Indeed, it is meant to be moved by finger pressure. In a competitive environment, where the wind might push a bullet a known distance across a target at a known range, "clicks" to adjust for the wind are helpful. In combat, not so much.

The A2 aperture body also differs from the A1. On the A1, the two apertures are on different planes. Changing from one to the other changes point-of-impact on a target (raising it). On the A2, the apertures are different sizes and diameters, but as much as modern manufacturing tolerances allow, their centers are the same height above the windage screw. The group sizes will change because the human eye can precisely aim better with the small aperture than with the large. But the center of the group should not shift on the target.

To make the A2 rear sight adjustable, it needed many more parts. The assembly is not significantly less robust than the A1, but sometimes the easy adjustment can be too much of a good thing.

A2 Sight Assembly

Unless damaged, there won't be much need to assemble an A2 sight. Many uppers come assembled, as do BUIS. However, knowing the parts involved and how to replace them if they become damaged is necessary if any rifle or carbine you bought has A2 rear sights.

Assembling the A2 sight body is the same pro-

■ The A2 sight is range-adjustable. The military (USMC) wanted a sight it could use at distance and dial in the yardage. The zero adjusts from 300 to 800 meters. On carbines, it was supposed to go from 300 to 600.

cess as installing sights on the A1 receiver, except there is less to hold on to. One difference between them is in the detent and ball for the windage knob. On the A1, the spring goes into the carry handle. On the A2, the spring goes into the windage knob.

Assembling the completed sight body into the upper receiver of the A2 is more involved. Place the A2 upper upright on the bench. Put the elevation detent spring and elevation detent in their tunnel. Place the elevation wheel upper and lower together and slide them into the rectangular slot from the side. Press the detent down to clear the wheel. Be sure to place the wheels with the detent holes down and the upper wheel so the numbers can be read upright.

Leave it standing for the moment. Pick up the rear sight assembly and insert the tensioner spring and ball into the sight housing. Hold the detent in place and insert the threaded end of the sight housing into the elevation wheel. Without losing either of the detents, turn the wheel to capture, and draw down, the sight housing. Once the housing has been caught, the elevation detent and spring will not escape. Once the housing has been drawn down enough so that the tensioner ball is trapped behind the wing of the carry handle, it cannot escape. Turn the elevation wheel until it bottoms out. Then bring it back up three clicks. This is the "mechanical zero." The sight dimensions have been calculated to start "three clicks up;" all adjustments are made from there.

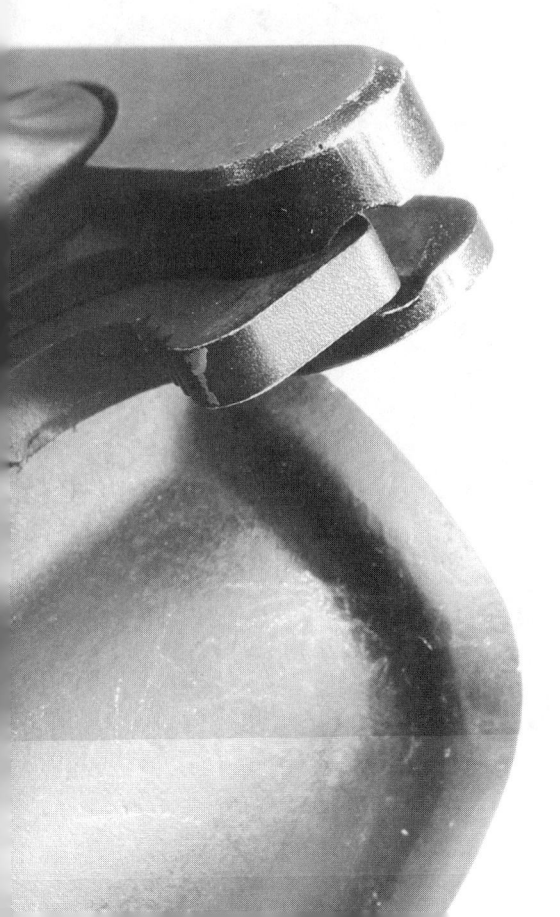

Now rotate just the upper half of the elevation wheel. It will turn without moving the lower half. Rotate it until the "3/8" (on rifles) or the "3/6" (on carbines) lines up with the index mark centered on the left side. Use a 1/16-inch Allen wrench to install the index screw. Once the index screw is in place, turning the wheel turns both the upper and lower halves and changes the rear sight's elevation.

The last step is the one requiring a special tool (available from Brownells, #080-000-079). Lay the receiver on its side. (The left is usually easier.) Push the spring in from underneath and use the special slotted sight tool and compress the spring. Place the roll pin in the hole and tap it into place. If you lack a vise or fixture to hold the upper (we almost all do), this is the time to ask for an assistant to hold the receiver in place (keep the spring compressed) while you drift in the roll pin. In a pinch, you can use a closely-fitting screwdriver to compress the spring. However, as with all such expedients, if something goes wrong, you end up losing parts, scratching the rifle or stabbing yourself with the screwdriver. If you're going to do this more than once or twice, invest in the proper tool.

The primary advantage of the A2 is its adjustability. However, that advantage brings with it many more parts and the possibility of mischief. Bored, idle or unknowing friends at the gun club can spin the windage knob back and forth.

To make the A2 less prone to inadvertent adjustments, you can acquire a locking windage knob (from Rock River) or drill and tap the knob. To drill and tap the knob, you'll need to remove it from the upper. Then, drill from the rear, between two plunger detent depressions but on the arc between them. If you use one of the depressions as your drilling point, the screw will eventually (if you do this to enough rifles) happen to fall right on the plunger when the rifle is zeroed. Then the locking screw will be depressing the plunger as it locks in place. It gets the job done but isn't the best solution. Drill in between instead.

You can also "paint in" the sight knobs.

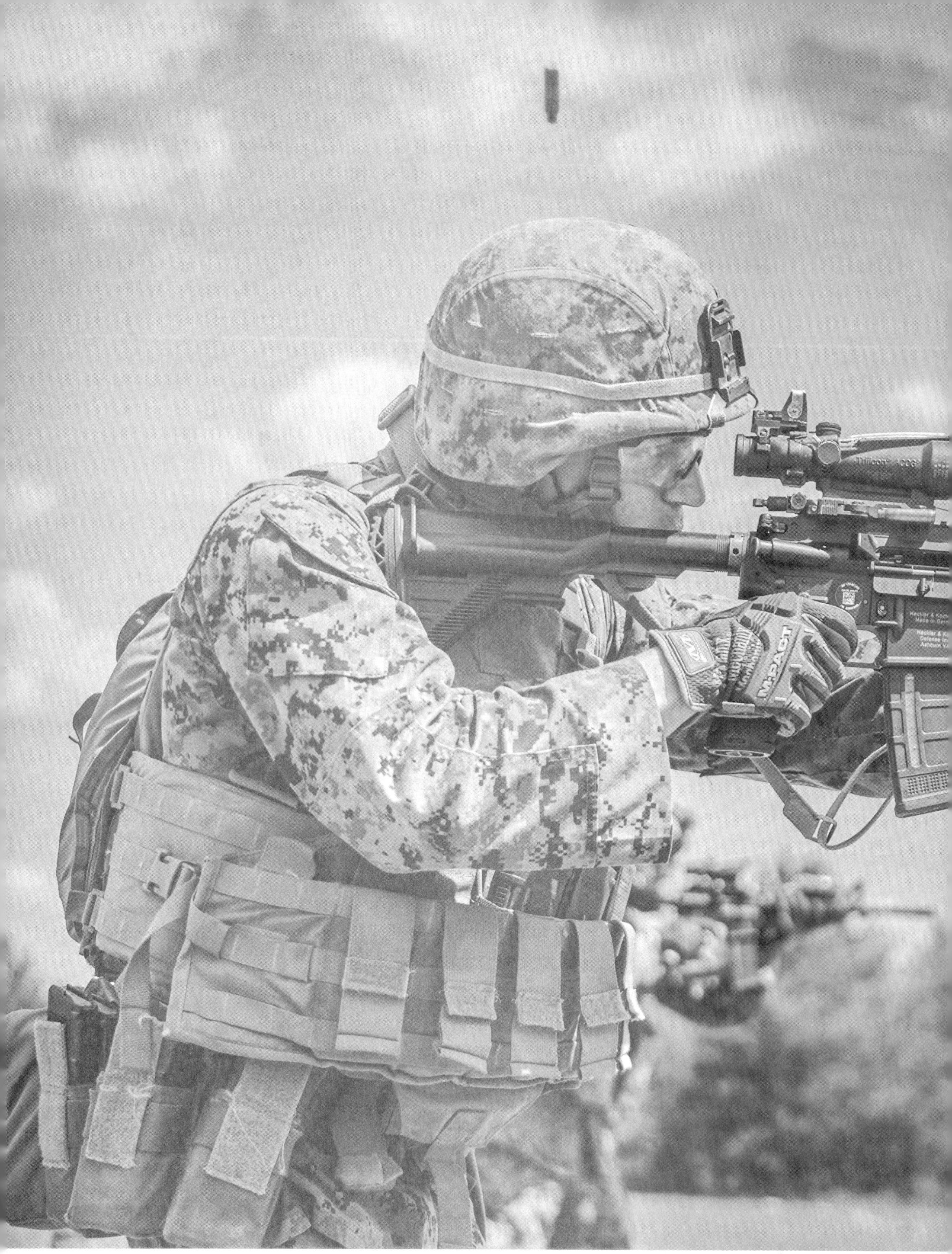
Trijicon ACOG
M-PACT

5

Barrels and Choices

Settle in with a favorite drink, maybe some popcorn (if you can keep the pages clean, of course) because we'll be here a while. We will be spending a lot of time on barrels because the subject is important, and most people take them for granted. The AR-15 barrel is an involved product of modern manufacturing, and it is both simple and amazingly complex. It will be, for most shooters, simply "the barrel," and it gets used, cleaned (or not) until it wears out or something better comes along. But if you're serious about AR-15 performance, the barrel deserves a closer look.

Barrel Basics

The barrel is what holds the cartridge and guides the bullet to the target. Barrels are made of steel (we haven't found anything better yet, but who knows?), and the bore has a set of grooves in it, called the rifling. These grooves impart spin to the bullet.

Barrels are defined (in no particular order) by their length and weight, composition, surface treatment, gas system, chamber size/caliber designation and the twist rate of the rifling. Picking a barrel is not always easy, as the choices seem infinite. There are, however, some relatively common combinations. And, as with so many

■ Heat is the real destroyer of barrels. The military figures a goodly part of the ammo consumption an M16/M4 is going to see will be full-auto or burst fire.

things, Pareto's Law — also known as the 80/20 rule — holds true here as well. It says that 80 percent of uses are handled by 20 percent of the available choices. An example would be that 80 percent or more of the AR-15s made or sold will have an M4 profile barrel, an A2 profile barrel, or a medium-weight comprised of one of those two profiles. These standard profiles serve so many users so well that it's a reach to justify some other, specialized barrel shape.

Barrel Manufacturing

Barrels are customarily manufactured in a preliminary step known as "barrel blanks." The blank begins as a steel bar of full manufacturing diameter (generally 1 or 1.2 inch in size) and 30 to 36 inches in length. The length and diameter vary based on the machinery used to make them and the desires of the barrel-making entity to which the blanks will be shipped. Each blank is fully rifled along its entire length. The barrel maker cuts it to length from this blank, uses a lathe to profile the exterior to the size and contour desired, threads the chamber end, installs the barrel extension, reams to headspace, and drills the gas port. Then, and only then, is it a barrel that you can use.

Length and Weight

Federal law imposes a minimum length on rifles, which is "greater than sixteen inches." The law does not care how much more than 16 inches, so some makers cut their carbine-length barrels 16.1 and some 16.25 inches. Going below 16.0 inches is a Federal crime (on a rifle) unless you have already applied for and received authorization to do so. One with a barrel shorter than 16 inches would be a "Short-Barreled Rifle" or SBR, and we'll get into that in a bit. Also, we'll be covering AR-15 pistols later. So, if you have a carbine-length barrel, do not do anything to make it shorter, or you could be in trouble.

> *"Federal law imposes a minimum length on rifles, which is "greater than sixteen inches." The law does not care how much more than 16 inches, so some makers cut their carbine-length barrels 16.1 and some 16.25 inches."*

The standard lengths that are greater than that are 18 and 20 inches. The 20-inch length is the original AR-15 rifle length, and it is common for those who want a full-sized rifle.

The barrel weight depends on the outside diameter. That full-diameter barrel blank, a rifled tube that has not otherwise been worked on for use in

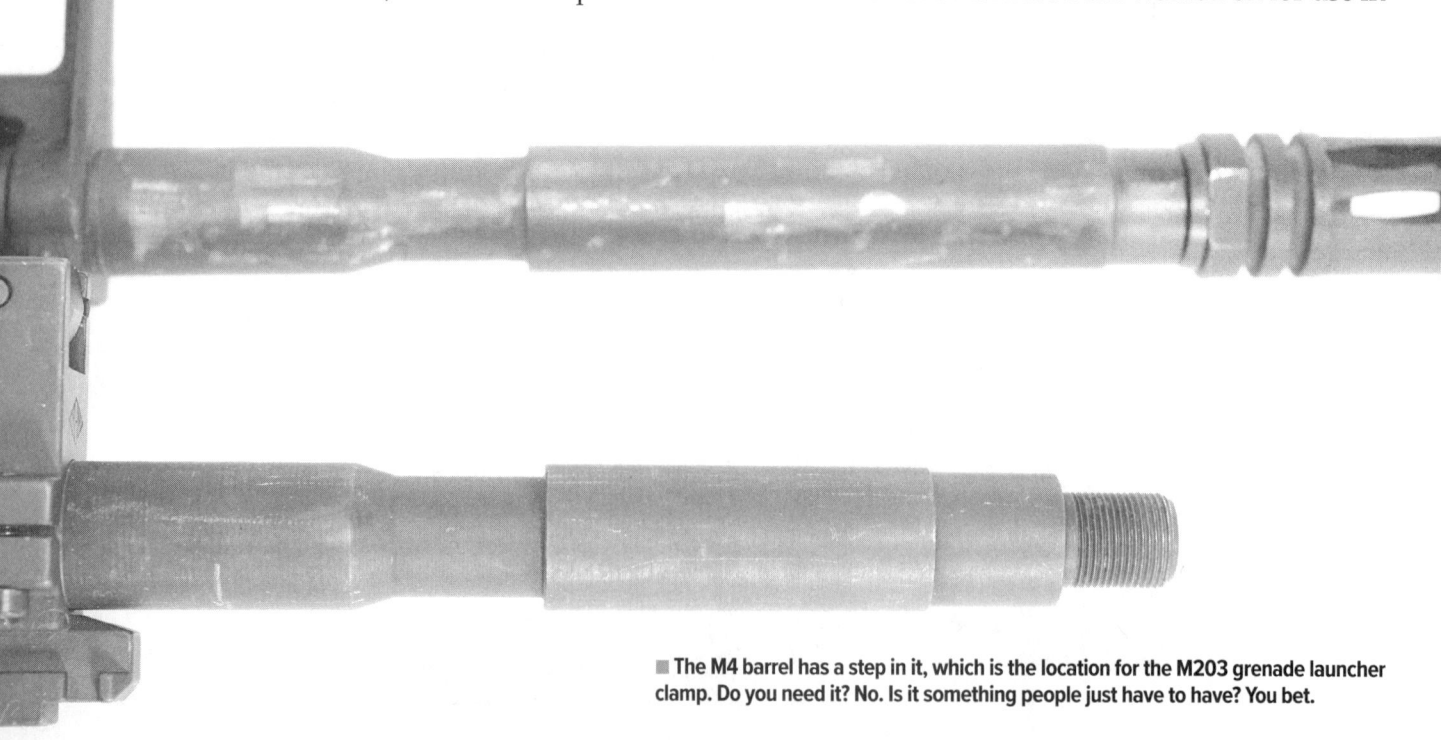

■ The M4 barrel has a step in it, which is the location for the M203 grenade launcher clamp. Do you need it? No. Is it something people just have to have? You bet.

■ This barrel has the barrel extension screwed onto it, and the extension has the locking lugs. Here, lugs to the left, chamber extending to the right.

a rifle, is a steel cylinder up to 1.20 inches in diameter, and it is heavy — over 6 pounds. It is a hefty chunk of steel, and it is not at all suited for installation. A barrel blank is "profiled," that is, turned down on a lathe to a specific contour to make it usable as a rifle barrel. The lighter it is, the easier it is to carry and the more difficult it is to shoot. (Lighter weight means less mass to combat recoil.) Also, the lighter it is, the thinner its walls are, and the faster it will heat up in use. Varmint shooters will choose a heavier barrel as they don't have to carry a rifle any farther than from the truck to the shooting position. A heavy barrel means less recoil and more shooting before the barrel gets too hot and must be cooled.

An AR-15 chosen for defense usually has as light a barrel as can be managed, making it easier to carry. If someone suggests a military profile, such as the M4 or A2 profile, remember this: the military selects the barrel profile that gives it the best performance when the rifle might be used as a tool until it absolutely quits. So, it might opt for more weight. After all, it will be carried by fit 19-year-olds who must shoot without respite until their ammunition is all gone. If all that describes you,

you may want a heavier barrel than an M4. If not, a lighter-than-M4 might serve you well.

The two military profiles are the A2 and the M4. The A2 has a smaller-diameter area under the handguards, so the warehouses full of M203 grenade launchers will fit on any rifles. (Yes, the Department of Defense chose to make several million future rifles less durable so it could fit grenade launchers on them, rather than modify the grenade launchers to work on the new, better rifles that were adopted in 1986. That's government for you.) The M4 profile has a recessed band forward of the front sight housing where the grenade launcher can be clamped. It serves no purpose on a carbine that never sees a grenade launcher, but people must have it.

Many current-manufacture carbines don't have the grenade launcher band since it serves no purpose, and without it, makers can produce barrels faster and easier.

There are several shorter barrel lengths that you may see. The common ones will be 14.5, 11.5, 10.3 and 7.5 inches in .223/5.56, and the same ones plus 8 and 9 inches in .300 Blackout. You have two choices when you are going to a length below 16

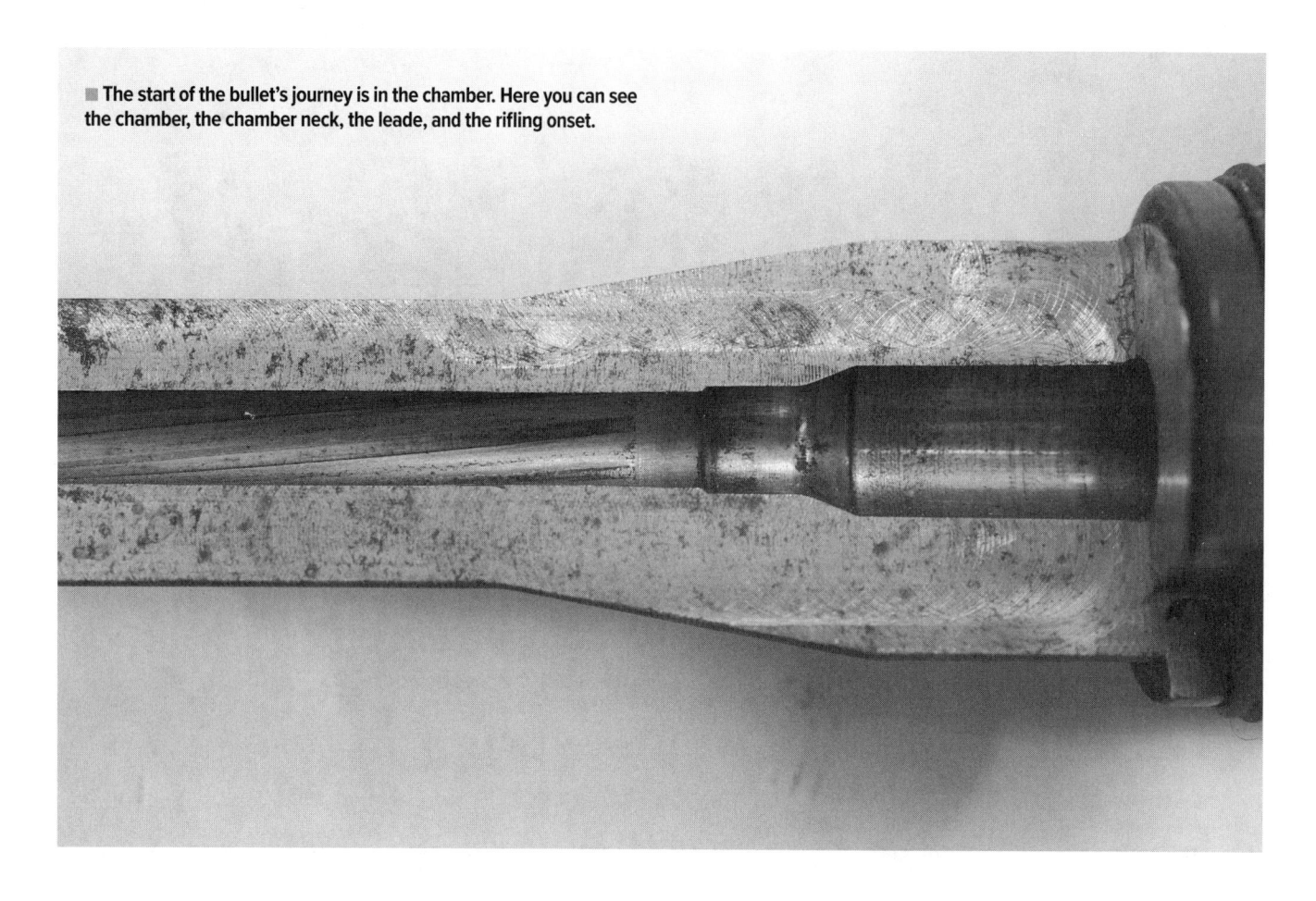

The start of the bullet's journey is in the chamber. Here you can see the chamber, the chamber neck, the leade, and the rifling onset.

inches. One is to build your AR as a pistol. (This will be covered in detail in the pistol-specific chapter.) It may not be permitted in some jurisdictions, and it may be something of a hassle. But it is easier than building a short-barreled rifle, or SBR. (Ditto on complete information in the Building an SBR chapter.)

The most significant obstacle in building an SBR

> "You can build an AR-15 with a barrel that is 14.5 inches long and avoid the SBR requirements. The trick is, you must permanently attach something to the barrel that makes it longer than 16 inches."

is applying for ATF approval on the build. Some states simply do not permit SBRs. And you cannot take the first step of building an SBR until *after* you have consent.

The additional lengths exist for specific reasons. The earliest, historically, is the 11.5-inch version, which is the "Vietnam carbine" length. It's the barrel length with the gas system that Colt found to be most reliable of the short-barreled M16s it was making back in the late 1960s. Colt originally made the AR-15 carbine with a 10-inch barrel. Shorter than 11.5 inches, and Colt found the reliability suffered.

The next length is the 14.5-inch variant, which is now the standard length of the US-issue M4. It exists for a simple reason: it's the length of handguards and front sight assembly of the 11.5-inch Vietnam-era carbine, and you can properly mount a bayonet onto it. Yes, a bayonet. There is no magical property with 14.5 inches; just being able to mount a bayonet is all.

The next in order is the 7.5-inch barrel, made for AR-15 pistols, which is obnoxiously loud and requires a new-length gas system because the carbine-length gas tube is too long. Not to get ahead of things, but the pistol-length gas system turned out to be perfect for subsonic-built .300 Blackout AR-15s.

The newest of the lengths is the 10.3-inch barrel, which the U.S. Navy developed as a complete upper assembly for when an M4 is too long and called it the Mk 18. This variant was created 30 years after Colt had given up on its 10-inch carbines. That was possible because of the development of the M4, improved parts and ammunition in the intervening time. An SBR or pistol built with an Mk 18 barrel can be a bit sensitive to the ammunition used, so if you build one, do not expect it to work reliably with anything and everything you can find at the big-box ammo store. But once tuned, it is reliable.

Barrel length is a consistent determinant of velocity but not of accuracy. A shorter barrel will always produce less velocity than a longer one, but accuracy depends on barrel quality, installation quality and ammunition quality. Shorter is not less accurate.

When is an SBR Not an SBR?

You can build an AR-15 with a barrel that is 14.5 inches long and avoid the SBR requirements. The trick is, you must permanently attach something to the barrel that makes it longer than 16 inches. The extra length of the addition — usually a flash hider or suppressor mount, but even a plain tube will do — must bring it past 16 inches. So, if you add a 1.5-inch long flash hider to your barrel but don't consider the half-inch threaded attachment, you will have a 15.5-inch barrel. Oops. So, measure carefully.

And by "permanent," the ATF means something that really is *permanent*. You must attach it with a high-temperature silver solder, not less than 1,125 degrees temp, or weld it. You can spot/tack weld in at least three places, but the most popular method is a "blind pin" weld. Here, the flash hider or mount has a hole drilled through the shank at the barrel, and the barrel is dimpled at the same spot. The welder presses a short section of steel rod into the hole, nestling in the dimple, and welds over the end. The steel pin keeps the part from unscrewing, the weld keeps the pin in place, and how it was done is obvious. And it does not pump excess heat into the barrel.

Barrel makers who turn out a great many high-quality 14.5-inch barrels will make them for precisely this purpose. There is, however, a downside.

Once the extension is welded in place, you cannot change the gas block, front sight A-frame, handguards or anything else that requires removal from the barrel. They won't slip over the flash hider or muzzle mount. Also, you cannot test-fire the built upper (if you are building one) with the extension not in place because that makes it an

■ When the bullet passes the gas port, it uncovers the port and allows gases to flow from the bore into the gas tube and back to the carrier.

SBR. You can, however, test-fire on a pistol lower. Once it is proven to work, have the extension blind-pin welded and install it on your regular lower carbine.

Barrel Stiffness

A barrel whips like a rope when you shoot. It bends, flexes, vibrates and generally goes crazy. However, the movements are minimal. The problem is that the movements happen while the bullet is still in the bore. A barrel that moves less or consistently will have a higher accuracy potential than one that is inconsistent or moves a lot. A heavier barrel, being stiffer, moves less.

Interestingly, a shorter barrel can be more accurate because stiffness is a function of both length and diameter. So, two barrels of the same diameter would find the shorter one being stiffer. Shooters interested in accuracy favor heavier barrels both for recoil reduction as well as stiffness.

The cost of a heavy barrel is weight. A varmint shooter, a target shooter or a ground blind hunter would find the weight to be less of a problem. Still hunters (stalking) and those using an AR for defense would find the weight more of a problem.

Alloy Steel

Before the AR-15 was developed, the standard barrel steel was an alloy 4140, or Ordnance Steel.

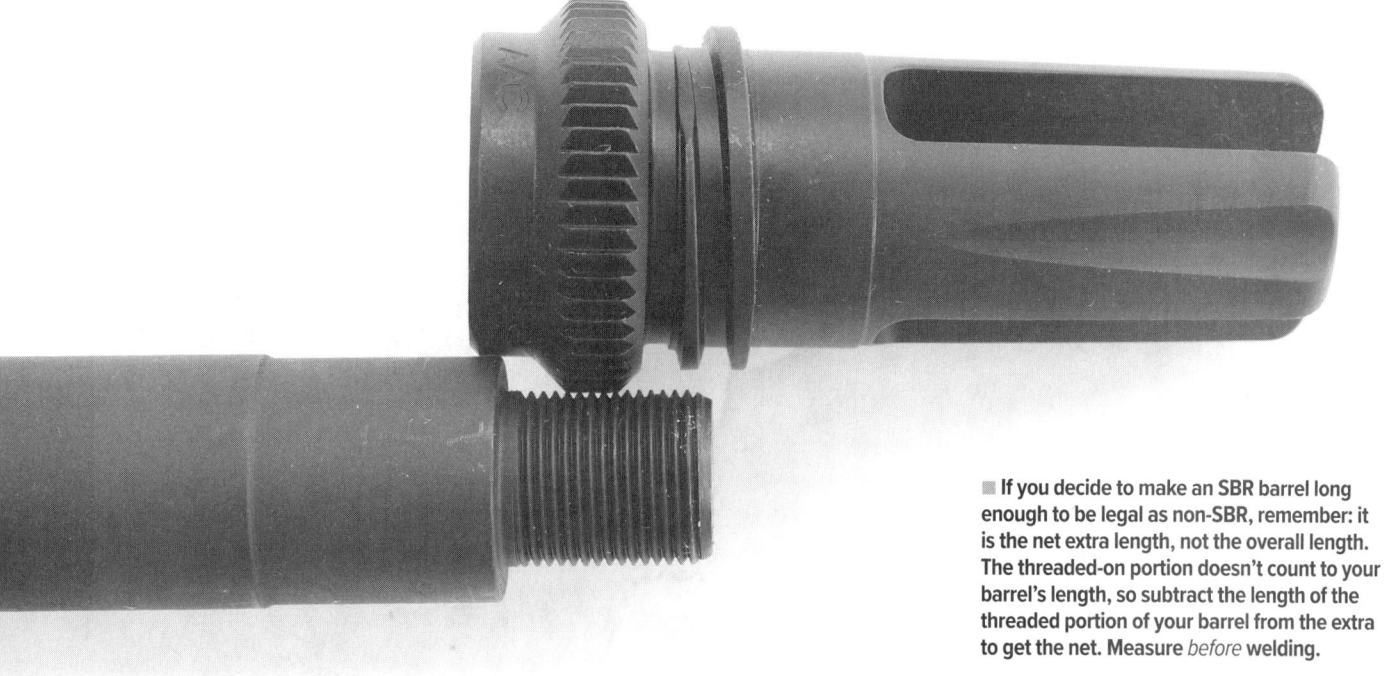

■ If you decide to make an SBR barrel long enough to be legal as non-SBR, remember: it is the net extra length, not the overall length. The threaded-on portion doesn't count to your barrel's length, so subtract the length of the threaded portion of your barrel from the extra to get the net. Measure *before* welding.

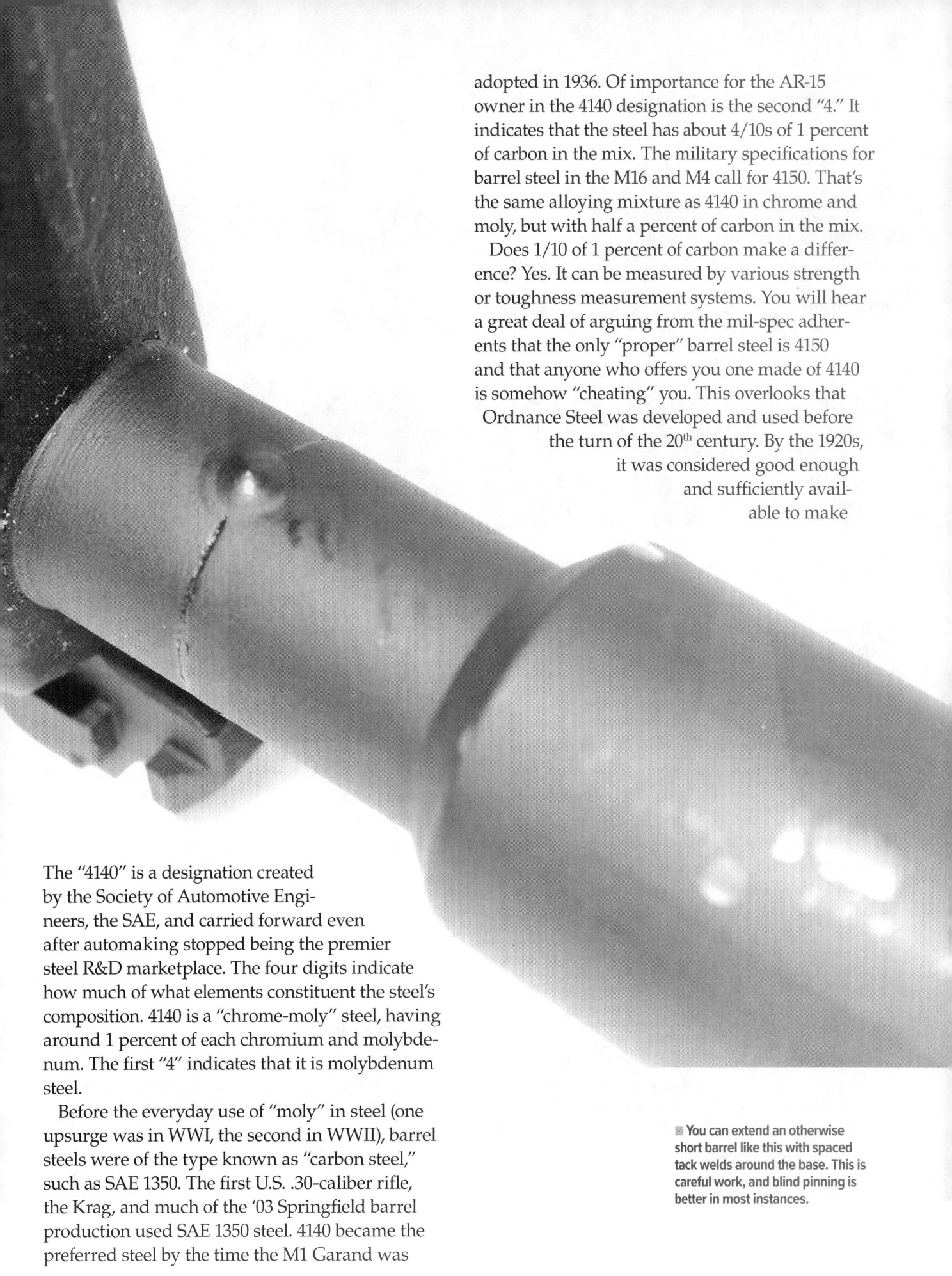

adopted in 1936. Of importance for the AR-15 owner in the 4140 designation is the second "4." It indicates that the steel has about 4/10s of 1 percent of carbon in the mix. The military specifications for barrel steel in the M16 and M4 call for 4150. That's the same alloying mixture as 4140 in chrome and moly, but with half a percent of carbon in the mix.

Does 1/10 of 1 percent of carbon make a difference? Yes. It can be measured by various strength or toughness measurement systems. You will hear a great deal of arguing from the mil-spec adherents that the only "proper" barrel steel is 4150 and that anyone who offers you one made of 4140 is somehow "cheating" you. This overlooks that Ordnance Steel was developed and used before the turn of the 20th century. By the 1920s, it was considered good enough and sufficiently available to make

The "4140" is a designation created by the Society of Automotive Engineers, the SAE, and carried forward even after automaking stopped being the premier steel R&D marketplace. The four digits indicate how much of what elements constituent the steel's composition. 4140 is a "chrome-moly" steel, having around 1 percent of each chromium and molybdenum. The first "4" indicates that it is molybdenum steel.

Before the everyday use of "moly" in steel (one upsurge was in WWI, the second in WWII), barrel steels were of the type known as "carbon steel," such as SAE 1350. The first U.S. .30-caliber rifle, the Krag, and much of the '03 Springfield barrel production used SAE 1350 steel. 4140 became the preferred steel by the time the M1 Garand was

■ You can extend an otherwise short barrel like this with spaced tack welds around the base. This is careful work, and blind pinning is better in most instances.

CHAPTER 5 – BARRELS AND CHOICES ■ **85**

Gas port diameters will vary depending on the barrel and gas system's length and caliber. There is no "one size fits all" diameter.

aircraft frames, M1 Garand and machine gun barrels. That's right, we kicked Hitler's butt with barrels made of 4140 steel.

4150 offers a stronger, tougher, more abrasion-resistant steel, but at a cost; it uses up machine tools faster. The military wants the extra strength and is willing to pay for it. Should you? A quick look at various barrel costs (January 2021) shows similar barrels, made from 4140 and 4150, where the cost "bump" up to 4150 is maybe $50. What matters more than carbon content is barrel quality and what is included in the barrel kit.

So, the extra cost isn't much, and if you want the 4150, go for it. But don't let someone at your gun club who is loud about mil-spec standards dog you into buying a barrel not-quite-what-you-want just because it is 4150, and the one you wanted (length, weight, etc.) was 4140.

More modern alloys are variants of the chrome-moly family, different in some extra alloying ingredients or the heat-treatment process they used. One such is 41V45, which is a subtle mix of 4140 and 4150. The makers split the difference in the carbon content (hence the "45" part, 0.45 percent, instead of 0.4 or 0.5 percent) and increased the molybdenum content slightly, plus tossed in a dash of vanadium (vanadium increases strength and improves wear resistance).

The various alloys used in barrel making are selected by manufacturers for their initial expense and cost in tooling wear, as much as the longevity and durability of the finished product. You can argue about the best tires on a Nascar vehicle, which last longer or hold tighter when driven at 220 miles per hour. But if your driving skills are such that you'd put the car into the wall at 100 mph, the differences in those tires are meaningless. The military insists on 4150 because it knows somewhere, sometime, someone they equip will be crawling up out of the surf, covered in beach sand, firing bursts of full-auto fire at the opposition. That M16 or M4 must work. If that's not your job description, then "4140 or 4150?" is not a life-or-death matter to you.

Chrome Lining

Before we move to stainless steel, let's cover chrome-lined bores. The sole purpose of a chrome-lined bore is to reduce corrosion. The "chrome" is industrial hard chrome, not at all like the decorative chrome on the trim or bumper of your car. The bore chrome is a thin, hard (in the mid-60s on the Rockwell C hardness scale) plating that seals the steel from corrosion. Well, almost. Chrome wears, and when it does, that worn section can corrode.

The process was undertaken during the Vietnam War. The earliest AR-15s (known as the M16 then) were supplied with unplated bores because, well, that was what barrels had been up until then. In the standard 105-percent humidity of Vietnam, and the lack of suitable cleaning supplies, the chambers rusted and cases stuck. Bores rusted, and accuracy went away. So, the standard was quickly changed to include a chrome-plated bore. (Not fast enough, though, and that's where the so-called "unreliable M16" reputation began.)

Chrome lining is not without its drawbacks. It isn't easy to uniformly plate a thin (measured in tenths of thousandths of an inch) coating the length of a small-diameter tube evenly. For the military, the protection is worth the cost of some accuracy loss. How much does it affect accuracy? I'm sure someone has tested it and can tell you how many fractions of an MOA it costs, but here's the essential detail: no one who has a choice will shoot the NRA High Power Championships with a chrome-plated bore if they can get a barrel that is not plated.

416 Stainless

Back in the old AR-15 days, you might get sneered at for using a barrel made of stainless steel. Then again, stainless barrels have always been accurate, mainly because the people who made barrels out of stainless steel were better than the cut-rate pirates of the old days who made cheap AR barrels. Stainless steel is produced by adding enough chromium and nickel to regular "carbon" steel to reduce the corrosion rate to acceptable levels. There is no such thing as truly "stainless" steel, just slower-rusting steel. The most resistant is the kitchen cutlery you own, marked 18/8, 18 percent chromium and 8 percent nickel, and it is too soft to

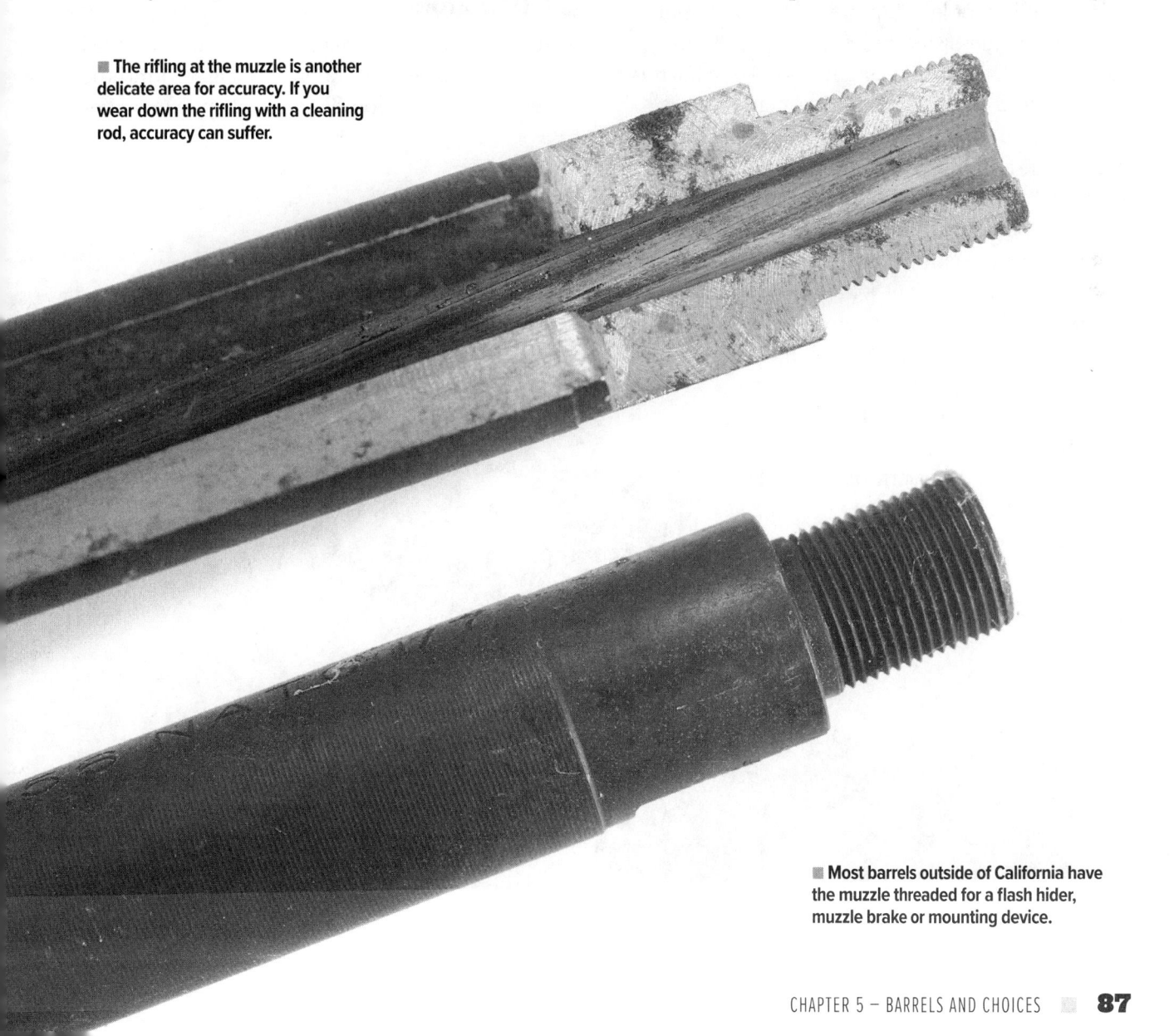

■ The rifling at the muzzle is another delicate area for accuracy. If you wear down the rifling with a cleaning rod, accuracy can suffer.

■ Most barrels outside of California have the muzzle threaded for a flash hider, muzzle brake or mounting device.

CHAPTER 5 – BARRELS AND CHOICES

BARREL MIXTURE/ALLOY

ALLOY	CARBON	MANGANESE	SULFUR	SILICON	CHROMIUM	MOLYBDENUM	VANADIUM
4140	.40	.85	.040	.3	.95	.2	
4150	.50	.85	.040	.3	.95	.2	
CMV	.45	.75	.040	.040	.28	.35	.25
416	.15	1.25	.15	1.0	13	.060	
17-4	.07	1.0	.03	1.0	16		

be used as firearms steel. You can sometimes find flatware marked "10/8" or even "18/10," indicating different amounts of chromium and nickel.

Stainless steel with that much non-corrosive alloying content can't be heat treated. Well, it can be run through a heat-treatment process, but it won't harden. By the time the steel maker dials back the percentages of chromium and nickel that it can properly heat treat and harden the steel for use in firearms, it is a lot less "stainless." It is far better than non-stainless steel but not like your forks and knives. The common stainless used in barrels is 416 or 416R. 416 has only 0.15 percent of carbon but up to 14 percent chromium. There's also manganese and molybdenum in small amounts. Not only that, 416 is selected for use in barrels because it perfectly balances between being easy to machine and lasting a long time when used as a barrel. 416R is a variant with the alloying composition shifted for high machinability, can be heat treated to a hardness of a bit more than 416, but it can also be polished to a very smooth finish. Custom barrel makers favor 416R because they can lap the bore (polish the interior) to a very smooth finish, reducing fouling buildup and promoting accuracy.

As with the choice between 4140 and 4150, stainless or non-stainless involves a slight price difference. You will likely find that you have the most options in stainless barrels from expensive manufacturers. That's because competition shooters choose stainless, who will opt for a barrel made to the most exacting specs before settling for something less expensive.

Carbon Fiber

Carbon fiber is not exactly used in the composition of the barrel, but rather the wrap around the barrel. While a carbon-fiber barrel appears to be

■ You can dimple the threaded portion of the barrel with a drill press to provide a location for the blind pin to rest and prevent the removal of the muzzle device.

the same diameter as a regular one, the barrel itself is a liner — a rifled tube of smaller size inside the cylindrical wrapping of carbon fiber. The carbon fiber adds stiffness to the barrel without adding the weight of a similar diameter of steel. Carbon fiber also aids in heat transmission, allowing a heated barrel to shed that heat and cool off faster.

Barrel Steels

The original source for steel info was the SAE, which for most of the 20th century, was the go-to source for steel info. SAE specs still stand, but there are a lot more sources now. Here are the specs for some of the steels you'll see listed for barrels, all numerical listings in percent of the mixture/alloy (chart above).

The remainder is iron. All alloying constituents are permitted a small spread, such as carbon in the 4150 allowed to be between .48 and .55 percent. Stainless alloys will sometimes have a small percentage of phosphorous and other trace elements, at the tenth of a percent level.

What is "Mil-Spec"?

The military standard for steel alloys used in barrels is Mil-B-11595E (a catchy title, no?). It specifies the alloying constituents, the heat-treatment process, and the testing procedures used to determine each in a shipped lot. This spec was codified in June 1988, and it is the standard to which barrel steel for the military is held. The document is 15 pages long, and it takes more than just a passing knowledge of steelmaking to parse its info.

Surface Treatment

Except for some stainless barrels, the exterior of your barrel will be given a coating or chemical treatment. For the non-stainless alloys, this is to reduce the corrosion rate.

Hot Blue

Hot blue is the traditional method of adding corrosion resistance to a barrel. It is simply a hot solution of bluing salts that reacts to the surface of the steel and provides thin and relatively marginal surface protection. Hot bluing was used a long time on non-ARs simply due to its good looks and tradition. I'm not sure you can find an AR-15 barrel that has only a hot-salt-blued finish on it today.

■ The small dimple drilled into the shank of this Surefire flash hider right behind the mounting collar is the location for your gunsmith (or you) to carefully drill for a blind pin insertion and weld it over.

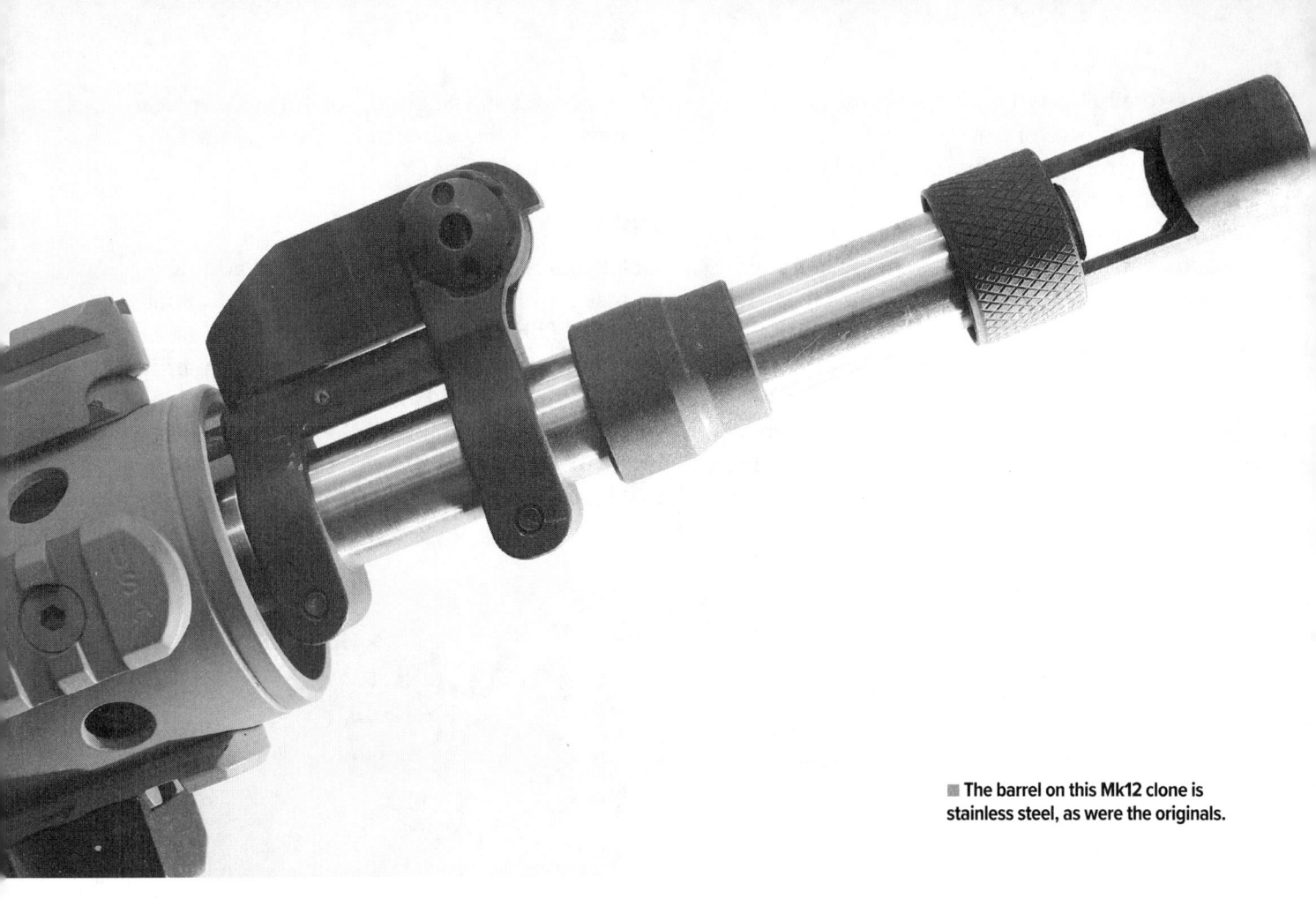

The barrel on this Mk12 clone is stainless steel, as were the originals.

Parkerizing

Parkerizing is an acidic phosphorous solution bath that produces a tough surface finish. It is the customary finish you might see on an M1 Garand, for example. It was also the finish given the early AR-15 and M16 barrels. Parkerizing is much more impervious than bluing and is more effective as a corrosion-resistant surface treatment. However, Parkerizing is more involved and costlier to produce (the waste products can be a problem), so it has been gradually replaced with black oxide. Part of that change was also driven by fashion. A Parkerized finish is a light or dark gray. When oiled for protection, the oil trapped in the sponge-like Parkerized surface will gradually oxidize. The resulting gray-green finish is what many associate with a classic WWII firearm, be it M1 Garand, M1 Carbine or 1911A1. AR-15 owners gradually shifted to wanting a gun that was all black with no gray on it.

Black Oxide

Black oxide is another chemical treatment that involves sodium hydroxide, nitrates and nitrites, and requires an array of dunk tanks. While the traditional hot-salt bluing could be done in a small shop with two or three tanks, black oxide requires more room, more tanks and more ventilation. So small shops could not do it, but barrel makers would have plenty of room for the tanks to surface treat their barrels. More corrosion-resistant than hot bluing and as good or better than Parkerizing, black oxide has the advantage of not creating a buildup. Parkerizing can add to the surface of a part and interfere with the fit if not accounted for. Black oxide does not. While Parkerizing creates corrosion resistance by adding a layer of non-corroding metal, black oxide creates a non-corrosive surface by chemically taking up the places in the steel that oxygen would attack in the corrosion process. If there's no place for atmospheric oxygen to "bite" into the steel, then it can't rust. This approach is also called *passivation*, as it makes the surface passive to oxidation.

Stainless steel can be given a black oxide treatment, and although the chemical solutions and processes differ, the approach, passivation, is the same.

Melonite

Melonite is a type of ferritic nitrocarburizing that was first known as Tenifer when used on Glock pistols. Here, the passivation is accomplished by diffusing nitrogen and carbon into the steel's surface. This finish also has the benefit of adding surface hardness and scuff resistance to the treated parts. When I attended the Glock Armorer's Course back in the early days, the instructors took great delight in rubbing keys on the slides and then scrubbing the brass off. They even sharpened pocketknives on the slides.

Indeed, Melonite makes for a very strong and corrosion-resistant part. However, it adds one problem: the surface is so hard that you can't drill or machine it readily.

This attribute would not be a problem except that it is a total immersion process. That is, the bore gets treated as well. The old hot-salt bluing was a full-immersion process, but Parkerizing and black oxide are applied only to the exterior. A barrel to be Melonite treated must have everything already done to it, including any muzzle threading, chamber headspace to final dimension, and any other drilling (gas port, gas block location dimples) completed. Then and only then can a barrel be Melonite treated. There are no Melonite-treated barrel blanks. *All* the lathe, threading and drilling work must be completed before a barrel hits the Melonite tanks.

The Best Barrel?

There is no best. There is best for your use, the best for your wallet, and your desired appearance. Many different barrel shapes, materials and lengths will work just fine for multiple applications. For example, I once went on an industry product unveiling where we used M4gery AR-15s for several days on a prairie dog hunt. Were these AR-15s the best tool for that job? No. Did they work? Just fine, *thankyouverymuch*.

M4 Feed Ramps

You will probably hear a lot about "M4 feed ramps" and how important they are. Depending on your gun club and the members, you may be

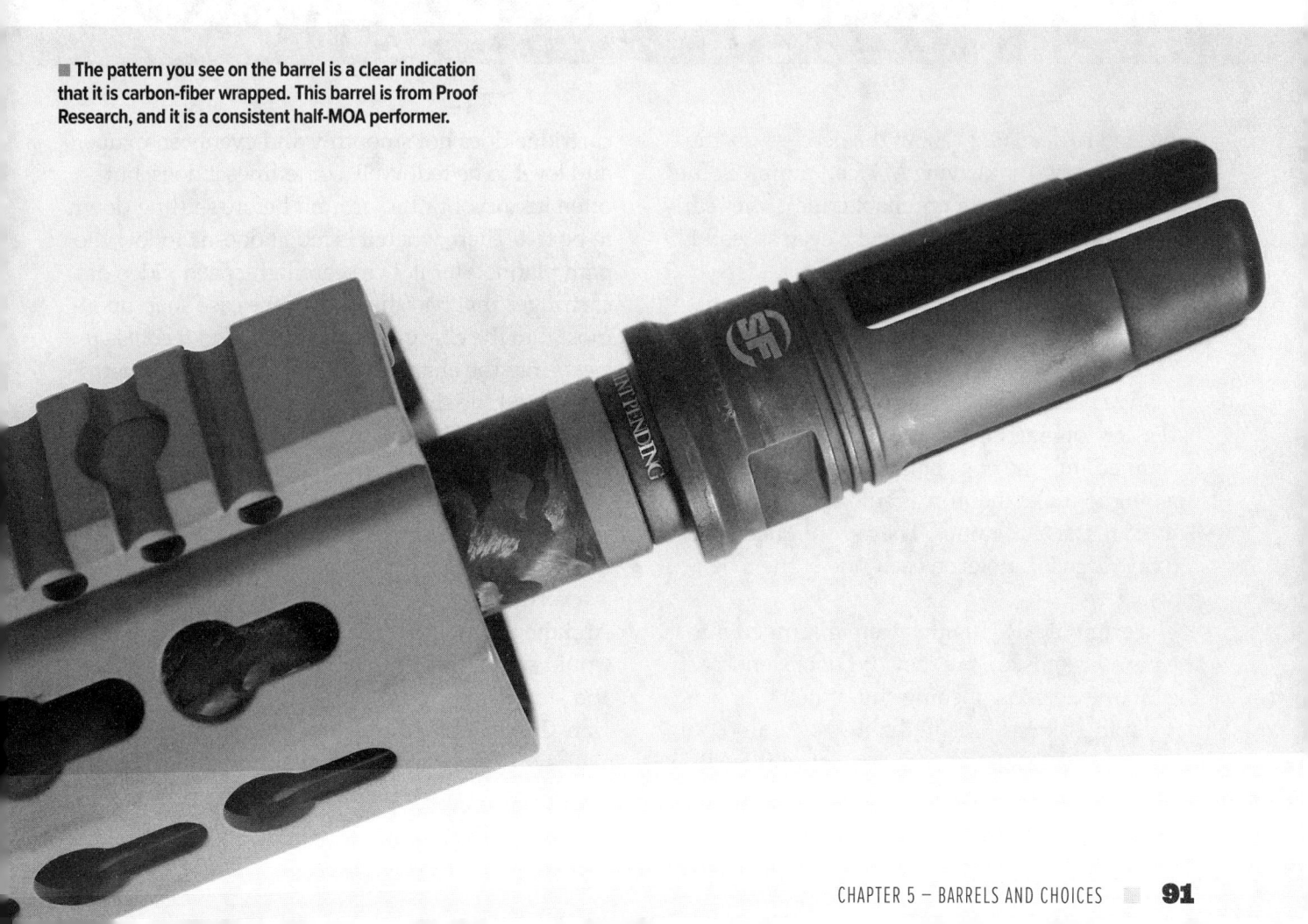

■ The pattern you see on the barrel is a clear indication that it is carbon-fiber wrapped. This barrel is from Proof Research, and it is a consistent half-MOA performer.

This upper is marked "M4" to show it has M4 feed ramps. Do all uppers need this? No. Does it help? Sometimes. Does it mean you are limited in barrel selection? A bit.

subjected to near-rants about the need — no, the very necessity — of having M4 feed ramps. Some claim you will have an unreliable rifle, suffer early male-pattern baldness and maybe even spread ED through the club membership.

And you are thinking, "What the heck is an M4 feed ramp?"

OK, in its trip from magazine to chamber, the cartridge passes through the opening of the barrel extension locking lugs. The AR-15 has two grooves machined into the edge of the barrel extension opening to make that trip as smooth as possible. These are the feed ramps. They are aligned with the cartridge locations on each side of the magazine.

The original AR-15 ramps were machined into the barrel extension, but they did not extend past the lip or extension opening rim. When Colt was developing the M4 back in the 1990s, it found out an interesting thing: the feed process of the AR-15 is not as smooth as people suspect. When uncovered by the carrier as the system cycles, the top cartridge does not smoothly and evenly snap up and level to be fed. Well, sometimes it does, but often it kind of rattles around before settling down to be fed. Then, when it is fed, it doesn't follow the path planned for it. I've seen high-speed video of cartridges that had the base of the case snap up almost into the charging handle slot and feed *downwards* into the chamber. All that got worse when Colt tested the shorter-barreled M4, especially with the SS109/M855 62-grain "green tip" ammunition. And it was worse yet in full-auto or burst fire.

On the original AR-15 barrel extension/receiver surface, the feed ramps stop at the edge of the barrel extension. Below that, near the magazine, there is a vertical aluminum surface, the receiver wall. And the tips of the M855 bullets in full-auto fire would sometimes stub or jam against that surface and stop.

So, Colt machined the ramp deeper into the extension, which extended the ramp down into the vertical receiver surface that also requires a machined ramp. *Voilà!* "M4 feed ramps."

■ The new hotness: M4 feed ramps, with the ramp to guide the bullet tip extending down into the front face of the upper receiver.

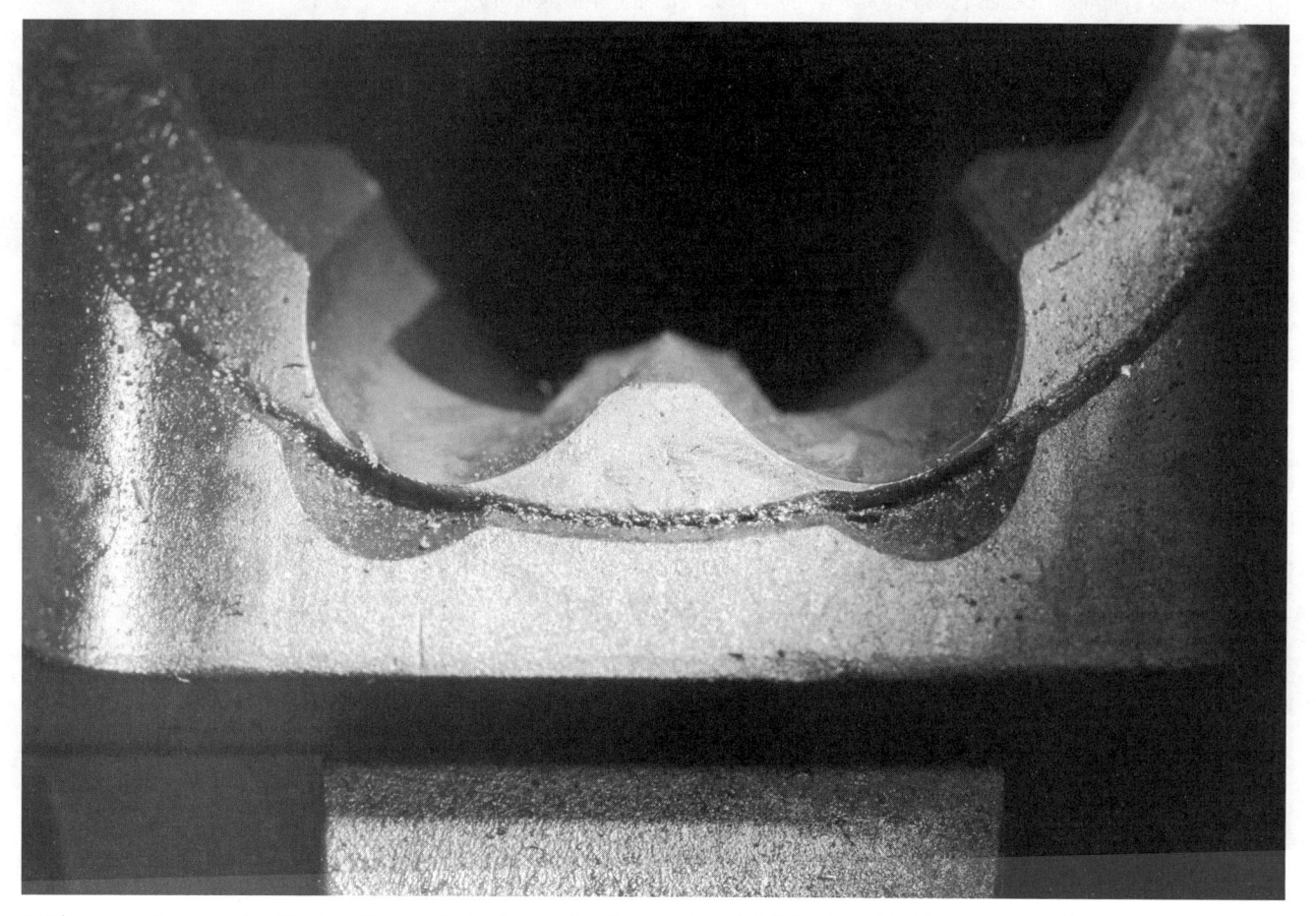

■ This example is a mismatch. The barrel has regular feed ramps, but the upper is an M4. This will (and it did) cause malfunctions.

CHAPTER 5 – BARRELS AND CHOICES

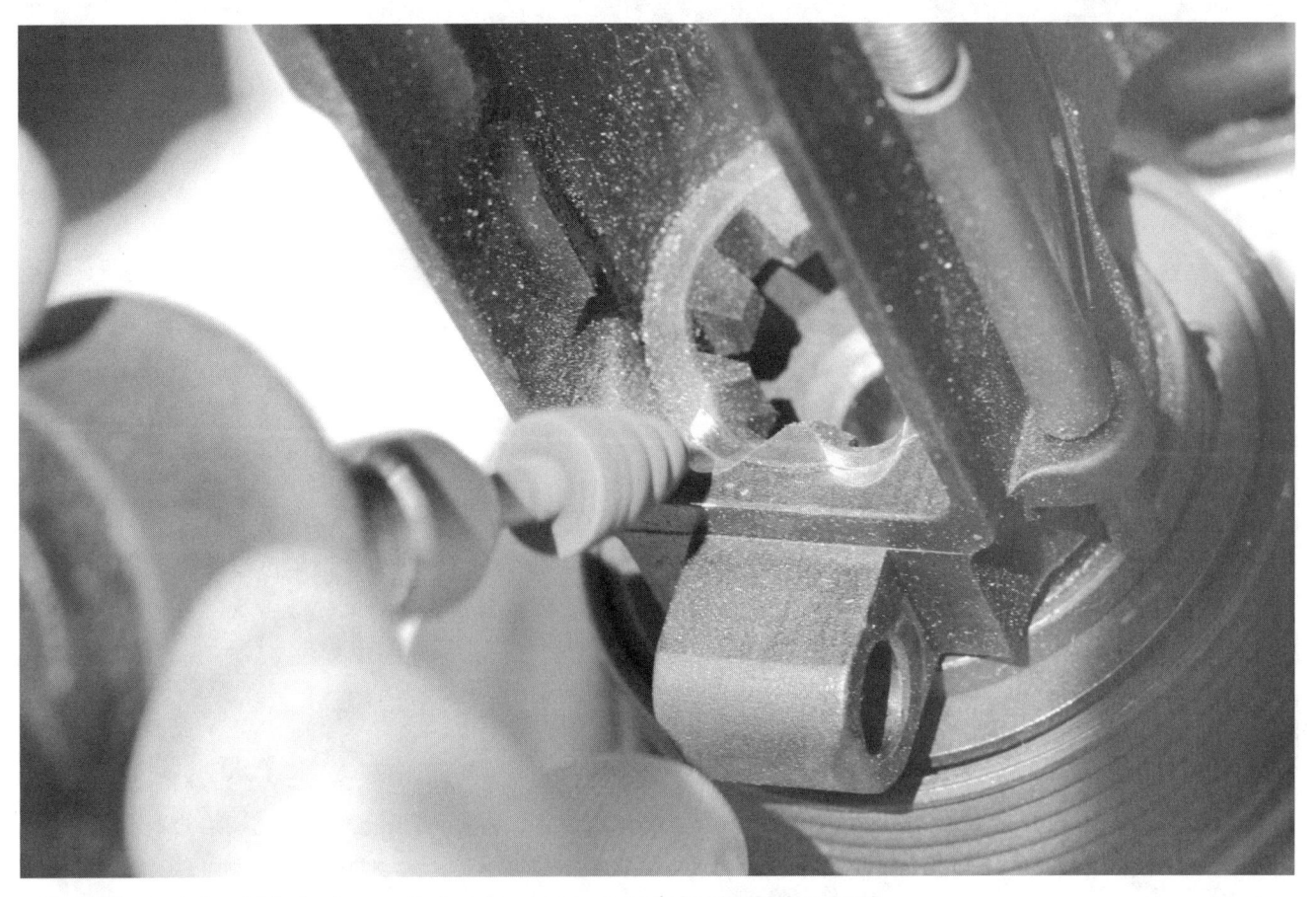

■ The solution to a mismatch is simple: swap the barrel or upper or use a grinder to make them match.

■ Here is the result of a short amount of careful grinding: a barrel with M4 feed ramps to match the upper's.

The markings here are B for Bushmaster, MP magnetic particle inspected, 5.56 chamber (yes, the author checked it, and it was correct, through some miracle), and the twist is 1/9. Sweeney used a 1/9 barrel for his retro project because he wanted to use heavier than 55-grain bullets.

Now, the government only specifies M4 feed ramps on M4 carbines. (Technically, the government doesn't, or didn't specify anything on the M4, as the technical data package was entirely Colt's. The DoD just bought what Colt made, called M4.) But the manufacturers were innovative. The idea of having a combination of M4 and (let's just call them) A1 feed ramps in the system was horrifying. Without any kind of industry-wide agreement or arrangement, everyone just switched over to M4 feed ramps, even for full-sized rifles. It is almost a universal standard now, and you can find full-sized rifles with M4 ramps. Why? Why not? The upper receiver doesn't care what length barrel you plug into it. If everything is an M4 ramp setup, everything works fine.

But not all ARs use M4 ramps, and you'll want to know the difference. A quick look will tell you once you've seen each. An M4-ramped barrel has distinct notches cut into the rim of the barrel extension, and the A1 does not. An M4-ramped upper will have two notches machined into the front lower surface of the inside of the receiver, and an A1 does not. (A1 in this context, referring to the ramps, not the exterior configuration of the receiver.) Also, the good upper makers will stamp "M4" on the external front face of the receiver above the gas tube hole so you can tell without peering inside.

Feed Ramp Combinations

Let's say we have two ramps and two receivers, which means there are four combinations of barrel/receiver setups. Will they all work? In a word: no. Let's go through them, and just for now, when I use "M4" and "A1," I will only be referring to the feed ramp dimensions.

M4 Barrel and M4 Receiver

Obviously, yes, it will match and will work. And today, this is the most common combination.

A1 Barrel and A1 Receiver

Again, yes, and in 99.999 percent of builds, as reliable as any rifle made.

M4 Barrel and A1 Receiver

Yes, this will look a bit ugly if you peer inside, but the M4 barrel ramps will, in most builds, still work just fine with the A1 receiver "ramps." You can, however, fine-tune it.

A1 Barrel and M4 Receiver

Most definitely not. The A1 barrel extension will hang over the feed ramp in the M4 receiver, creating a trapping pocket that will cause malfunctions.

CHAPTER 5 – BARRELS AND CHOICES

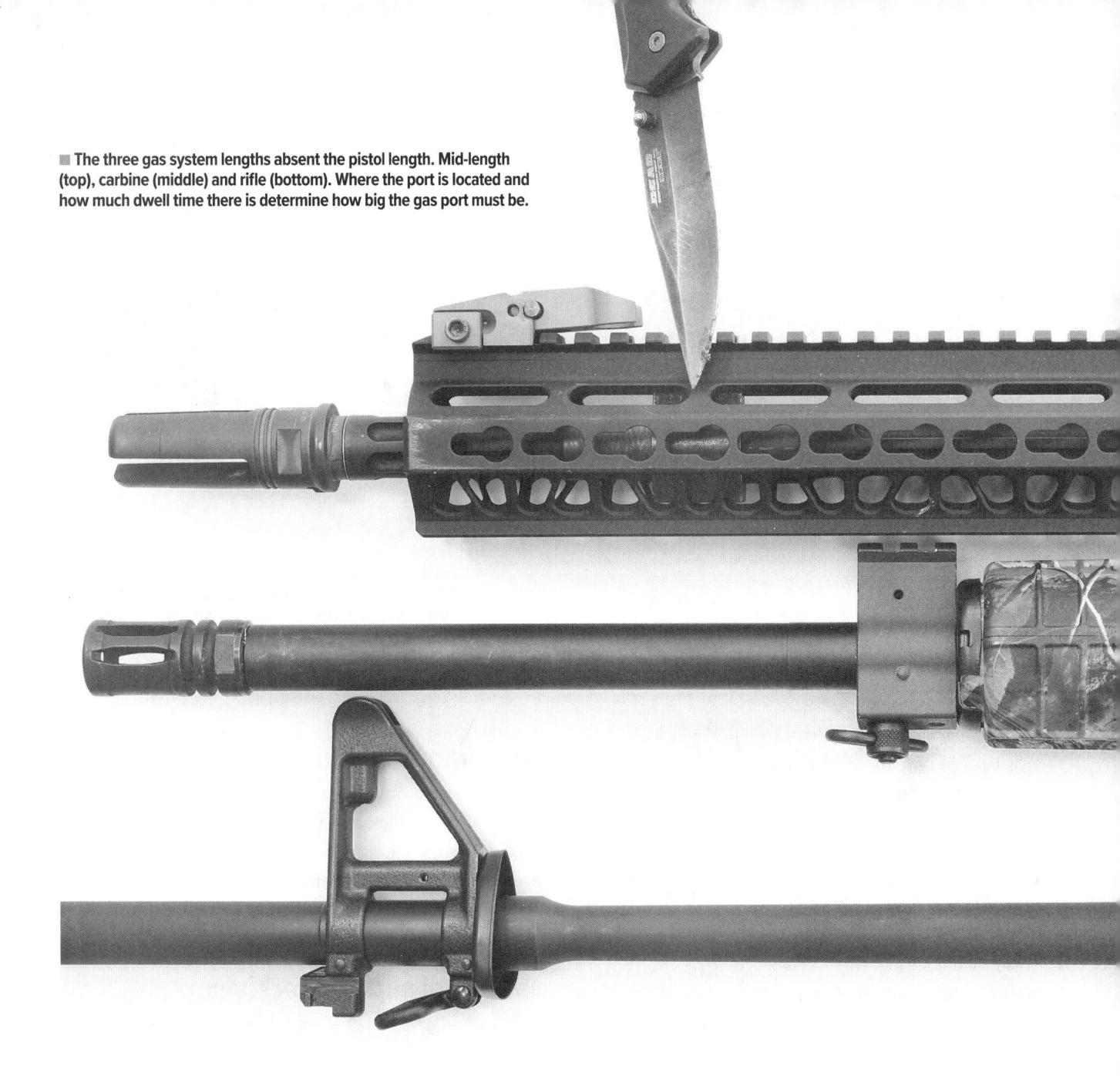

■ The three gas system lengths absent the pistol length. Mid-length (top), carbine (middle) and rifle (bottom). Where the port is located and how much dwell time there is determine how big the gas port must be.

Fixing a Problem

An A1/A1 rifle might be a tad unreliable and need fixing in feeding. An M4 barrel and A1 receiver benefit from a re-fit. And the A1 barrel and M4 receiver must be fixed. One solution is to simply re-barrel with a different barrel/receiver combo. If you are faced with an existing rifle that you must fix, and it can't be re-built, the solution is simple, if a bit delicate: you cut the feed ramps.

You will need a Dremel tool or other high-speed cutter and non-tapered carbide cutters. Looking like little end mill cutters, the Dremel gives you the RPM to cut, and the carbide provides you a clean cut. This operation is not a "Do it by hand" setup. You have the upper clean and clamped in a padded vise. You want the vise to also have a place to rest your hands while cutting. This process is exactly like painting a room where all the work and time is spent in prep, and the actual painting/cutting is done in short order.

So, keep arranging the receiver in the vise until you can simply tip your hand down to the cutting surface with the carbide cutter at the correct angle and hold it steady. Why? Because the Dremel's angle means that if the cutter "bites" into the metal, it can push your hand off to the side and make a mess of things.

How likely are you to need to do this? I did it

once in the 1980s before Colt had developed the M4 because I had a rifle that would sometimes stub a round in feeding. It is unlikely to be something you'll need, but I include it because it can be helpful. And should you feel the need to polish the feed ramps of your AR-15 (a detail necessary almost none of the time), you will follow the exact same process, but with a polishing bob on your Dremel instead of a carbide cutter.

Do you need M4 feed ramps? Maybe, maybe not. Your rifle, magazines, ammo and shooting will tell you if you do. The simple truth is: you'd have to search pretty diligently to find an upper receiver these days that doesn't have M4 feed ramps. I suspect that even the makers of retro uppers meant to duplicate the look and features of a pre-1986 AR-15 would have M4 feed ramps, just to avoid the hassle of a customer later plugging in a barrel with them and having problems.

Gas Systems: DI vs. Piston

The AR-15 uses gas to operate the mechanism. The design that engineers settled on for all gas-operated firearms was a small port drilled in the barrel, which bleeds a small amount of gas from behind the bullet and powers the system.

There are two methods: direct impingement (DI) and the piston system. First, the piston, as it is historically older. Here, the gas strikes the end of a rod, the piston, and the rod pushes the bolt. On a rifle like the M1 Garand (or M14/M1A), the piston is also the operating rod, which cams the bolt lugs and pushes the bolt back, then forward, and cams it closed again. On the AK-47, the piston and operating rod work like the Garand, but the rod is above the barrel instead of below it.

A slightly different approach is the "tappet" piston, the exemplar being the M1 carbine. The carbine piston is trapped in its housing under the barrel. When the gas hits the piston, it moves a fraction of an inch, pushing the operating rod. But once the piston has moved its entire distance, it stops. The operating rod then continues to cycle with the momentum the piston has delivered to it. When the bolt closes, the operating rod pushes the piston back to its starting point.

The direct impingement or DI system does not use a piston. Instead, the gas is directed down a narrow tube called the gas tube, and once in the receiver, it pressurizes the carrier. The gas pressure blows the carrier off the gas tube — like a wrapper off of a straw — and starts the cycle. The carrier has a built-in cam track that rotates and unlocks the bolt and cams it closed when the carrier and bolt return.

Which is better? You will be subjected to much discussion on the subject if you care to listen. The main advantages given for each are: DI is the known, accepted, reliable and easy-to-run system. Parts are all known and available. The DI system does not put extra parts or weight on the barrel and thus is easier to accurize. The disadvantage is that the gas gets blown into the upper receiver, making things grubbier. But the regular application of lubricant and cleaning keeps that from being a problem.

The piston advantage is that the gas and its heat are not blown into the upper receiver. However, the piston system brings its own problems. The extra parts clamped to the barrel can (but not always) hurt accuracy. The gas is often bled out of the forward gas block as part of the gas flow control, making a piston AR slightly louder when suppressed. There is no mil-spec for piston systems, so once you buy a piston-equipped AR-15, you are locked into that manufacturer's supply system for parts.

The heat from shooting is also a point of contention. Piston advocates like to point out that the heat of the gases is not blown back into the receiver.

> *"Regardless of DI or piston, your rifle will have a given length to its gas system, something you must keep in mind if you are ordering replacement or repair parts."*

True, but I've measured the heat of carriers in DI rifles, and they don't get hot enough that it matters. The piston system, however, usually has a larger gas block, which does get hot. They both generate heat; you simply have to decide where you want that excess heat dumped.

There used to be a lot of arguments over the subject. Mostly that is over. Who won? No one, everyone decided to just stop arguing. The Marine Corps adopted the HK416, in the version known as the M27, a piston system. The rest of DoD sticks with the M16, M4 and its variants. And they all may be replaced soon by some uber-weapon that has yet to be settled on. (No, it isn't a phased plasma weapon in the 40-watt range. At least, not yet.)

Regardless of DI or piston, your rifle will have a given length to its gas system, something you must keep in mind if you are ordering replacement or repair parts.

A Brief Discussion of Gas Ports

The gas port allows gas to leave the bore, enter the operating system and work the parts. How far forward of the chamber it is located and what it is expected to do determines the port diameter. A larger port bleeds off more gas. The gas pressure in the bore will be higher the closer to the chamber the port is when the bullet passes the port.

But there is also the matter of gas dwell time. You see, until the bullet has passed the port and left the bore, the gas is still pressurizing the system. Designers and barrel makers have to consider the dwell time of the bullet when determining which diameter they should be drilling the port. There are no fixed port sizes for a barrel, a discussion we will go in-depth into later. Just be aware that port diameter, like many other aspects of the AR-15, is a subject that you may find annoyingly argued to death.

Rifle

The rifle-length gas system is the original, and you can use it on 18- and 20-inch barrels. It is possible to shorten a 20-inch barrel to 16.5 inches and use the rifle gas system. I have done so in the past, but it was for a specific time, place and need. The rifle gas system produces the smoothest and softest-recoiling operation of all the designs.

Carbine

To make a barrel shorter than 16 inches, Colt moved the gas port back. This change meant a shorter gas tube. Its engineers located the gas port on the carbine to provide enough room to get shooters' off-hands onto the handguard and still function with a barrel just over 10 inches in length. The gas port location remains the same even though your carbine will have a 16.5-inch barrel.

Mid-Length

With many shooters choosing to have a 16- or 18-inch barrel on their AR-15 but not liking the sometimes jarring cycling of the carbine-length gas system, custom makers developed a "mid-length" system. This length started out as an R&D and custom option, as the riflesmiths doing the work had to take a rifle-length gas tube and cut it shorter but build it as a working gas tube. Mid-length is now a standardized system, and you can go to Brownells and order a mid-length gas tube for your AR. However, if you're building or re-building and going with a barrel produced for a mid-length system, you will find it easy to just add the barrel maker's mid-length gas tube to the order.

■ The markings on this barrel tell us many things: C means chrome-lined, MP means magnetic particle inspected, 5.56 is the chamber, and 1/7 denotes the twist rate. This example is a Colt barrel, so it really is a 5.56 leade.

Some high-end makers use proprietary gas tubes anyway. Geissele uses a gas system designed for a given barrel length that its testing has proven produces the best reliability and smoothest function. If you are re-barreling a Geissele rifle, you are probably going to be using a Geissele barrel, and it can provide the proper gas tube as well. Since Geissele makes its own barrels, this is not a problem.

Pistol

When the barrel length drops below 10 inches, you need an even shorter gas system. These shorties are the realm of AR pistols and ARs built to be subsonic-ammunition-only in .300 Blackout. Nothing is to be gained by making an AR with a 10-inch barrel using a pistol-length gas system.

Piston Gas Ports

Note that piston systems use the same operational lengths (gas port locations) as the DI gas systems. That's for a simple reason: the piston manufacturers (rifles or aftermarket, drop-in piston systems) want to have the commonality of the DI gas port locations to work with. It would be silly to make a piston system an odd length, so no one could replace a worn barrel with anything but the piston maker's own barrels.

There is also the matter of mil-spec. As in, there is no industry standard for piston systems. So, if you opt for a piston-driven AR-15, you are wedded to that manufacturer. You may be able to re-barrel and remove and install the piston system from the old barrel to the new. But, if something breaks in the piston system parts, you have one place, and one place only, to go to — the maker. As an example, Remington bought Para-Ordnance, AAC, Bushmaster and DPMS. If you now need replacement parts for a Para-Ordnance pistol, you'll have to find a custom 1911 builder to help you. Your AAC suppressor is an orphan. If you have a Bushmaster or DPMS rifle, and the part you need was proprietary to that brand, well, ask the custom 1911 pistolsmith if he knows of a custom AR-15 gunsmith because you'll need one.

Chamber Size/Caliber Designation Headspace

Headspace, simply put, is the room in the chamber for the cartridge. To set standards, the rifle and ammunition makers have gotten together through SAAMI (Small Arms and Ammunition Manufacturers' Institute). A source of confusion on headspace (and other chamber dimensions) is that the Department of Defense is not a member of SAAMI. Nor does it care what SAAMI says. However, the people and companies that provide products (rifles and ammunition) to DoD are, so for the most part, the two agree. More or less.

Headspace is the distance from the face of the bolt to where the shoulder of the case will stop when it enters the chamber. To allow manufacturing tolerances, the chamber is made within six-thousandths of an inch to this dimension. That is, it must be within 0.006 inch of the centerline of the headspace measurement. That's the total, so that would be plus or minus 0.003 inch.

Ammunition is manufactured to never exceed the smallest allowable chamber size. That way, the largest case will always fit the smallest chamber.

The problem arises when you shoot your ammunition. The shorter-than-the-chamber case (all cases are) will stretch when fired. They must stretch; they are subjected to 50,000+ PSI. If you reload your empty brass, that shoulder needs to be "bumped back" during the re-sizing step, but not by too much, only a few thousandths. Do that enough times, and the case will need to be trimmed as it will have "grown" too long, and the edge of the case opening might hit the case neck ledge in the chamber. (Not something a headspace gauge can measure, by the way.) The stretching acts to thin the case down near the base, and if done enough times, the case will break in two. Brass cases only have so much useful life in them, and that life is shortened if your headspace is too great or you bump the shoulder back too much, which effectively creates too much headspace.

One problem, and a subject of much argument, arises because the military does not reload empties. In fact, it requires the empties to be policed up (with sometimes obnoxious thoroughness) to be turned in instead of lost or "appropriated" by the end-users.

This lack of reloading means the government's acceptance of chamber dimensions is wider than ours might be. Headspace gauges come in sets known as Go and No-Go. A bolt and chamber *must* accept a Go gauge (if they won't fit the chamber, it is too small/short), and they *must not* accept a No-Go gauge. (If they do, the headspace is too great.) The military has a third gauge, called a Field gauge. The military assumes that all chambers will pass a Go/No-Go inspection. That's what the strict mil-spec dimensions are all about. There is a headspace extreme at which the brass will regularly break on the first firing given properly made ammunition. The military has settled on a less-than-that dimension but greater than the non-military No-Go length. This dimension is what the Field gauge measures.

5.56x45mm Versus .223 Rem.

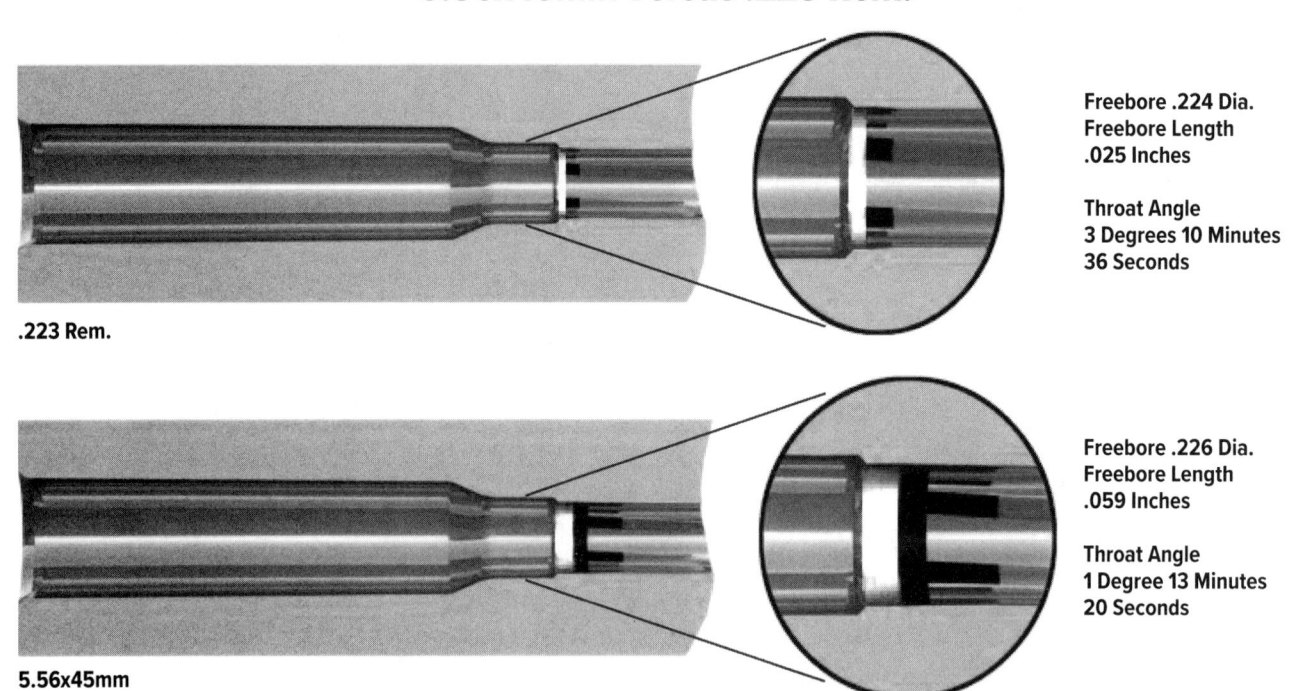

.223 Rem.

Freebore .224 Dia.
Freebore Length
.025 Inches

Throat Angle
3 Degrees 10 Minutes
36 Seconds

5.56x45mm

Freebore .226 Dia.
Freebore Length
.059 Inches

Throat Angle
1 Degree 13 Minutes
20 Seconds

■ Both of these popular calibers feature a .224-inch-diameter bullet and an identical overall length. However, the throat length for 5.56x45mm is longer than that of .223 Rem. As a result, you can safely shoot .223 ammunition in a 5.56 chamber, but not 5.56 in a .223 platform, as it can result in excessive pressures upon ignition.

This detail is essential, so keep it in mind from a strictly military point of view: an M16/M4/whatever in government use might well gobble up a commercial No-Go gauge and still be considered suitable for use by the government. Remember, no reloading. The case stretching t   c.) does not close on a Field gauge, it is considered suitable for issue. If it will close on a Field gauge, it is deemed to be unsuitable. Go and No-Go do not enter the equation. I stress this repeatedly: this is a military thing, meant for emergency wartime considerations. Most M16/M4-*whatevers* the government uses will pass a Go/No-Go gauge test. The Field gauge is only for an "Is this so worn/out of spec that it would be hazardous to hand to a soldier and ask him to go shoot commies with it?" test.

Some will tell you that the only gauge you need is a Field gauge, and it will tell you if your rifle is acceptable. They are wrong.

Not all bolts and barrels are made to mil-spec, as much as the makers try. The quality of bolts and barrels is much higher now than it was years and decades ago, and it is a rare combination that will not pass a Go/No-Go inspection. Plus, if your new barrel comes with a bolt from the same supplier, they will have checked that for you. (In all likelihood, anyway.) If you embark on a lifetime of AR building, re-building, assembling or maintenance, investing in a set of headspace gauges is a small cost. And it's a satisfying thing to check.

Chamber Agreement

There are a host of dimensions that are used in making barrels. Every maker produces barrels the way it sees fit and to the customer's specifications. This process can involve small changes, and as long as they are within the allowed spread that SAAMI has settled on, everyone is happy. Here is what Federal says about chambers and the ammunition used in them.

If Yours Fails

OK, you just bought a barrel or a barrel and bolt combo, which fails the test. Now what? Start over. Scrub the chamber. Scrub the bolt. You did remove the extractor and ejector, didn't you? (If not, then do that and re-test.) If it fails again, you have two choices: if you have spares, keep swapping (keep track of the originals, of course) until you find a combo that works. You can sometimes find a combo that corrects an out-of-spec pairing. Of course, when you do that, you now have a non-interchangeable combo. That bolt can't go into another barrel (if you have multiple rifles in the rack), and that barrel can't use some other bolt.

Contact the supplier and lay it out for them if you want to do it right and have fully interchangeable parts. You didn't shoot the parts, you haven't modified anything, but the combo fails a Go/No-Go test. Request an exchange, and would they please double-check the replacements before shipping?

All reputable suppliers will swap the parts and probably raise hell with their suppliers.

Interchangeability

Which brings us to: Can you swap parts? Specifically, can you change bolt/carrier assemblies from one rifle to another? Well, yes and no. Yes, if everything involved passed a Go/No-Go test. The military tells troops not to swap the bolt/carrier assemblies because, well, it doesn't want them to. The troops aren't even allowed to disassemble the firing mechanism in the lower; that's how controlling Uncle Sam is. If two rifles have passed a Go/No-Go test with the same gauges, they will work fine with the bolts swapped. But what if yours passes the test because you found out it was too short on the first test and you reamed the chamber to fit? Well, then it won't be a good idea to swap the bolt/carrier combo with another rifle.

HEADSPACE COMPARISONS	GO/NO-GO GO	NO-GO
Commercial .223	1.4640	1.4670
Military 5.56	1.4646	1.4704
USGI Field*	1.4730	
Colt Field II	1.4736	
M249	1.497	1.4982
M249 Field*	1.5020	

■ The "223 Wylde" on the receiver tells us several things. Primary Arms used this in-between leade, with the length of the 5.56, but the snugness of the .223.

This was more common in the old days when we had to make things fit. Today, with most if not all of the bad parts makers out of business, and everyone making quality stuff, it is much more likely that interchangeability will be OK. But I'd check first.

.223/5.56 Headspace and Leade

The .223 vs. 5.56 issue is another subject with a great deal of confusion and misinformation. The designations ".223" and "5.56" are the commercial and military designations for pretty much the same ammunition. Pretty much, but not exactly. The mistake many make is in looking at the headspace dimensions. The dimensions are listed as "X" inches, plus-or-minus a smaller "X" spread. The government is willing to accept a larger spread in those measurements since it does not reload cases as we have just mentioned. We civilians do reload them. So, the .223 invariably has a smaller spread than whatever 5.56 set of dimensions you may find. (And yes, Virginia, there is more than one definition of "5.56" headspace dimensions.)

There is no Go/No-Go for a Field gauge; it simply is a pass-fail proposition. The overlap between the commercial (and there is a spread there, believe it or not, in what various rifle makers of .223 call "good enough;" the USGI dimensions mean you really need not worry). And the Field gauge is a non-issue for those of us not running military armories.

You can use a Field gauge as your one-and-only gauge, but you can do so only within certain conditions that will ensure your safety. You have to buy all (and I mean *all*, bolts and barrels) of your parts for real-deal, honest-to-God mil-spec providers. You only build your rifles or carbines with these parts. And, you use brand-new, factory-made .223

or 5.56 ammunition, never shooting reloads and never loading your own.

Because that's what the Field gauge and mil-spec standards are predicated on. If you use outside parts, reloads, or load your own, you really need to be careful and spend time checking leade and headspace.

Oh, and the gauges for the M249 SAW? I include those to show how you can sometimes find once-fired brass that is so abused that it nets you one reload, and then the cases break. The government is plenty happy with a chamber that big on the M249. Ignore that difference.

What matters in the .223 vs. 556 subject is the space called the leade. (Pronounced "leed," sounds like weed.) The bullet projects forward of the case in the chamber, and the chamber is reamed to accommodate the bullet. You have the chamber shoulder, chamber neck, a smooth cylinder where the bullet rests and finally, the beginning of the rifling. The difference between .223 and 5.56 is:

The distance forward of the bullet's start, where the rifling begins, and the angle of the ramp of the start of the rifling.

5.56 has more of a distance, a longer bullet jump, than .223. Why? In short, back in the 1960s, the Army resisted the adoption of the M16. The .223 had been designed in the 1950s. The Army, in trying to keep the M16 out of inventory, insisted on better performance. Having bought the M16 (then the AR-15, the designation hadn't been changed yet), Colt could not change it to accommodate a larger cartridge. As such, Colt lengthened the leade.

When a bullet starts its journey, the burning gases push the bullet forward, and once the bullet reaches the rifling, it in essence stalls, as it takes some additional force to engrave the bullet into the rifling lands. That stall creates the maximum pressure the cartridge will experience.

By moving the leade forward, Colt was able to reduce the pressure spike. With the spike decreased, it increased the loading of the case and gained

> *"So, yes, there is a difference between .223 and 5.56 ammunition. There is a difference between .223 and 5.56 chamber/leades. And yes, using hotter 5.56 ammunition in a .223 leade increases pressure even more than it should be."*

more velocity at the now-the-same-as-the-original pressure spike it was previously creating.

So, yes, there is a difference between .223 and 5.56 ammunition. There is a difference between .223 and 5.56 chamber/leades. And yes, using hotter 5.56 ammunition in a .223 leade increases pressure even more than it should be. We'll go into that in-depth in the barrel fitting and gauging chapter.

Here, I'm just giving you the straight skinny: there is a difference, it can matter, and those who say it doesn't are wrong.

.223 Wylde

Competition shooters developed a chamber that gained the name .223 Wylde to control pressure but not give up accuracy. You may see this stamped on the barrel or listed in the specs of your rifle. Essentially, it is a chamber with the length and rifling angle of the 5.56, but the freebore diameter is more like the .223. That is, closer guidance of the bullet while giving it the running room to keep pressures down.

If you poke your M-guns 223/556 Gauge into a .223 Wylde chamber, it may read as if it is a .223

CHAMBER PART	.223 REM.	5.56X45	.223 WYLDE
Neck diameter (in.)	.2510	.2550	.2550
Freebore diameter (in.)	.2242	.2265	.2240
Throat angle (deg.)	1.5 to 3	1.2 to 2.5	1.25
Neck length (in.)	.2034	.2200	.2220
Freebore length (in.)	.0250	.0500	.0620

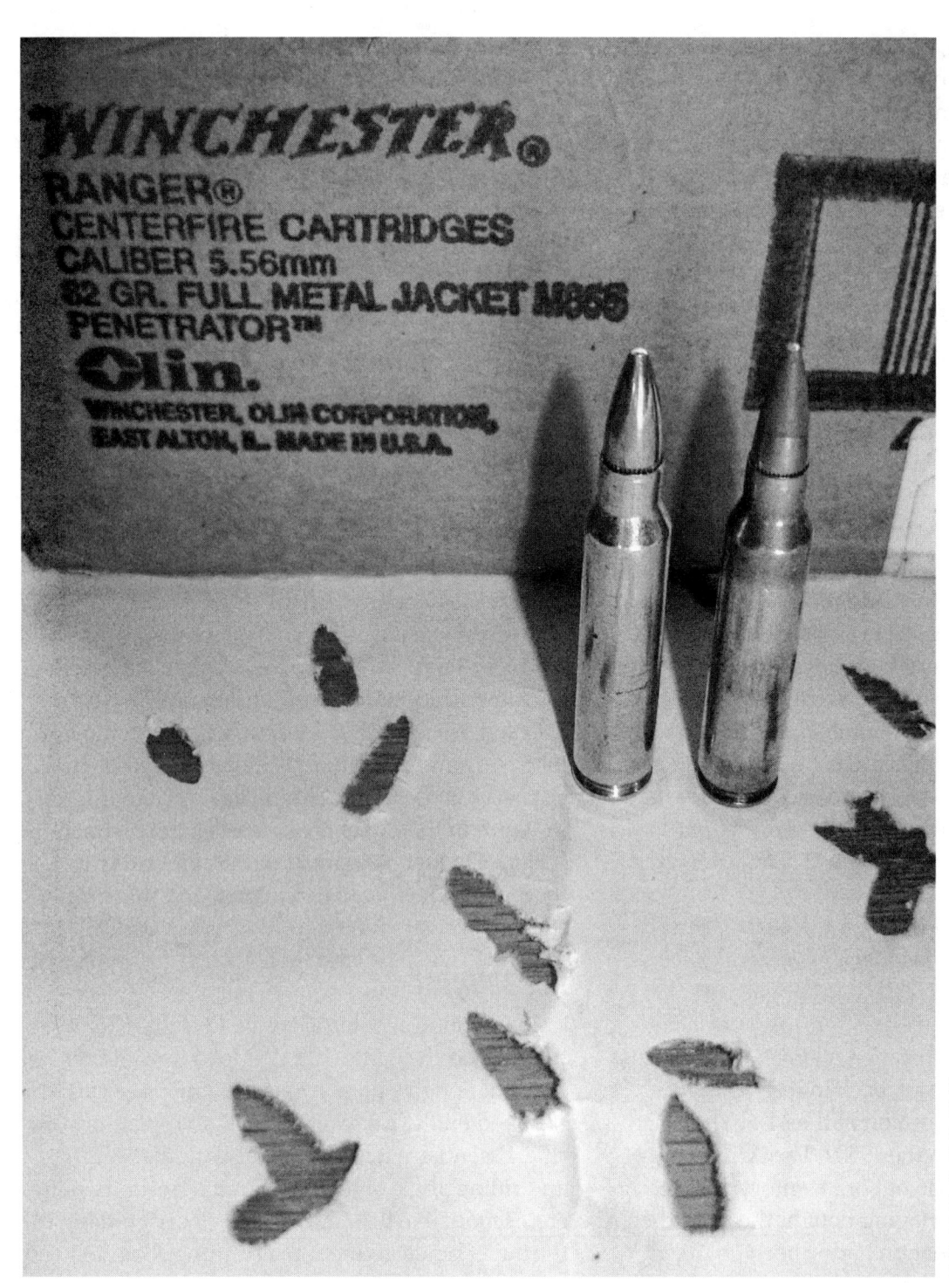

■ This target depicts the result at 25 yards of using a 62-grain "green tip" bullet in a barrel with a 1/12 twist. The bullet is unstable, and by 25 yards, it is already going sideways or tips as soon as it hits paper.

and not the combination chamber that it is. You will not need to ream such a chamber unless it is popping out primers with factory ammo. In which case, you must ream.

Rifling Twist Rate: What It Does

The rifling in the bore imparts a rotation, or spin, to the bullet. This spin creates gyroscopic stability that keeps the bullet point-first in its travels. Without that spin, the bullet will be subject to the vagaries of every puff of wind along its path. Also, as soon as it deviates from point-on travel, its shape will cause it to veer off-path. In baseball, a knuckleball pitcher throws the ball without imparting any spin on it. As a result, it wanders toward the batter, taking the path every errant change in the air adds to it.

There is also the matter of bullet shape and the barrel. You see, when the bullet is forced down the bore, it rotates about its center of form — or the mechanical center of the bullet. Once it leaves the bore, it transitions to rotating around its center of mass. A high-quality bullet will have a microscopically slight difference between the center of form and center of mass, but it does exist. As a result, the bullet will be slightly unstable when it first leaves the muzzle until it "settles down" over a short path and rotates on its center of mass.

An ordinary child's gyroscope is a perfect example. When you pull the string to start it, it will wobble slightly. When the bullet leaves the muzzle, it will similarly wobble. Once each of them "settles down," they will spin stably until friction (or, in the case of a bullet, an obstacle) causes them not to.

That means that a bullet will not be as stable as at close range and will not penetrate as deeply. This effect is counterintuitive, as we'd expect a faster bullet to penetrate more. But at close ranges, the instability is a more significant variable than the velocity. The classic example comes from *Hatcher's Notebook* by Julian S. Hatcher, who took a .30-06 military round and, out of an M1 Garand, shot it into oak planks at 50 feet and 200 yards. At 50 feet, it penetrated 10 inches, and the bullet traveled in an arc in the stacked planks, a half-circle. At 200 yards, it penetrated 30 inches of oak planks on a straight line.

How to Measure

The simplest way to measure twist (assuming the barrel isn't marked) is to use a cleaning rod with a free-rotating handle and a tight-fitting patch. Insert the patched tip of the rod into the bore, and once it is in place, stop and attach a "flag" of masking tape to the rod pointing straight up. Now push the rod in, watch the rod turn, and the tape rotate. When the tape is back up top (one complete revolution), the rotation rate is the distance in inches the rod has moved.

The standard measurement is denoted as the distance for one turn in inches. For example, the rate is given a shorthand marking of 1-10, 1/10 or 1:10, where the "10" means 10 inches.

Markings

Your barrel will likely be marked as to the twist (and chamber, .223 or 5.56) someplace on it. Usually, a 1/12, 1/9, or a 1/7 stamped, etched, laser-engraved or roll marked forward of the front sight housing. The earliest Colts did not have any markings, as there was only one twist. Later, they would have a "12" or a "1-12" roll-marked on them. Why the difference now? In the early 1980s, the big worry was body armor on Soviet infantry in the coming war in Europe. NATO developed heavier bullets to get better penetration, which we adopted. This bullet was known by NATO as the SS109 and the U.S. as the M855, aka "green tip." It is basically the 55-grain FMJ but with a 10-grain steel pyramid inserted inside the jacket at the tip to increase penetration.

The NATO testing covered many designs, and to ensure they would all be stable in testing, the R&D was done with the fastest twist NATO thought it'd need, a 1 turn in 7 inches twist. That was the twist rate and ammo adopted for the M16 A2.

Many shooters then thought the twist was too fast for 55-grain FMJ (target bullets), so a compromise of 1/9 twist found its way into the marketplace.

They all work in .223 and 5.56, and while some combinations are less than ideal (lightweight varmint bullets in a 1/7 twist, for example), don't obsess over twist rate.

Calculate Stability

Not just any rate of rotation will do. Objects only have gyroscopic stability within a specific rate of rotation. Too slow, and it will not be stable. In the case of bullets, stability is directly related to length. The longer the bullet, the faster the rotation, and thus the twist rate, must be. It is difficult for us because bullets are not designated by length but by weight. Depending on the shape, a given-weight bullet can be of different lengths.

So, when discussing bullet stability, barrel twist and bullet weight, we do so with common and known exemplars. For example, when we speak of a "55-grain bullet," we mean, for the AR-15, a pointed boattail, full metal jacket or soft-point bullet. We do not imply a bullet with a flat base and a blunt, hemispherical nose, like the contour of a .38 Special 158-grain lead round-nose pistol bullet.

For those who do not want to go in-depth, here's the short form:

A 1/12 twist barrel will stabilize all bullets up to 55 grains and some that are heavier.

A 1/9 twist barrel will stabilize all bullets up to 77 grains.

Here we have a comparison between the leades of .223 and 5.56. And NEMRT, the one the M-guns 223/556 reamer creates.

A 1/7 bullet will stabilize all bullets up to 85 grains.

If that's all you need, you are done here. Skip to how barrels are made. If you want to know the details, to revel in technical geekiness, continue.

Greenhill Formula

Sir Greenhill was a professor of mathematics at the Royal Military Academy at Woolwich, London. He developed a formula to determine the rifling twist needed to stabilize the new cylindrical artillery shells. (This was in the 1870s.) Spherical cannon balls required only a very slow twist to stabilize, but the longer shells needed more. His formula was developed empirically, that is, through experimentation, and is:

$$T = \frac{C x D^2}{L} X \sqrt{\frac{S_g}{10.9}}$$

T is the twist
C is a constant, either 150 or 180
D is the bullet diameter in inches, which is then squared
L is the bullet length, in inches
And then, as the extra, we have:
Sg, the specific gravity of the bullet. For lead-core,

copper-jacket bullets, the Sg is 10.9, thus making the second half the square root of one, which is one. For most uses, we can simply drop the second half of the equation

The constant Greenhill used, 150, gives us a twist rate in inches when the other dimensions are inches. The constant works with velocities up to 2,800 fps. Above that, we change to the constant of 180, which gives a better result.

Using Greenhill

Let's jump right to our question: the original M16 bullet and twist rate. Measuring a selection of 55-grain FMJ bullets, we see lengths of .728 to .755 inch. Let's use the longer of the extremes, just to be safe. Plug in the numbers using a constant of 150, and you get 9.9 inches as the Greenhill-calculated twist rate. Interesting! The standard government twist rate as determined by the tests for the M16 is a bit on the slow side.

But wait, you may have noticed what was off — the constant. The M-193 bullet left muzzles at 3,100 fps or more. That means the Greenhill Constant should be 180, not 150. Let's re-calculate. We get a twist of 11.98 inches. Spot on.

But we can do more.

One of the beauties of symbolic logic — in this case, mathematics — is that if you follow the rules, you can move the parts around to structure the equation any way you want. That's the process by which Einstein came up with his breakthrough:

$$E = MC^2$$

Starting with the idea of the speed of light being a constant, he simply kept cranking the allowable changes that mathematics permitted into the equations he knew to be correct until he came up with one that took his breath away. Once he had devised it, it was up to mathematicians and physicists worldwide to prove him wrong. No voting, no "consensus," just here it is, prove me wrong or sit down and pour yourself a big, steaming mug of "shut the frak up."

So, instead of making the twist rate the equation's results and a constant, we turn it into one of the variables. Instead, we use the *constant* as the variable. That is, we want the equation to read, so the result is always 150. (Or, in the case of a cartridge over 2,800 fps, 180.)

To do this, we shift things around. Initially, we have:

$$T = \frac{C x D^2}{L}$$

Multiply both sides by length, negating the length on the right side of the equation.

$$L \ x \ T = C x D^2$$

Next, divide both sides by the square of the diameter, negating diameter squared on the right;

$$\frac{L \ x \ T}{D^2} = C$$

Flip it, so our result is on the left, and we have:

$$C = \frac{L \ x \ T}{D^2}$$

The Greenhill constant results from the bullet length multiplied by the twist rate, and that sum is divided by the bullet diameter square. I'm going to be bold here and name yet another technical aspect of firearms after myself.

I will divide the regular Greenhill constant by the above formula results and call the resulting ratio the Sweeney Stability Ratio, or SSR, a technical symbol of M, or capital Mμ, the greek letter used for the coefficient of friction.

$$M = \frac{C_g}{C_c}$$

Where C_g is the Greenhill Constant, and C_c is the calculated constant by our above equation.

Why? Just because the thought of the friction between the desired/appropriate spin rate, and the actual one, is amusing.

So, if the twist rate of a given barrel and bullet is correct as calculated using the Greenhill formula, then Mμ will be 1. If the twist rate is too slow and stability decreases, the ratio, or Mμ, will be less than 1. If the twist rate is faster than the Greenhill formula calculates, the ratio, or Mμ, will be greater than 1.

In researching this, (after having done the algebraic work), I found that there had been other work done expanding on Greenhill's formula. Don Miller elaborated on the Greenhill formula, but it still produces a twist rate while his formula adds in variables. Berger comes closer, with a plug-in software formula that uses Miller's formula, having the same desired result as the Sweeney Mμ.

■ Note the short gap from the case mouth to the start of the .223 rifling.

Let's take a look and see what we get by calculating Mμ.

As we established above, if we calculate the desired twist rate of the 55-grain FMJBT, as found in the M-193 bullet, we get a predicted twist rate of 11.96 inches. Turned into a Mμ ratio, the M-193 out of a 1/12 twist barrel produces a figure of 1.003.

If we take that bullet and push it down a 1/9 twist barrel, we have a Mμ of 1.33. And out of a 1/7 twist barrel, the Mμ is 1.71. In all three instances, the bullet will be stable and accurate. We are not, however, considering the effects of RPM on bullet structure itself. A lightly-constructed, varmint-type bullet will be stable out of a 1/7 barrel right up until centripetal forces tear it apart. I have seen that happen with my own eyes; it is not an urban myth.

So, having established that we have not yet encountered an upper limit for stoutly constructed bullets, let's see if we can set a lower limit. We have two classic cases in the history of the AR-15/M16. One is the original twist rate of one turn in fourteen inches (1/14). There, the 55-grain FMJ was barely stable, and any degraded variable caused a loss of accuracy so bad that the Army would not have it. We can establish that as our boundary. The problems of dense Arctic air, worn barrels, pretty much anything but a new rifle in shirt-sleeve weather caused accuracy to deteriorate. So, the calculated Mμ in this instance is the original and classic dividing line.

Second, the use of a 62-grain SS-109/M855 bullet in a 1/12 twist barrel. The practice has established that this is less than marginal, and it is a case of the stability being insufficient to produce accuracy. M855 ammunition, fired through a 1/12 twist barrel, will make keyholed impacts on a target at 25 yards. We are clearly below a threshold for Mμ of stability with this combination.

A 55-grain FMJ out of a 1/14 barrel produces a Mμ of 0.8547.

An M855 out of a 1/12 barrel produces a Mμ of 0.8272.

■ The 5.56 leade gives the bullet more of a running start, and the angle or "ramp" of the rifling start is more gradual.

We can thus determine that we are on the stability threshold with a Mµ of 0.85 or 0.86 or less. (The engineering schooled will assert that we have only proven the case for .224-inch diameter bullets. If that's you, then good for you. We'll not overlook that.)

We can then use this to extrapolate and compare to experience.

The hot 5.56 load for many uses is the Mk 262 Mod 1, which features a 77-grain bullet and is typically used in a 1/7 twist barrel. Will it be stable in a 1/9, the more common twist rate found on many ARs? The math tells us that the Mµ for that combination is 0.979. That is much closer to our ideal of 1.0 than the threshold of 0.86 that we have empirically established. And experience has shown that most rifles with a 1/9 twist will shoot the Mk 262 Mod 1 at least as well as the user can.

Those that can't, we can lay the blame not on bullet stability but on it being a barrel made with a cost figure in mind — that is, a crappy barrel. Or poor handloading habits. Or something, but not twist rate and stability.

If we then work the equation in other instances, we can calculate the stability of 77+-grain bullets, commonly used in long-range rifle competition. NRA High Power shooters single load bullets up to 90 grains. What is the stability of these bullets in a 1/7 barrel?

First, remember that these are not faster than 2,800 fps, so the Greenhill Constant drops to 150. (At least, I hope out of .223 cases, they are not trying to exceed 2,900 fps. If they are, I want to leave the range before firing commences.)

The 80-grain bullet is over an inch long, as much as 1.080 inches. Its Mµ from a 1/7 barrel will be

CHAPTER 5 – BARRELS AND CHOICES ■ **109**

0.996. That's close enough to the Mµ for a 55-grain FMJ out of a 1/12 barrel and pretty darned close to our desired Mµ of 1.00. Hmm. The 90-grain bullet, at 1.198 inches in length, gives us a Mµ of 0.897, which is still in the stable range, as we have calculated.

In talking with the high-end High Power shooters, I find that the 80-grain bullets pushed as fast as people dare are best for long-range. It is touchy, however, as you are pushing everything to the redline. The 90s are not so popular, simply due to the limited case capacity of the .223. You just can't push the 90s fast enough to take advantage of their greater ballistic coefficient.

With the re-worked Greenhill formula, we can calculate the stability for several bullets with different twist rates.

An Exception

Oh, and the 1/12 twist not working with bullets heavier than 55 grains? I know of one heavier. Winchester used to offer a 63-grain softpoint in .224-inch diameter. This bullet was for those who deer hunted in areas where the .22 was permitted. Despite being "too heavy," the bullet (no longer made) was a flat-base, not boattail. And the round nose was blunt. It was short enough, despite being heavier, that it worked in a 1/12 barrel. For me, the tricky thing was that Winchester or wholesalers would regularly put these bullets on sale to get them moving through the supply system. If I waited for the sales and bought in volume, I'd get them for less than any other bullet for the .223/5.56.

In fact, I bought so many of them that I wore out a fistful of barrels shooting those bullets in 3-Gun and bowling pin competition.

■ The NEMRT reamer lengthens the leade to make it a 5.56, and it also cleans it up to ensure all traces of the previous leade are changed to the new and improved one.

Now, back to our regularly scheduled programming.

Barrel Making Methods

Barrels are made of steel (until something stronger comes along, anyway), and they all start as rods with holes drilled down their centerline. The process requires two drillings, one from each end to the halfway point. It's that "halfway point" that adds complexity. The process usually involves spinning the barrel while the drill bit remains stationary. The drill bit is hollow and has cutting lube pumped through it at a high rate to cool the drill and carry away the metal chips created. The hollow tube-to-be-barrel is reamed and polished on the inside. It is straightened and, depending on the quality desired, these steps might be done several times to the bore. It may also be stress-relieved, either with heat (not usually, as it can cause problems with the heat treatment of the bar, and thus its hardness) or cryogenically.

Then the barrel maker cuts the rifling.

Cut Rifling

Cut rifling is also known as "single-point" rifling. Here, a single cutter is used. The cutter has a hook shape and is pulled through the bore, guided by a spiral-shaped groove in the guide mechanism. The rate of the groove is the rate of the twist produced. Depending on the barrel maker, steel, quality desired and time spent, the cut might be a thousandth of an inch, and it might be a tenth of a thousandth. Once the cutter makes one pass, it is pulled back, shimmed or hydraulically adjusted to cut another path, and the cut is repeated. Once the groove is deep enough, the whole thing is done again on the next groove. Repeat for as many grooves as the barrel calls for — from two to eight grooves.

This is the province of high-end, absolute precision barrel-making, and such barrels are costly.

Broach Rifling

For broach rifling, the single-point cutter is replaced with a multi-step "Christmas tree-shaped" cutter. The broach has all the grooves in one, as individual cutter groups. Each step in the cutter removes a fraction of the groove depth, with the one following it the next step taller, cutting the groove deeper, and so forth. Think of it as a round

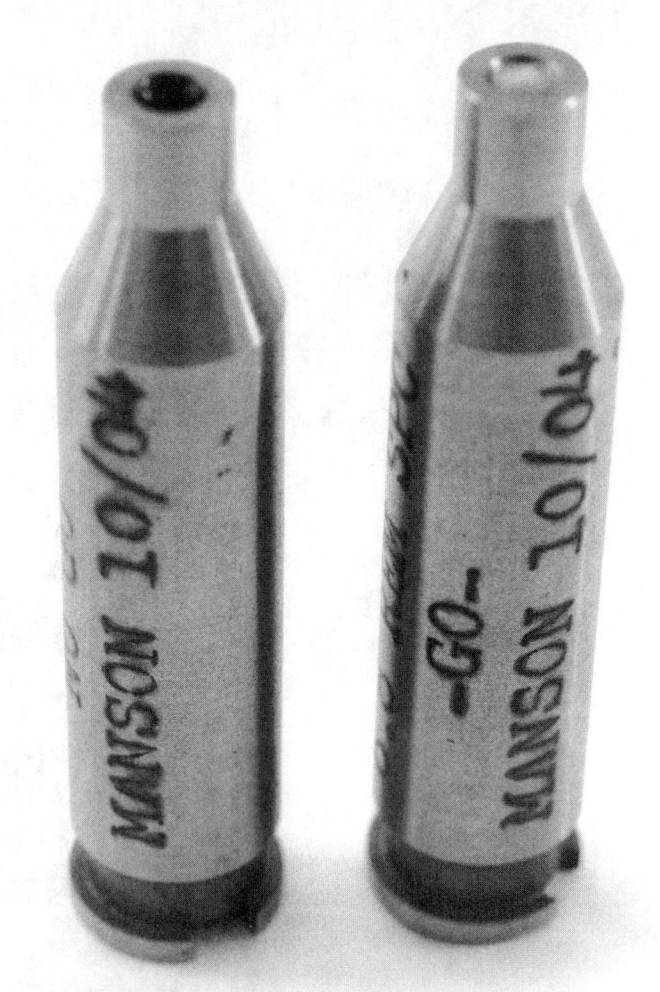

■ Headspace gauges only measure the distance from the bolt face to the chamber's shoulder. They tell you nothing about the leade. It is passing rare for a barrel-bolt combo to not be in spec these days. The old days of *craptastic* bolts and barrels are gone.

file shaped like a cone with the teeth aligned for the rifling grooves, and you won't be far off. The broach is pulled through the reamed and polished bore once, and that's it — it is rifled.

Button Rifling

A super-hard button is shaped like the rifling desired and is pulled or pushed through the bore for button rifling. The tops of the button swage the steel (yes, really, steel swaged to move it out of the way), and the moved steel fills the gaps between the high spots on the button. Like the broach, the button goes once through the barrel, and it is done.

Cold Hammer-Forging

In forging, the barrel blank has a "mandrel" run down into it. The mandrel is shaped like the rifling desired. In some instances, it can include the shape of the chamber. Once in place, the multiple hammers of the machine pound the

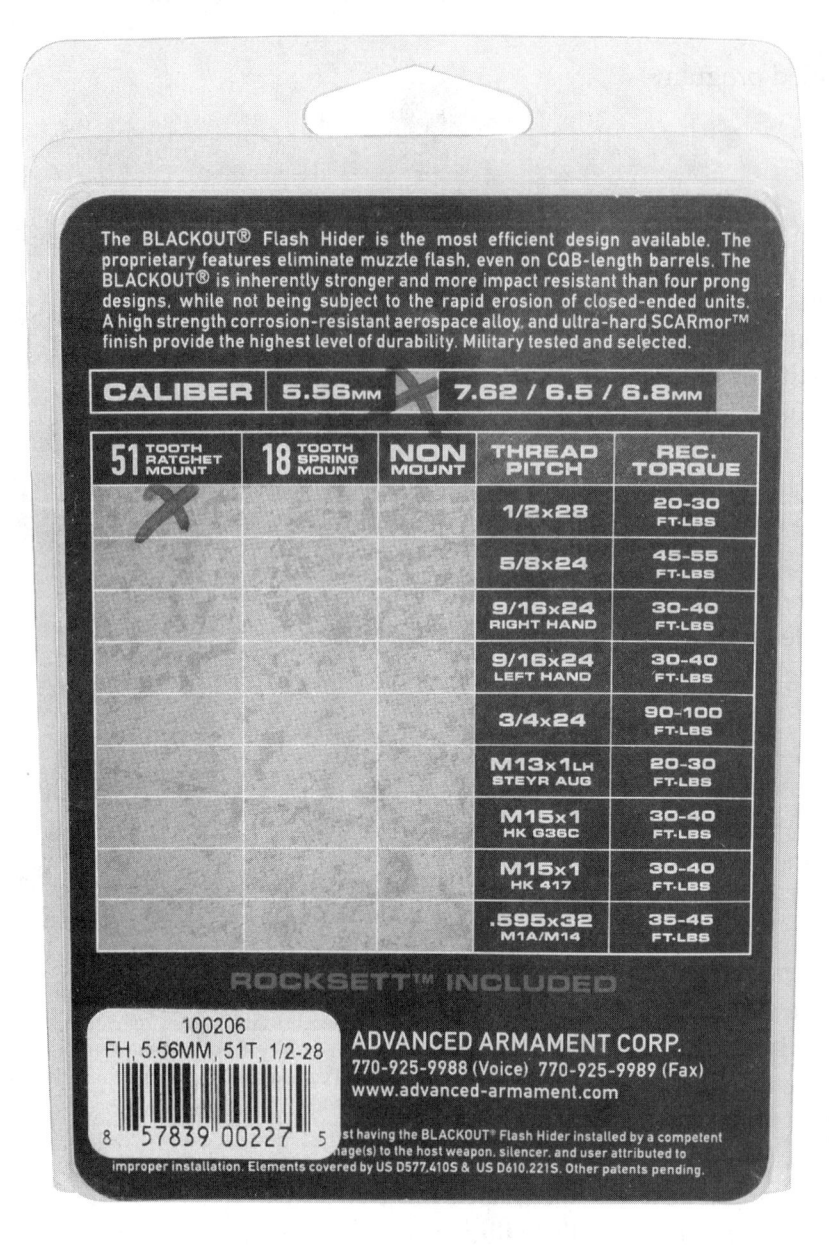

The BLACKOUT® Flash Hider is the most efficient design available. The proprietary features eliminate muzzle flash, even on CQB-length barrels. The BLACKOUT® is inherently stronger and more impact resistant than four prong designs, while not being subject to the rapid erosion of closed-ended units. A high strength corrosion-resistant aerospace alloy, and ultra-hard SCARmor™ finish provide the highest level of durability. Military tested and selected.

CALIBER	5.56mm ✗	7.62 / 6.5 / 6.8mm			
51 TOOTH RATCHET MOUNT	18 TOOTH SPRING MOUNT	NON MOUNT	THREAD PITCH	REC. TORQUE	
✗			1/2x28	20-30 FT-LBS	
			5/8x24	45-55 FT-LBS	
			9/16x24 RIGHT HAND	30-40 FT-LBS	
			9/16x24 LEFT HAND	30-40 FT-LBS	
			3/4x24	90-100 FT-LBS	
			M13x1 LH STEYR AUG	20-30 FT-LBS	
			M15x1 HK G36C	30-40 FT-LBS	
			M15x1 HK 417	30-40 FT-LBS	
			.595x32 M1A/M14	35-45 FT-LBS	

ROCKSETT™ INCLUDED

100206
FH, 5.56MM, 51T, 1/2-28

ADVANCED ARMAMENT CORP.
770-925-9988 (Voice) 770-925-9989 (Fax)
www.advanced-armament.com

■ All accessories, including flash hiders and muzzle devices, have manufacturers' torque specs. Read and follow.

outside of the barrel tube, compressing it down onto the mandrel and forcing the steel to take the mirror image of the mandrel.

EDM

EDM means electrical-discharge machining. If you pump a substantial electrical current into a setup, the electricity will jump across a gap. The gap is small, and the distance can be controlled. So, you make a rod with electrodes on it and pull it through the reamed tube while the electrical charge jumps the gap, eroding steel as it goes. You can "cut" grooves this way. This is not an everyday method employed for rifle barrels, but it is used.

All barrels, once rifled, will be inspected, straightened again (and again after every step past this). And the top-quality ones will be bore lapped. Lapping requires a cast lead shape of the bore, which has a lapping compound smeared on it. The lap is run back and forth down the bore, polishing it. Mil-spec ones might not be lapped (usually not, the added cost isn't something the government is willing to pay for) and then have the interiors chrome-plated once the chamber has been reamed.

Barrel Finish

The exterior of the barrel blank will be cut to length, then lathe-turned to the desired contour, the gas port located and drilled, the rear threaded, the barrel extension screwed in place, and the indexing pin drilled and swaged into place. If it is a military barrel or a military clone, it will be placed in a fixture and have the front sight pin locations drilled and then taper-reamed. Somewhere along

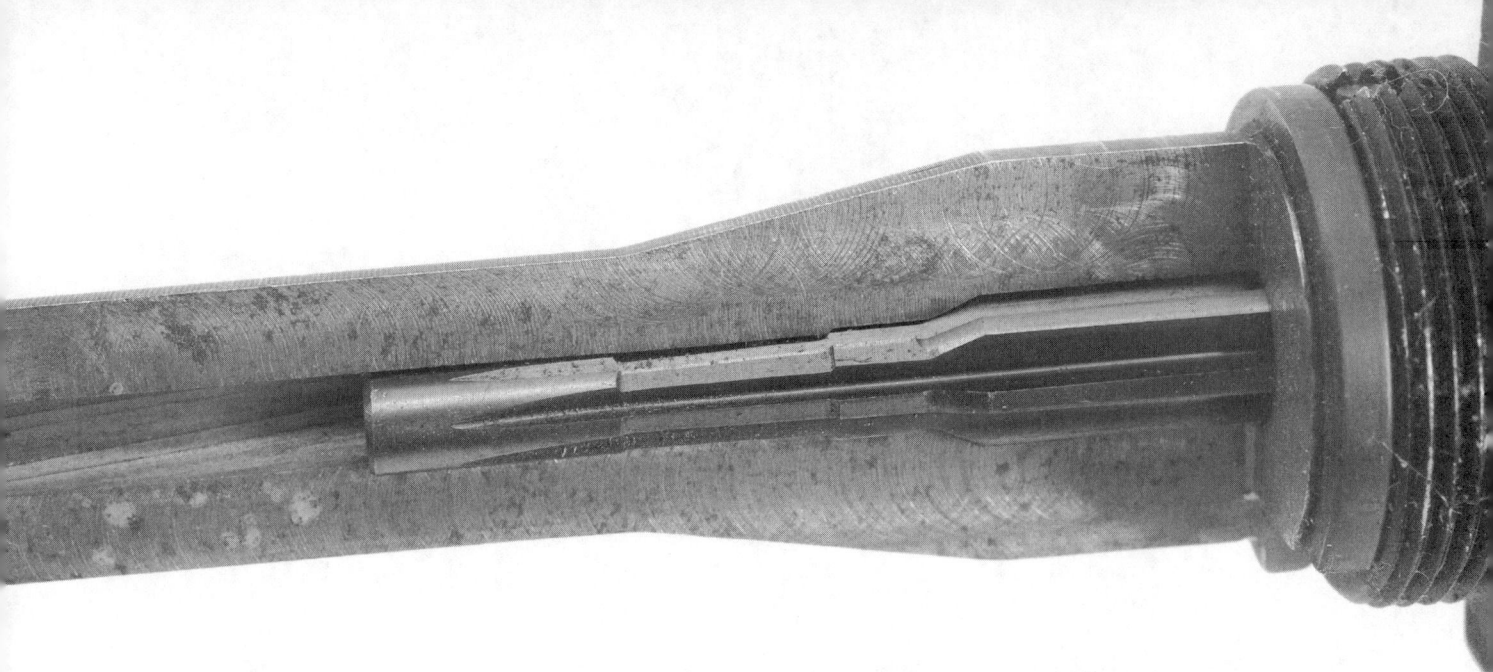

■ When barrels are made, the chamber reamer cuts to the chamber shoulder. The length of the leade depends on the specifications of the reamer in the leade, not the shoulder.

the way, the muzzle will be crowned and threaded for a flash hider or other muzzle device.

The quality of CNC lathes these days makes all these operations much superior to the original barrels. As a result, it is rare to find misaligned muzzle threads or cockeyed barrel extensions. Also, the multiple ups and downs of the AR market have driven the poor-quality barrel makers out of business.

Why Do Barrels Cost So Much?

Simple: machines cost money. Running machines takes skilled operators. Let's take, for example, a standard-size deep-drilling machine, like the Precihole GVN08C. We're talking about a machine with a 211-gallon holding tank for the drilling lubricant, which delivers said oil to the bit tip at 1,500 PSI. That's a big, heavy machine. It takes a skilled operator to run it, and if it isn't operated correctly, it will eat tools, scrap barrel blanks and create losses for the shop.

How Accurate is "Accurate"?

Those who live and die by the mil-spec standards are less willing to look at what the government allows for accuracy. The measuring systems used in mil-spec are not the same as we use. Our method is simple: shoot a group, slap a ruler across it and measure the distance between the two farthest-apart holes. This method gives groups in sizes of inches, and a 1-inch group is just that. Also called a Minute of Angle or MOA.

The military method measures each shot distance from the geometric center of the cluster, then divides, multiplies, adds in the gravitational

> *"Those who live and die by the mil-spec standards are less willing to look at what the government allows for accuracy."*

constant and comes up with a figure. (OK, mild exaggeration.) Generally speaking, the Army (I cannot speak for the USMC, I don't have sources there) is happy with a rifle/ammo combination that delivers on the order of 4 inches at 100 yards. From a machine rest.

No, I'm not kidding. Colt is proud that their rifles do half that.

This precision is predicated on one detail: the military is more invested in rifles that work all the time, every time, and will not fail. It will give up some accuracy (except for snipers, of course) to ensure that.

Keep that in mind when you are obsessing over getting your rifle to shoot sub-MOA. Or the local gun club expert rants about the superiority of mil-spec.

6

Barrel Fitting

■ For barrel fitting, you'll need clamping blocks or a Reaction Rod, a good wrench and sometimes shims. A Reaction Rod is a handy tool for many tasks, but don't skimp on the wrench.

Let's start at the beginning: a new upper and a new barrel, neither previously assembled. Yes, a parts kit. You will need the following tools:
- Reaction rod or upper receiver fixture
- Barrel wrench
- Gas tube alignment gauge or a #16 drill
- Pin punch for the gas tube roll pin

■ A good vise, clamping block and insert will serve you well.

If you're using a barrel that already has a front sight assembly attached but will have a low-profile gas block, then you'll need the Brownells front sight block to remove the old pins and front sight.

If you are also going to use the old bolt, or a bolt that is not one sent by the barrel provider, you'll need:
- Bolt fixture
- Extractor pin-sized punch
- Ejector pin-sized punch
- Headspace gauges

Let's start with the most common receiver, a flat-top, and an upper assembly with the forward assist and ejection port cover installed, but no rear sight or optics on it. First, pull the barrel out of its packaging and confirm it is what you bought. Check that it is the correct length, contour, twist, material and external finish. If you're using a basic mil-spec-type barrel, it will have the front sight attached, and the "Delta ring" spring-loaded handguard retainer will also be on the barrel. If you remove the handguard to install a non-mil handguard, then the Delta ring assembly can only come off by first removing the front sight assembly. You can remove the front sight "A" pillar before or after installing the barrel into the upper receiver. We'll cover that later.

Headspace

The easiest way to measure headspace is with the barrel off the upper receiver. If you intend to do it, tackle it first. If you bought a special headspace gauge set that does not require bolt disassembly, great. Otherwise, you'll need to a) Remove the bolt

> *"If the bolt does not turn on the Go gauge, the chamber is under minimum, or the bolt is over maximum, and you and the barrel or bolt maker will need to have some words."*

from the carrier assembly; B) Remove the extractor; C) Remove the ejector; D) Scrub or wipe the bolt clean, as well as the chamber. This process is easier with a bench vise. Clamp the barrel — with padding — in the vise, muzzle down. Drop the Go

CHAPTER 6 — BARREL FITTING ■ **115**

gauge into the chamber and press the bolt into the barrel extension as if it closed during the firing sequence. You should be able to rotate the bolt once it is in place, as the locking lugs should clear the barrel extension lugs. If it does, loosen the barrel, remove the gauge, re-clamp the barrel and proceed to the No-Go gauge.

If the bolt does not turn on the Go gauge, the chamber is under minimum, or the bolt is over maximum, and you and the barrel or bolt maker will need to have some words. As you will read many times here, this was a problem in the old days, and now it is pretty much not one. But if it is a problem, you must fix it by replacing the bolt or barrel.

Now, with the No-Go gauge in place, press the bolt into the extension. It should not turn, but you should be able to feel a slight engagement. The bolt lugs and barrel extension (the bolt more so) have shallow, short angles machined into the backs of the bolt and the front of the barrel extension to make the camming of the bolt closing easier. This is the "catch" you'll feel if the bolt and barrel are correct. If you do not feel any camming, with the bolt lugs basically bouncing off the extension lugs, then your chamber is on the short side of correct. If you can almost force the bolt home, camming up on the tiny little ramps, then your chamber is on the long side of correct. In either situation, you have a correctly headspaced bolt-barrel combination.

■ Hand-tighten the barrel nut.

■ Shown here without the Delta ring assembly, put the upper into the clamping blocks or onto the Reaction Rod and press the barrel into the receiver. Align the tab on the barrel extension with the slot in the receiver.

■ Use a quality barrel nut wrench and tighten the barrel nut to just shy of the minimum torque. Loosen, tighten again, then draw up to full torque or until you've aligned the barrel nut notch.

CHAPTER 6 – BARREL FITTING

■ If your barrel nut turns too far, loosen it if you can stay above the 30 ft-lbs minimum torque. If not, then it is shim time.

This process is a touch-and-feel operation, not a brute force exercise. Over time, you will develop the feel of a proper headspace dimension.

What not to do? Don't toss a headspace gauge into a chamber on an assembled rifle and let the action spring crash home to close on it. The bolt is likely to fully close on even a No-Go gauge even if the headspace is correct. It could also wedge closed so tightly that you can't get it open. If your buddy tells you, "This is how we did it in Iraq/Afghanistan/SEALs," don't let him work on your rifle.

What if you want to check the headspace on an upper that is already assembled? Do you take the upper receiver and barrel apart? No. Go down to the big-box store and buy a one-foot section of PVC tubing of nominal .405-inch outer diameter. The interior will be more-or-less .249 inch, while the bolt tail will be more-or-less .250 inch. You can press the bolt's tail end into the inside of the tube and use the tube as an extension to reach the bolt down to the chamber and turn it.

Barrel Nuts, Old and New

Now is the best time for a brief overview of barrel nuts, history and design. Let's assume you have a new, bare barrel that does not have a barrel nut and Delta ring assembly installed. We'll go through installing those. The Delta ring assembly and barrel nut are four parts: barrel nut, Delta ring (or in the retro builds, slip-ring), waffle spring and "C" clip. You will need a special set of pliers known as "reverse" pliers. If your barrel doesn't have a barrel nut already installed, you'll need to remove the front sight or gas block. If your barrel arrived with a front sight "A" frame, it almost certainly already has at least the barrel nut and probably the entire Delta ring assembly in place. If not, jump to the front sight/gas block removal section and non-destructively remove it.

Slide the barrel nut onto the barrel, with the toothed end toward the muzzle. If it has a barrel nut, good. Now, clamp your barrel in a padded vise with the muzzle pointing straight down. With one hand, slide the barrel nut up to the barrel seat shoulder. Place the Delta ring over the chamber end of the barrel, making sure it slides down to and over the barrel nut. Pick up the waffle spring, place it inside the Delta ring, around the barrel nut, and press it down. It will spring back; that's its job. You hopefully noticed the groove machined around the barrel nut. That's where the C-clip goes. Place the C-clip on the end of the barrel nut, then pick up the reverse pliers, which act to spread the ring when you squeeze the handle. Poke the pliers' tips into the holes in the C-clip, squeeze to spread the ring and slide it over the barrel nut. Make sure it clicks into the groove. Relax, and let go, and set the pliers down.

The Delta ring is now a self-contained unit.

The Delta ring's waffle spring pushes it over the rear lips of the two pieces of the mil-spec handguard. The C-clip holds it all together. Modern, free-float handguards do not always use the regular barrel nut, and none use the Delta ring assembly. Many now have a proprietary barrel nut, one designed to work with the free-float handguard. Once you leave the Delta ring assembly as a handguard-holding part set, you are into proprietary-land designs. Many are good; some are only average. But they are each their own parts assembly, and you will have to go to that manufacturer if you have any problems.

Barrel Installation

Once you are sure the barrel is correct, wipe the exterior off with a shop cloth and hand-fit the barrel into the upper. It should be a snug fit, even take some pressing, to slide into place. Slip the indexing pin into the slot on the upper and press the barrel into place. Now hold the upper with the muzzle pointing away from you, with the upper receiver opening facing you. Is the front sight vertical to the receiver? If not, you have something seriously wrong and need to exchange either the barrel or the upper. This issue was common years ago but is pretty rare today. Still, it is worth checking.

Pull the barrel out of the upper. Secure the upper receiver in your clamshell fixture or on the reaction rod. Use a stiff-bristle plastic brush to clean the upper's interior at the barrel seat and barrel extension. Also, cleanly brush the threads on the upper receiver. Put a few drops of light oil onto the threads of the upper receiver and press the barrel into the upper. The Delta ring assembly is a spring-loaded setup, and the barrel nut is inside the various parts. The Delta ring and its spring will rotate around the barrel nut, so when you turn the barrel nut, make sure you turn it and not just the outside Delta ring.

Hand-turn the barrel nut until it stops. Fit your

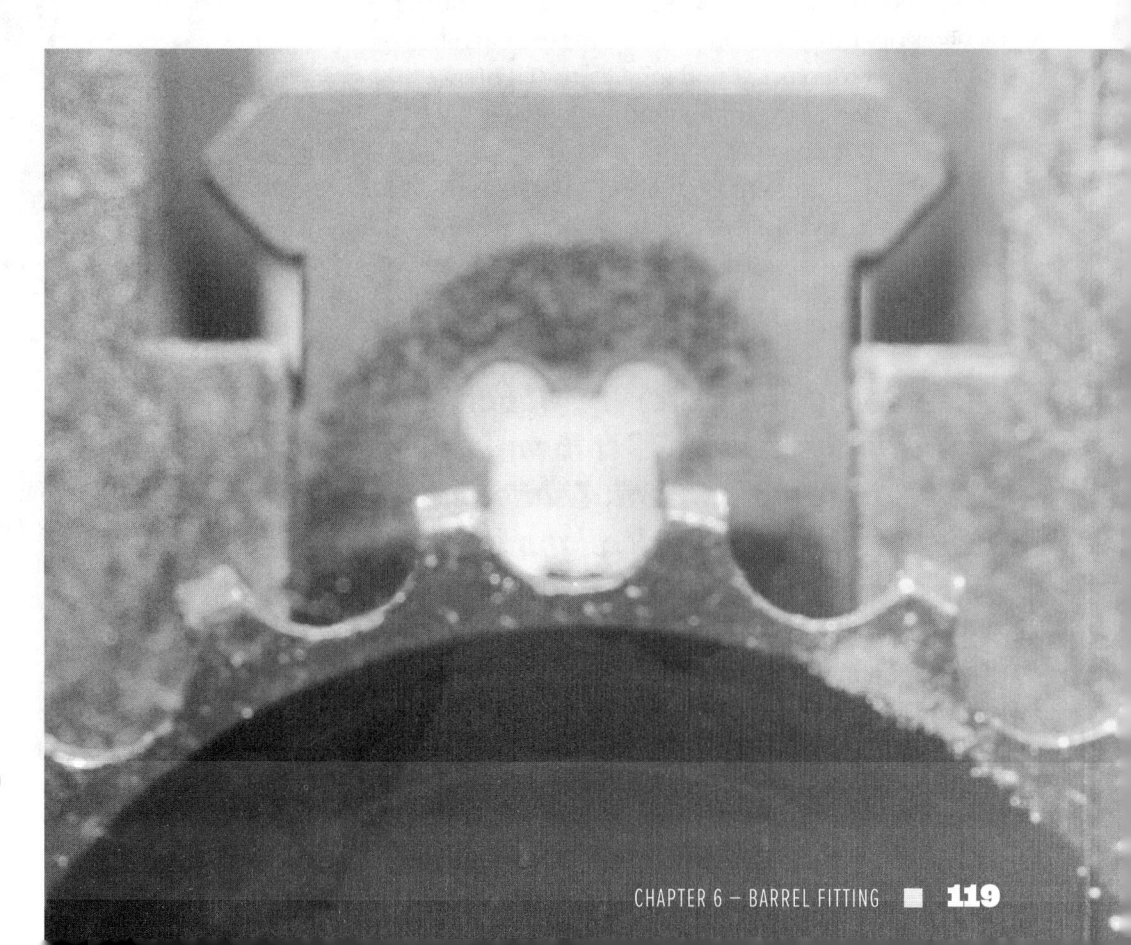

■ A perfectly timed barrel nut with the notch allowing the gas tube to pass through without touching.

barrel nut wrench securely into the notches on the barrel nut. (The Delta ring will be pushing the wrench away from the nut flanges, so this takes some care.) Tighten the barrel nut up to just short of the torque limit indicated. Now loosen it and tighten again. Loosen a second time, and on the third tightening, bring it to the upper torque limit. You do this to burnish the thread surfaces to each other and make sure any high spots or machining marks are ironed out.

The torque limits for the GI barrel nut are shockingly casual: 30 ft-lbs minimum, not to go over 80 ft-lbs for alignment. That's right, you crank it up to 30 ft-lbs and check alignment. If it needs a bit more torque, keep going until things line up. Disassemble and start with different parts if you can't get it to line up by 80 ft-lbs.

Assuming the flange notch and gas tube hole aligns, use a small punch to rotate the Delta ring, the internal spring, and the retaining ring on the rear so they all line up with the gas tube clearance hole in the receiver. Remove the assembly from the reaction rod or fixture.

To check proper barrel nut alignment, take your assembled bolt-carrier assembly, install the barrel nut alignment gauge or the #16 drill into the gas tube opening. Slide the carrier into the upper receiver and look at how it passes through the upper receiver opening. It should pass over the barrel nut without touching the flange teeth. Tighten or loosen the nut in small amounts to adjust the alignment if it does.

Barrel nut alignment is an almost philosophical question. If you assemble an M4gery and are happy with "good enough" accuracy (which can be pretty accurate in many instances and often better

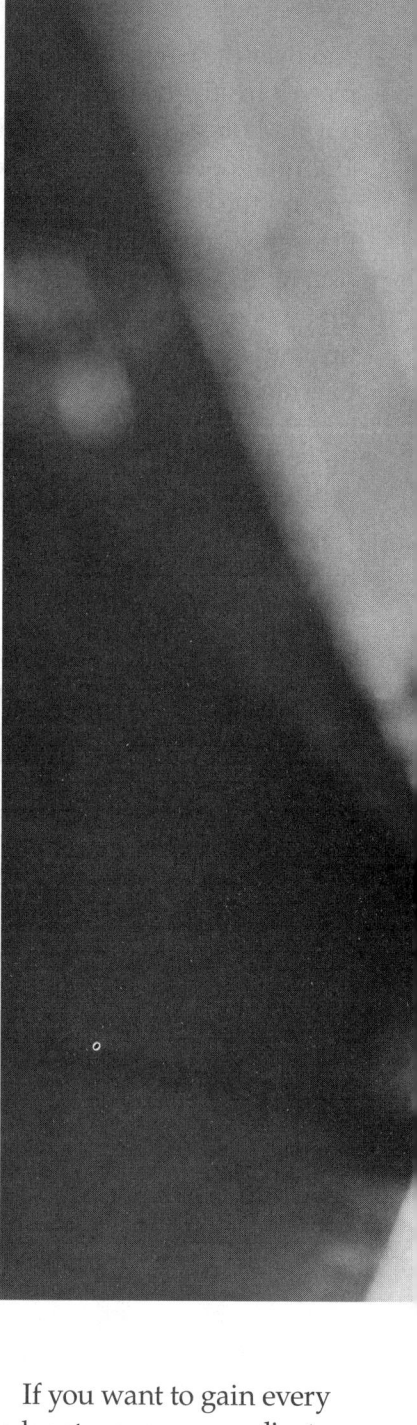

■ A shim is in place to correct a barrel nut timing problem.

> **"The torque limits for the GI barrel nut are shockingly casual: 30 ft-lbs minimum, not to go over 80 ft-lbs for alignment. That's right, you crank it up to 30 ft-lbs and check alignment. If it needs a bit more torque, keep going until things line up."**

than the owner can shoot), then the gas tube touching but not binding on the barrel nut is fine. The allowable torque range for the barrel nut permits fine-tuning of the barrel nut teeth alignment while staying tight and within torque limits.

If you want to gain every advantage, you can adjust barrel nut torque (staying within the torque limits listed) until the barrel nut is in place and the gas tube does not touch.

You cannot allow the gas tube to be pressed out of alignment by the barrel nut teeth. This condition causes it to bind or even fail to align with the carrier key, and that can cause malfunctions.

Once the barrel nut is timed correctly, align the

Delta ring, waffle spring and C-clip so the gas tube can pass through. Weasel the gas tube into the upper, rotate it to align with the gas block (gas port in the tube faces down, remember) and press it in. Then drive the gas tube roll pin in place.

Not Lining Up?

What do you do if the flanges of the barrel nut won't align to clear the gas tube while within the torque limits? You have several options. You can try a different barrel or receiver depending on which is the one you "must have" or have spares of. If you have a box of uppers of the type you want to build on, pull the current receiver out of the fixture/reaction rod and try the next one. If the upper is a must-use, and you have spare barrels, then try another barrel. If both are must-use parts, pull the barrel nut/Delta ring assembly off the barrel and try another barrel nut.

You have two other options if all that fails: square the receiver surface or use a receiver shim.

Despite being precision-machined, the front face of the receiver may not be square. Brownells offers a piloted reamer that will square the surface. This tool uses a lapping compound to lap down the high spots. At $35 for the tool, it is a bit pricey for

CHAPTER 6 – BARREL FITTING   **121**

Sometimes, a correctly timed barrel nut leaves a gas tube misaligned, which you can correct with a large screwdriver. Use the bare carrier as a gauge and feel for change as it slides over the gas tube when you tweak the gas tube alignment.

one-time use. The other option is to use shims. Again, Brownells, and this time it is all of $6. You get five shims, two of them .001 inch, two .003 inch, and one of .007-inch thickness. You now can adjust the thickness in one-thousandth of an inch increments up to .010 inch. (I would not want to be using more than two shims in any assembly, but that's just me.)

You can use the shims one of two ways: calculate how much thickness you need, or just put one in and see how much it changes your setup, and then take your best estimate of which one or pair you'll need to make things perfect.

And obviously, if you are using a proprietary barrel nut that doesn't have the flange with notches, don't worry about gas tube alignment. Just torque it up to the high end of the 30-80 ft-lbs range to keep things tight and call it good.

Epoxy, Thread Locker, Anti-Seize Compound

You will be given contradictory advice by "experts" about thread lockers and epoxies, and the like. On the one side, you'll be advised to use an anti-seize compound on the threads so the steel-to-aluminum interface can't gall the aluminum, bind things up and make it unsalvageable when you replace the barrel.

On the other side, you'll be told that using Loctite or even epoxy will make the fit tight and improve accuracy. Some will even advocate using steel foil sheeting as shim stock wrapped around the exterior of the barrel extension to fill the gap between it and the interior of the upper receiver.

■ If the barrel nut doesn't draw up far enough, even at 80 ft-lbs, you can shim it. In addition, you can face the edge with a piloted trimmer or try a different barrel nut.

CHAPTER 6 – BARREL FITTING ■ **123**

■ The gas tube must pass through the flange of the barrel nut, but it also needs to pass through the Delta ring, waffle spring and C-clip.

Both sides are correct, and both sides are chasing tiny differences.

The anti-seize advice comes from the military side of things, where a given rifle or carbine might have the barrel installed right up to the 80 ft-lbs torque limit and be subjected to heinous abuse. A rifle that goes through the surf on a beach assault regularly or is shipped to the Arctic (or one and then the other, repeatedly) might need thread-locking. The threads can get sand, grit and corrosion into them, and when it comes time to re-barrel, they just … won't … come … apart. A quick question: will that be you? If not, then all you really need is a light coating of oil to keep from torquing up dry, bare threads, and you'll be good.

The epoxy/Loctite advice comes from those seeking the utmost accuracy. A ten-thousandth of an inch (.0001) in movement in the barrel shank as it sits in the receiver can translate (doing the arithmetic here) to three and a half inches at 1,000 yards. Or two inches at 600 yards. More or less. Now, for the competition shooters going after match standings, giving up a two-inch increase in the point of impact error is anathema. Yes, the 600-yard target Ten ring is 12 inches across, and the X ring is six inches, but that doesn't leave much margin. That two-inch slop of fitting means you are, in effect, giving up one-third of the diameter of the X ring and just over 15 percent of the Ten ring. Shooters who obsess over one or two X-counts plus-or-minus in their score just won't have that.

To reduce that problem, competition shooters will epoxy, shim, Loctite or otherwise make the fit as tight as possible. They do so for competition reasons, and for economic ones as well. A match barrel for long-range shooting can quickly run you $700 to $1,000. An upper will cost maybe $80.

> "It is worthwhile to plan ahead by using some penetrating oil on the barrel nut threads."

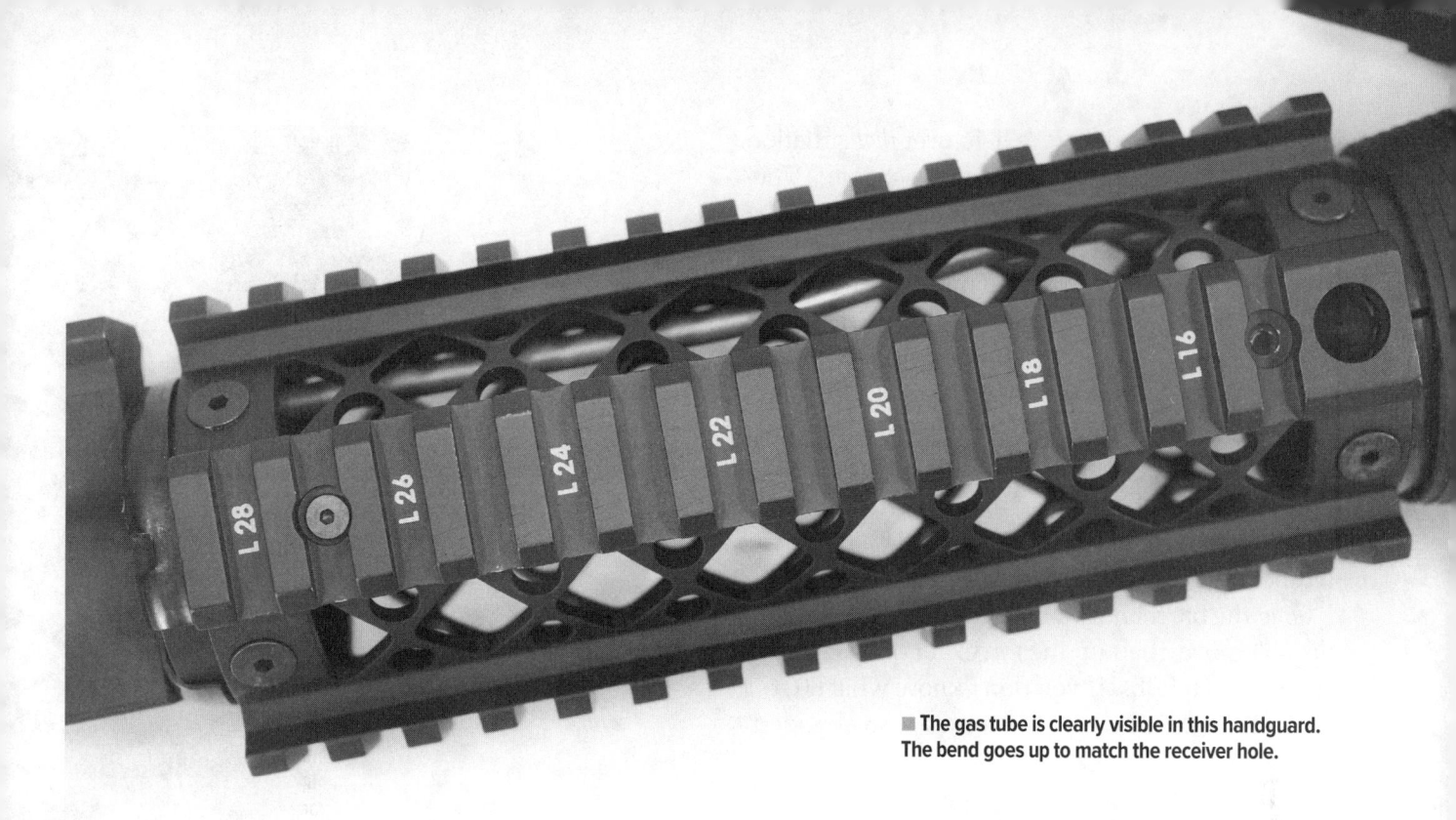

The gas tube is clearly visible in this handguard. The bend goes up to match the receiver hole.

For them, not removing the barrel from the upper when the barrel is worn out is not a big deal. If it can be salvaged, well, then good. But it won't break their hearts to scrap an $80 upper once they have used up the accuracy of an $800 barrel. A bare minimum of cost puts the bullets alone used at $1,200, and once you add in the primers and powder (we'll just call the brass free), they will have spent on the order of $3,000 in barrel and ammunition costs. An $80 upper? Pu-leeze.

The questions you have to ask are: will scrapping an upper break your heart? Do you need that extra slim addition of accuracy? Can you install the barrel with epoxy without other problems? For most shooters, the extra precision is a non-existent bonus. You aren't going to see it, shooting on-sale (if ammo ever goes on sale again) 55-grain FMJ ammunition.

Again, use a light coat of lube on the threads, torque to the proper specs and make sure your gas tube isn't binding. And if you do epoxy or Loctite the upper and barrel together, make sure the goo doesn't wick someplace else and cause problems. And when it comes time to get them apart, a heat gun is your friend.

Starting with an Old Upper

Now that you understand the basics of barrel installation, what should you do if you are replacing a shot-out barrel? The first step is to remove the handguard and then remove the gas tube. Some people drive out the gas tube retaining pin, but I figure that if the barrel is gone, the gas tube is also worn enough to be scrap. A new gas tube, at current prices, is just $18 or so, and with a new barrel running you at least $150, a new tube is a prudent investment. If the existing tube looks serviceable, I'll make one attempt at removing the gas tube pin, and if it's recalcitrant, I cut the tube in half and remove the rear half. (Some fussy details of salvage I just can't be bothered with, at least not on my own builds.)

It is worthwhile to plan ahead by using some penetrating oil on the barrel nut threads. The day before (or more), stand the upper receiver on its muzzle (someplace where it won't fall or get knocked over) and apply some penetrating oil to the back of the barrel nut where it threads onto the receiver. Even if you haven't had the rifle very long, if you have shot it enough to have worn out the barrel, the barrel nut has had plenty of opportunities to become locked in place.

Once you're ready, lock the upper either into the clamshell or the Reaction Rod, and apply your barrel nut wrench to the nut. There is no standard procedure here. You have no way of knowing (unless you're the one who installed it) how much torque was used to tighten the nut before it got to you — or just how much it will take to remove it. And, you don't know if it may have been given a

CHAPTER 6 – BARREL FITTING

dose of thread-locking. (We'll go over *that* situation, and solutions, again at the end of the chapter.) The Delta ring assembly can push the barrel wrench away from the barrel nut. Keep one hand on the barrel nut end of the wrench while you press the other. The easiest way to do this is to position the wrench, so it is (right-handed directions here) more or less horizontal and pointing out on the ejection port side. Stand with your back to the charging handle end of the receiver, use your left hand to keep the barrel wrench tight into the Delta ring assembly, and press down with your right hand on the barrel wrench. A two-foot-long handle helps here.

Give the barrel nut wrench a test press. If it doesn't move, then up the force, but quit when it surpasses 80 ft-lbs. If you don't know what 80 ft-lbs feels like, quit when it becomes a two-handed operation.

At this point, you have one of four situations: You have a dry, galled, binding barrel nut; a massively over-torqued barrel nut; one treated to Loctite; or one treated to epoxy. The dry and binding situation could be because someone didn't apply oil during the installation, or it simply got used, abused and neglected so much that the oil, if any, has long since left the station. The over-torque scenario could have happened when someone couldn't get the barrel nut spline lined up at 80 ft-lbs and just kept going. The other situations? Probably someone wanted to "gain accuracy."

You're going to need heat. Use a heat gun, not a propane torch, and gently apply heat to the barrel nut. In the case of an M4gery, with the Delta ring assembly in place, you will have a tough decision to make: you can't heat the nut effectively with the nut in place. You can't take the Delta ring assembly off while it is on the receiver. You will have to destroy the delta assembly to get to the nut. (Sometimes life is like that.) The straightforward way is to use a Dremel tool and cutoff wheel. Wear a mask, glasses and hearing protection, and slice right through the Delta ring, spring and clip. A new Delta assembly is $20. A new upper receiver is $80 to $100. Your choice.

Once the ring parts are off, apply heat to the barrel nut. You have a two-branch decision tree here. If you see white smoke come out of the barrel nut/receiver interface, then you have Loctite or epoxy in there. Keep going until the smoke stops, but don't overheat the receiver. (I know, not easy, but

■ **A good-quality wrench is worth the weight it brings and makes you haul. Use the multi-tooth side, not the three-post side.**

that's the task.) If you don't see smoke, then you have a dry or over-torqued nut. If the latter, stop here. Apply penetrating oil to the barrel nut/receiver gap and let it sit muzzle down.

With the barrel nut heated and oiled (the heat helps the oil penetrate into the threads) or the locking goo burned out, you can apply more torque.

But now you know it will work. A barrel nut wrench with a two-foot handle is best here. Again, stand back from the charging handle, the left hand holding the wrench on the barrel nut, and the handle horizontal to the right. Push down on the handle. Once you reach the limit of your pushing strength, lean on it and put bodyweight into the leverage. Be careful; if it lets go with a snap, you might fall forward. Usually, it will grindingly and reluctantly start to move. Once it starts, the work will get easier. Then you can wrestle it off.

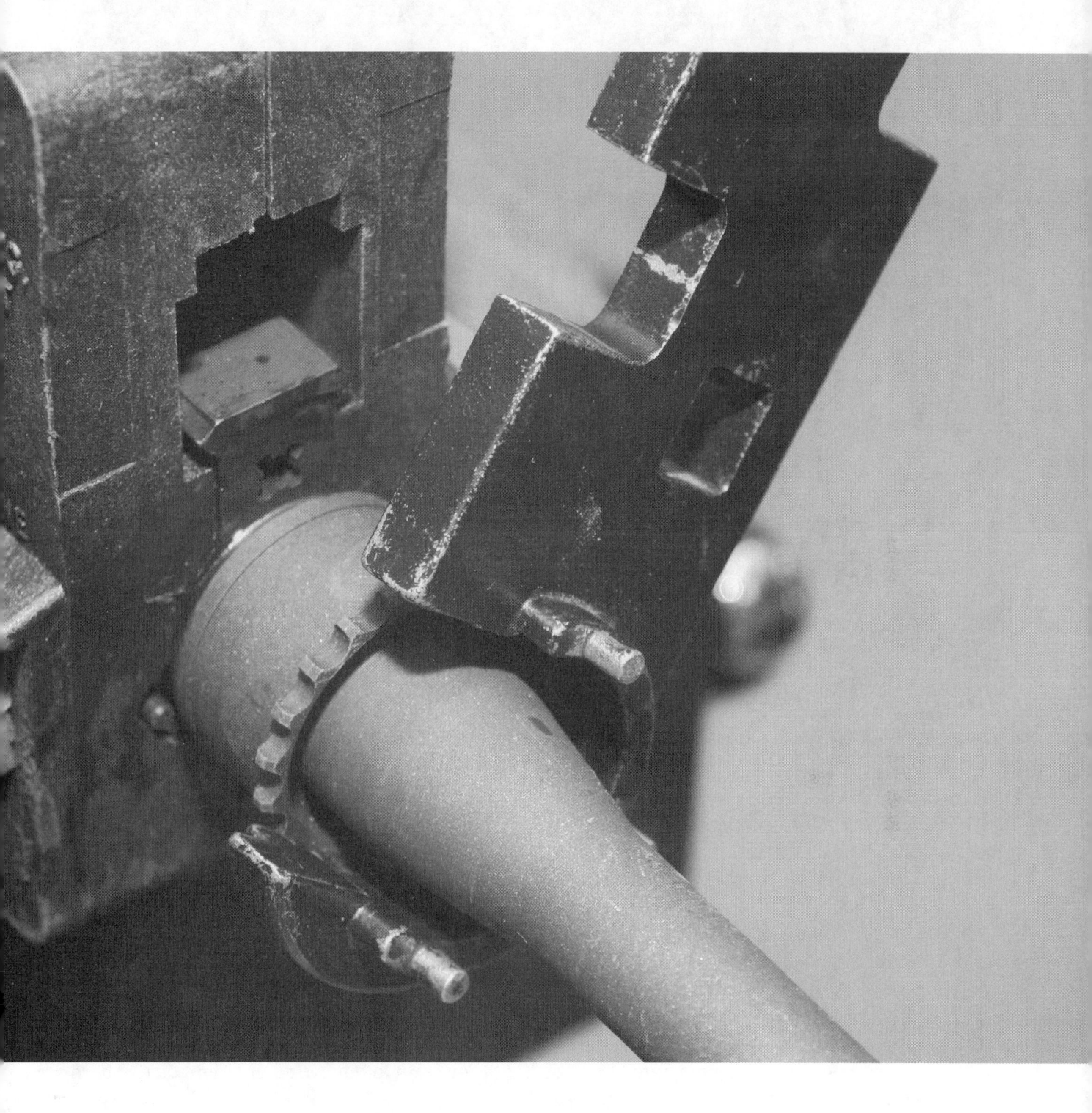

What if it still refuses? You'll need power tools. Get out the Dremel and a cutoff wheel. Gear up. That means a face mask or protective glasses (and despite the advice of ZZ Top, a pair of cheap sunglasses is not your friend here), hearing protection and a breathing mask. Maybe even gloves. Very carefully slice into the barrel nut on the side parallel to the bore axis. Be sure to slice through the front flange. Gradually work your way down until you can just start to see the gaps of the threads appearing in your cut. You do not want to cut the barrel nut completely because that would mean you also cut deeply into the threads of the upper receiver. But do cut through the front flange.

Next, put the barreled receiver back into the

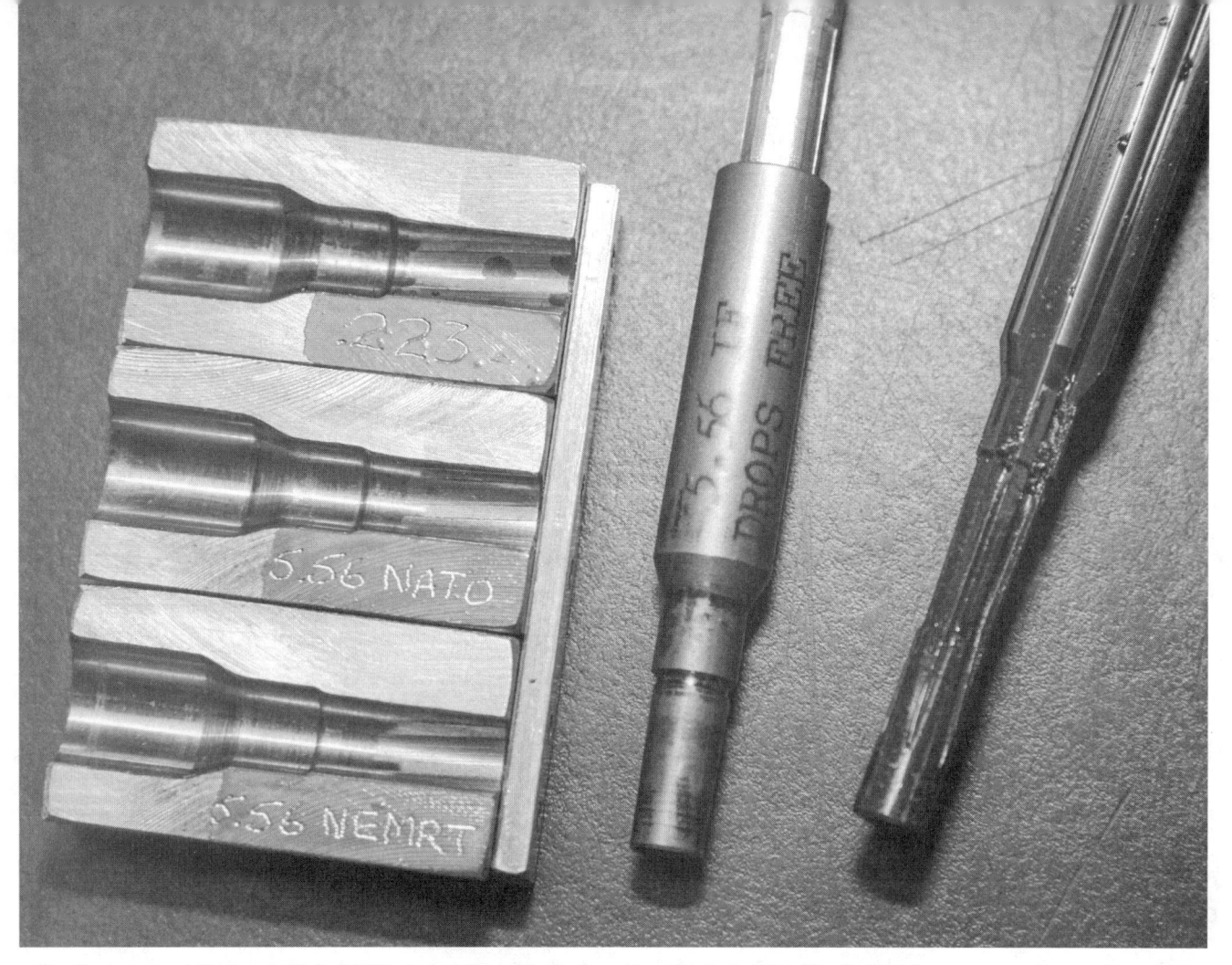

■ If you're concerned that your leade isn't 5.56, the best time to measure and treat it is before installing the barrel.

fixture or Reaction Rod. When you try to remove the barrel nut, it will break at the cut. (Well, that's the plan. Sometimes it still resists, but it is so weakened now that it will rotate.) Congratulations, you have just done perhaps your first actual gunsmithing operation, and not just a parts-swapping armorer's task.

Now do some close inspection. You want to pore over the upper receiver closely. Use a stiff-bristle plastic brush to scrub all the debris from the threads. I also suggest using a pointed tool like an awl to flake the last bits of Loctite or epoxy out of them. What you are looking for are cracks, breaks or chips. Also, you want to see if the barrel pin indexing slot is still intact and unaltered. You may well have gone through all this only to find that the receiver is cracked, the threads are mangled, or the barrel index slot is hogged out, either to "make it fit" or in the many uses it has experienced. There will be a scored line across the tops of the threads from the cutoff wheel. This line does not scrap the receiver if you have done it correctly.

If the receiver is damaged, it is scrap. One of the technical details of 7075-T6 alloy is that it does not respond well to welding.

Next Step

Now you have the old barrel out. What next? Scrub the receiver thoroughly. Clean the threads. If you have access to a receiver thread die, a quick spin onto and off the receiver can ensure they are clean. Scour the inside where the new barrel will go. You want to remove all grit, remnants of hardened oil, grease, Loctite, epoxy or God-knows-what that is in there.

While you're at it, look inside the receiver to make sure there aren't any gouges, scars or other problems that happened during use and might cause a problem in the future.

Check the fit of the new barrel. It should be snug. And yes, you are now right back to where we were when you started with a brand new barrel and receiver, otherwise un-assembled.

You can take advantage of this opportunity to replace the ejection port cover if you so wish. You can also strip the old cover, and the forward assist off and degrease and give the now-bare receiver a coat of paint. "Rattle-can camo" is the term many use, and this is one way to make a flat black upper receiver a tan, green or camo receiver. Next, put the forward assist and ejection port cover back on, and you're ready to go with the barrel installation. Also, keep the receiver threads covered when you paint. Paint there doesn't help and can cause problems later.

It's essential to align the barrel nut properly. Not just for the gas tube, but for the handguards and everything on them. The regular handguards lock into and align from the barrel nut. If the nut is incorrect, the handguards will be twisted as they try to fit between the barrel nut at the back and the front handguard plate, which aligns and locks in the handguards.

A railed handguard on a misaligned barrel nut will have a top rail that is not lined up with the top rail of the upper receiver. Also, any vertical pistol grip will be off-vertical.

Make it straight at the start, and you'll never need to bother with it again.

Gas tubes must be the appropriate length for the barrel and gas system. There are three lengths, two traditional and one new; Shorty or M4/carbine, full-size or 20-inch barrel and the new mid-length. Regardless of how long the barrel is, those are the lengths of the tubes and gas systems. The gas tube extends from the receiver to the front sight. It is mechanically possible (but not advisable) to have a barrel more than 20 inches in length, with the front sight located where an M4 would be. You would use a shorty or M4 gas tube on that barrel.

The gas tube has an open and closed end. The open end goes into the receiver. Slip the open end through the topmost notch in the barrel nut and into the receiver. Push it back until the closed end clears the front sight housing. Press the gas tube over and aligned with the front sight housing and rotate the tube to bring it in line with the gas tube tunnel in the front sight housing. The gas port hole in the tube goes on the bottom. The correct orientation of the gas tube is *down* from the upper receiver toward the barrel. It is possible, with much effort, to install the gas tube upside-down. Since there is only one gas access port in the front sight end of the tube, gas will not move down the tube (the port will be pointing the wrong way), and the rifle will not cycle.

Press the closed end of the gas tube into the front sight housing. Look through the retaining pin hole, and you will see the end of the tube pass by. Push the tube until the retaining pin hole of the gas tube lines up. Place the barrel in the Brownells barrel fixture, hold the retaining pin with a small pair of needle-nose pliers and tap the retaining pin into place. A dab of black paint will cover the ends of the pin and disclose any later attempts at removal.

In wrestling with the gas tube, it may have become slightly bent. Check the alignment by removing the bolt from the carrier. Slide the carrier into the upper and ease it forward over the gas tube. If there is no change in resistance or just the slightest hesitation as the gas tube slides into the key, the alignment is correct. If you can feel the gas tube flexing to match the key, but it goes together, you will still need to adjust the tube. If the key will not slide over the tube at all and the barrel nut is not centered, the nut must be tightened before you

> **"It's essential to align the barrel nut properly. Not just for the gas tube, but for the handguards and everything on them."**

can install the gas tube. Remove the gas tube and tighten the nut until the topmost notch is aligned.

If the barrel nut is centered correctly, but the gas tube will not easily slide over the carrier key, then the tube itself is slightly bent or kinked. Gas tubes that rub or fail to enter the key can be bent to fit. First, see which way the gas tube flexes as the key rides over it. If it does not enter the key at all, it will be visibly out of alignment, and you can see which way it needs to be bent to fit. Using a large screwdriver, gently bend the tube in the direction it flexes. Check the fit. Repeat until the resistance eases.

Recheck sight alignment. It should be vertical. A sight alignment gauge (a long steel bar) is helpful. However, the gauge is only a guide (and you need an upper with a carry handle). For best effect, check the alignment of the old barrel before removing it. A particular rifle may be vertical when it appears to the eye to be tilted. If the new front sight aligns like the original one, the gun will shoot to the same point of impact as the old, regardless of how tilted the front sight might look.

■ To properly clean your barrel, take it off the lower and remove the internals so you can get in there and thoroughly clean.

7

Barrel Cleaning

As a new AR-15 shooter, you'll be barraged with advice about how, when and how often to clean the barrel of your rifle. The broad outlines are, indeed, broad. On the one hand, you will have people who almost condescend to those who don't clean the bore down to the bare metal after each practice session. On the other hand, there will be those who feel an annual cleaning, even with a lot of practice, is overdoing it.

Why Clean?

Each time you fire a round, the bullet traverses the bore at high speed. The coefficient of friction between the barrel steel (or hard chrome) and the bullet jacket is low, but it isn't zero. If the bore is smooth, the amount of copper rubbed off into the bore will be minimal. Those areas will accumulate more jacket material if there are tool marks, pits, or other irregularities.

There is also the matter of powder residue. Yes, we use modern smokeless powder, but it isn't "ashless." There is some residue left behind, which you can see if you look at your flash hider. The expanding gases, cooling, will precipitate onto the flash hider. That and the "carbon" on the carrier is where most of the powder residue accumulates. But some remains in the bore. Most of that is swept out by subsequent rounds, but there's always some.

That residue buildup can decrease accuracy while the repeated friction wears the bore, also gradually hurting accuracy. There is one more accuracy-decreasing action going on in your bore:

heat. The hot, abrasive gases rocket out of the case mouth and pour directly over the beginning of the rifling into the area known as the throat. The heat erodes the steel, and the heating and cooling crack the surface of the steel, making it look like a dried mud patch on a hot summer day. No amount of cleaning will restore the throat. When a throat is worn to the point that accuracy suffers, all you can do is replace the barrel.

However, if enough copper and powder residue — known as "fouling" — builds up, accuracy can suffer even if the barrel still has service life left in it. How much of a hit can accuracy take? That depends. And, it depends on what you deem "accuracy" to be. We'll use our apex shooter here, the NRA High Master in rifle competition. They will be using a rifle and ammunition combination that can easily shoot sub-MOA groups. That is, under 1 inch at 100 yards, and thus under 6 inches at 600 yards. If they find that a rifle/ammo combo that could previously be counted on for 5-inch groups at 600 yards suddenly produces 7-inch groups, that is cause for worry. That change could cost them in their "X" count. Any larger, and it can start costing them points. As such, they will make sure that the exquisitely expensive barrel they installed is as clean as it needs to be to maintain accuracy.

At the other extreme, we have a weekend shooter or a competitor in multi-gun or 3-Gun who shoots at clubs that do not have a rifle range greater than 100 yards. With their red-dot sight and 55-grain

> **"The bottom line? When you clean depends on your expectations. And as far as how often, that is determined by how much you shoot."**

FMJ ammunition, they shoot a 4-inch group at 100 yards. If, at the end of the competition season and several thousand rounds later, their rifle is now shooting a 5-inch group at 100 yards, they might not even notice. If they do, a good scrubbing will restore that "accurate" 4-inch grouping capability.

The bottom line? When you clean depends on your expectations. And as far as how often, that is determined by how much you shoot.

How to Clean

If you do it incorrectly, you can wear your bore more by cleaning than by shooting. Ideally, use a single-piece cleaning rod long enough to go entirely down the bore from the chamber end of the upper receiver assembly. This rod should be coated so it won't collect grit. Use a rod guide, a tube that fits the inside of your upper receiver and which has a center bore just large enough for the rod and brush. The proper-sized brushes, patches, chamber brush and copper or powder solvent complete the ensemble.

Use a one-piece rod because it will reduce wear. The joints on a multi-piece segmented rod do not match perfectly. That means there will always be an edge sticking out to scrape the bore. When the brush meets resistance, the rod will flex (it must; there's no way to make it strong enough not to), and the flex will rub against the bore. The rod guide reduces flex in the bore. And the guide also eliminates flex at the usual flex point — the throat. Yes, that's right, the irony of the flexing, jointed rod is that it flexes (and thus scrapes) most at the point in the bore that can least afford it, the throat.

Chamber First

Unload the rifle and open the upper from the lower, remove the bolt/carrier assembly and charging handle from the upper, and separate the upper and lower. Clamp the upper securely in a padded vise or holding fixture upside down. The chamber brush has a long bronze-bristle section and a shorter but wider "collar" of stainless steel bristles. Only use the chamber brush on a handle, and a "T" handle is best. Push the chamber brush fully into the chamber and start rotating. Clockwise or counter-clockwise, it doesn't matter, but that is the only direction you rotate. Never reverse the rotation, or you'll break off bristles.

Keep pressing forward and rotating until the collar of the brush enters the locking lug recesses of the barrel. Keep turning. Give the brush several rotations before backing it out, still turning in the same direction. Once you've pulled the collar free of the locking lug recesses, you can pull the brush straight to the rear and out. If you want to wipe out the loosened gunk, use special chamber mops made of fabric and shaped like the brush.

Mount the receiver upside-down (top rail facing the floor, parallel to the floor), so you can get a clear view of the chamber area as you do this step.

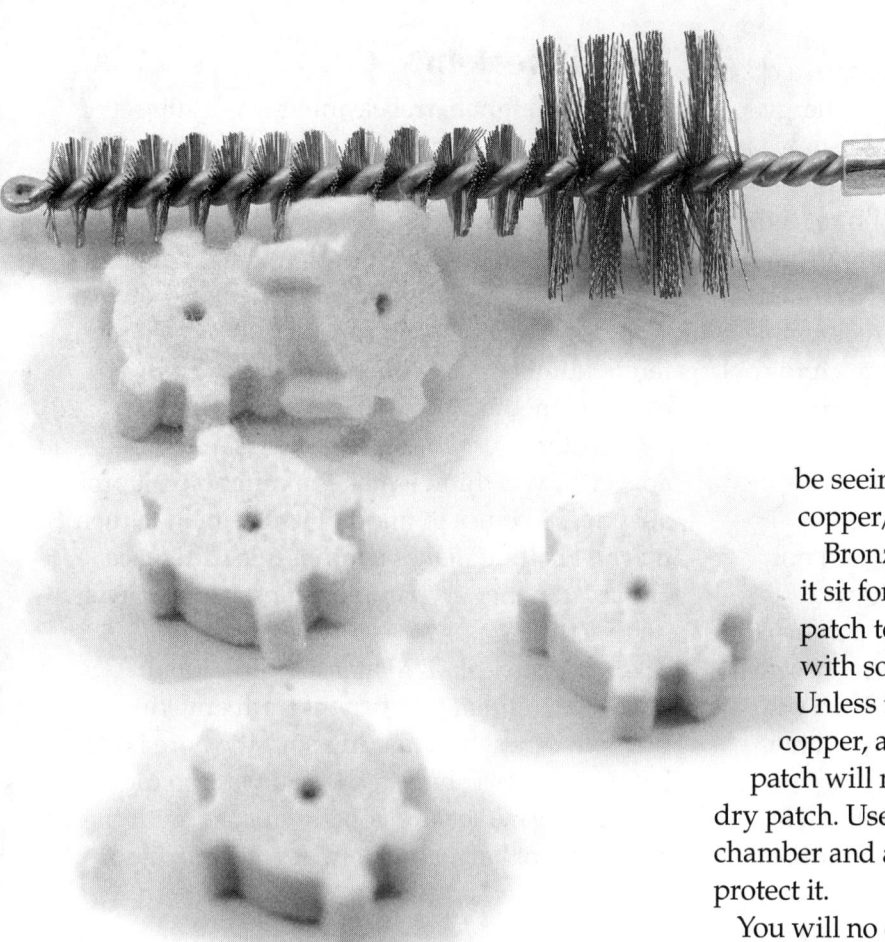

■ The chamber brush is your friend. The Real Avid felt locking lug cleaners are a very nice addition.

Now, press your rod guide into the upper receiver. At this point, the already arcane and near-religious aspects of bore cleaning can become even more so.

Some will say brush first, then run the patch. Others will run the patch first, then the brush. Some do each in turn, back and forth. Some will argue about how much wet patching versus dry patching and brushing, and by this time, no one in the gun club can stand to be in the room as the adherents of each viewpoint argue it out. I'll give you my process and why and let you take it from there.

This is my process after a day of practice or a day or two of a class. The in-the-class process is different; we'll go over that later.

Brush first, dry. If there is dry powder residue in there, I want to break it up. Then, a dry patch to get it out. Back to the brush, this time with some powder or copper solvent. Oh, and a quick digression at this point: brushes are copper. If you use copper solvent and then run a patch through to use them in combo until you "don't see green/blue" (the color the solvent creates when dissolving copper), you will never see a "clean" patch. You'll always be seeing the reaction of the solvent to the copper/bronze brush.

Bronze brush through with solvent. Let it sit for a minute or two, then send a dry patch to swab it out. Next, a patch damp with solvent, let it set, and a dry patch. Unless the bore is extremely gunked with copper, a couple of cycles of wet-patch/dry-patch will make it clean enough. Finish with a dry patch. Use your chamber swab to clean up the chamber and a lightly oiled patch down the bore to protect it.

You will no doubt see that the insides of the upper are really caked with gunk. One cool tool to deal with this is made by Wilson Combat. It is a cylindrical plastic tool that is proportioned such that it and a cleaning pad can just fit inside the upper receiver. Use a brush and some powder solvent to scrub the interior of the upper. How much depends on how OCD you are or how much your training officer will inspect and "ding" you for not cleaning. You can also remove a bunch of nasty stuff with aerosol cleaners, but do so in a place where the draining, gunky slurry is safely disposed of. Wrap the pad around the tool, and press in, turn and extract. Yuck.

Now, in a class, during a break in the shooting, or lunch or lecture time, you may not have time enough to do a thorough cleaning. What I do is this: Unload. Open the action but leave the upper and lower connected by the front pin. Remove the bolt/carrier and the charging handle. Use the chamber brush to scrub and dry the chamber. If there is time, drop a Boresnake down the bore, and pull it out of the muzzle. Put a couple of drops of lubricant in the cam pin slot and the neck of the bolt where it enters the carrier. Reassemble, and get back to the class. A properly built AR treated this way will continue to function 100 percent in a class for as long as you have ammunition and energy.

If you have the cleaning solutions and some more time, I'll run a patch wet with bore or copper solvent through on a hot day. I'll set the rifle aside for a minute to scrub the gunk from the carrier and bolt. Then, chamber-brush and dry-patch the bore. Lube the bolt/carrier, reassemble and get back to shooting. I do this as much to cool the barrel with the solvent via its evaporation as anything else.

Another Way

There is one way to use a jointed rod and not scar your barrel. But you clean it "backward." Separate the upper from the lower, and remove the bolt and carrier and the charging handle. Assemble a set of rod sections that are longer than your barrel. You don't need all of them. Screw a bore brush into the rods, and drop the rod's *non-brush end first* down the barrel from the chamber. The brush will stop the rod when it hits the chamber. *Pull* the rod out of the muzzle. By pulling, it won't flex and cannot rub the bore like being pushed. Repeat with patches.

Barrel Break-In

If you thought barrel cleaning was a subject of rumor, argument and contention, then "breaking in" a barrel is even more so. The idea is that you are supposed to be using the bullets themselves to burnish or polish the bore by firing them one at a time and thoroughly cleaning the bore between shots. Every source you consult will have a different number and sequence of shots to fire and cleaning methods to use.

Does it matter? For some shooters, yes. Another adage: "If you think it makes a difference, it probably does," comes to mind. If it does matter, then mechanically, it makes a minuscule difference. However, national championships are often won on tiny differences.

Your vanilla-plain M4gery AR-15 will not have a barrel that will benefit from any kind of break-in other than making sure the bore is clean before you start shooting. If you want to indulge yourself or make sure you are in solid with the adherents of barrel break-in at your gun club, knock yourself out.

■ When scrubbing the chamber (this barrel is removed from the receiver for clarity), it is essential to get the stainless bristles all the way into the locking lug section.

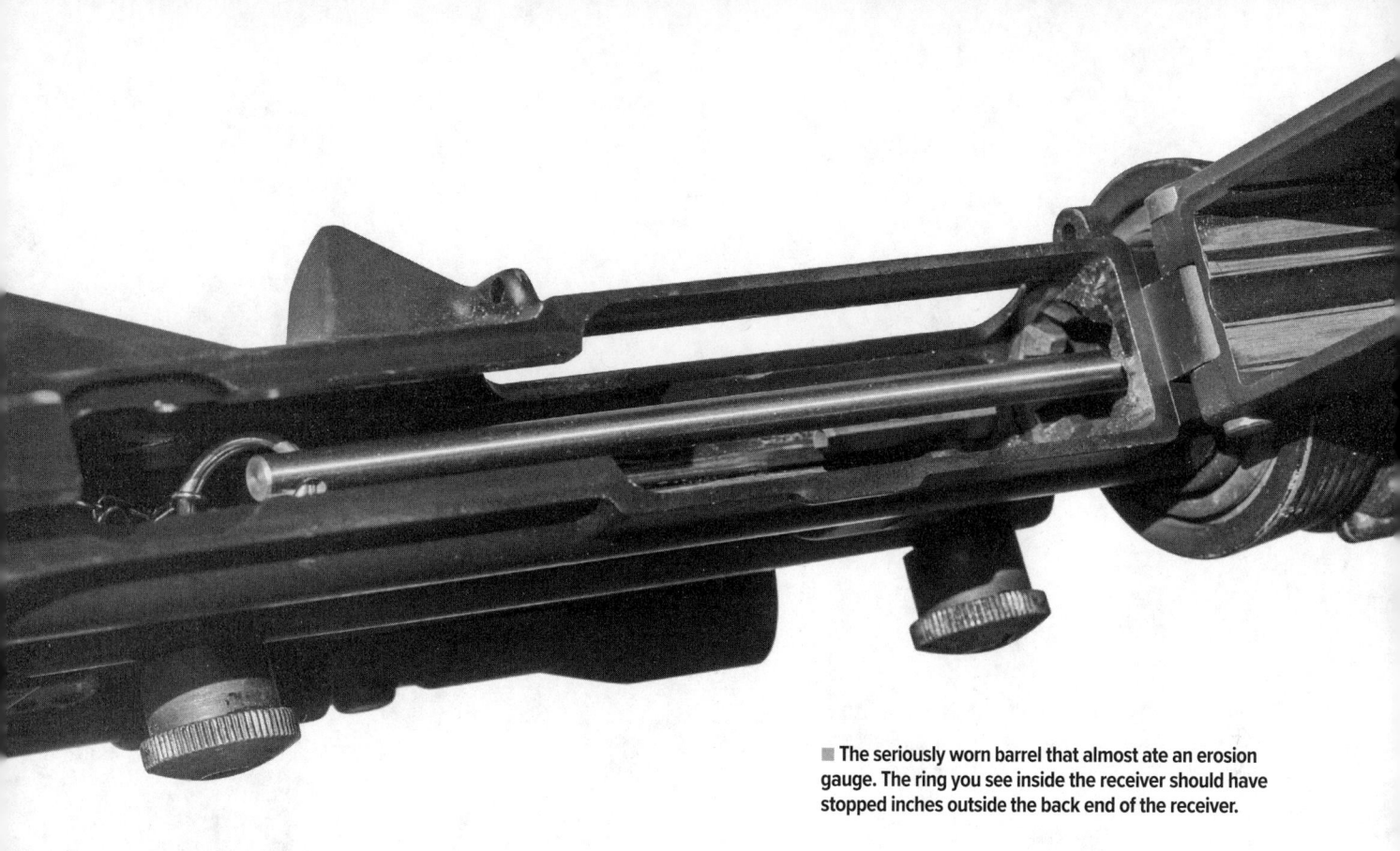

The seriously worn barrel that almost ate an erosion gauge. The ring you see inside the receiver should have stopped inches outside the back end of the receiver.

Wear and Erosion

Both heat and bullet travel will wear your bore, and eventually, accuracy will suffer. How can you tell? The simple solution is to shoot for groups. You would have a baseline if you did that at the start (and your skill level was up to it, no insult intended). You may hear of an "erosion gauge" that is used in the military. This gauge is a simple rod, precision-ground to a specific diameter. That diameter matches the onset of the rifling in a mil-spec bore.

The gauge simply goes into a clean bore and stops when it hits the rifling.

When your bore erodes, chips off and gets blasted by heat and grit, the rifling is gradually worn away. The gauge has a mark on it, and when that mark comes up level with the receiver's rear, the bore is deemed worn out by the military.

If you're precision-oriented, you will be aghast at the crudeness of this kind of system. If you're accustomed to measuring in thousandths of an inch, a "stick a rod in the bore, and eyeball off the back end of the receiver" is tantamount to reading tea leaves. Well, that's what the military does. Does it measure anything? Yes, the point where the rifling begins. Does it matter? Perhaps.

We had an officer come to a Patrol Rifle class with the *Frankengun AR* he had been using as his squad car rifle for a couple decades. It was a full A2 rifle (getting in and out of a car with it must have been a hassle), and in the class preliminaries, he was having some trouble checking his zero. The rifle just wouldn't settle in on a small group on a given place on paper. So, we gunsmiths pored over it, trying to find some cause for casual accuracy.

Nope, nope and nope were the answers to our checks.

Just on a whim, I poked my erosion gauge down the chamber. It didn't stop. In fact, it stopped only when the aluminum data plate on the end banged into the receiver. I untangled the plate and chain, and we finally determined that the rifling had eroded to a point some 8 or 9 inches down the bore. Up until that class, he had carried it and shot a clean score on the departmental qual course. He used his spare for the class and re-barreled that rifle later.

The point? Erosion, in and of itself, will not necessarily cause a loss of accuracy. If you are happy with 3-4 MOA (the military is), then some erosion is not a big deal. But however much or little you are satisfied with, it is time for a new barrel when accuracy disappears.

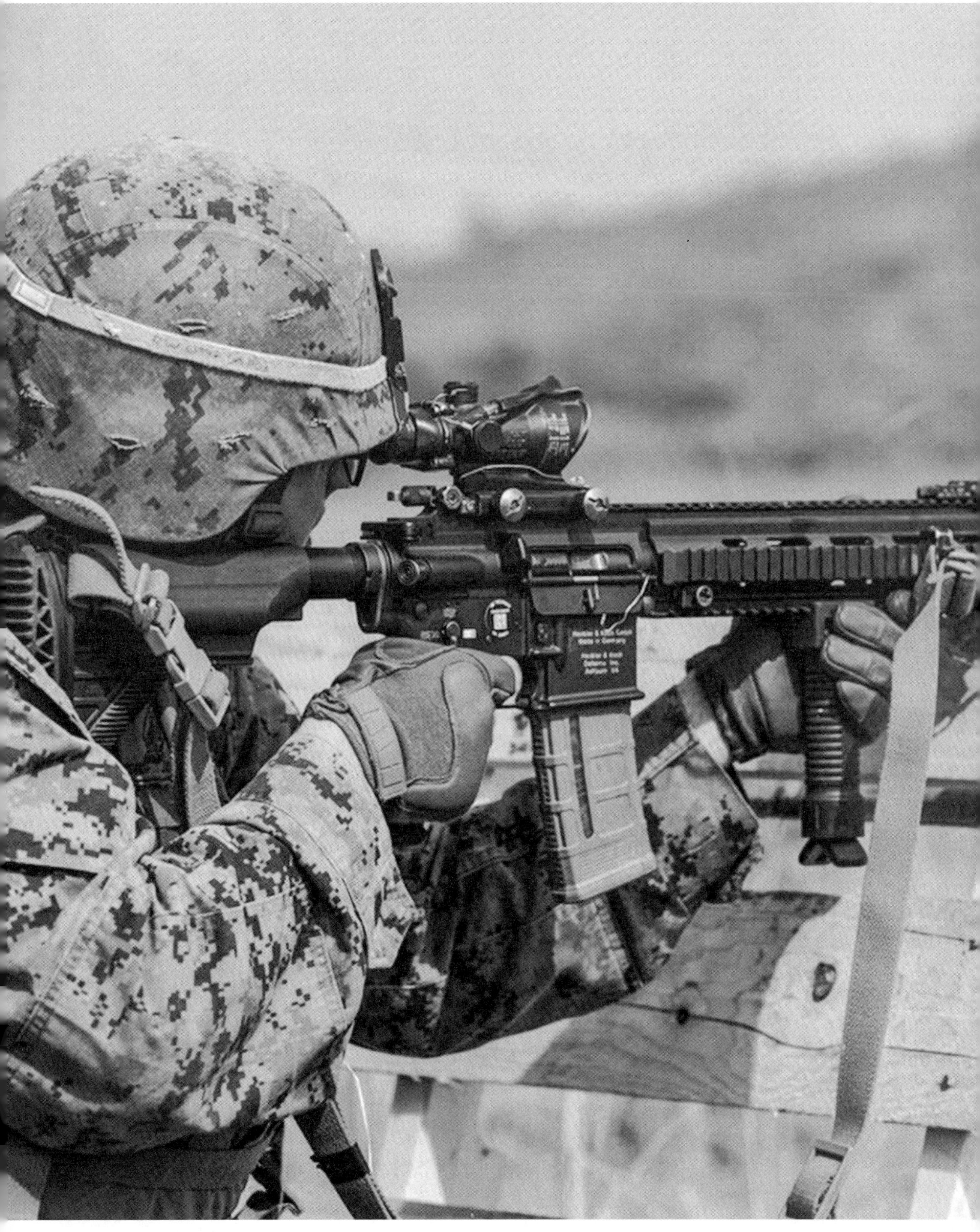

8

Bolts and Carriers

Before we can discuss the bolt/carrier assembly, we must disassemble it. With your AR unloaded, press the rear takedown pin to remove it and pivot the upper and lower apart. Pull back the charging handle until you have enough of the carrier sticking out to grasp it and pull it out of the receiver. Pull the charging handle back until you line up the ledges on its edge with the clearance slots in the upper receiver, and you can then tip it down and out of the slot and remove it from the upper.

Disassembly

Set the upper (or upper/lower still attached by the front takedown pin) aside, along with the charging handle.

You'll see a cotter pin on the carrier, with the looped end on the left side. Hook a pointed tool into the loop and pull the pin out. The pin holds the firing pin in place. If your rifle is reasonably clean, simply tipping the carrier will cause the firing pin to fall out. Otherwise, you'll need to tap the carrier down into your cupped hand or onto a solid surface to jar the grubby, oiled and carbon-caked firing pin free. Once free, set it aside.

■ Just when it looked like the direct impingement (DI) vs. piston argument was settling down, the Marine Corps went and adopted a piston gun, the HK M27, aka the 416.

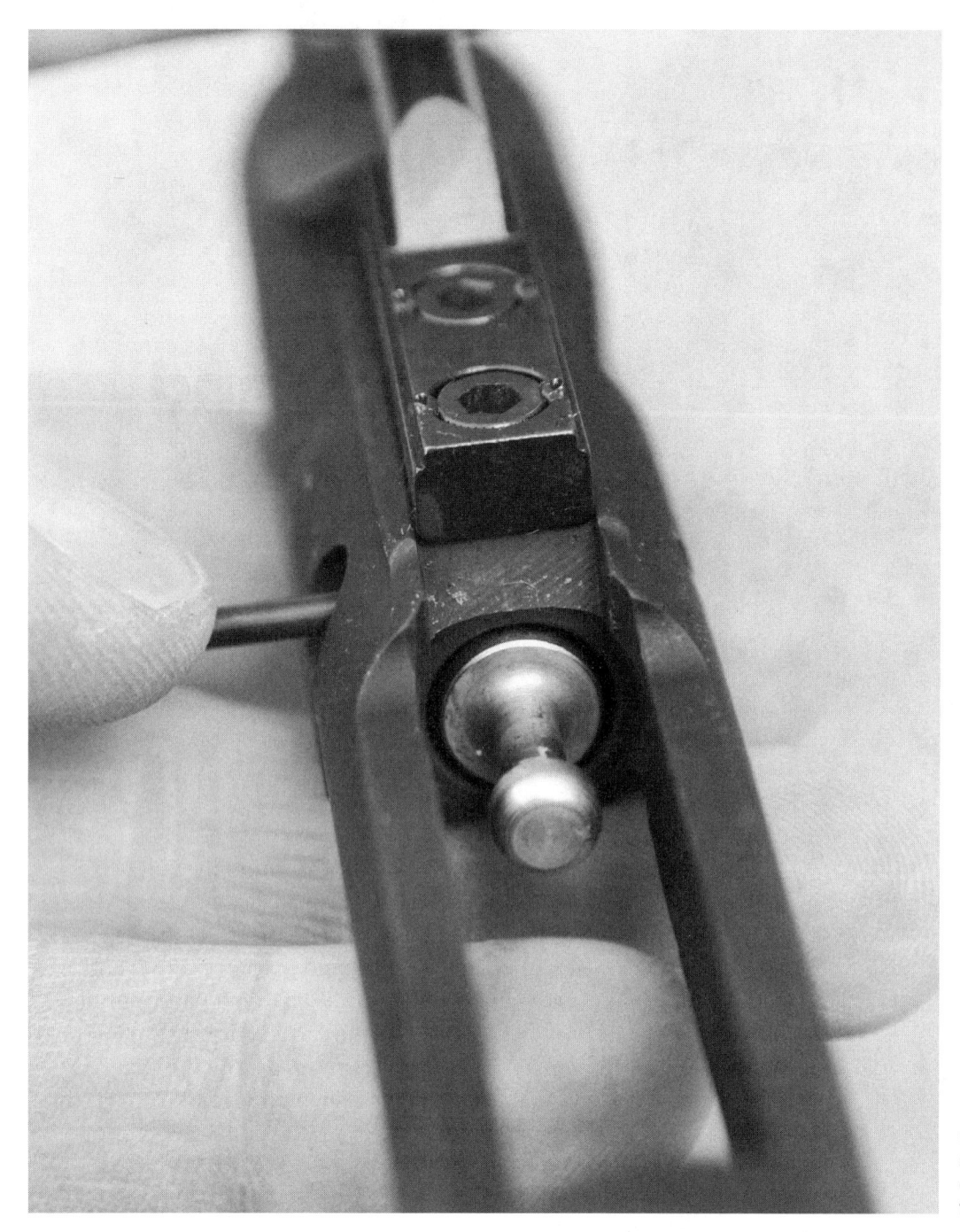

■ To remove the bolt, start by removing the cotter pin, then the firing pin.

On top of the carrier, under the gas key, is the cam pin. The head is rectangular, and the firing pin passes through the cam pin. In this ready-to-fire assembly, the cam pin head is too wide to clear the gas key. So, give the cam pin head a quarter-turn to position the longer flat parallel to the gas key and lift it out. (The head is there solely for you to take the cam pin out. If it were simply a steel cylinder, it would work just fine to function, but be murder to try and disassemble.)

With the cam pin extracted, you can pull the bolt from the front of the carrier. Like the firing pin, if your rifle is clean, this will come out easily. But if you've done a bunch of shooting, then it will be caked with powder residue and oil and will need to be squirmed out.

With the parts out, you can begin studying them and seeing what needs inspection, repair or replacement, and start the task of cleaning.

Carriers

Let's do the carrier first because it is easier. The carrier is simply a steel cylinder that is open at each end. One end is the clearance tunnel for the firing pin. The other end is the opening for the bolt. On the bottom, it is cut out for hammer

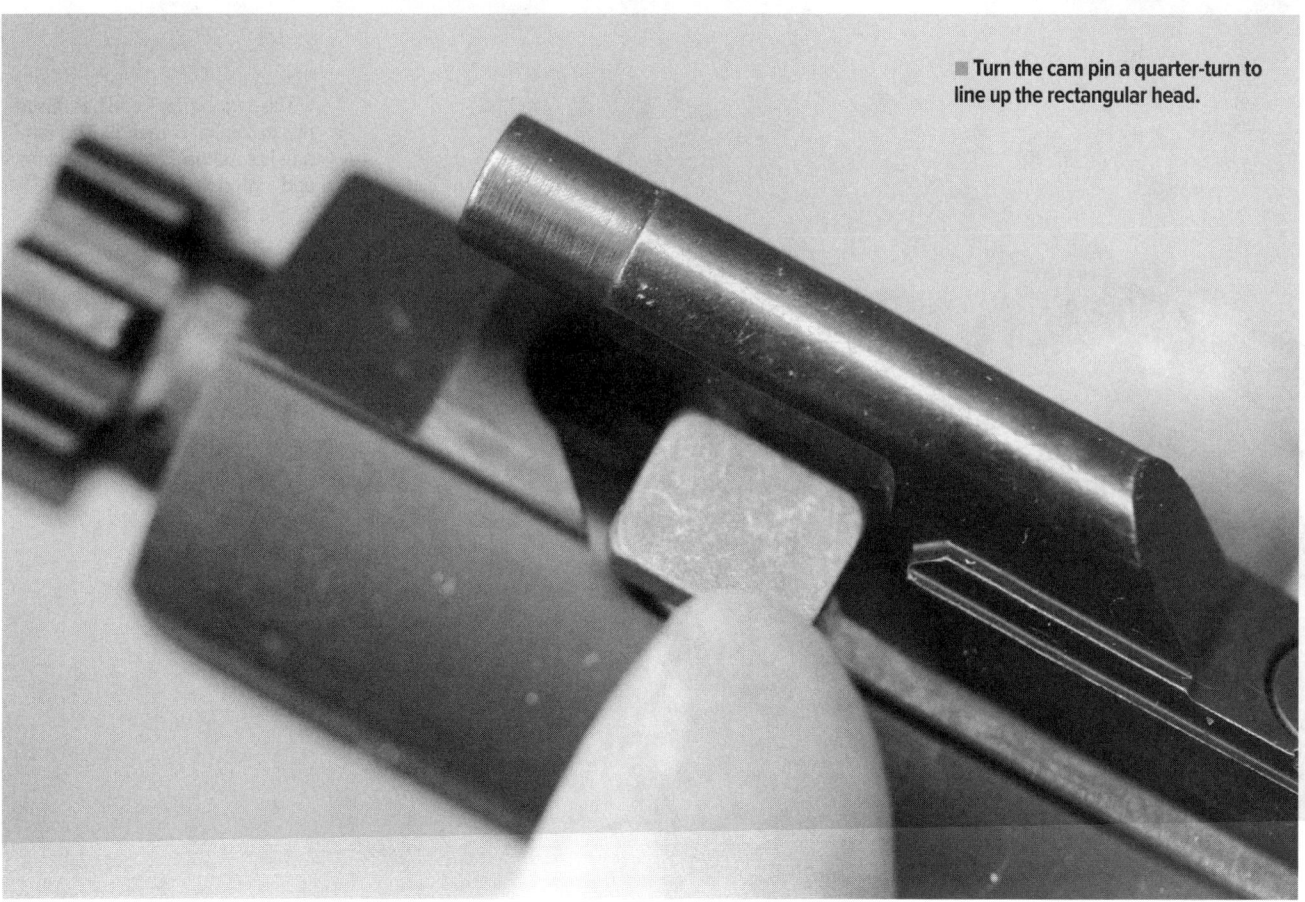

■ Push the bolt back in the cam slot until it reaches the back of the slot.

■ Turn the cam pin a quarter-turn to line up the rectangular head.

■ Lift the cam pin out. If it's grubby, you may need to gently wiggle it.

■ The dark carrier's end has raised ribs to combat carrier tilt. This feature is essential in a piston system and a good thing in a DI system.

■ The Fail Zero carrier and bolt are plated with a nickel boron alloy. Slick, easy to clean and tough.

clearance. On top, it is machined to accept the gas tube key.

The carrier is made of a very strong and hard steel alloy known as 8620, and it does not undergo much stress, as these things go. In addition to being a hard alloy, the carrier is surface-hardened and almost impervious to mishandling or abuse. Almost. It is so sturdy that absent abuse or detonation, it is a lifetime part. Most end-users will be served admirably by a mil-spec carrier with a black oxide finish. If you want, you can splurge for one with a slick modern coating and even newer designs that are more in keeping with the machining cues your billet-machined upper and lower might show.

The carrier does five things. It holds the bolt and cams it to lock and unlock. It contains the firing pin, so the hammer can hit it. It cocks the hammer once fired, rotating the hammer back to engage the disconnector. It positions the bolt to strip the top round off the magazine in feeding. And it holds the gas key, accepting the gas coming back from the gas port, to cycle the mechanism.

There are, however, some details you will want to know and keep in mind when considering buying, upgrading or simply experimenting.

Materials

The steel alloy of the mil-spec carrier is given a super-hard surface heat treatment. It is a complete and utter waste of time to polish up the guide rails of the carrier. It will make no difference whatsoever in the function of your rifle. You cannot get a black oxide mil-spec carrier coated with a new high-tech coating unless your buddy works in a shop that does that sort of thing. And if you did, you'd gain no benefit. If you want coatings, get them from the start.

Some carriers will be made of metals other than steel. Titanium is one. These are lighter than the mil-spec ones, but they are specialized and primarily used in competition rifles. The AR gas system depends on the bolt, carrier and buffer having a particular mass to function correctly. Making the moving parts lighter simply increases the speed they move when cycling, and a faster-moving bolt may cycle back, slam with vigor into the rear of the buffer tube and zoom forward before the magazine can lift the stack of cartridges. This cycling speed will often be unreliable.

Then why do some shooters use them? If

installed in conjunction with an adjustable gas block, they can decrease felt recoil. By adjusting the gas block flow, dialing back the gas, and using lighter parts, a competition shooter can reduce or eliminate the "thump" of the cycling parts bottoming out inside the buffer tube. Like everything, this refinement comes at a cost, however. The lightest-to-heaviest power band of "ammo that works reliably" narrows. Indeed, competition shooters will often use just one load, with one powder and one pre-selected bullet, to get this benefit. Once they find the bullet/powder load that is most accurate and makes the Power Factor they need, they can tune the gas flow to just barely lock the rifle open when empty and reduce recoil to a minimum.

Of course, this means they must keep the rifle reasonably (or spotlessly) clean, so it will still function 100 percent.

You can lighten parts by machining steel out of the regular carrier, which is an approach some

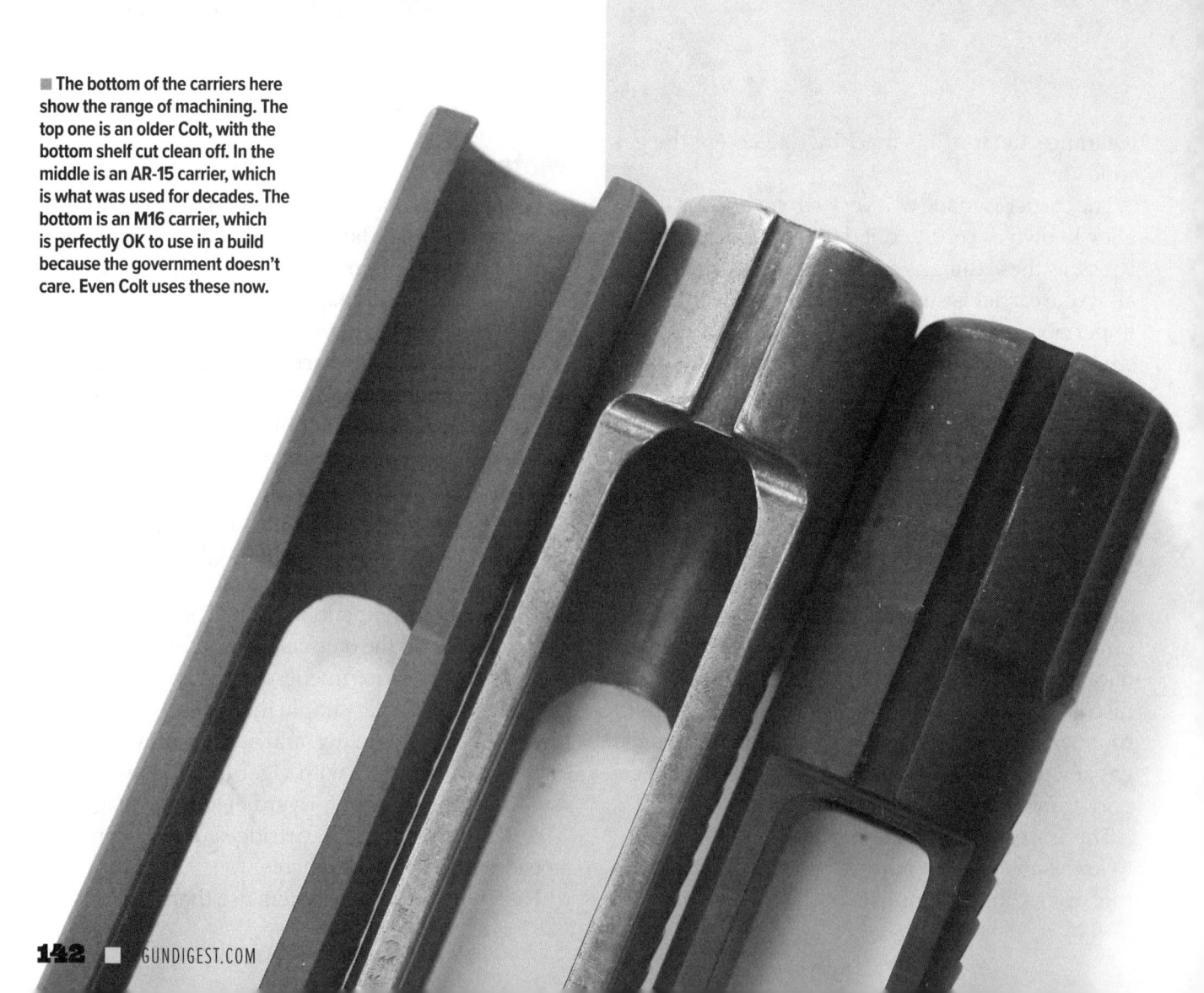

■ The bottom of the carriers here show the range of machining. The top one is an older Colt, with the bottom shelf cut clean off. In the middle is an AR-15 carrier, which is what was used for decades. The bottom is an M16 carrier, which is perfectly OK to use in a build because the government doesn't care. Even Colt uses these now.

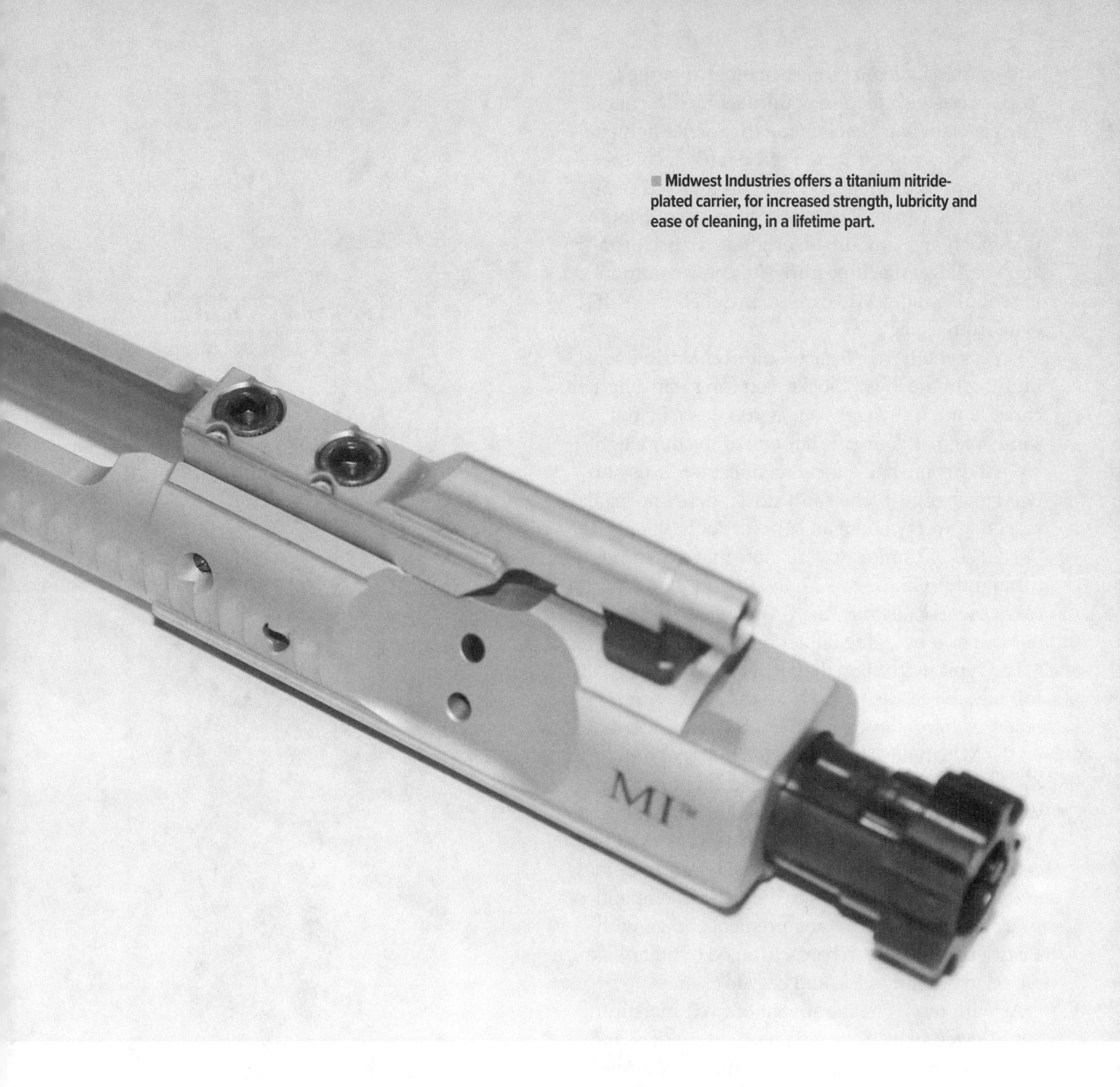

■ Midwest Industries offers a titanium nitride-plated carrier, for increased strength, lubricity and ease of cleaning, in a lifetime part.

take, those keen on keeping the strength of steel while achieving lighter weight.

If you're going into a competition, these steps might be necessary sometime in the future. In the beginning, when you're learning, they won't help much, if at all. If you're using or building an AR for duty or defense, avoid competition-specific parts or systems.

AR-15 vs. M16 Carriers

The bottom-rear of the carrier has a shelf machined into it as part of the hammer clearance cut. If this shelf is the same length as the top shelf, it's an "M16" carrier, even if it has never been in the same zip code as an M16. The bottom shelf of this length is used in select-fire guns, where it trips the auto sear when the selector has been rotated to Auto or Burst. (To do this, it must have all the other M16 parts installed as well, a subject covered in the M16 chapter.)

To keep experimenters and unlawful modifiers from having things easy, it was common for makers — Colt primary among them — to machine the carrier shelf short to trip the auto sear if one was (unlawfully) installed. In fact, Colt went so far as to machine the carrier's bottom off entirely

CHAPTER 8 – BOLTS AND CARRIERS ■ **143**

and even installed a pinned-in block into the lower to interfere with the use of unmachined carriers. The problem was that it made the carrier lighter, which could cause function problems. As of the last decade-plus or so, the ATF has allowed them because the carrier itself doesn't really contribute that much, if un-modified/original, to the "problem" of illegal machine guns. It is now common to see full-weight M16 carriers installed in AR-15s, even from Colt.

Unless you have a legacy Colt from when it was pinning in the lower blocks, you can swap a lighter carrier for a full-weight one if you wish. By the same token, if your rifle has one of the more lightweight carriers and functions fine, there's also no need to change it. The short story: there's no legal reason to worry about an M16 carrier in your AR (well, Federal, anyway, your state may see things differently). On the other hand, if your non-M16 carrier works just fine, there's no reason to search one out to replace the lighter one.

The typical finish on the carrier is black oxide. Initially, the carrier (along with the gas key and bolt) was hard-chromed. When the Army adopted the M16 in the late 1960s, it felt that the shiny carrier, seen through the open ejection port door, was too easily observed. It insisted that the carrier be changed to a Parkerized finish dyed black. It is common for those building retro rifles and carbines and those interested in an easy-to-clean competition rifle to ignore the Army requirement and go with a carrier that has been hard-chromed or otherwise plated to be shiny slick, and easy to clean.

As with receivers, the advent of CNC machining has allowed manufacturers to sculpt carriers into attractive and eye-catching contours. The shape makes no difference, as long as the weight is correct and the carrier has contact surfaces where it needs them.

Carrier Steel

Carries are made from SAE 8620, an alloy with nickel, chromium and molybdenum, with a nice addition of carbon, but not too much. The percentages are nickel 0.30 percent; Chromium 0.50 percent, and Molybdenum 0.20 percent. The hardness of the carrier is due to the heat treatment, which gives it a hard surface with a tough core that resists stress and impact. Given even minimal care, a carrier is a lifetime part.

■ The 2A bolt carrier assembly uses a titanium carrier. It's designed to be used with a regular buffer and gas system, so you can just "plug and play" without having to tune a gas system.

Gas Keys

Here's a problem we didn't know about for a long time. The gas key is the spout on top of the carrier. It slides over the tip of the gas tube, which pokes into the upper receiver. When you fire a round, the gas comes down the tube, the key and the carrier. The pressurized carrier is blown back (like how an

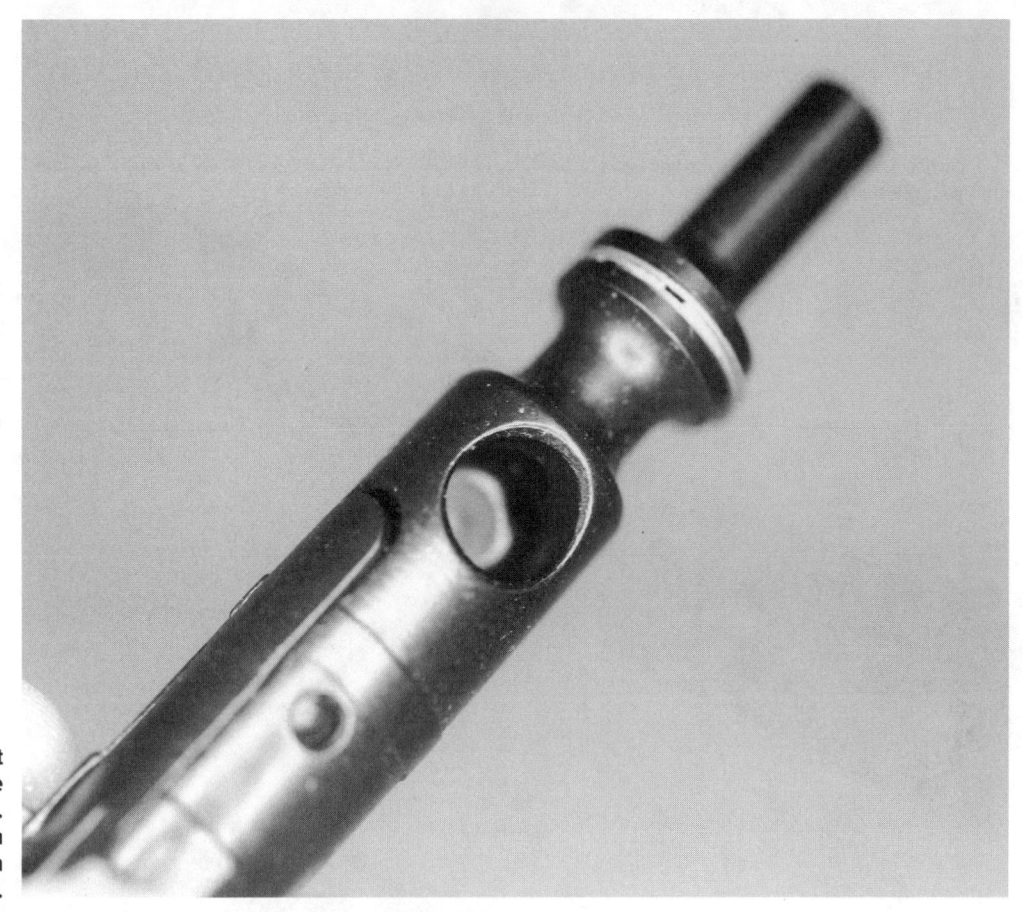

■ The HMB bolt does not have the cam pin hole drilled all the way through. It uses a proprietary cam pin with increased strength over the regular bolt.

obnoxious kid in a restaurant blows a straw sleeve from a straw).

If the key leaks, your rifle will be unreliable. The main reason for this is that the cycling parts don't have enough energy delivered to them by the gas system, and the bolt/carrier/buffer will cycle a shorter distance or with less vigor than it needs.

For a long time, many AR-15 malfunctions were attributed to other causes. The "short-stroking" AR was blamed on an undersized gas port (seldom the problem, even in the old days), improper headspace, ammo loaded with the wrong powder, incorrect buffer weight, or buffer spring problems. There were even those who blamed it on the magazines, and they would go to great lengths to test, sort and protect the "reliable" mags they had "found."

Most of it was due to gas key leakage, for which we have a solution.

The gas key is a precision-machined steel part, and the interior is hard chrome plated to preclude corrosion. (Corrosion would bring the system to a grinding halt.) It is held onto the carrier by two cap screws. The installation and fitting of screws, and the carrier key, is the subject of much interest, attention and study.

If the key is loose, you will have problems. The test is simple: hold the carrier in one hand. Grasp the key with your other and try to move it. Wiggle it, twist it, do what you can. You do not have hand strength great enough to damage it. If it moves, it

> *"Many people re-fit the key just as a matter of course, but that isn't necessary if it works as-is."*

is too loose. Now, even if it is tight, give it a visual inspection. This is best done after test-firing your rifle. Look at the base of the key where it rests against the carrier. There is a leak if you see any soot jetted around the bottom of the key slot. Inspect all the way around. Soot means you must re-fit the key.

Many people re-fit the key just as a matter of course, but that isn't necessary if it works as-is.

One detail that must be given careful consideration is how you stake the screws. On top of the key, you will see hammered gouges at the opening for the screw heads. These gouges are good to

CHAPTER 8 – BOLTS AND CARRIERS

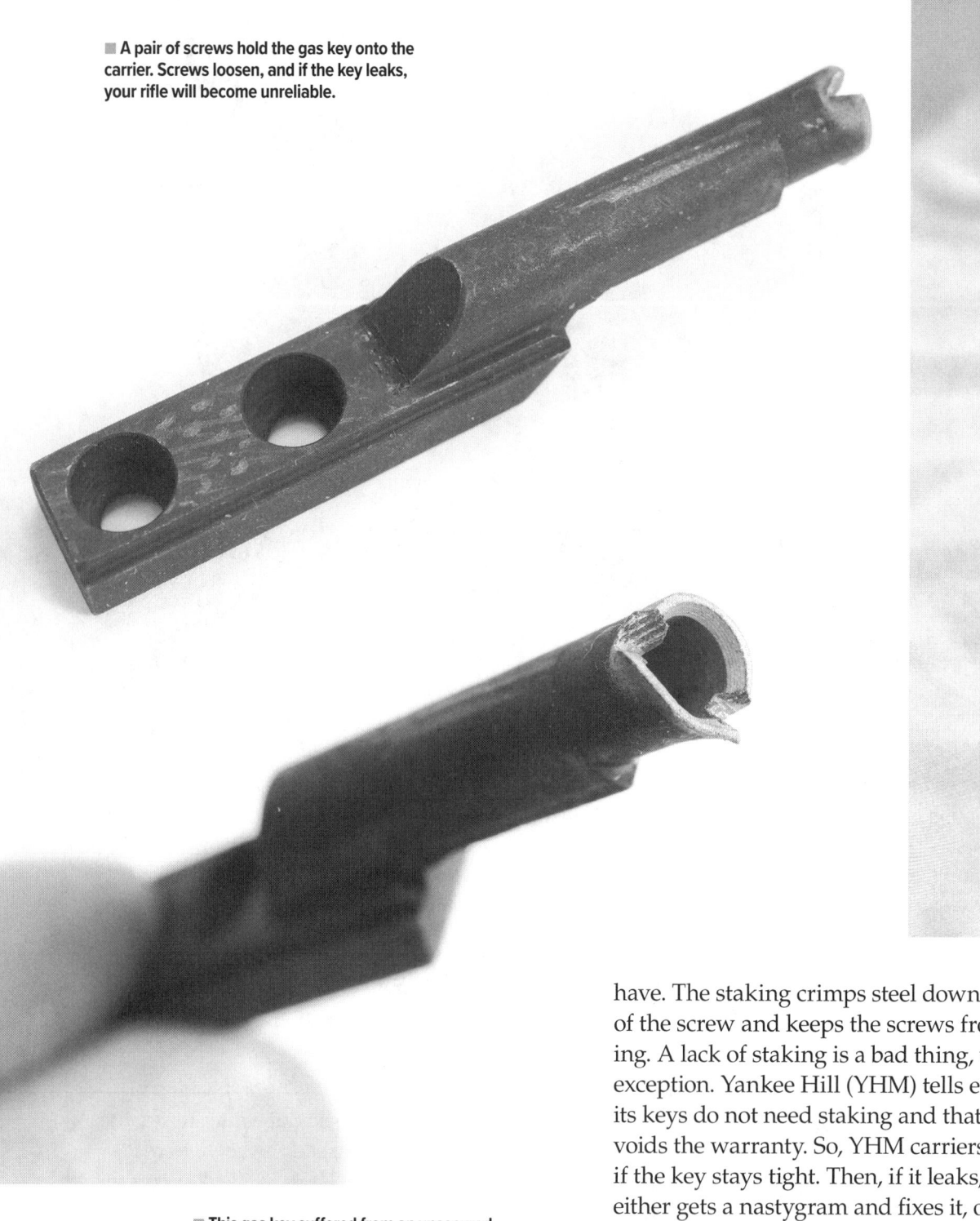

■ A pair of screws hold the gas key onto the carrier. Screws loosen, and if the key leaks, your rifle will become unreliable.

■ This gas key suffered from an unsecured handguard. Gas keys can be delicate; take care when cleaning.

have. The staking crimps steel down onto the head of the screw and keeps the screws from unscrewing. A lack of staking is a bad thing, with one exception. Yankee Hill (YHM) tells everyone that its keys do not need staking and that staking them voids the warranty. So, YHM carriers get a pass if the key stays tight. Then, if it leaks, Yankee Hill either gets a nastygram and fixes it, or the key gets re-fitted and staked.

Key Problems

If your key is tight, but your rifle still has gas flow problems (a very specialized diagnosis, and not one to be jumped on as the first source of an issue), then it might be worn. The gas key slides over the tip of the gas tube each time the rifle

■ To properly stake the gas key screws, the best tool is a MOACKS from m-guns.com. Once you've cleaned the key, and have installed the screw tight, use the MOACKS to crimp the key edges over the screw heads.

cycles, even if it isn't fired. So yes, every time you chamber-check to see if it is loaded or disassemble it to clean, or whatever, you are rubbing the tube and key. Do that 10,000 to 20,000 times, and there will be wear. A significant source of wear is misalignment. If the tube is so out of alignment that it needs to be flexed onto the center when the key slides over it (but not enough to crash into the key and stop things), it will wear more on one side. As that side rubs down, clearance will be created on the other side, and you will get gas leakage.

To check for this, start with a clean upper receiver and bolt assembly. Place the upper upside down on the bench. Slide the bolt/carrier assembly into the upper and ease it forward until the gas key slides over the gas tube. If there is a slight misalignment, you can see and feel it. The gas tube will move slightly, and the carrier will need more force to move the key over the tube.

Adjusting it is easy though it may seem a bit brutal. [Editor's note: Be sure you wear safety glasses anytime you handle tools.] If the flex is side-to-side, simply stick a large-blade flat screwdriver into the gap on the tight side, twist the screwdriver, and bend the tube over a bit. If the flex is up or down, you will have a more difficult time telling which it is. (Which is also quite rare, as the mis-fit is almost always side-to-side.) If the tube needs to be pushed down, then the same screwdriver, held at an angle to the axis of the tube can be used to push down. If it needs to be lifted up, use a long-enough screwdriver — one thin

■ Properly staked screws installed with the MOACKS.

enough to ride in the charging handle slot — to reach from the back end of the receiver.

In decades of building and fixing ARs, I might have had to adjust one or two gas tubes that needed an up or down change. All the rest were left or right, which is easy.

Usually, when you replace a barrel, you change the gas tube, as it wears faster than the key even when properly aligned. Routine tube replacement solves the problem. However, by the third or fourth barrel — yes, some people shoot enough to do that — the key will probably have worn enough to have a gas problem. There are two ways to determine if it is a problem. One is to replace the key. If the problem goes away, then that was the source. If it doesn't, then you are left with solving the problem. The other is to check with a gauge.

LWRCI Key Solution

LWRCI solves the key leakage problem by making the key base an integral part of the carrier. The key spigot is screwed into the gas key shoulder and pinned in place. If the key shoulder wears (after three to five barrels or more), simply drive out the pin, extract the key nozzle, replace and re-pin. You are, however, using a non-standard carrier. If something goes wrong, you'll need to go to LWRCI for a replacement nozzle. And if your rifle already has a carrier in it, then you are buying a replacement part that costs a lot more than a replacement gas key of the mil-spec variety. This is America; you get to choose.

Cleaning the Carrier

Carrier cleaning is perhaps the most straightforward job in the AR-15. Simply use a stiff-bristle

> "The first time I cleaned an AR, I used the included pipe cleaners in the military cleaning kit. In the nearly 40 years since, I haven't used a single one."

plastic brush to scrub the carrier clean with whatever solvent is easy, least smelly or handy. The outside will be heavily caked with powder residue as the gas tube vents the residual gas pressure with the carrier cycling. This aspect is the one most complained about by the piston advocates. Scrub and brush and let dry or blow-dry. The interior of the rear is not as easy to clean but has no consequence to not cleaning. (Unless your training Sergeant inspects there, in which case it becomes vitally important to get it clean.)

The front of the carrier is more important than the rear. The bore the bolt rides in gets a jolt of gas every time you fire. The bore is chrome-lined to aid in proper function and ease of cleaning, and there are several tools made to scrape out the caked-on carbon. While cleaning the rest of the carrier is either easy or unnecessary, you should scrub the carrier bore clean and scrape the carbon out. The bore has another aspect that we'll go into when we discuss gas rings on the bolt, but for now, the critical thing to know is this: you want this part *clean*. The AR can be pretty forgiving in matters of maintenance, but this one is worth doing thoroughly.

The gas key and cam slot benefit from scrubbing, but they won't be as easy to get clean as the carrier exterior. And pipe cleaners down the gas key? That is something that only training officers and those cleaning after taking a dunking in swamp water or super-sandy environments need to go through. If your rifle has taken a bath in silty water, or you have been in a sandstorm, then you might want to tend to the gas key that way. Otherwise, it's a waste of time. The first time I cleaned an AR, I used the included pipe cleaners in the military cleaning kit. In the nearly 40 years since, I haven't used a single one.

■ With the carrier and key aligned, tighten the Allen screws to stake the key screws.

Bolt Coatings

The very first ARs had bolts and carriers that were chrome-plated, which made them easy to clean. When the Army adopted the M16A1 (and begrudgingly so, I might add), it changed the finish to Parkerizing because it didn't want the shine of a carrier through an open ejection port door. Since then, we have come full circle. It is now common to see plated carriers with updated platings. Nickel boron, titanium nitride, various nickel Teflon coatings have all become common, and for a good reason. They make an easy cleaning job even easier.

Two Special Carriers

Technology moves on. The now widespread use of suppressors (aka "silencers") has changed carriers. Gemtech has a carrier with an adjustable setting that lets you dial back the gas flow for shooting suppressed. The indicating arrow is on one side, and to change it, you remove the bolt carrier from the upper and use a small screwdriver to turn the slotted head on the other side to a different setting. That bleeds off gas that might otherwise over-drive your rifle or carbine. The excess gas does make the gunshot noisier, but only by a decibel or so. That's a small price (since you are knocking what, 30-35 dB off the shot sound with the suppressor?) to keep the rifle from self-induced malfunctions by high-speed cycling.

The other one is a complete bolt, carrier buffer

and spring system from Surefire. Designed by Jim Sullivan, it has a re-engineered carrier cam pin slot that takes longer to unlock the bolt, and the carrier has a more extended travel when it cycles. The result is a smoother, slower-cycling rifle or carbine that doesn't bounce around as much.

> "The bolt has a lot more places where crud can hide. And those spots are more important to function than the large flat surfaces of the carrier."

I had a chance to test both these carriers in a select-fire AR-15. By shooting bursts and recording the cyclic rates, I determined just what the carriers could do. The test gun was a mil-spec M4 upper with a 14.5-inch barrel. This test was done with an H3 buffer, the heaviest to be had, just because I wanted to test the limits. The ammunition was Federal XM-193. With no suppressor on, the Gemtech carrier in the unsuppressed setting cycled at 641 RPM. Switching it to "suppressed," which bleeds out a fraction of the gases, it would not run reliably. So clearly, that setup required a lighter buffer. The same testing with a Gemtech Halo suppressor on it got 755 RPM with the carrier "unsuppressed" and 538 RPM with it set on "suppressed."

A standard H3 buffer, standard carrier and the 14.5-inch upper with various suppressors gave me cyclic rates from 850 to 925 RPM.

That result is not surprising, as I was deliberately stacking the variables against proper function to find the limits. For that setup, I would most likely dial back the buffer weight to H or H2 instead of the H3.

For the Surefire system, I replaced all the internals with the Surefire ones. The test gun used the same 14.5-inch upper, but to make life as difficult as possible for the Surefire to win, I reinstalled the H3 buffer. With the same XM-193 ammunition, the standard buffer setup cycled at 753 rpm while the Surefire OBC turned up 702 RPM.

Both carriers do precisely what their makers say they will do.

Cleaning the Bolt

The bolt has a lot more places where crud can hide. And those spots are more important to

■ LWRCI makes a carrier with a gas key that can't leak. It's integral to the carrier, and only the replaceable front is separate. Smart guys.

function than the large flat surfaces of the carrier. To clean your bolt, first, remove the extractor. Use your thumb to compress the rear half of the extractor into the bolt to ease its spring tension. While holding it, use a drift punch to hand-push the extractor pin out of the bolt. Lift the extractor out and set it aside. We'll be covering that in detail in a bit. Scrub the bolt body and bolt face of carbon. Use a pointed (but not sharp; hard brass is best here) tool to scrape the carbon out of the corner of the bolt face shoulder.

The bolt's tail will be heavily caked with carbon, as it is directly in the gas flow path from the gas key. Getting this clean takes a specialized tool. Using the edge of a knife will scrape the Parkerizing off the bolt and risk cutting yourself. And the steel-toothed gun-cleaning toothbrushes risk hooking a gas ring and bending them or flinging one off the bolt. Instead, use a specialized tool.

The ejector is spring-loaded and held in with a small pin that requires a fixture to hold the bolt to remove the pin and ejector. That is a rare need. To clean and check the function of the ejector, place the bolt in a holding fixture, or clamp it in a padded vise, face up. Use a drift punch and pump the ejector. Push the punch in, and let the ejector push the punch back up. You can put a drop of oil onto the ejector to start, and the movement will pump the oil in and out, cleaning and lubing it. If it is at all sluggish, you'll need to remove, scrub and reinstall it. If it isn't sluggish, then pumping with oil will be all you need.

The ejector should have a slight bevel around the top edge of the pin. In rare cases, we have seen ejectors lacking that bevel, and the result is the ejector nipping brass off of the case head when fired. If you see a collection of brass shavings on the bolt face when cleaning, you'll benefit from removing the ejector and using a stone to break the edge of the ejector top so it won't have a sharp edge to shave brass. The fastest way is to clamp the ejector rod in the jaws of a hand drill and, with a careful touch, lightly kiss the edge of the ejector with the drill where you want the bevel to be.

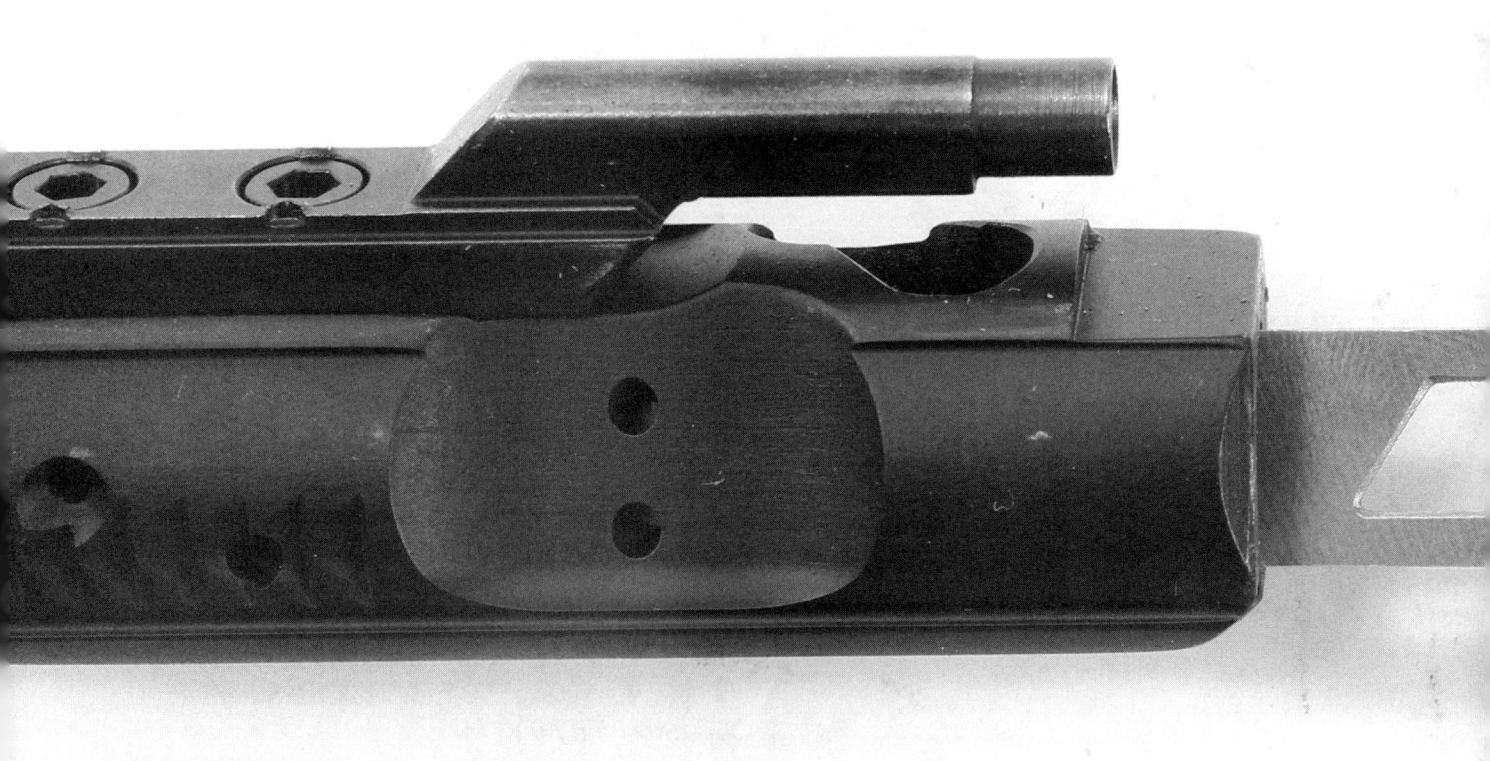

■ The carrier is simple to clean, but the one area that needs scrubbing is the bore's interior. Here, the Real Avid tool gets in there and scrapes out the carbon.

■ A scraper like this one from M4CAT will do a great job of cleaning the bolt and carrier.

Ejector Work

Before we go into the metallurgy and history of the bolt, let's assume you need to do some ejector work. For this, you'll need a bolt fixture. Oh, you can take the ejector out and even replace it without one, but you will not have fun doing so — you risk losing parts, and lost parts mean downtime until the next box arrives from Brownells. The fixture is a simple cradle that holds the bolt, aligning it so you can drive out the retaining pin. The bolt fixture is one of those tools that you will rarely need, but when you need it, the thing will save you

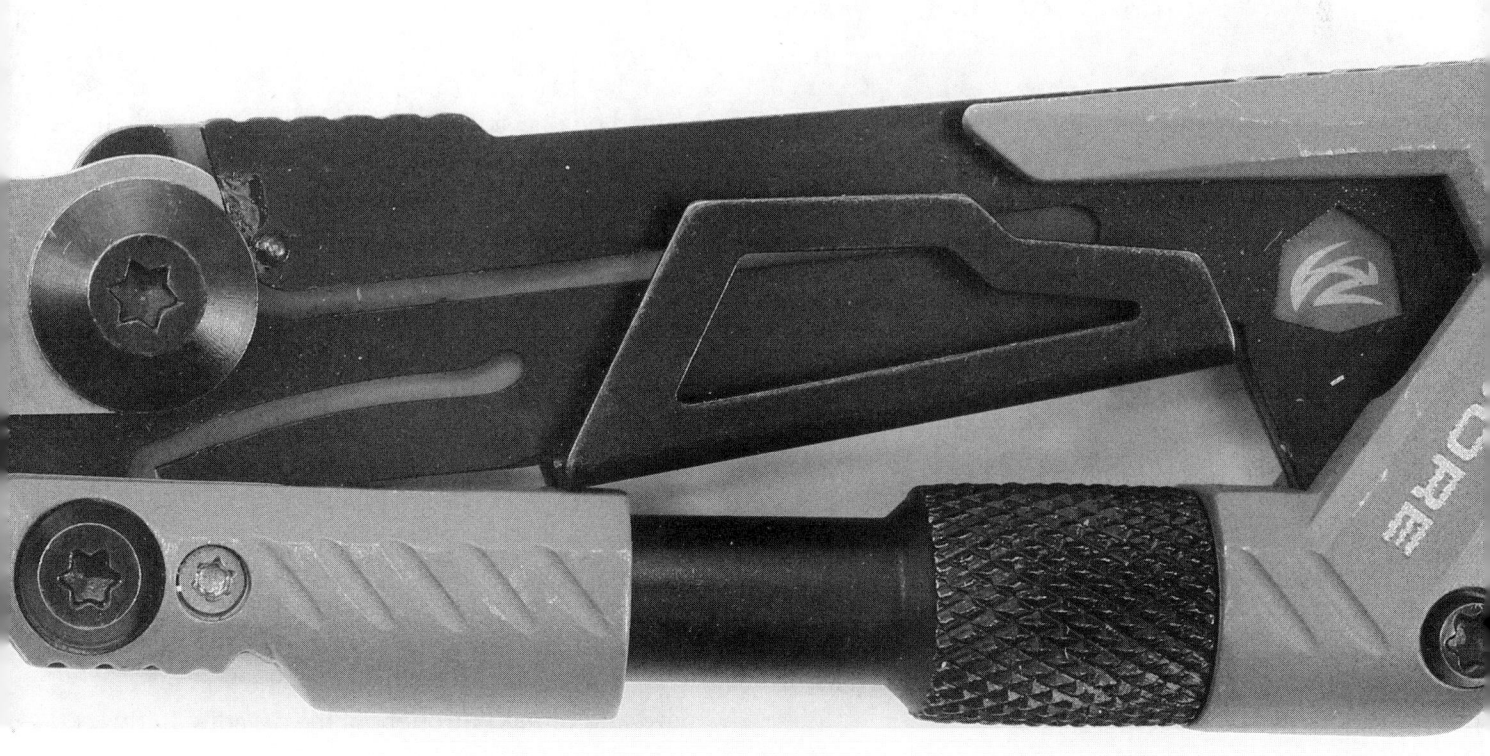

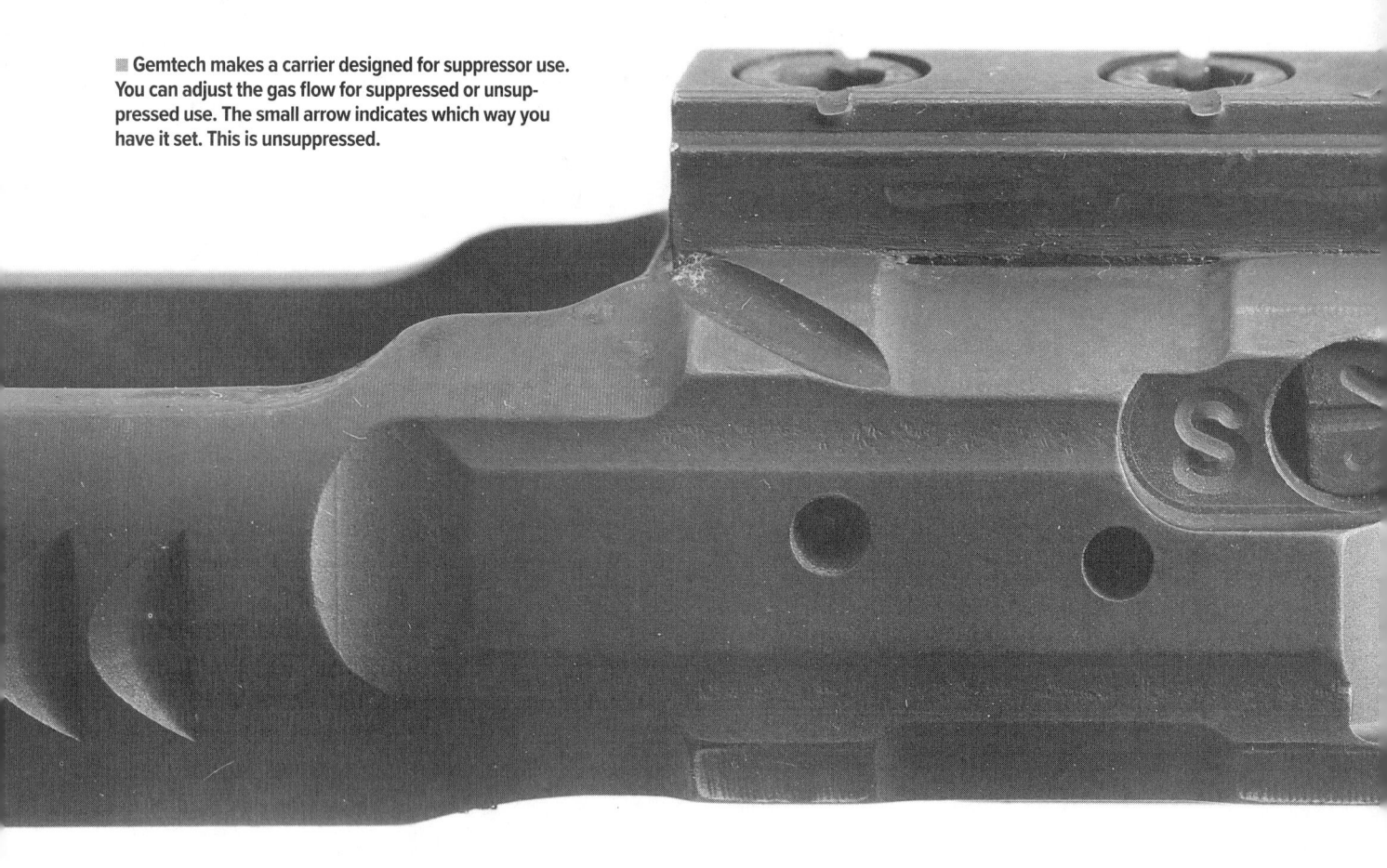

Gemtech makes a carrier designed for suppressor use. You can adjust the gas flow for suppressed or unsuppressed use. The small arrow indicates which way you have it set. This is unsuppressed.

much time, lost parts, banged knuckles and aggravation. Place the bolt in the fixture and turn the knob until the bolt is tightly compressed. The knob compresses the ejector as it presses against the bolt body. Now use a correctly fitting punch and your hammer to tap out the retaining pin. Unscrew the knob, and the ejector will ease out of the bolt far enough to grab it and pull it out.

Bevel the ejector if needed. Scrub the bolt. (This might be a good time for the pipe cleaners, but I've never felt the need.) Check the ejector spring. It should not be rusty or broken. If it comes out with a bunch of brass shavings (the ejector bevel needs attention, as mentioned), you should use an aerosol cleaner to hose the interior clean and insert and remove the ejector spring several times to ensure you have them all out.

For reassembly, use the fixture again, but attend to one detail: the ejector has a clearance slot machined on one side. The pin will only go through the bolt and capture the ejector if you have that clearance slot oriented to the pin. It's worth a few moments of your time to handle the bolt and ejector, sliding the ejector into place without the spring to understand which way the clearance slot goes for the pin to pass by it.

Next, put the spring in place, ejector on top, bolt into the fixture and tighten the knob until it stops. Check the ejector clearance and adjust it if it won't let the pin pass. Start the pin, tap it into place flush with the bolt and remove it from the fixture.

Extractors

The extractor is one of the AR-15's parts that had to be re-assessed several times as the gun was used and refined throughout the decades. In the beginning, it was just a part that hauled empties out of the chamber. Next, we obsessed over shape, sharpness, longevity and "did I use any steel-cased ammo with this extractor" — things that didn't matter.

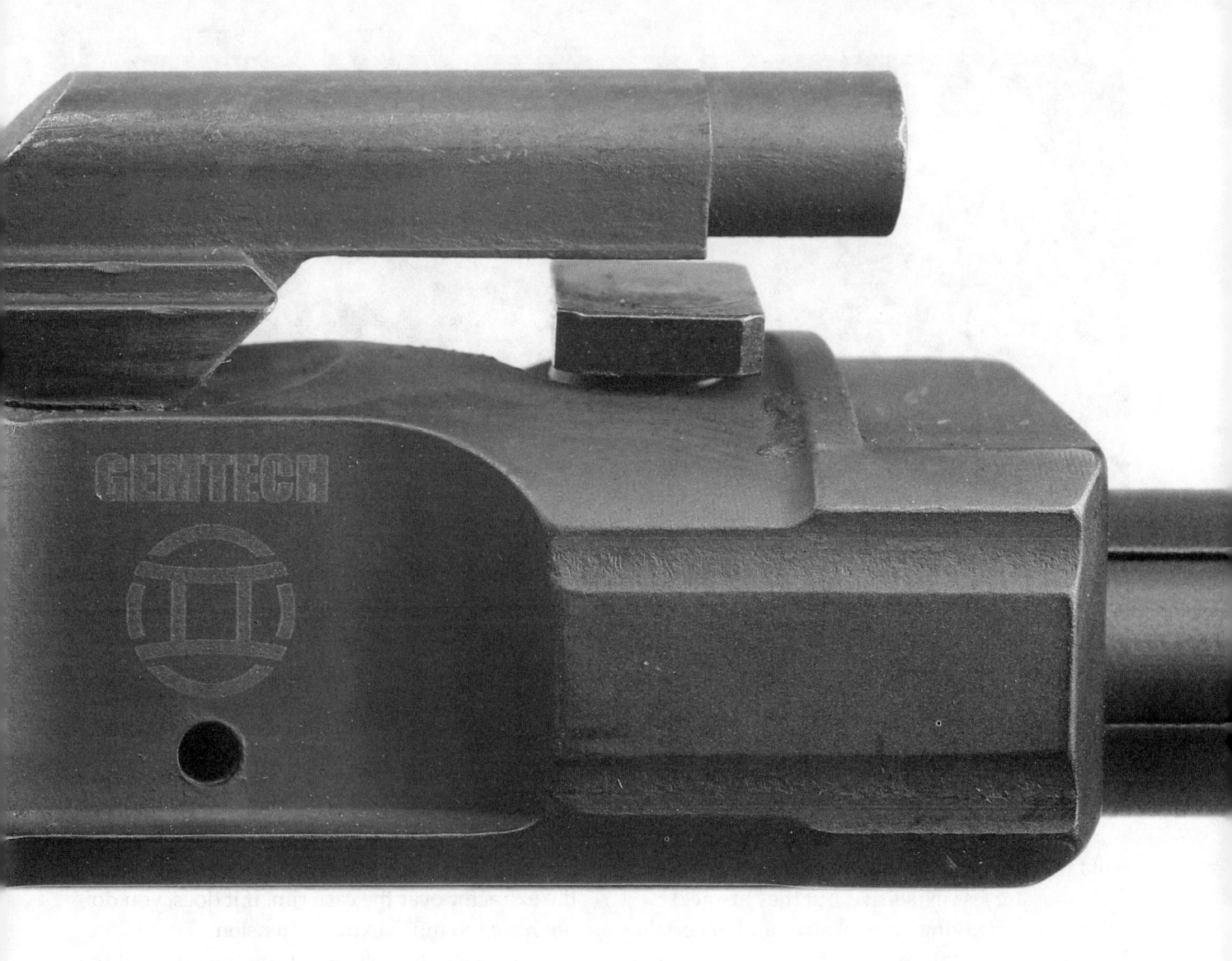

Then we figured out that the problems we had were due almost entirely to lack of extractor tension. Once we used enough spring tension, the problems went away, and now we're back to it being the part that simply hauls the empties out.

Initially, the extractor was two parts: the extractor blade and its spring. It didn't take long for the Army to discover that the extractor needed more tension, and it added a small plastic cylinder inside the spring to boost tension. Historically, boosters have come in an array of ever-darkening colors — from white to yellow to red to blue to black. The darker it is, the more boost (known in spring circles as the "durometer" of the material used), and you want to be using black. I have seen USGI M16A1 rifles with just springs, no booster, that functioned just fine with M193 ammunition (that's the 55-grain full metal jacket, full-power ammo). But adding the interior booster gives you a more considerable margin of function. You should make sure your extractor has the internal booster, preferably a black one.

However, in harsh environments or with shorter barrels, that wasn't enough. The original extra ring is the D-Fender. This is a D-shaped ring that goes around the extractor spring. It's wedge-shaped, so it follows the angle of the pivoting extractor and boosts extractor tension even more. It is the best option. The government wanted to increase extractor tension further, but rather than pay for an existing part designed for the task, it opted to go with a cheaper but harder-to-deal-with choice: an "O" ring. The O-ring also goes around the spring, but — because it doesn't taper — it requires a strong grip to get the extractor compressed into the

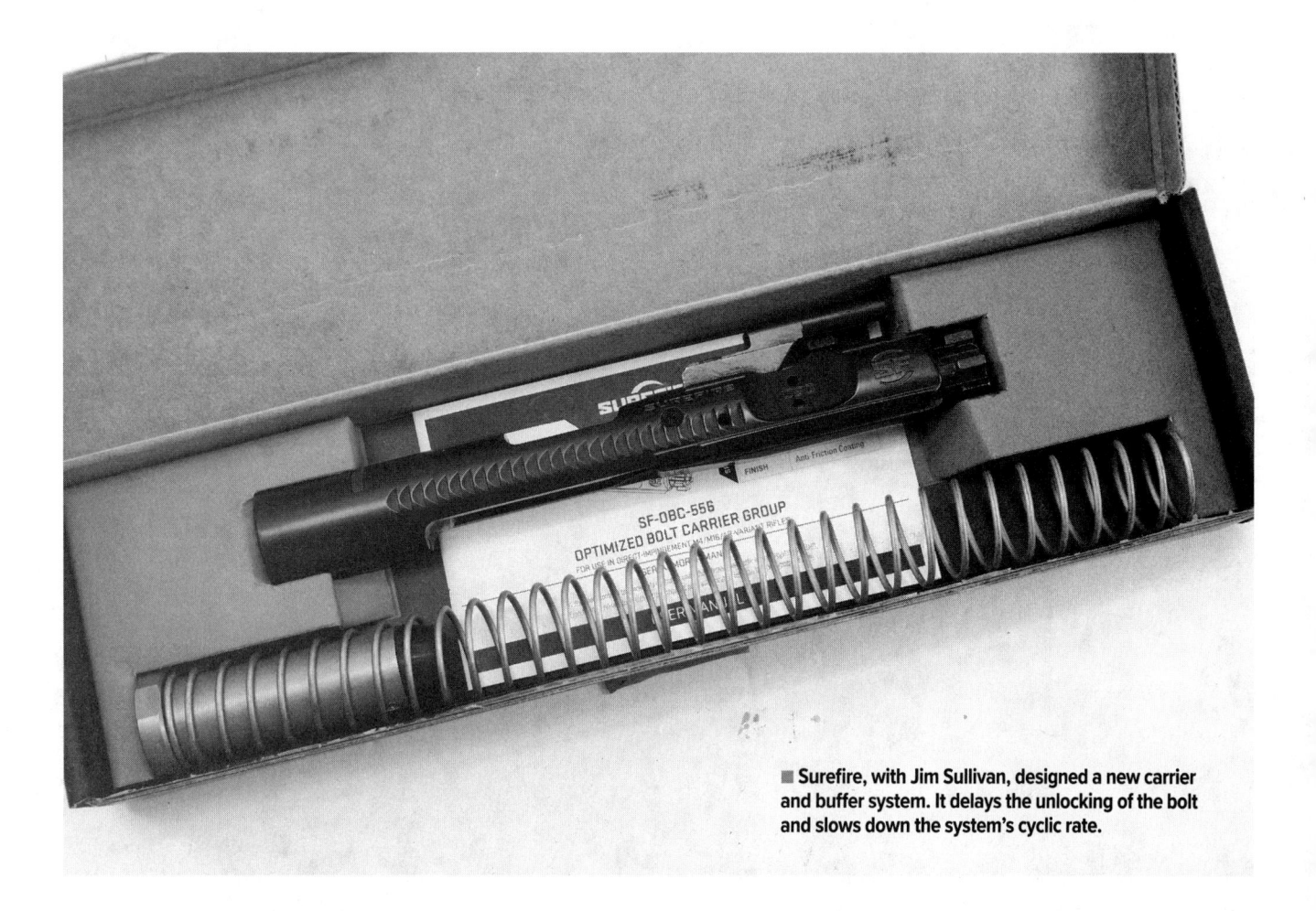

Surefire, with Jim Sullivan, designed a new carrier and buffer system. It delays the unlocking of the bolt and slows down the system's cyclic rate.

bolt far enough to insert the retaining pin.

O-rings are less expensive, but they are also offered in a dizzying array of sizes and materials. You need the right size and correct durometer material resistant to solvents, oil and heat. Brownells carries them, so you can order as many as you need, from $1 to $2 each. You can, if you wish, go to an industrial supplier like McMaster-Carr and order a box of 100 of them for less than $3 (plus shipping, of course).

A fully boosted extractor will not fail to extract a case. It will even rip a case rim if the brass is lodged in the chamber. There is some concern that you can have too much of a good thing — excessive extractor tension. Here's a test that you can perform (but do so at the range):

With your fully tensioned extractor installed in the bolt, lock the bolt to the rear. Put the selector on Safe. Drop a cartridge into the chamber. Now, grab the charging handle and use it to unlock the bolt, but don't let it drop. Ease the bolt forward against the pressure of the buffer spring until you can feel the extractor bump against the rim of the chambered round. Slowly let go of the charging handle.

The buffer spring must have enough force to cam the extractor over the case rim. If it does, you do not have too much extractor tension.

If, however, the bolt just sits on the case and the extractor won't cam over, you have too much extractor tension. You'll need to remove the internal buffer or the O-ring. This occurrence is rare. How can it happen? Simply put, you stack everything up to the maximum: in addition to the internal booster, the O-ring or D-Fender, you've added an extra-power extractor spring. You can, indeed, have too much of a good thing. So, of the three variables: spring strength, internal booster and external booster, you only need to increase two of them, not all three.

As I was writing this, I got word from one of the other instructors in our Patrol Rifle class that they had a student arrive who had done just that: all three. His rifle not only failed the test; it failed regular feeding, stopping short of camming the extractor over the case rim.

Unluckily for all of us, the third variable — the extra-power extractor spring — is the most difficult to correct and install. So be content with enhanc-

■ Do you need to clean a bolt? This one isn't even filthy, just a full day's shooting in a class. In a pinch, lube it and keep shooting. Otherwise, scrub it clean.

■ The Otis Bone tool for cleaning bolts and firing pins.

CHAPTER 8 – BOLTS AND CARRIERS

The bolt tail is being cleaned by the Bone tool.

ing the internal and external boosters.

The Army took a long time to come around to admitting its firearms needed extra extractor tension. It solved the problem by coming up with a new extractor spring, the "gold" spring (the coating color looks gold-ish) and the new spring was deemed good enough by itself for full-sized rifles. The M4, however, is to get the gold spring *and* an

> **"If the extractor has insufficient tension, it won't leave an empty in the chamber but will lose grip on it before the ejector can deliver it to the ejection port edge to hurl it free."**

O-ring. Knowing the Army, I'd bet that there are many M16A2s with both gold springs and O-rings in them and many M4s with just one or the other.

The Army is wrong. You should have as much extractor tension in your rifle/carbine/SBR/pistol as you can and test it to prove it isn't too much. In this case, the rock 'n roll motto of "too much is not enough" is almost exactly true, except as seen above.

I can hear someone remarking, "All this talk of the importance, but no explanation of why and what lacking tension does to cause problems." OK, the extractor holds onto the case's rim as the bolt moves back and extracts the case from the chamber. The ejector is pressing on the case constantly, and as soon as the case mouth clears the barrel extension, that push begins to tip the case out of the ejection port, mouth first. Usually, the case has not yet cleared the ejection port by the time the bolt has hauled it to the rear of that port, and the case slams into the rear edge of the ejection port, ricocheting the case to the side or forward.

This situation was common with the older HK rifles like the G3, HK33, 31, etc., but in those, the bolt speed was so fast that the impact put a distinct crease in the empty case. Some empties were almost bent at the crease, the HK so abused them. The AR doesn't crease the case, but it still causes case ricochet. The pyramidal lump on the side of the A2 and later receivers is there to control the angle the case bounces.

If the extractor has insufficient tension, it won't leave an empty in the chamber but will lose grip on it before the ejector can deliver it to the ejection port edge to hurl it free. If you find that you occasionally have an empty in the feedway blocking the progress of the next round out of the magazine or hanging out of the ejection port as the bolt goes forward, then you lack extractor tension. One clue that isn't that "OhMyGodMyRifleMalfed" is after shooting, going to police your brass and finding that while most of it is in one area, there are strays

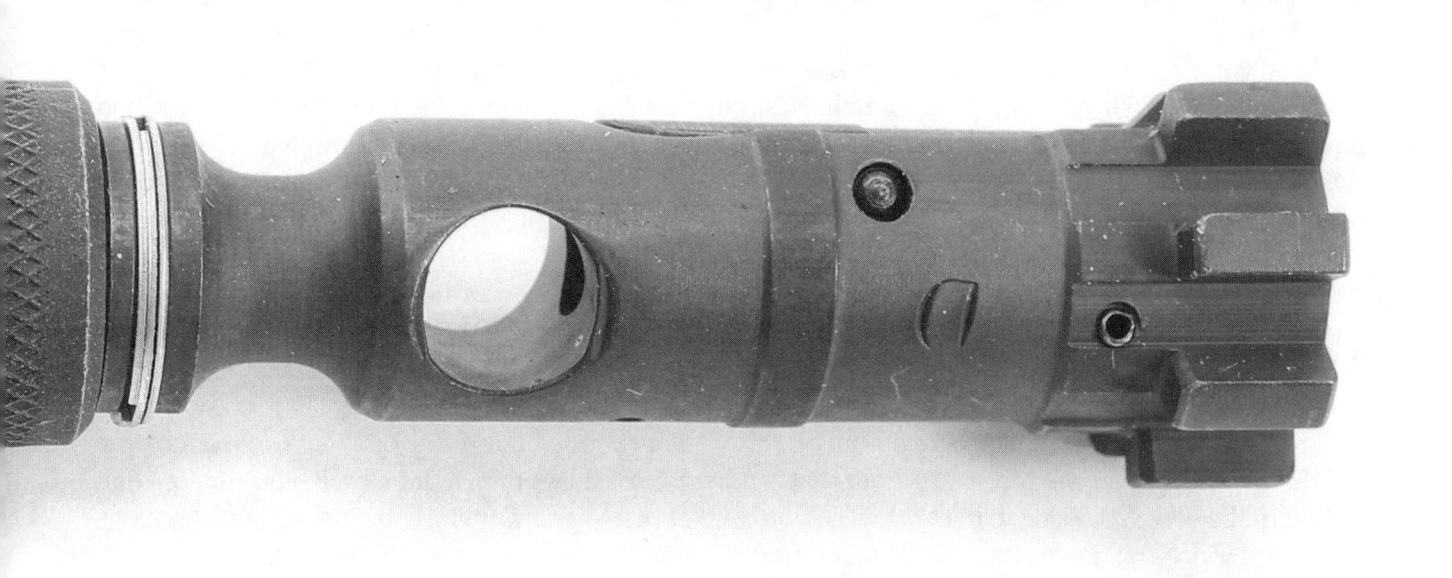

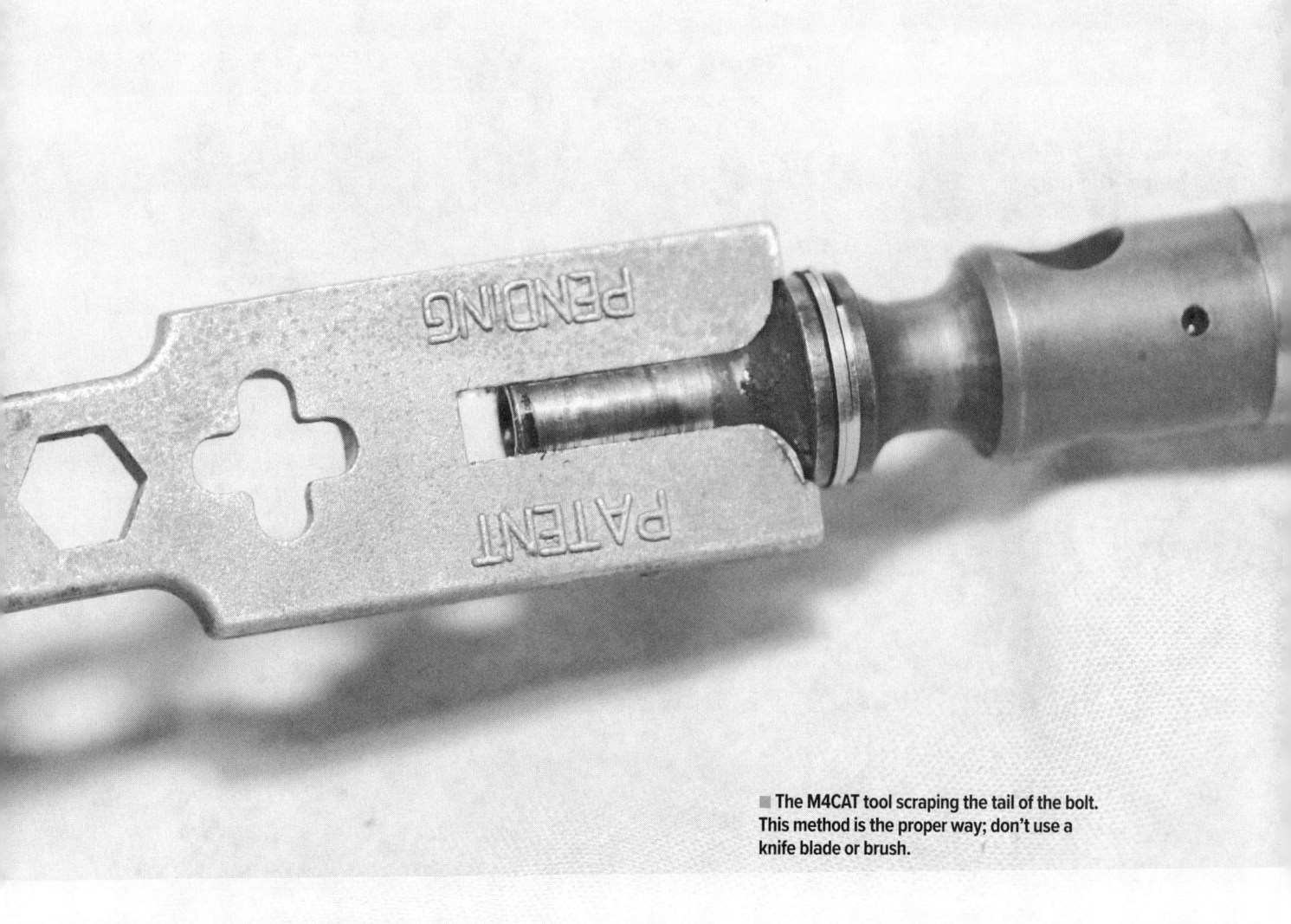

■ The M4CAT tool scraping the tail of the bolt. This method is the proper way; don't use a knife blade or brush.

CHAPTER 8 — BOLTS AND CARRIERS

that are not as far from your shooting position and at a different angle. Those are the ones that slipped but still made it out.

OK, so you need an O-ring. Which one? The environment is harsh, and the space is small. First, it must withstand lubricants, cleaning solvents and the grit of the powder residue. It is subjected to the heat of the chamber and brass and is constantly flexing.

O-rings come in diameters, ring widths, cross-section shapes, hardness and compositions. The size you need to fit around the extractor spring is known as Dash Number 006. (No, going with Bond, James Bond, won't do you better. That one would be too big.) You need the ring width that will fit in the space available to the O-ring, so you need a 1/16-inch fractional size, which is an actual .070-inch width. You'll need the circular cross-section with a hardness that is "medium" on the "soft-medium-hard" spectrum. And then there is composition: To withstand the solvents, heat, etc., you'll need a Viton Fluoroelastomer composition.

That translates to a 006 Durometer 75A Viton O-ring. Where to get one? Alas, you can't get just one easily. You can, however, purchase a bunch of them.

As mentioned earlier, go to McMaster-Carr. The part number you want is 9464K11 (a package of 100 O-rings for $6.21 plus shipping and handling). I know what you're thinking: "Dude, I don't need a hundred of these. I've only got three ARs." So what? At less than a dime each, you can lose half of them just by opening the package and not significantly cut into your lifetime supply. You and all

■ The two tools for taking the ejector out work the same way. Open the compression screw, insert the bolt, close the compressing screw, and the ejector will no longer be pressing on the roll pin.

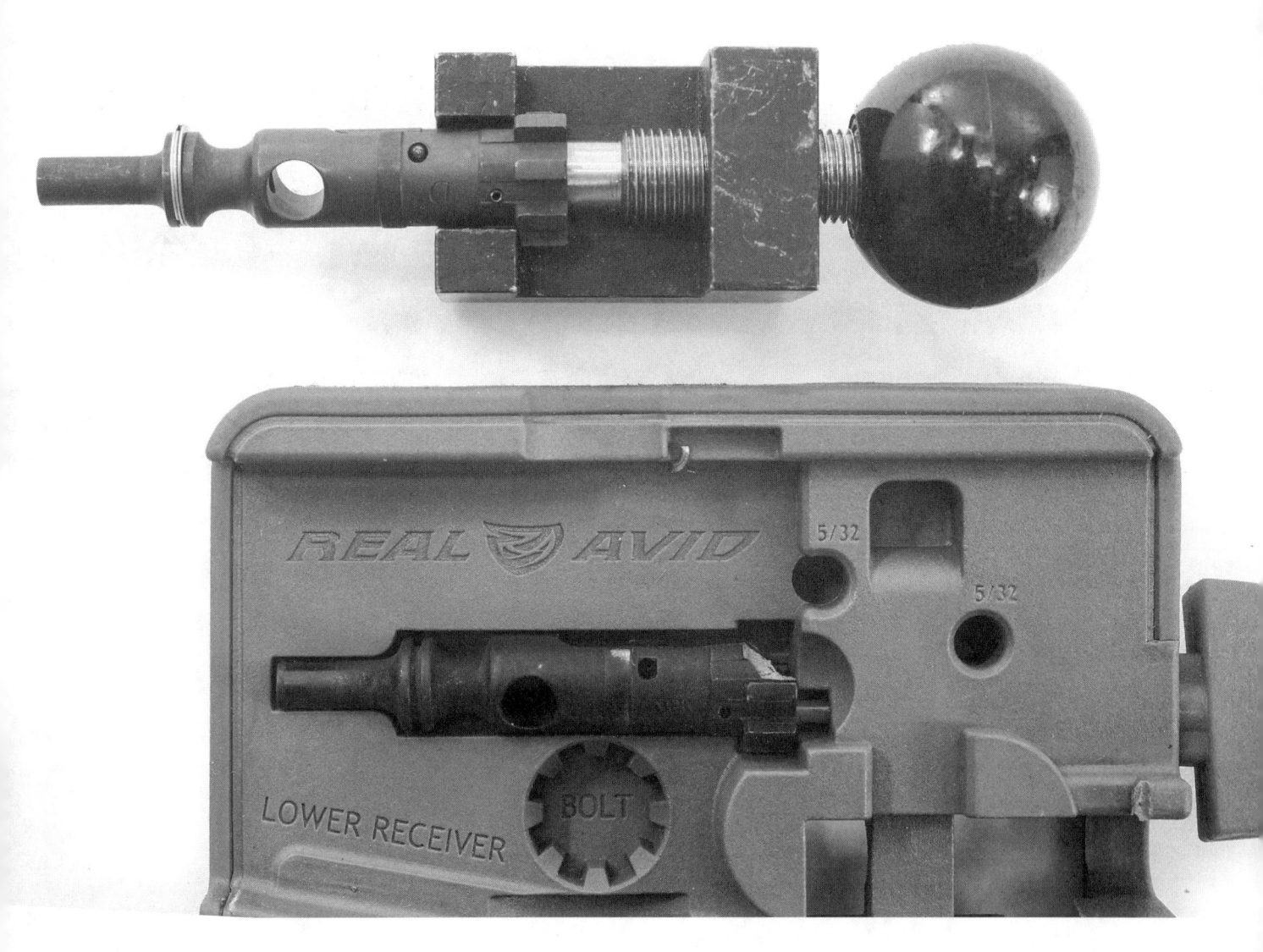

■ Extractors can break. They are exposed to high stress, and there isn't much anyone can do about making them beefier. So, inspect yours, and at the first sign of trouble, replace it. They don't cost much, and you won't have to do this very often.

your buddies at the gun club will each have all you need, for $10 total. Geez, don't be so cheap. One magazine of ammo costs you more than this.

O-ring installation is easy. Take the extractor out of your bolt and press the O-ring down over the extractor spring. When reinstalling the extractor in the bolt, firmly compress the tail of the extractor at the pivot pin to fit the pin through. Once you install the O-ring and reassemble the bolt and carrier, do the extractor tension feeding test at the range.

Super Extractors

LMT makes a bolt with a special extractor. Karl Lewis (the boss of Lewis Machine & Tool) made the tail of the extractor wide enough to hold two extractor springs. Referred to as a "lobster tail" extractor, the two springs do what the combined assemblage of the single-spring does: provide enough extractor tension. However, to get the LMT extractor, you must have an LMT bolt. Now, if you're building a new rifle and getting each part to your exact specs, you can do that. If, however, you have your basic M4gery and want the LMT extractor, you'll have to buy the complete bolt assembly. It will fit into a regular carrier, so you don't have to do that upgrade, but those going LMT lobster-tail probably will.

Bolts

The bolt in your AR is the hardest-working part in the gun biz. And just to make things worse, it is perhaps the smallest and most complicatedly machined part for the expected work. How is it made, and what does it do? How well does it stand up to work expected of it? When it wears or breaks, how can you tell? Can you get a better bolt or one made of improved steel?

The bolt starts out as a steel rod; mil-spec ones are of Carpenter 158 alloy. If you scan a steel alloy

■ With a properly fitting punch, drive the roll pin out, unscrew the compression, and you now have the ejector and spring.

chart to discover Carpenter 158's composition, you will not find it on the SAE chart, not on an aerospace chart, not on Wikipedia. The SAE steel alloy index is, for "carbon" steels (not "stainless" or "exotics"), denoted by a four-numeral designation. The barrel of your mil-spec M4gery will be composed of 4150 alloy. Each of the numerals indicates the mixture and proportions of alloying materials with the iron.

Carpenter 158 is made by the Carpenter Company, and it has the mysterious "158" number for reasons known only to Carpenter.

That's right, the government only buys bolts made from steel that is a proprietary product and a sole source. Even if you owned your own steel mill, you could not make Carpenter 158. Well, you could figure out what is in it and the treatment necessary to duplicate it, but you could not call it "Carpenter 158." That is a protected trademark. You'd probably be in trouble for saying something like "Carpenter 158 equal" or "substitute," or "just as good as."

The C-158 alloy dated from the late 1950s when it was excellent steel, even perhaps aerospace-grade for the time. Since then, steel production has advanced dramatically, but the mil-spec has not been updated; thus, your bolt is made of the best steel to be had when Eisenhower was president.

What's in C-158?

The alloying constituents of Carpenter 158 are relatively easy to ascertain. A qualitative analysis tells us that. A magnified view of the ground, polished and etched surface reveal the crystal size. But the secret is in how they get there. And that, Carpenter, isn't saying.

Carpenter 158 alloy qualitative test:
- Iron 94.1%
- Carbon 0.10%
- Manganese 0.50%
- Silicon 0.30%
- Chromium 1.50%
- Nickel 3.5%

I'd call it a "chrome-nickel alloy." The manganese and silicon are probably there for crystal formation and machinability.

A brief aside here. Steel is more than just a proportion of alloying ingredients, just as cuisine is more than the list of the foods and spices that went into it. Steel is a crystalline form of iron, and the

■ Here is the bolt, with the removed roll pin and the ejector and ejector spring extracted.

size of the crystals, their shape and distribution, all matter. On the one hand, I'm being clever when I say it is the best steel from the 1950s, but at the same time, I'm sure the Carpenter Company has been keeping up to date on heat-treatment and anything else that could improve the quality of its 158 steel. But it can't stray too far from what 158 originally was, for if it did, it would not be "Carpenter 158," and the government would be very cross with them.

An example would be an automobile. Ford made the Taurus sedan from 1986 to 2019. While it was all the same Taurus to Ford, it wasn't the same vehicle in 2019 that Ford made in 1986. Ford kept changing things, and the design kept drifting. The government does not want that. An M16 bolt made in 1971 out of Carpenter 158 must fit and function in an M4 delivered in 2021, or else the government will find out why and punish those responsible.

The steel bar bolt-to-be is precision-machined, heat-treated for surface hardness, then precision-ground to the final dimensions.

Once fully machined and ground, it will be surface-treated to a Parkerizing solution and sent on for further testing and production.

The exterior is subjected to a shot-peening process. This process involves basically sandblasting it, but with small iron spheres instead of sand. The impact of the shot further hardens the surface and relieves any stress points caused by the various machining steps. Every single unit in a production batch is subjected to a proof test for a true mil-spec bolt. Each bolt is placed in a barrel extension fixture and a proof round fired. The proof round produces 130 percent of the expected peak chamber pressure of a standard cartridge. Once fired, each bolt is given a magnetic particle inspection (MPI). The bolt is placed in yet another fixture. A magnetic field is generated in the bolt, and a solution of magnetic particles is brushed across it. The magnetic field will alter the particle pattern, which shows the flaws. If there is a crack in the bolt, it will be discarded.

In an actual military contract production run, each bolt is tested at every step. This QC process requires specialized equipment and highly trained operators. And if more than a certain number of bolts in a production batch fail the proof test, the MPI test or any other evaluation, the entire lot must be destroyed. Why? The markings. The hard-

■ The extractor needs all the boosting it can get. This one has the internal buffer, black, a regular extractor spring, and an O-ring as the icing on the cake.

ness-increasing methods applied to the bolt make it too hard to mark after passing the proof station test. So, each bolt has to be marked "MPI" for Magnetic Particle Inspection, "HP" for High Pressure (the proof test) and all other markings given for passing the various tests *before* it is hardened. If too many fail, the lot is obviously sub-standard, and the government does not want properly marked-as-if-they-were-OK bolts if they aren't correct. They get scrapped, not sold as "surplus."

All this work is expensive. And dates from, you guessed it, the 1950s. Modern statistical sampling and QC on CNC-precision machining means that a bolt maker can produce AR bolts and only proof test some of them. It knows — from experience and statistics — that the sample is more than good enough to derive statistical confidence in the sample. You will hear some people exclaim that only genuine mil-spec, 100-percent proof test bolts are good enough. Actually, you could make a much better bolt using something other than C-158 and not proof testing each one. But I'm getting ahead of things.

What the Bolt Does

The bolt has a multitude of jobs. For starters, it uses one of the two bottom lugs (as it is in the upper receiver when cycling) to strip a cartridge out of the magazine, shove it up the feed ramp and press it into the chamber. The bolt's locking lugs pass through the lug recesses of the barrel extension as the bolt pushes the cartridge fully into the chamber. Once there, the closing carrier rotates the bolt through the cam pin's angled track to close it.

The bolt lugs are now lined up with and supported by the barrel extension lugs. When the hammer strikes the firing pin, the pin protrudes enough to ignite the primer. A brief aside here: the firing pin is just one of the exact sets of dimensions it takes to produce a proper AR-15. The firing pin must protrude enough from the bolt to set off the primer. If it is too short, no bang. If it is too long, the primer gets "pierced" (here, the combination of excess firing pin length and chamber pressure blows through the thin primer cup wall, and the jet of gas erodes the bolt face over time) and causes accelerated wear on parts.

The firing pin protrusion is determined by the bolt's length from the bolt face back to the bolt tail and the length of the firing pin from the front face of its shoulder to its tip. The manufacturers of each have a few thousandths of an inch of leeway to get it right. That so many firing pins are made, and so many bolts by different companies, and they

■ On the left is an original extractor spring, much-used, with its blue internal buffer. On the right, a new spring. If your rifle fails extraction, get as much boost as you can.

all work, should not be shrugged off as a regular occurrence. It is a minor miracle of modern manufacturing.

Also, if you somehow end up with a combination that does not work correctly, you can do nothing to correct it except to buy replacement parts. The parts are hardened, and the dimensions too critical to attempt filing, stoning or machining them. If parts-swapping solves the problem, then do that and never change those parts out to other rifles. If

The O-ring, or the D-Fender, goes on the outside of the extractor spring. In the case of the D-Fender, the flat part goes toward the extractor hook.

swapping doesn't resolve things, then it is time to return them and get replacements.

Having fired the cartridge, the bolt waits. While it waits, the chamber pressure on the cartridge case decreases as the bullet travels forward. Case springiness allows it to relax some from being pressed to the chamber walls at 50,000 PSI. Once the gas flow has come back down the tube, the carrier is blown back. Utilizing the cam pin, the cam slot rotates the bolt open and pulls it out of the locking recess. The bolt, by the extractor, yanks the empty case out and, once that case clears the barrel extension and ejection port, the ejector pushes the brass free of the bolt.

The bolt travels to the rear as part of the carrier assembly, compressing the buffer spring. Once it reaches the bottom, it is propelled forward. If the magazine is empty, the bolt stop will lift, and the bolt stops against it. Otherwise, the bolt goes forward to strip the next cartridge out of the magazine and repeats the cycle.

Bolt-Gas Timing

The gas flows back to the bolt in a known timespan at a known pressure, assuming all things are operating correctly. The case has had time to relax from the chamber walls. The bolt rotation creates what is known as "primary extraction"— where the now-somewhat-loose case is given a rotational nudge, further breaking it free of the chamber walls. The bolt speed in extraction does not unduly stress the case rim, and the speed allows the case to tip far enough to hit the ejection port edge or pyramid on an A2 and be tossed free.

Changes to the system can throw the timing off. Such changes include a shorter barrel (barrel makers adjust gas port size to accommodate this alteration in timing), or an incorrect powder, causing excessively high or low port pressure. Or it can be a gas port drilled too large, so the gas arrives early or at a higher pressure.

Symptoms include a bright, circular smear on the case head across the headstamp, indicating the bolt rotated while the case was still tight. Or bent rims, meaning the bolt had too high a speed. Or creased cases from a high-velocity impact on the ejector edge.

Also, installing a suppressor can sometimes change a well-running system into an unreliable setup with no margin for error.

Finding the root cause of an overly energetic extraction/ejection problem isn't always easy.

All that said, how well does the bolt withstand hard usage?

For its size, and what we ask of it, surprisingly well. You will encounter more urban myth and wrongheaded info here as well. You will have people tell you that only mil-spec bolts are "good enough" for your rifle or your build project. Then they will claim that your bolt needs to be swapped out after 7,500 rounds. Wrong on both counts, for the most part.

Many years ago, we saw sub-standard bolts. Making bolts isn't easy, and companies who were new at it would get some things wrong. Those days are gone, as all the bad makers have pretty much been driven out of business (a point I've made several times in this book because it bears repeating). The advent of CNC machining has made top-quality bolts (and other parts) the norm. Plus, many new bolts are better than mil-spec. Remember, mil-spec is simply the lowest acceptable level of quality the government requires. Absent abuse, a well-made bolt will last a lot longer than 7,500 rounds. I wouldn't be surprised to see a good bolt that hasn't been abused last 20,000 rounds or more. Depending on the use and expected accuracy level, that is three or four barrels worth of shooting.

And when it goes, it won't wear out, get loose, sloppy or show signs of age; it will just break. Bolts are too hard to wear, at least by the standards of AR users. No, when it decides its contract is up, it will crack, or some part of it will crack and fall off.

Why the 7,500-round figure? That is the accepted use threshold in the military and is adopted without critical thinking by some who either don't know better or just want to look cool. The bolt experiences accelerated wear if you change the system (how the rifle/carbine is configured) from a 20-inch barrel rifle and the corresponding rifle gas system to a shorter one. Add in the jolt a suppressor adds and throw in regular dollops of full-auto fire, and the bolt gets worked a lot harder. Now do this in a sandy, dirty or low-maintenance environment, and you are really making life hard on bolts.

Lastly, consider the use and needs of the end-users: if a bolt fails, the rifle stops working, and the soldier and unit lose that contribution to firepower. The government would rather swap bolts out before they break than have a gun go down in a firefight. Imagine there you are, a highly trained and experienced service member, going through a village in some dusty place. You're packing an M4 with a short barrel and a suppressor. Or an Mk18 because it is convenient to have and maneuver in tight spots. You've gotten there either by helicopter or Humvee, and you and your carbine are coated in dust. Bad people suddenly try to do bad things, and you spend the afternoon shooting large amounts of ammo. Starting the excursion with a high-mileage bolt in your M4/Mk18 is probably not prudent.

The question you have to ask is this: how many of those wear-accelerating aspects I've just described happen in your regular shooting? I thought so. Consequently, scrapping an otherwise functional bolt because it has reached the "magic" 7,500-round use point is wasting money. That's money you could be spending on ammo and more practice.

Bolt Inspection

How do you tell if your bolt is good? Look closely after getting it absolutely clean. Here are two common (well, "common" as in, if and when it breaks, these are the places it breaks) areas that bolts break. The first and easiest to inspect is the cam pin hole. The cam pin hole is a large hole drilled and reamed across and through the bolt body. Occasionally, when I'm working on an AR bolt, I'll stop and look at that cam pin hole. I've had the good fortune to meet Jim Sullivan, the engi-

■ Mil-spec bolts are magnetic particle inspected (MPI) and so-marked.

neer who worked with Eugene Stoner and who was the one who scaled the AR-10 down to be the AR-15. "What was Jim thinking?" will pop into my head. And the answer will be: "That was as small as the cam pin could be and survive the workload that the rifle asks of it. And the bolt is just strong enough that it works with that big hole through it."

If the bolt has been properly made, the cam pin hole will have the edge of one end peened in, so the cam pin can only be assembled one way, the

> **"Those looking for the absolute gilt-edged accuracy that a premium barrel can muster will obsess over full locking lug engagement."**

correct way. The hole will have sharp edges all around its opening when it is first machined. The edge is supposed to be beveled after being drilled and reamed, but this is a delicate operation, and some operators are clearly better at it than others. The bolt can crack at the cam pin hole. That usually happens — such cracks are extremely rare — at a nick or toolmark on the edge. So if you are looking over bolts to buy, inspect that location. If you see one with no nicks or toolmarks, with a smooth beveled edge, then grab that bolt.

High-mileage, or hard-used, bolts usually stop working when one or more locking lugs crack or break off.

Look closely at your bolt. You'll notice that it is designed as an eight-lug bolt, with one lug replaced by the extractor. The unavoidable result is that the bolt will attempt to bend, or flex, or tilt, because of the missing locking lug. For most rifles, this is not a problem. The bolt is strong enough that it can take the shifted load. However, anything that increases the load uses up that operating margin.

Another brief aside here about accuracy. Those looking for the absolute gilt-edged accuracy that a premium barrel can muster will obsess over full locking lug engagement. If only four or five or six lugs fully engage, and the others have partial or no support, then the bolt will shift each time you fire it, which can decrease accuracy. By how much? Only enough that it matters to someone who can shoot High Power at the top level, someone who depends on getting more X-ring hits than anyone else to win. Short of that, you will not see a difference.

Specifically, a carbine puts more stress on those two lugs (the ones flanking the extractor) than does a rifle. An SBR increases the load (AR pistols with barrels below 11.5 inches are even worse), and a suppressor adds even more stress. Add up all this extra stress, and the two lugs on either side of the extractor can crack or even break off. I know fellow gunsmiths who spend a lot of time with users of suppressed SBRs in professional environments. They report finding broken bolts regularly in those organizations' fleets of AR/M16/M4s. So much so that the first thing they do on arrival is inspect bolts.

Back at the workbench, you have a clean, dry bolt. What to look for? Inspect the edge of the cam pin hole to see if there are any cracks. Look closely around the base and at the back of the two high-stress locking lugs for cracks. The cam pin hole usually is an all-or-nothing crack. That is, it probably looked fine for the shot right before it cracked. Suddenly, it cracked a bit, then it cracked completely through on the next shot — even broke the bolt in half. Locking lugs differ. You can have a small crack that stays small for quite some time, then gets bigger, then finally the lug breaks off. (Unless you are one of those suppressed SBR users, and then it just stops working.)

The correction is: replace the bolt. There is no repairing it or easing the stress.

How to Get a Better Bolt

I'm going to outrage a lot of people at this point and say that pretty much any bolt you buy that isn't a mil-spec bolt, that isn't made by a price-conscious maker or retailer, is better than a mil-spec bolt. Why? Metallurgy, heat treatment, dimensional tolerances and modifications to deal with stress. All of those have advanced dramatically since the AR was introduced.

Steel technology has advanced significantly since the late 1950s. So has heat treatment. With modern computerized design and testing, you can subtly shape a bolt so that it still fits a standard carrier and a standard barrel extension but is more robust and longer-lasting.

The question, however, is this: is the extra cost (because better always costs more) worth the enhanced performance? That is an answer only you can give.

Gas Rings

Now we enter another area of urban myth, mystery and intrigue, despite accurate info that is much easier to find these days. But here's the skinny: You need to have three gas rings, in good order, in your bolt for it to function correctly. Can a rifle run with only two? Yes. I have a rifle that runs reasonably well (it won't lock open with some ammo) without any gas rings at all. I suspect that the gas port is too large, but until I remove the front sight and check with a pin gauge, all I can say is, *it works*.

The gaps in the gas rings needn't be staggered. That's just nonsense, although I saw it in an Army training pamphlet as late as the end of the 2000s. There are continuous rings made as one spiraled gas ring that you install, which solve gas problems. Some people swear by them, but I've never seen the need.

Gas rings are consumable items. When they wear out, you replace them. Replace them as a set; there's no point in trying to get "a few more rounds" out of one or two in a set that isn't as worn. How can you tell they're worn? The rings have a gap in them, and the ends of the rings look like small snakeheads. When the ends are worn to points, replace the rings.

There is a test, as well. Take a clean, lubricated bolt/carrier assembly. Snap the bolt extended, as it would be when open. Stand the assembly on a hard surface, on the face of the bolt. If the weight of the carrier causes the assembly to collapse to the closed position, your gas rings are long gone. You should have changed them earlier.

What causes the rings to wear? They are acting like the piston rings in your car. They expand to fill the inner diame-

■ After cleaning, inspect the bottom rear of the locking lugs for cracks.

CHAPTER 8 – BOLTS AND CARRIERS

The cam pin hole can chip or crack if not correctly beveled (this one has been), and that crack quickly means a dysfunctional bolt.

ter of the bore in the carrier and seal the gas that drives the system. They rub directly against the surface of the bore and should be lubed. (They rarely are lubed, or if they are, they don't stay that way long.) The interior of the carrier bore is supposed to be drilled, reamed, polished and smoothened. But what really wears gas rings is a cheap carrier. If the maker leaves tool marks when the bore gets chrome-plated, those tool marks act as a file, and the gas rings quickly wear.

The only solution to a rough bore carrier is a new carrier. Just remember relative costs. A new carrier costs as much as what, a hundred gas ring sets? Fifty? How fast are you going to go through fifty or a hundred sets of gas rings? You could send the carrier back, but you aren't going to figure out that the carrier is the problem until you've sent hundreds of rounds through the rifle, and at that point, the seller probably isn't going to entertain returns.

Removing rings is easy. Use a dental pick or the point of a small knife, and hook the end of the rear-most gas ring. Pry it up and out of the slot, pushing it toward the tail of the bolt. Then run the tool around the circle of the bolt, and by the time you get to the halfway point, the gas ring will fall free. The second and third rings are removed the same way, and it will be easier to get the point into the groove and hook them.

Installation is also easy. Hook the end of the first ring into the groove. Holding it in place, run your fingertip or fingernail around the bolt, pressing the ring up and into the groove. Then do the second and third rings the same way.

It's not necessary to remove the gas rings when cleaning the bolt. Unless you're replacing the rings, the more you handle them, the more likely you will damage or lose them. Oh, and when scrubbing the bolt tail to remove carbon, keep an eye on the rings. If you use a steel-bristled cleaning brush, the one that my friend Jeff Chudwin jokingly remarks "makes your gums bleed," you risk flicking a ring out of the bolt. Don't use a steel-bristle brush, and don't use a knife blade. Use a proper bolt-cleaning tool.

Bolt-Carrier Assembly

Putting it all back together is easy. Note that this is the same process you'd use if you were assembling the set from a bag of parts while building your first AR-15.

Take the assembled bolt and stuff it into the front of the carrier. The extractor will go to the left, as the carrier would be when in the rifle. Look down the cam slot for the cam pin and align the hole through the bolt with the cam slot at the back end. Push the cam pin down into it, with the long side of the top rectangle parallel to the gas key. Then turn it a quarter-turn (either direction works). Once the cam pin is in, pull the bolt all the way forward. Turn the assembly bolt-down and insert the firing pin into the back of the carrier. Let it slide all the way in, and press the cotter pin in from the left side.

Of all the steps here, the cotter pin is the one that causes the most hassle. The tip of the pin is a pair of wires that are not always the same length. The pin hole crosses the bore for the firing pin. It is not unusual for one of the cotter pin legs to hit the bore wall and ride out of alignment with the pin hole. When that happens, you cannot press the pin through. To solve that problem, Press the cotter pin gently (with time, you will learn the required pressure needed to press, it varies from rifle to rifle) into the carrier while also rotating it. Doing so will force the leg that is riding out of alignment to slide around, match up with the pin hole, and reluctantly be pressed through.

Next, test it.

The first test is to ensure the firing pin is retained by the cotter pin; yes, that is the sole job of the cotter pin, to keep the firing pin from falling out. The firing pin shoulder must go *ahead* of the cotter pin. If the firing pin hangs up when you install it, the cotter pin will also fit ahead of the firing pin shoulder but not keep it in place. Hold the carrier assembly in one hand and gently slap the back end of it into the palm of your other hand. If the cotter pin doesn't catch the firing pin, the firing pin will fall out. If it stays, you are done here. The next test is one we've already explained: stand the extended bolt/carrier on its face. If it stands, it is also done. You're ready to move on.

The 5.56 Question and Solution

We've discussed the differences between .223 and 5.56. In a nutshell, the short, tight leade of the .223 design causes an excess of pressure when 5.56 ammunition is used in it. That pressure expands the case head, and in some instances, the primer can fall out. Yes, fall out. The "blown" primer rattling around in the lower can cause problems. It can bind the trigger. It can bounce up and get into the path of the hammer or carrier. It can fall out and end up in the locking lug area, and even once, we had to fish a primer anvil out of the open end of the gas key. If it falls underneath the bottom of the trigger, it can keep the trigger from pivoting enough to fire.

In one memorable instance, the anvil from a primer lodged itself underneath the trigger of the firing mechanism, back by the selector lever. (I have to mention that this rifle was built with *all* AR-15 internal parts, not a single M16 piece or even a modified M16 part to be found.) He had finished firing the string, and when the shooter attempted to engage the selector to Safe, it kicked off a three-shot burst and then quit.

Now that is a real problem, but it has a known solution. As mentioned in the barrel selection chapter, just because your barrel says "556" on it does not guarantee that it is a 5.56 chamber. Some companies can be counted on. Others, not so much.

The solution for gauging and correcting both is the 223/556 Gauge from M-Guns (m-guns.com). The gauge is precision-ground to be just under the maximum 5.56 dimensions allowed. If you stick the gauge into a .223 chamber, it will bind in the narrow, short leade, and you will find you have to pull it out. If it "bounces" and drops out of its own weight, you are good to go. I find that coating the gauge with a Sharpie lets me see *where* it is binding. If it doesn't contact the rifling but is rubbing on the freebore — the smooth cylindrical section of the leade — you may well have a .223 Wylde chamber.

If it turns out to be a .223 leade, then the NEMRT reamer comes into play. This reamer is made with a non-cutting headspace shoulder — you cannot increase headspace with it. It only cuts the leade, and it cuts it far enough to make a correct 5.56 leade. It also cuts a bit more, so it just "cleans up" any residual problems the leade might have had.

We have had a rifle that "popped" primers corrected by applying the M-Guns reamer to the leade more than once. The reamer will cut all barrels except for those treated by Melonite, which has such a hard surface that you cannot cut them, though they will dull the reamers. The reamer is heat-treated such that it will also cut chrome. This alarms some people who have the chrome lining to protect the bore. However, if they have a chrome-lined .223 leade, they will pop primers, which is a bigger problem.

If you're picking up your fired brass and finding that now and then one of them lacks a primer, then you have a problem. Your rifle is experiencing excessive pressure. Also, the loose primer pocket makes reloading the brass problematic. If it fell out the first time, the second primer won't stay in place. When it does fall out, the powder inside is free to flow out and make a mess of things.

9

Front Sights and Gas Blocks

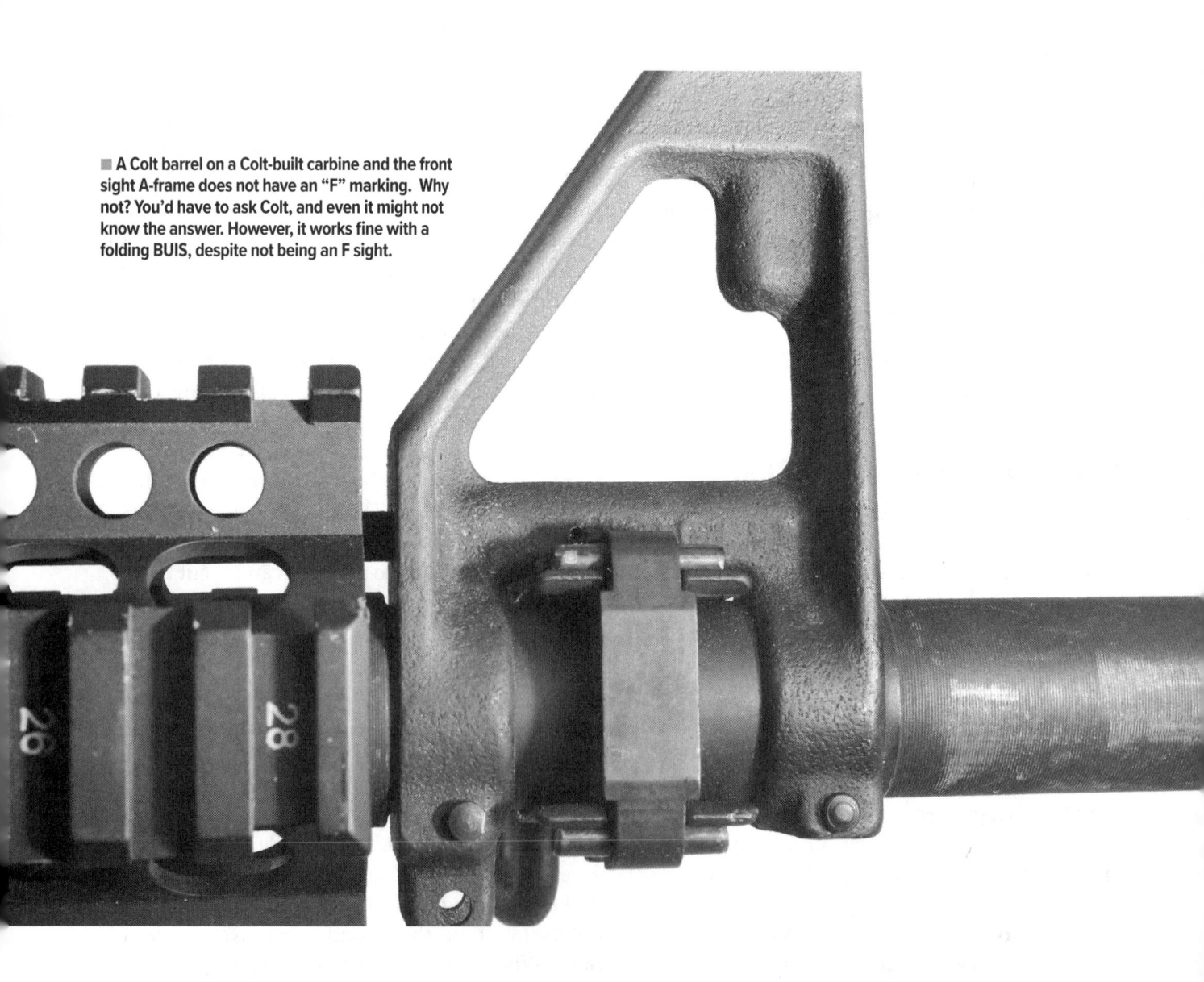

■ A Colt barrel on a Colt-built carbine and the front sight A-frame does not have an "F" marking. Why not? You'd have to ask Colt, and even it might not know the answer. However, it works fine with a folding BUIS, despite not being an F sight.

■ M4 means feed ramps. It does not necessarily mean you need an "F" marked front sight, but it may require one.

In the early years, a barrel with a front sight was also the gas block. The only options for handguards were A1 or A2. Now, with all kinds of handguard choices, and free-float handguards the norm, we must consider the gas block as a readily serviceable item.

The regular front sight assembly is a forging or casting machined to fit the barrel and accept the front sight parts. Manufacturers first machined the barrel hoops to the expected barrel diameter, either .750 or .625 inch, then the front sight parts. That means the hole for the plunger, spring and the sight is drilled and tapped.

The GI method of attaching the front sight involves precise fixtures. With its barrel extension attached and the gas port drilled, the barrel is set into a fixture that aligns the gas port and index pin, so the front sight is vertical. The front sight A-frame is pressed on, and everything is held firmly. Next, the maker drills the holes for the cross pins and reams them with a tapered reamer. A gunsmith drives the tapered pins home, pulls the barrel from the fixture and sends it on its way.

■ The original front sight housing is held on with tapered pins. You need the Brownells block to hold it and to remind you which side is which.

CHAPTER 9 – FRONT SIGHTS AND GAS BLOCKS

■ The front sight posts are threaded to screw into the A-frame. Here is a pair of A1 posts flanking an A2 post.

■ The front sight screws into the A-frame. This A2 post has flat sides and four notches for elevation adjustment. It has been painted in.

The front sight is vertical, and if everything has been correctly calculated and measured, the front sight will be in the right place for you to accurately aim.

In the early years, I found front sight housings tipped out of vertical often enough that I made a fixture I could take to the range and, after removing the pins, adjusted the sight and test-fired until it was vertical on that rifle. That process involved custom pins fitted to the barrel, but there wasn't much anyone could do back then.

OK, more Colt trickery. When Colt made the flat-top receivers, the receiver and the bolt-on iron sights were supposed to work out to the exact location in space as fixed sights. That didn't happen. The front sight flat, machined in the A-frame, was too low. To get the front sight up high enough, you had to unscrew the sight until it was close to coming out. What did Colt do? It simply raised the location of the flat on the A-frame and marked the new sight bases. That is the reason for the "F" marked front sight housings. If you have a flat-top receiver (which will be marked "M4" above the gas tube hole if it is a correct receiver), you'll need an F-marked front sight housing to get the sights to work correctly.

So, we have four combinations to consider: two older

uppers, the A1 and A2 with sights in place and the M4 with bolt-on sights. And we have the regular, original front sight housing height and the F-marked. Non-F goes with the A1 or A2, F goes with the M4.

Let's suppose you've decided that you don't want the A-frame front sight that came on your M4gery. Or you want to change handguards, which requires a different gas block. What to do?

First, remove the old one.

If it is a taper-pinned A-frame, simply use your Brownells front sight assembly backing block (the orange one) and drive the pins out. (You do have a Brownells block, don't you?) Use a tapered punch to start the pins and a smaller-diameter pin to punch them out. Depending on how many rounds have been through it, you may need to use a rubber or rawhide mallet to knock the gas block forward off the barrel. If you're going to re-use the gas tube, remove it once the sight housing is off the barrel.

If it already has a low-profile gas block, and you need to remove it to do the handguard swap or whatever, you should do some inspecting. How is the current one held on? It could be a cross-pin or pins,

■ This front sight mount is also the gas block. It has a rail on top to attach the sight. The block is held on with a straight pin, which you can see below the barrel boss.

■ Set screws that are too tight need to be heated or drilled. This procedure often means the gas block gets scrapped, but you were removing it anyway.

CHAPTER 9 – FRONT SIGHTS AND GAS BLOCKS **177**

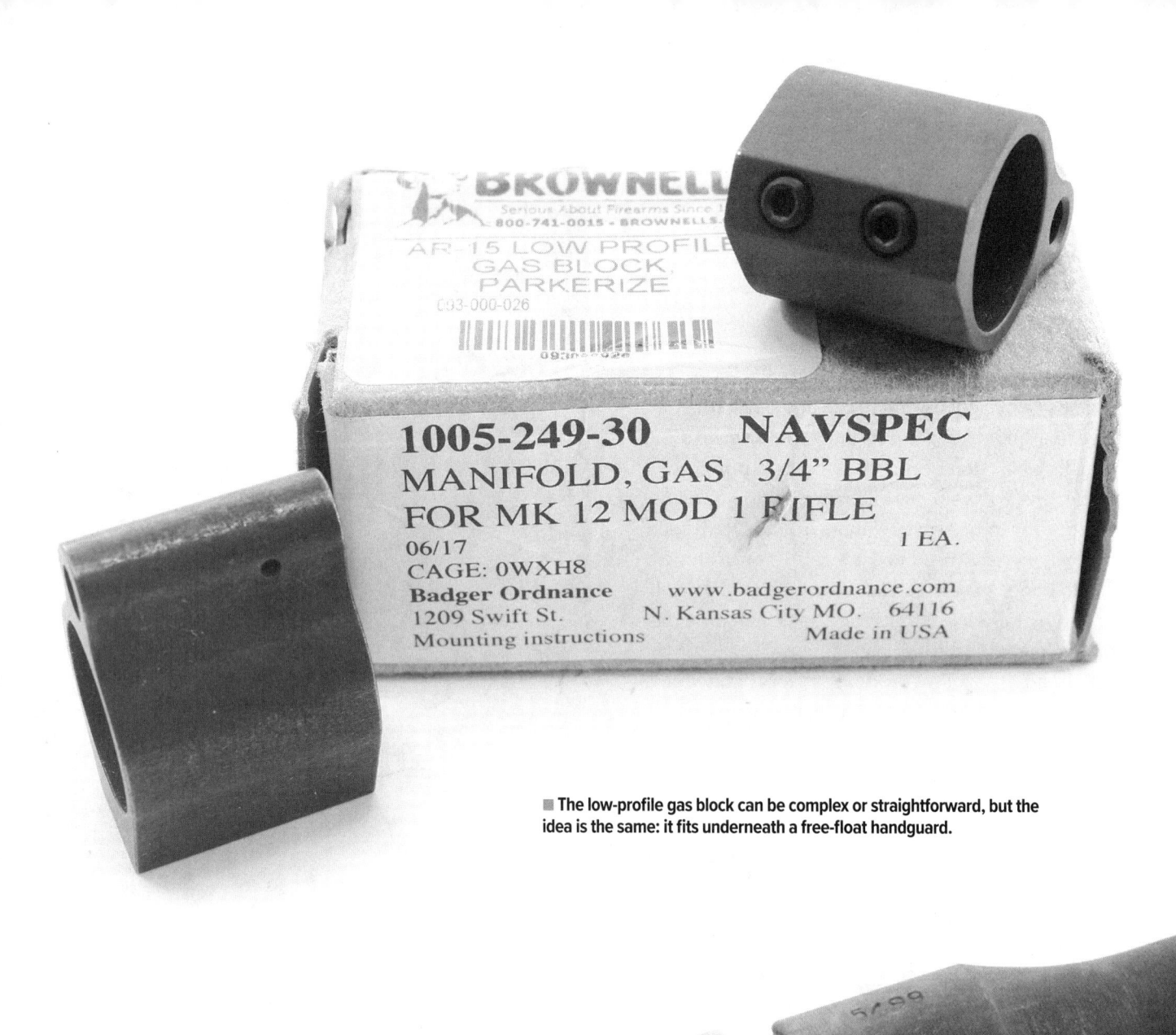

■ The low-profile gas block can be complex or straightforward, but the idea is the same: it fits underneath a free-float handguard.

■ The Gas Block Genie lets you easily measure and mark where the gas port is so you can correctly install your gas block the first time.

■ The front sight gas block assembly on this Mk 12 clone uses a pair of clamping screws. Since there's no bayonet lug, the military clearly feels that this is sufficient for the task. This kind of front sight assembly needs a careful application of Loctite.

which are almost certainly not taper pins. If so, put the barrel in the Brownells block and knock them out. They might be held in with Loctite or epoxy (non-taper pins can loosen), and you may need some heat to break those compounds. It could be held on with set screws, a secure attachment method, but many are marginal at best. We'll go into why when we install your new one.

Set screws are almost always Allen head screws (I have yet to see a set screw with a Torx head), and they won't be large. If you force a locked-in screw out and strip the head, you'll have to break out the power tools. So, regardless of what seems simple, assume they are locked in and get out the torch and penetrating oil. Heat the gas block and allow the heat to penetrate and loosen the set screws. Once you have determined that there is no Loctite or epoxy (no smoke comes out of the screw area) or if there was, it has burned off, apply penetrating oil to loosen things.

Then unscrew the screws and use a mallet to tap the gas block from the barrel.

> "If you force a locked-in screw out and strip the head, you'll have to break out the power tools. So, regardless of what seems simple, assume they are locked in and get out the torch and penetrating oil."

Likely, the replacement is a type known as a "low-profile" gas block. It's called that because it's no larger than it needs to be, and it fits underneath even slim handguards. However, it cannot hold a front sight; it is there solely to keep the gas tube in place. However, some gas blocks are larger and have a rail on top to hold a front sight. These are historical oddities, as

CHAPTER 9 – FRONT SIGHTS AND GAS BLOCKS 179

■ The front sight location is only a marginal accuracy factor. Yes, placing it farther away increases the sight radius, but learning to use it properly matters more.

front sights now are customarily bolted to the free-float handguard and not to the gas block.

Some barrel makers like Geissele, which also makes gas blocks, provide us an excellent service here. Geissele barrels are drilled with dimples that align with the set screws on Geissele's low-profile gas blocks. It's simple to install the gas tube, slide the gas block on, line it up, and tighten the screw. Once you've checked that the rifle functions properly, remove the screws one at a time, Loctite (blue, here) and reinstall them. You can also cross-drill the gas block for a locking pin. And again, Geissele makes it easy, marking the location for the pin.

A few details to keep track of. First, the front cap for the standard handguards is meant to fit between the front sight housing/gas block and a step in the barrel that holds it in place. If you take the cap off to install a

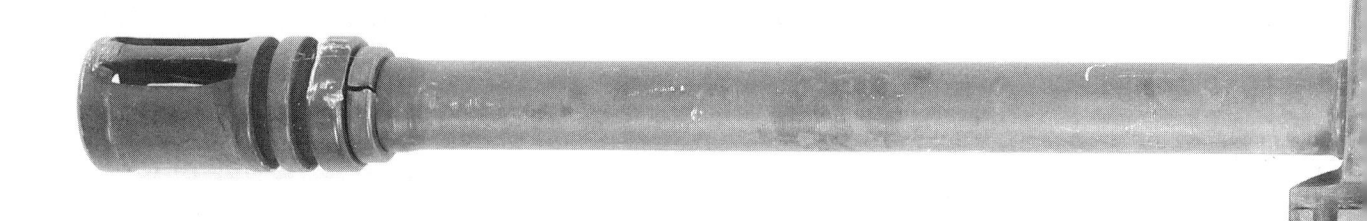

■ The gas block marries the gas port to the gas tube. These parts all must agree on distance and location, or your rifle will work poorly, if at all.

■ **The folding front sight, mounted on the free-float handguard, is becoming the new standard. You still have to zero your rifle after mounting the sight; such sights are not "plug n' play."**

free-float handguard, the gas block *does not* go snug up against the step in the barrel. If you do this, the gas block will be too far back, and the gas port might be partially blocked. A clever tool to ensure you have your gas block in the right spot is the Gas Block Genie (gasblockgenie.com), which allows you to measure and mark locations, and get your gas block top dead center and aligned over the gas port. ■

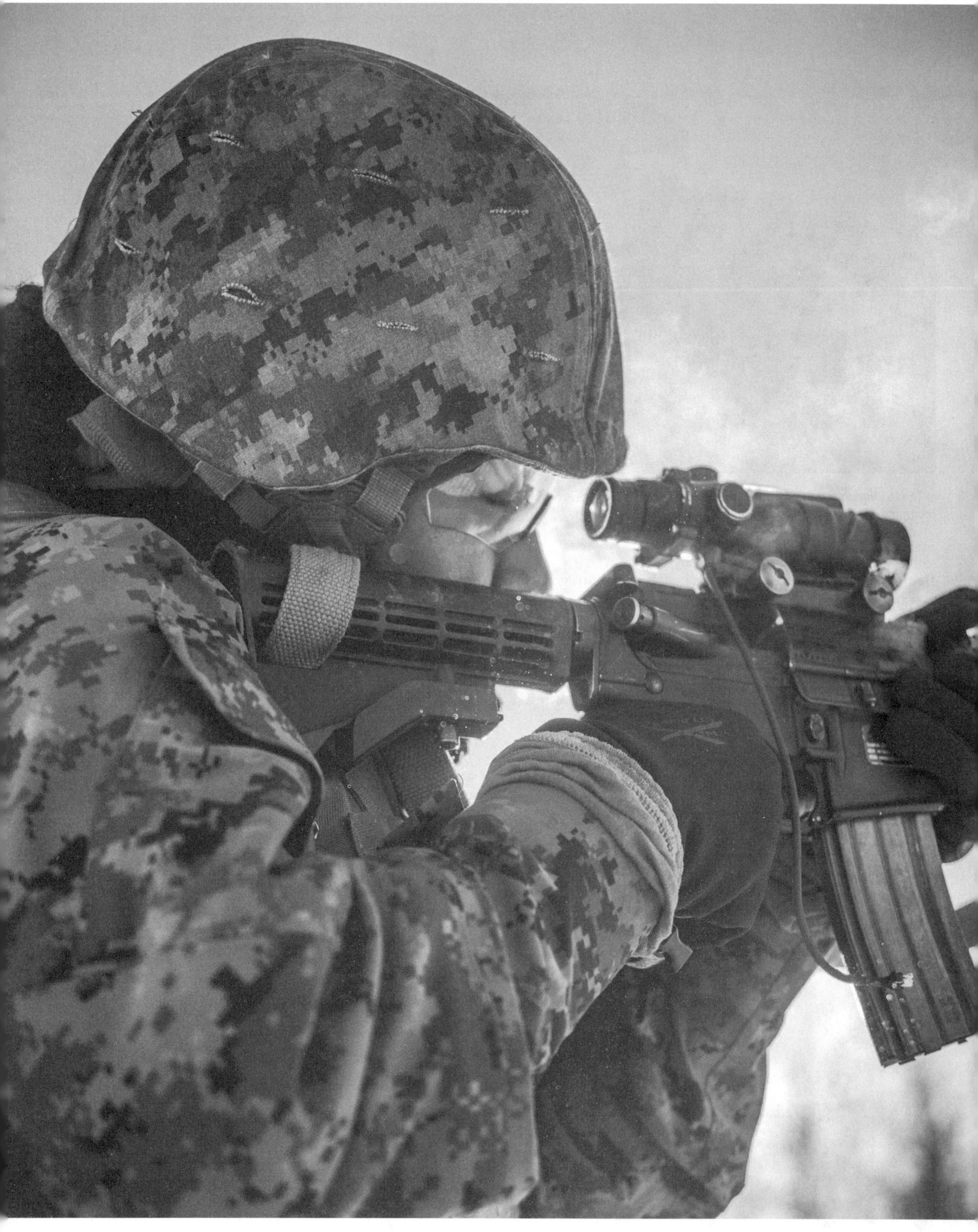

The military expects rifles and carbines to work in any kind of weather. So, the bitter cold of an Alaskan winter is not a problem for the carbine or the optics.

10

Sights

When it comes to AR-15 sights, your initial reaction might be, "I don't need iron sights; I have a cool optic on my carbine just like the Seals/Delta/SWAT." Good. But do you have the rest of the team? That photo you see of the uber-cool operator who doesn't have a rear sight on his M4, does it also show you the other troops nearby? And don't forget, those other soldiers or marines have grenades, belt-fed machine guns and a radio to call in artillery or air support. Because if the guy without the rear sight has a problem, one of the other team members will step in to help solve the problem. Or someone will get on the radio and get that extra-special assistance that is so satisfying to make a mess of someone else's plans. (And mercilessly rib the guy without the sight when it turned out he needed one.)

None of that is available to you. You are on your own until help arrives. As the saying goes, "When seconds count, help is minutes away." You are your own first-responder. The whole point of having a rifle is that you can precisely deliver a bullet to a point at a distance. You're not shooting a shotgun, blasting a cloud of projectiles. You're not shooting a belt-fed machine gun and creating a beaten zone; you are shooting one shot. It must hit where you need it to, or your efforts will be in vain.

In the last decade or so, I have seen and heard from other instructors that the number of students who arrive in an AR class with only iron sights is getting perilously close to being "nobody." The police officers who show up in classes with irons-only are already in the process of convincing their department to permit or buy red-dot sights. Everyone is using red-dot or magnified optics. But

■ Yes, this Mk18 upper is very cool and really correct. But the people who use AR-15s like this in service have lots of friends with guns, radios, grenades and artillery on call. You? Not so much. Get iron sights as backups.

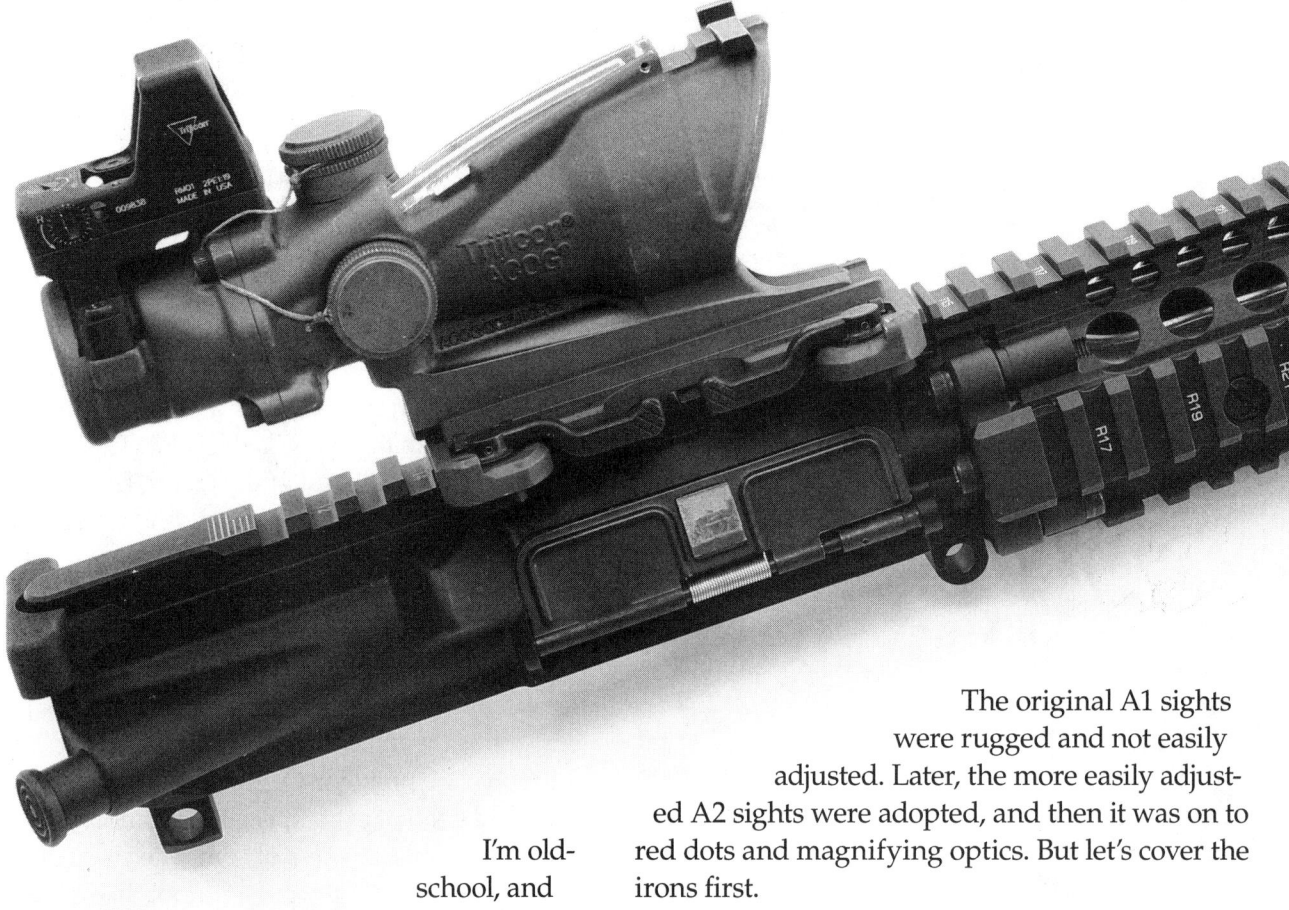

I'm old-school, and irons don't have batteries or fragile optics to break.

So, we start with iron sights. The sights on an AR-15 are the type known as *aperture* sights. The rear sight is a small circular hole, also known as a "peep" sight. Smaller is better for precision, yes, but you needn't use a sight aperture that is too small. If you relax and let it, your eye (actually, your brain, guiding the eye) will find the aperture's center. And if you focus on the tip of the front sight, your eye (again, your brain) will put the tip of the front sight in the center of the opening, and then you have an aimed rifle. All that's left to do is put the tip of the front sight where you want the bullet to go and press the trigger. Bingo! You got a hit. Work too hard at it, focus too much on making the center of the rear aperture the focus of your attention, and you'll be too slow or miss.

The original A1 sights were rugged and not easily adjusted. Later, the more easily adjusted A2 sights were adopted, and then it was on to red dots and magnifying optics. But let's cover the irons first.

Iron Sights

Iron sights can be the A1 or A2 type, folding backup iron sights (aka BUIS) or a combination of the two. The front sight is adjusted only to establish a zero for your AR. Once that is done, you will not be touching it, probably ever again, as long as that barrel is on that rifle. So you want to get it right and do it with the least hassle. Perhaps your barrel arrived with the front sight parts installed. If so, you're a step ahead. If they are zeroed, then your job here is done. (Lucky you.)

I'm going to assume your sights aren't installed and walk you through installation. The front sight assembly consists of the sight housing, spring, plunger and sight itself. Screws secure the sight to the sight housing. The spring and plunger are attached in one of four (or with the A1, five) recesses machined into the front sight flange edge.

I learned a long time ago that many A-pillar front sight housings are castings, and the threads can be rough. That's why I always use an 8-36 bottoming tap run down into the threaded sight hole to clean out the gunk and knock off any rough spots on the threads. That one step can save a lot of work, hassle and cosmetic "oops" in the future. A "bottoming" tap? That's the one with little or no taper at the bottom. It cuts/cleans threads all the way down into the bottom of the hole.

■ Your sights, backup or otherwise, can be fixed or folding.

Front Iron Sight Installation

Let's install the front sight. First, drop the spring down into the small hole drilled in front of the threaded sight hole. Press the plunger down on top of the spring. Use a small punch to press the spring and plunger down, and screw the front sight in. Once the top deck of the sight flange is level with the sight housing flat, line up the closest flange notch and ease the plunger up to lock the sight in place. Historical point: the "mechanical

■ The M68 red dot on this M4 is backed up by a folding rear sight. If the battery dies or the scope gets busted, the soldier is expected to take #79 off her carbine (the optic has a rack number on it) and continue with the iron sights.

> **"When you zero at the range, you cannot make fine adjustments. You can only change the point of impact by the amount of the next notch in the flange."**

zero" of rifles and carbines in government armories requires the front sight post flange top deck to be level with the front sight housing deck. The rear sight is on the indicated center. Any fine-tuning for actual zero after that is left to the service person to whom it is issued. (Or not, you'd be surprised.)

Oh, and the cruel joke here is that, while it appears that the bullet's tip will be a useful tool for adjusting — the TM (as in, official Training Manual issued by a military organization) might even demonstrate such — it never works. Never. You'll gouge the bullet tip and scratch brass all around the sight parts you are trying to adjust. Instead, use the correct tools when adjusting for zero.

When you zero at the range, you cannot make fine adjustments. You can only change the point of impact by the amount of the next notch in the flange. Thus your group's center at 100 yards might be half an inch off the center of the aiming point. However, that is a problem only for the top-end Service Rifle competitors. Why? Unless you are an NRA High Master, the ammo/rifle/shooter combination at best will mean groups at 100 yards with iron sights of maybe two inches, more likely three. In that case, a

Sight adjustment amounts (in inches) at 100 yards, per notch change

SIGHT, FRONT	CARBINE	RIFLE
A1	1.25	1
A2	1.5	1.25

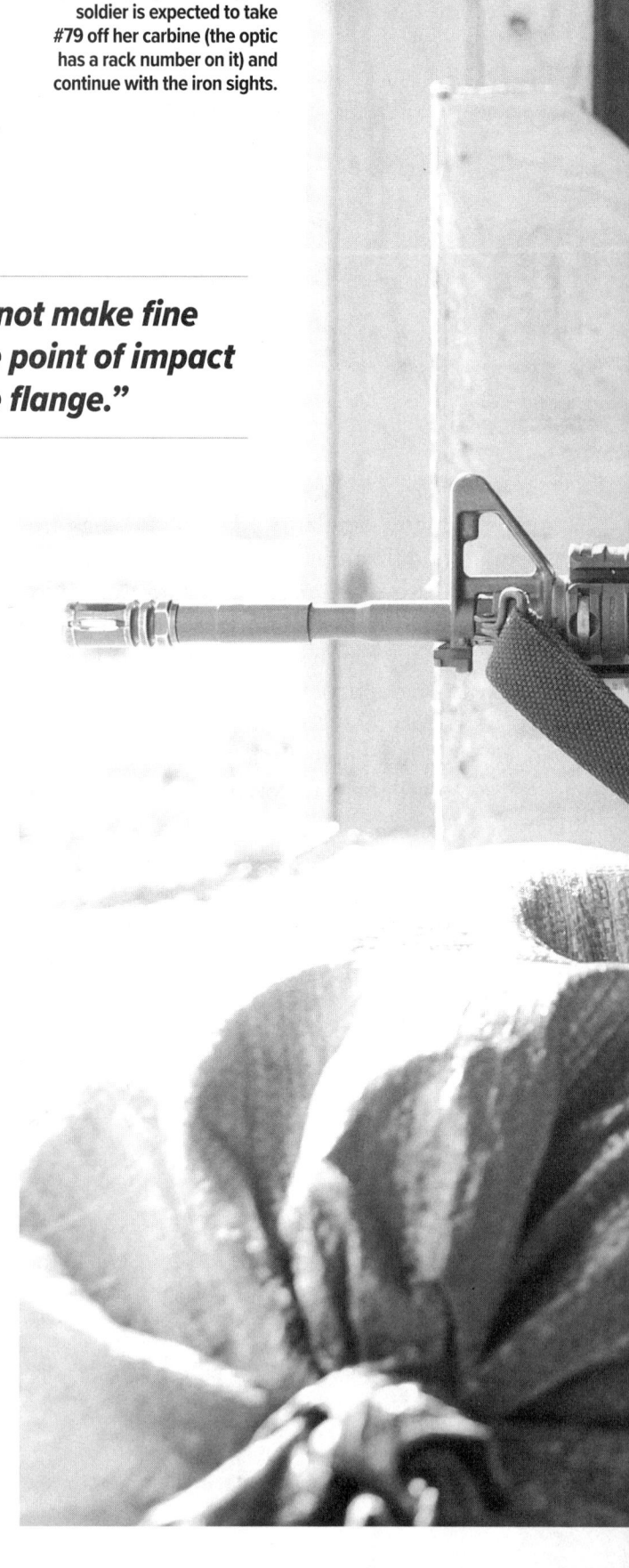

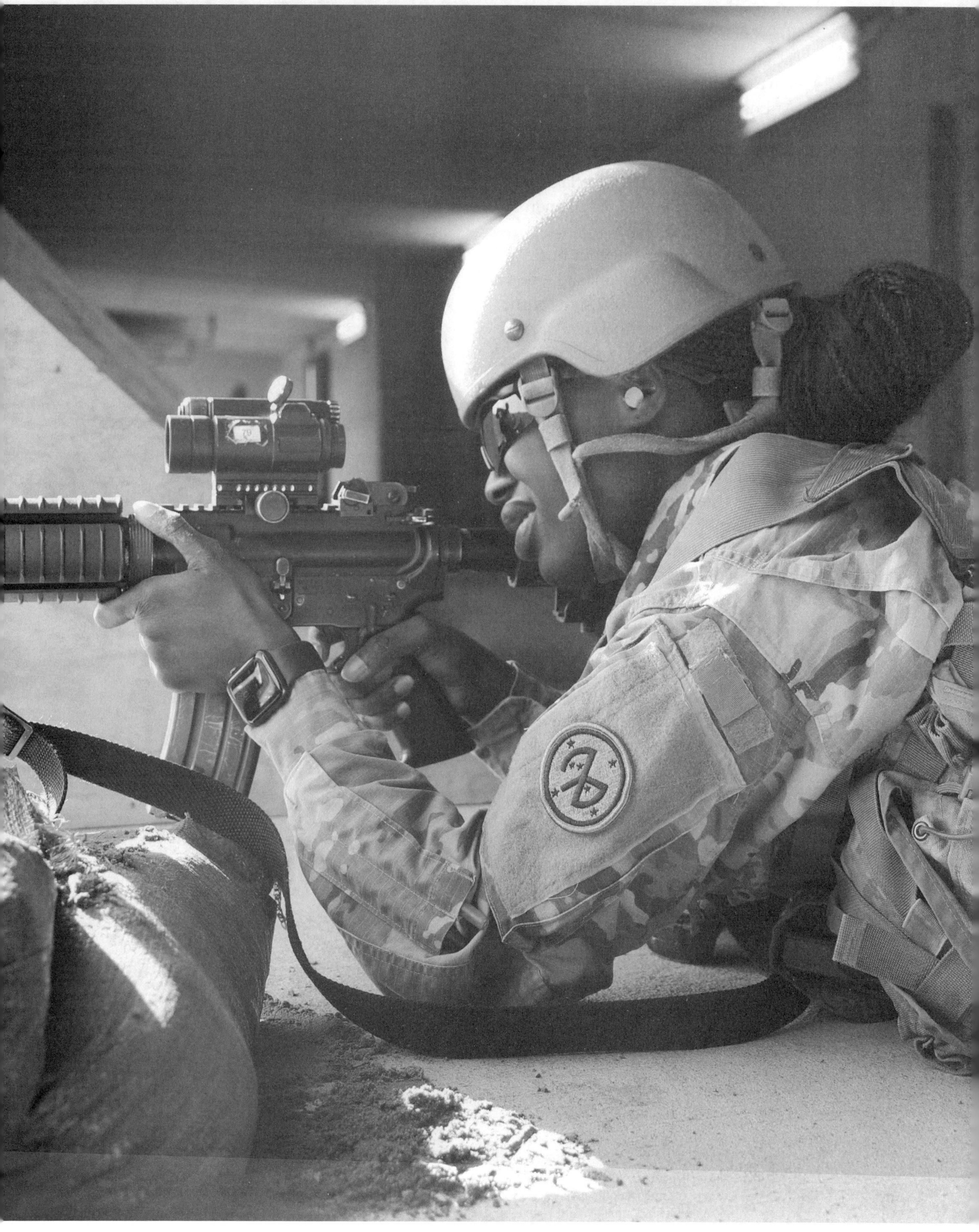

half-an-inch of offset gets lost in the noise. Until you can consistently shoot close-to-an-inch groups, the zero "error" is at best a theoretical problem.

The A1 has five notches, the A4 has only 4. That's because the A1 post is a tapering cylinder, and in target competition (and USMC qualification), competitors found the glare on the post would "pull" their aim into the sun. The A4 has four flats and doesn't do this. But it makes the A2 adjustments coarser than those of the A1.

The rear sight is where you make your horizontal adjustments for zero. Like the front sight, you're limited to click adjustments on an A2 sight or the locator holes in the rear sight plate of the A1. And again, you can have half an inch of offset here as well. If you put the rifle in a machine rest, the group might be half an inch high-right, or low-left or some other combination from the point of aim. Again, this is a theoretical problem.

On A1 sights, use the external plate to adjust zero. On the A2, the exterior knob is on the right side of the sight assembly. On BUIS, simply treat the sight (front or rear) as if it were permanently attached to the rifle and adjust accordingly. Nothing is different unless you remove the sight to do some work. Bolting it back on might or might not shift your zero, and you'll have to range-check to verify.

Red-Dot Sights

These are the ones that use batteries. The earliest red-dot sight didn't use batteries, but that was a particular method or design known as the "Bindon Aiming Concept," where one eye saw the red dot, the other saw the target, and your brain combined the two images. You then would "see" a red dot superimposed on the target. Today, we have red-dot aiming devices that create a red (or green) dot or reticle, and you aim using the dot.

The process is aided by the red-dot design not having any parallax. It has such slight parallax as to be negligible. Parallax happens when aiming through an optical system that uses lenses. The lenses can only be focused to a certain distance. They can also only be optically parallax-free at one distance. When viewing something at other ranges through the optic, the reticle moves as you move

■ All zeroing work involves moving the front sight for vertical adjustments. This entails specialized tools because the tip of a bullet hardly ever works.

CHAPTER 10 – SIGHTS

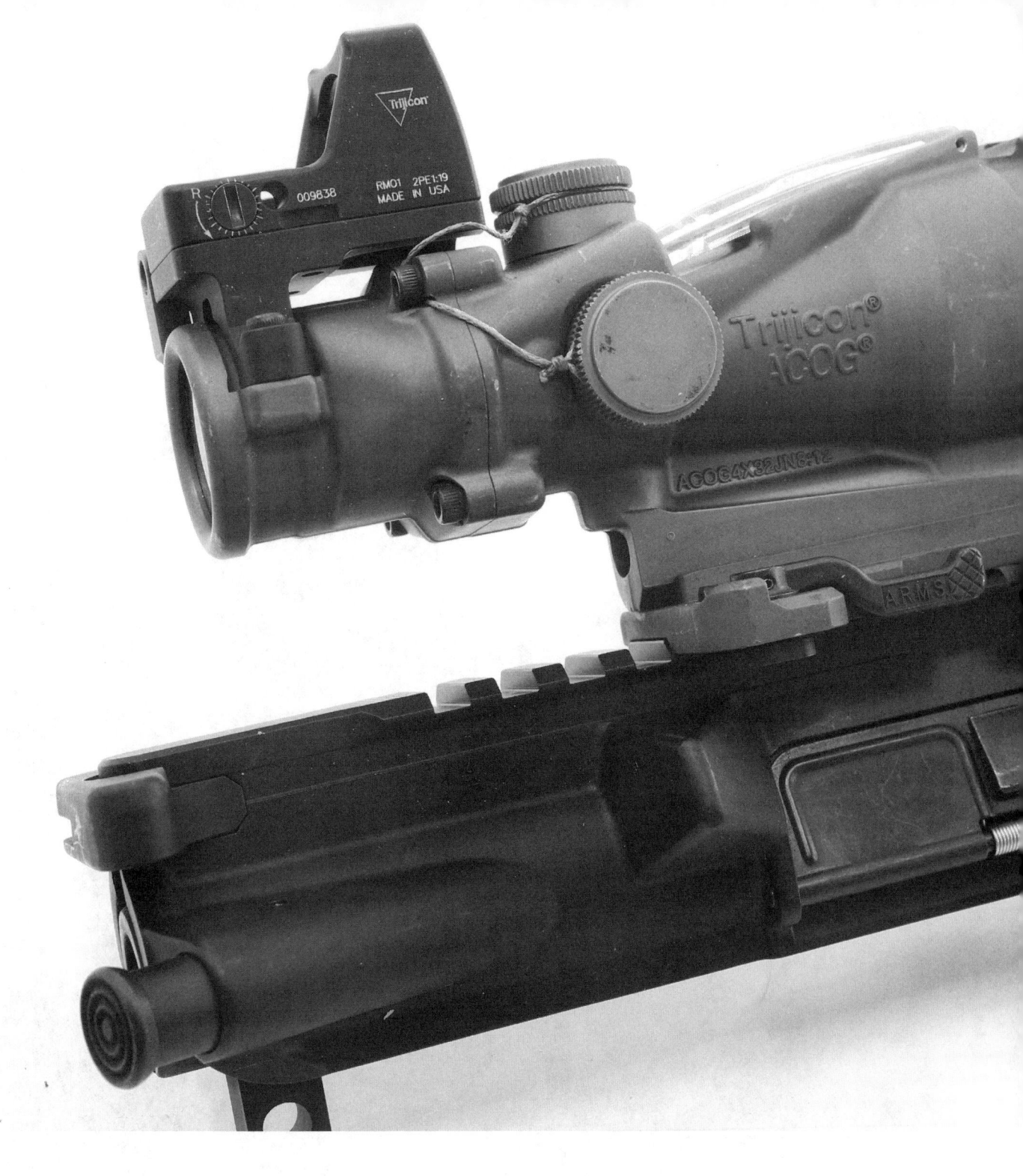

your eye off the centerline of the optical path. In fact, it moves at the parallax distance also. But at that range, the image and point of image move as seen through the scope. At other distances, the reticle moves, but the point of impact does not move as much. So, an aiming error happens. Errors are bad with rifle shooting.

Red-dot sights have some parallax error, but the amount is so tiny it doesn't really matter. What does matter is that if you can see the dot within the field

> **"Co-witnessing is an administrative process. You're cross-checking the validity of the two aiming systems against each other."**

of view of the optic, where that dot is when the trigger breaks is where the bullet hits. (Once you have it zeroed, and adjusting for trajectory, of course.)

We have two types of red-dot optics. The reflective type projects a small dot onto a lens or screen inside

Any optics you put on your rifle must clear the iron sights you install as a backup. Trijicon designed this ACOG to fit over any folding rear sight.

the optic, reflecting it toward you, which you see as an aiming point. The other is the holographic projection, made by EOTech. While they work differently, their external use as an aiming system is the same. Once zeroed, put the dot where you want the bullet to go, and press the trigger.

Mounting optics is easy. Red dots and scopes bolt directly to the top upper rail or fit onto a rail adapter. The adapter is needed simply because many of today's red-dot optics are so small that they would sit entirely below your line of sight without the riser or adapter. The red-dot optic must be raised up to the 2.6-inch line of sight of the iron sights.

To install, pick a spot on the upper not otherwise occupied by iron sights or other accessories, and clamp the dot and its adapter (if needed) in place. Don't place it too far to the rear, even if you aren't using iron sights. You want it forward of your face far enough that you can still benefit from binocular vision as your non-aiming eye looks around the red dot. You also don't want to put it so far forward that it bridges the gap onto your handguard rail. The minimal movement between the upper receiver rail and the handguard rail (even the best will wiggle a few ten-thousandths of an inch) is undesirable. Even the smallest amount will add aiming error to your point of aim/point of impact alignment. More significant movements can add stress to the red-dot or magnifying optic and cause malfunction or failure. A one-piece mount, bridging the gap, is less likely to have a problem but is still undesirable. If you need to move the optic forward past the joint between the upper and handguard, use a cantilever mount with a base that clamps solely to the upper but angles forward far enough to move the aiming device ahead.

Once mounted, use the same zero you would for irons or optics described at the end of this chapter.

Co-Witnessing Sights

You will quickly have someone ask you about co-witnessing sights; have you done it, can you tell them how to do it, what the heck is it?

Do the following with an empty rifle in a safe place. Mount your red-dot optic or iron sights. Zero them as described below. Take your irons (most likely BUIS) and stand them up. Turn on your red-dot optic. Dial it down in power, so it isn't blasting your eye with a glowing fireball. Now aim using the iron sights. Get a tight cheek weld as if you are shooting a group at the range. Once you are comfortable, look at the red dot. If everything is correct, the dot will be perched top dead center of your front sight post.

That is co-witnessing.

Co-witnessing is an administrative process. You're cross-checking the validity of the two aiming systems against each other. Let's say you co-witnessed your sights in the past. But now you take the rifle out of the gun safe and do a co-witness check, and the dot is no longer at the top dead center of your iron sights. Something is wrong. The red dot, the irons, or maybe both, have been jarred, banged, damaged or otherwise knocked off-zero. Which one? No way to tell, short of hammer marks or tire tracks. But at least you know one of them is wrong and can check next time you are at the range.

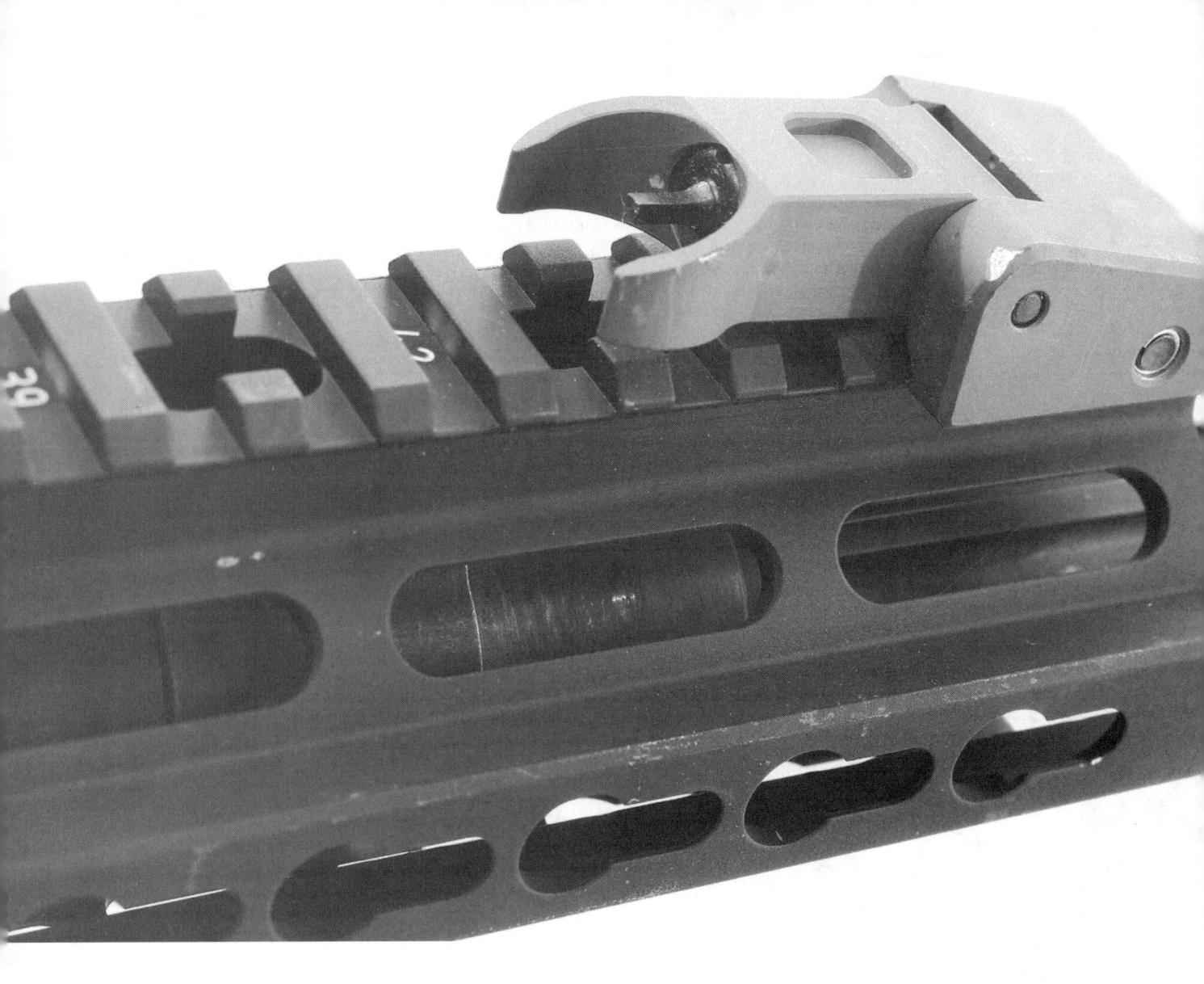

I have had students take inordinate amounts of time aiming, trying to check a zero, or otherwise shoot a drill, only to find out the reason for the excessive time is that they were trying to shoot while co-witnessing. When shooting, use one set of sights or the other. Irons or red dot — not both at the same time.

Co-witnessing can be done one of two ways: center or lower third. In center co-witnessing, the iron sights will be in the middle of the red-dot optic field of view when using the irons, and the dot is at the top dead center of the front sight post. In lower third co-witnessing, when you line up the iron sights to do the check, you will see them in the bottom third of the red-dot optic's field of view. Which is better? Neither! It is simply personal preference. Some shooters are distracted by seeing the iron sights above one-third of their red-dot field of view.

Magnifying Optics

Magnifying optics are what people typically think of when you say "riflescope." A riflescope is a tube (generally) with lenses in it. It features knobs at the mid-point to adjust the position of the aiming reticle and to adjust focus or to change the power of an illuminated reticle or dot. The primary descriptor of scopes will be something like "1-4x40." The first two digits are the power ratio. A 1x scope has no magnification. A scope described as 1-1x40 would be a 1- to 4-power scope. The last numeral is the width of the front opening, the

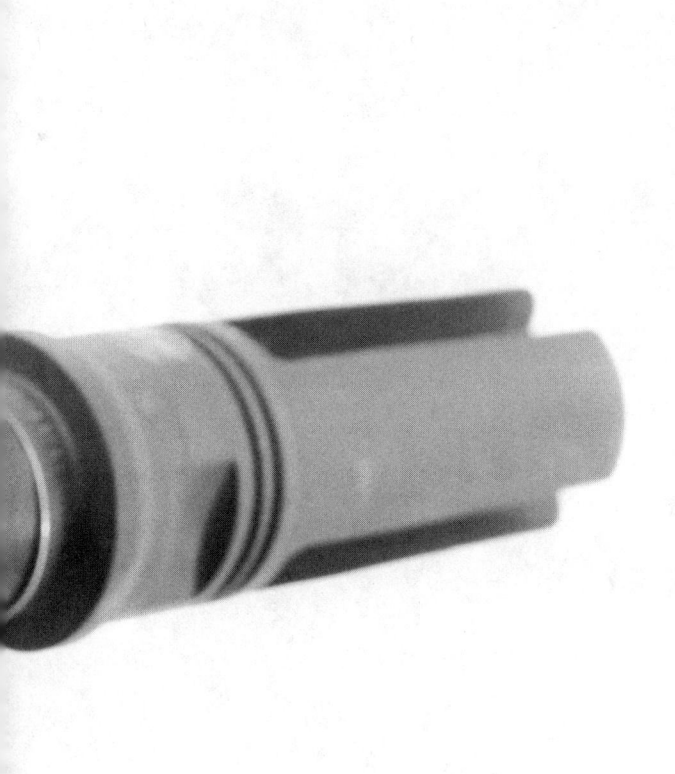

A folding front sight is ideal because you can move it out of your line of sight and still use your optics.

objective. The larger the objective lens, the more available light for your eye. But also, the greater weight, cost, and height the scope must be mounted to clear the barrel or handguard.

Scopes also have another numerical description like 1 inch, 30mm or 34mm. This dimension describes the diameter of the main scope tube. Again, the larger the number, the larger the tube and the more light transmission — but also greater weight, cost and mounting height. A larger tube is more valued by long-range shooters, as it affords them a wider adjustment range. More adjustment is good when "dialing up" to change the point of impact to correspond with the point of aim past 1,000 yards.

Each scope will have an optical detail known as eye relief. This value is the minimum and maximum distance your eye can be behind the scope and still aim. Ideally, you want to be as far back as possible and still see an entire field of view through the scope. Too far back, and all you see is a small image in the middle of a black donut in the scope lens. Too far forward, and you risk having the scope strike your face in recoil.

How far forward you mount the scope depends on your shooting style. I tend to "crawl" a stock; that is, I extend my neck and head forward more than most. As a result, I have my scopes mounted farther forward than many shooters. It isn't unusual for me to arrive at a gun writers' industry event, only to find the rifle scopes mounted so far back (probably someone short mounted them, and they "looked good" to them) that I can't shoot them until I adjust them to my style.

Magnifying optics require a mounting system for attachment to the rifle. I know of no scopes that come with a built-in AR mounting system, at least not the regular tube-based riflescopes. Mounts will come one of two ways: QD (quick detach) or not. The exemplar of the QD is the LaRue mount system, which uses a pair of throw levers built into the base (with the rings as part of the assembly) to clamp to the upper receiver. The throw levers make it possible to quickly remove a scope without tools if it fails, and you need to continue with iron sights.

The exemplar of the non-QD mount is from Geissele. Here, you use a wrench on a pair of bolts with half-inch hex heads to tighten and clamp the mount to the upper. Geissele machined its mount from an aluminum billet, and it is so stout it probably can't be damaged with a ball-peen hammer. It is also on your rifle until you can find a half-inch wrench to loosen the bolts.

Mounting a magnifying scope is more of a fuss than a red-dot optic, simply because the magnifying type requires more space. First, install the mount rings on the scope in front of and behind the adjustment knobs. Given your shooting style, the scope must be located on the upper receiver for proper eye relief. And it cannot bridge the gap between the upper receiver and handguard. As with the red-dot optic, having one part of the base on the upper and the other (worse if they are two separate rings on bases) on the handguard, the scope will be twisted and tweaked by the handguard movement. And there's always a few ten-thousandths of an inch movement.

CHAPTER 10 – SIGHTS

BUIS for the Optics

If you have a magnifying optic on your rifle, and the mount is a bolt-on like the Geissele, you have an interesting problem with backup sights. Unless you have a half-inch wrench in your pocket, there is no real-time way to transition from a broken magnifying optic to backups, either iron or red dot. A method that competition shooters first adopted is now the norm: mount a compact red-dot optic (like the ones used on pistols) on a short adapter rail that puts it at a 30- to 45-degree angle to the right. To use it, rotate the rifle on your shoulder, bringing the compact red-dot optic into your line of sight. There are also iron sights made for the same purpose.

Why there? The only other place to install backup irons or a red dot is on top of the magnifying optic. And that does two bad things: it places the red dot even farther away from the bore (and since the emergency is likely a close-distance one, the offset is now even more of a problem), and your face is farther from a solid cheek weld. That slows aiming.

So, angled and tipped it is.

Establishing a Zero

What is a "zero"? And why does it matter?

Your bullet travels on an arc. Your line of sight is straight. The bullet falls below the line of sight, moves up to or above it. It then drops back down to and past the line of sight.

The simple truth is the details matter only in some instances. And it matters pretty much only because the AR-15 design is to mitigate felt recoil and put the sights 2.6 inches above the center of the bore. On previous rifles, the sights were kept low to the bore. Let's take the classic '03 Springfield. The tip of the front sight is less than an inch above the bore's centerline. The bullet and the line of sight start out close to each other.

The problem arises because bullets don't travel in straight lines, unlike laser beams. Depending on the distance, your bullet can travel on an arc, called a *parabola*, that begins to look like a fly ball to center field. The difference between the line of sight and the arc of trajectory doesn't matter within a relatively close distance. Known as the point-blank range, this distance is where the bullet's arc stays within the line of sight, above and below, no more than the target size you wish to hit.

For example, we have a bore-to-sight distance of 2.6 inches. We want a sight setting (zero distance) that will allow the bullet to rise no more than 2.6 inches above the line of sight as it goes downrange, and we want to know the distance at which it drops back down to 2.6 inches below. That would be a "2.6-Inch PBR (point-blank range)." If your

■ The original CCO, Aimpoint's close combat optic red dot, improved marksmanship and combat results so dramatically that the military went almost overnight from "scopes are for snipers" to "we need a scope on everything, including machine guns."

target is a three-inch diameter steel plate, then you could count on a hit on the plate (trajectory alone being considered here) from the muzzle to the PBR.

Easy, right? Not really. Everything matters. What about velocity? More velocity means a flatter trajectory. Which bullet weight and ballistic coefficient (BC)? BC is the mathematical figure given to a bullet to describe how smoothly it moves through the air. The higher the number, the less it slows down as it travels downrange. (I know, you'd think you'd want a scale that reflects the action: high drag, high number, low drag, low number. Alas, that is not the case. So, a higher BC means a flatter trajectory.) But we can only get so much BC and velocity out of the .223/5.56 cartridge, so we're still left with calculating a trajectory.

CHAPTER 10 – SIGHTS 195

Complicating this is that we want to know the precise differences at close distances because those are the ones where it matters. Not to be too gruesome, but at seven or 10 yards, how much lower than your point of aim will the bullet strike the person you are defending yourself from?

So, zero matters.

> **"You do not zero a rifle while shooting offhand. Sit at the bench with a solid rest and shoot a three-shot group on your target at 25 yards."**

The traditional distances are 25, 50, and 100 yards or meters. The military distance is 25 yards (with some organizations using 36 meters, for reasons too involved to go into here). That's because, with a 25-meter zero, the bullet is back down to the point of aim at 250 meters. That means that if you hold your sights in an enemy soldier's belt buckle, you will get a disabling hit all the way to 400 meters without having to mentally calculate the distance involved.

In a practical shooting competition, trajectory matters. You may be shooting at small steel plates at 200 yards, and not knowing the trajectory can cause a miss even though your hold and trigger press is correct. Or, at closer distances, not knowing how much lower your bullet strikes than where you are aiming could cause you to hit a no-shoot target and incur the penalties.

The process is simple, but it is also exacting, and there is no easy way nor any shortcut. You simply must do the work. You will also find that the process takes most of a day on some ranges due to the procedural requirements. First, make sure you have the correct ammo, your sights are mechanically zeroed, the bore is clean, and you have a solid shooting position to work with. You do not zero a rifle while shooting offhand. Sit at the bench with a solid rest and shoot a three-shot group on your target at 25 yards. If you've done it correctly, you'll have three shots almost touching each other. If you don't have a nice 3-shot group, there is not much point in trying to establish a "zero." Mathematically, trying to find the center of a one- or two-inch group at 25 yards is a waste of time. That two-inch group (and I've seen worse) at 25 yards translates to a minimum group of eight inches at 100 yards. That's five shots, barely all on a sheet of typing paper at 100 yards, not exactly rifle-like performance.

Once you can post that cluster of three shots of less than an inch, it is decision time.

Do all the preliminary work at 25 yards, regardless of what zero distance you want in the end because 25 yards is close enough to shoot a tight group and close enough that walking back and forth won't take up the whole day.

The Three Trajectories

We'll do the 25-, 50- and 100-yard zeros and run the number out to 300 yards. Let's use a 55-grain FMJ (also known as the XM193 loading) with a velocity of 3,200 fps out of a 20-inch barreled rifle. Changing bullet weight/BC and velocity will change the absolute numbers, but not the relative ones.

Trajectories in Inches

You can see from the table below that the 25-yard zero keeps the bullet on an arc of travel above the line of sight for quite some distance, as it doesn't come back down to the line of sight until just before 400 yards. However, it is almost a foot above the line of sight at 250 yards from the muzzle. The 50- and 100-yard zeros have a noticeable drop once you reach 300 yards, but out to 250 yards, not enough to be a problem. So, do you need a relatively flat and not-far-from-line-of-sight trajectory to 200 or 250 yards, or do you need the ability to hit a large-ish target at 400 yards?

Trajectories in Inches

Zero distance	YARDS						
	25	50	100	150	200	250	300
25	0.0	+2.4	+6.4	+9.3	+10.9	+11.1	+9.5
50	-1.2	0.0	+1.6	+2.2	+1.4	-0.8	-4.7
100	-1.6	-0.8	0.0	-0.3	-1.8	-4.9	-9.6

50-Yard Zero, Trajectory in Inches

	YARDS	25	50	100	150	200	250	300
Velocity (fps)								
2,900		-1.2	0.0	+1.5	+1.7	+0.6	-2.1	-6.4
2,750		-1.2	0.0	+1.3	+1.3	-0.3	-3.6	-8.7
100	-1.6	-0.8	0.0	-0.3	-1.8	-4.9	-9.6	

A carbine has slightly different numbers, an SBR has others, and pistols more so. Change the bullet velocity or the ballistic coefficient, and you have different numbers as well. However, inside 100 yards, the trajectory differences won't be more than an inch or two for a given distance-zero. If you go from a load using a 55-grain FMJBT and its rock-like BC to a 77-grain open-tip match with a higher BC, the calculated trajectory at 100 yards won't change much. Just to check my recollection, I ran the numbers on a 77-grain OTM with a BC of .355, at a rifle velocity of 2,900 fps and a carbine velocity of 2,750 fps.

50-Yard Zero, Trajectory in Inches

From the table above, you can see that inside 200 yards, the trajectory difference for any of the three combinations is less than an inch. And at 250 yards, it is at a max of just 2.8 inches. If you can see a 2.8-inch difference at 250 yards with the naked eye, you need to be doing something other than building your own AR-15s for fun.

The Rest of the Work

OK, you've determined your zero range, thus trajectory. You've shot a three-shot cluster at 25 yards and adjusted it to the predetermined point. That is, with a 25-yard zero, precisely on the point of aim. For a 50-yard zero, 1.2 inches low, and for a 100-yard zero, 1.6 inches low. (Based on a 20-inch rifle and XM193 ammunition.) Now, you can set up a target at 100 yards and shoot again. You will likely find that you need to do a bit of fine-tuning at 100 yards, as your groups will require a click or two of additional adjustments to get them on zero. The reason is simple: measurement. A half-inch error in finding the center of your group at 25 yards becomes a two-inch error at 100 yards.

Sight Adjustments

Your optics — red dot or magnifying — have a specific rate of correction, and the literature with it will tell you. For example, "four clicks per inch" means four adjustment clicks on the dial of the scope equates to one inch of change at 100 yards. The iron sights will not; theirs depends on the distance between the front and rear or sight radius. A longer barrel places the front sight farther from the rear sight, so any change will end up being smaller at 100 yards.

An A1 front sight has five adjustment notches in its rim, while the A2 has four, which means the A2 has coarser adjustments. Adjust the front sight toward the group and the rear sight away. If you find your group is hitting too high, raise the front sight. If the group hits to the left, move the rear sight to the right. How much? Again, to keep things basic, I'll list the rifle iron sights and the carbine rifle sights at 100 yards:

Rifle:	A2 rear sight 0.5 in.	front sight 1.25
	A1 rear sight 0.4	front sight 1.0
Carbine:	A2 rear sight 0.75	front sight 1.5
	A1 rear sight 0.6	front sight 1.2

Sight Offset

Inside of 25 yards, all sight setups have a problem: the bullet strikes the target below the line of sight. This can be an issue in some situations, and it can only be handled with training and practice. *Remember that your bullet is rising to the line of sight.* If you have a 50- or 100-yard zero for your rifle or carbine, then the bullet will still be around an inch and a half low at 25 yards.

Without proper sights and knowledge of how they work, you might as well be pointing and shouting "BANG!" for all the good it does you. Plus, you will be subjected to a large amount of advice on sights, sighting systems, assembly and use, so you really need to have a grasp of the subject, or else you'll be whip-sawed by the varied opinions you'll get at the gun club.

11
Lowers

■ A billet-cut lower receiver from Wilson Combat. By machining uppers and lowers, the manufacturer can add reinforcements where they wish, like on this magazine well.

The lower receiver or "lower" is where all the action is, legally speaking. When Congress passed the Gun Control Act of 1968, all firearms were required by federal law to apply a unique serial number. (No, seriously. Before that, there was no federal requirement for a serial number.) They also had to have the manufacturer's name on the firearm as well.

The designation of what gets the number, for most firearms, is straightforward. Your bolt-action Mauser, for instance, will have the receiver marked. However, a rifle like the FN SCAR will have the upper receiver of the pair numbered, and the lower is just a part among others. Colt adopted the Armalite method, which numbered the lower, and 60+ years later, here we are.

The lower does a slew of tasks, and it does them without excess metal or weight. It has two cross-pins held in by spring-loaded plungers that hold the upper in place. The lower holds the firing mechanism, hammer, trigger, selector and disconnector. It has a tab to which you attach the pistol grip. It holds the magazines and has the mag attachment parts as well. The bolt hold-open catch is on the far side of the standard AR lower; it locks the bolt back when you've fired the last round. And finally, on the lower's rear is a threaded loop, into which the buffer tube is screwed and the stock assembly installed.

Material and Manufacture

Like the upper, the lower is made of 7075-T6 aluminum and was traditionally produced from forgings. It is also now common to find billet-made lowers on the market. The billet lowers are the same as those forged in function and assembly, with a tiny difference. You could pivot the triggerguard on the original downward for use in cold weather when wearing mittens. It's not uncommon for a billet-made lower to have the triggerguard re-shaped, machined as an integral part of the lower, and not hinged. Otherwise, forged or billet, it's the same other than appearance.

There was a time when manufacturers were experimenting with polymer lowers for the AR-15. Everyone found out that the high-stress areas of

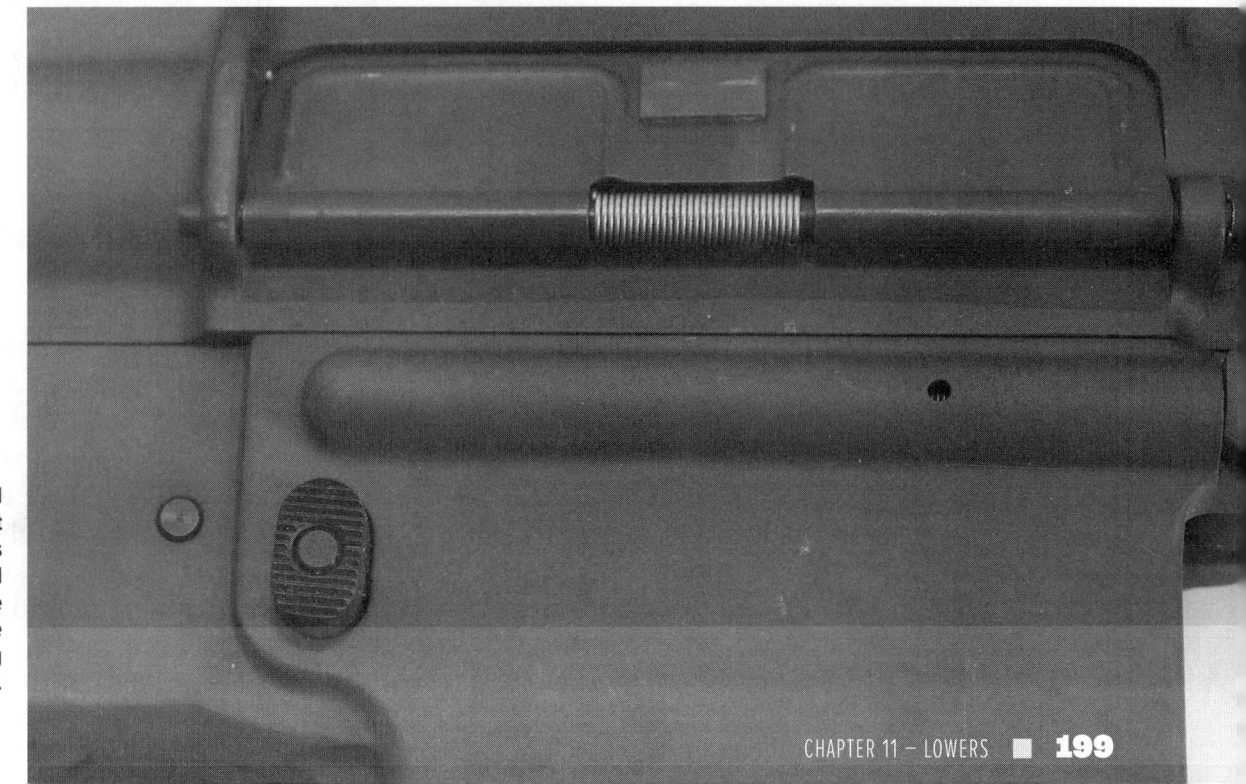

■ A lower forging, ready to begin the machining process needed to make it into a firearm.

■ The original lowers didn't have fences. This one, a transitional clone, only has the upper fence for the takedown spring and plunger.

■ A lower parts kit contains all the parts to assemble the lower, but not any hammer/trigger components. That means takedown parts, bolt hold-open and magazine catch.

the lower and upper were strong enough for the task when the parts were made from aluminum but not polymer. Some lowers were produced with metal inserts held in the molding to strengthen those parts, but the general result was: stick with aluminum.

Like the upper, the lowers are forged, then the platter blanked. Once that's done, the external finish texture of the lower is applied. Yes, the pebbly texture is part of the forged die surface, and the ridges you see on some lower parts are where the rest of the platter was clipped off, the seam, if you will, left over after production.

Then the manufacturer drills and broaches the magazine well. The first step is to drill an access hole where the magazine well will be located. Next, the machine operator places the lower into a fixture and guides the broach through the hole. The broach is a four- or five-foot-long steel bar that looks like King Kong's nail file. Each set of teeth on the broach is slightly larger than the one before, with the last set of teeth sized and shaped to the final magazine well dimension. The hydraulic system, with lots of lubricant being pumped in, pulls the broach through the lower. That happens once, and it's done.

Another way to form the mag well is with a wire EDM. Here, a wire is threaded through the hole. The system pumps an electrical charge into the wire and across to the lower. The spark jumping the gap erodes the aluminum, but only by a few thousandths of an inch. The EDM machine operator directs the wire through the lower forging, eroding a cut path like a wire cheese cutter.

While the process used to make the magazine well doesn't much matter, its size does. A tight mag well will be picky about which magazines it accepts. A loose magazine well can cause feeding problems if the mag is wobbling around as the bolt

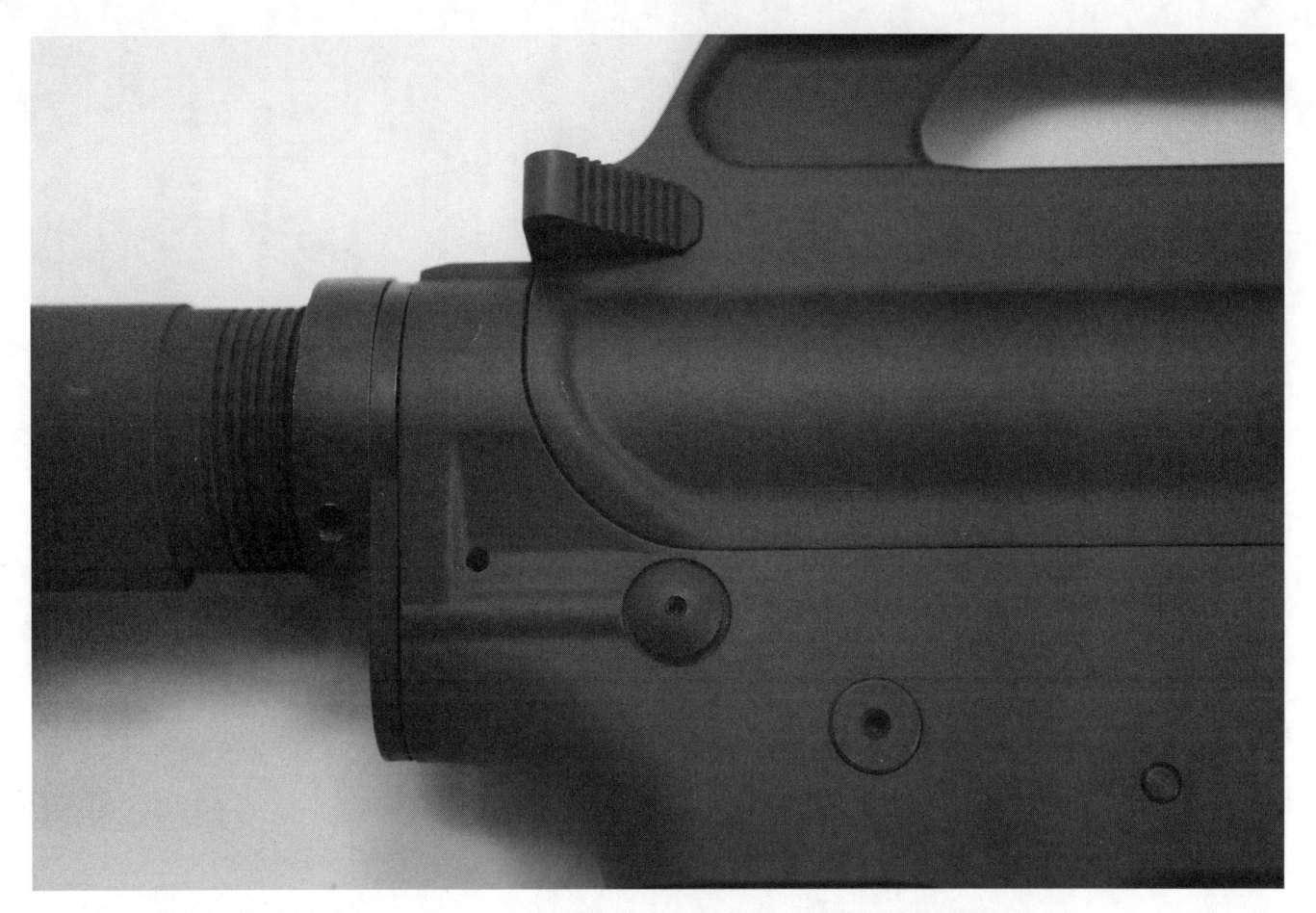

■ To build a retro AR, you'll have to source an A1 lower like this, which lacks the reinforcement added to the A2 lower.

■ The A2 lower has a reinforcement of extra aluminum in the forging around the buffer tube hoop.

CHAPTER 11 – LOWERS   **201**

■ The takedown pins each come with a spring and plunger.

tries to strip off a cartridge. Ideally, every lower would work with every magazine, but life isn't like that. If you find your lower is picky, then you'll have to get picky. If it hates "XYZ" magazines, it doesn't matter what kind of bargain you can get on them. Stick with what it likes or replace the lower.

You can often tell which system was used in your lower. Peer down the mag well in good light and see the direction of the tooling marks. If they are up and down, then it was broached. If they are around the inside, wire EDM. Both systems work. It is simply a matter of what kind of machine setup the manufacture uses.

The final step in making a lower is a CNC operator mills the trigger mechanism pocket and the trigger slot through the lower's bottom. The pivot holes are drilled, and the magazine catch pocket is drilled and milled, along with the bolt hold-open slot.

■ The front takedown pin has a flat on the head.

■ This lower was machined from a billet. The surface finish and the lines of the fences tell you that. It only takes a few looks at forged and billet lowers side-by-side to learn how to spot them.

Finish

Once fully machined, the lower receiver is anodized. Anodizing is an electro-chemical process that creates a hardened surface on aluminum. The process also causes the part to "grow" or expand by a known amount. That amount is built-in to the manufacturing process, so the result meets specs. However, you may run into a lower with pivot holes that are out of tolerance. In addition, anodizing decreases hole diameter and tightens them. You'll have to live with that. Over time, wear will loosen the fit. But opening them up now risks making them too loose in the future.

As a reminder of what we discussed earlier, the mil-spec process is known as Type III Hard Anodizing. There are also Type II and Type I, but these do not produce as hard and durable a surface. As I mentioned earlier, there's a catch: anodizing doesn't change the color. Anodized aluminum is as bright as non-anodized aluminum. The color you see is due to dye added at the end of the process.

■ The assembly tool has a hole in one end. Insert this end through the hoops from the left.

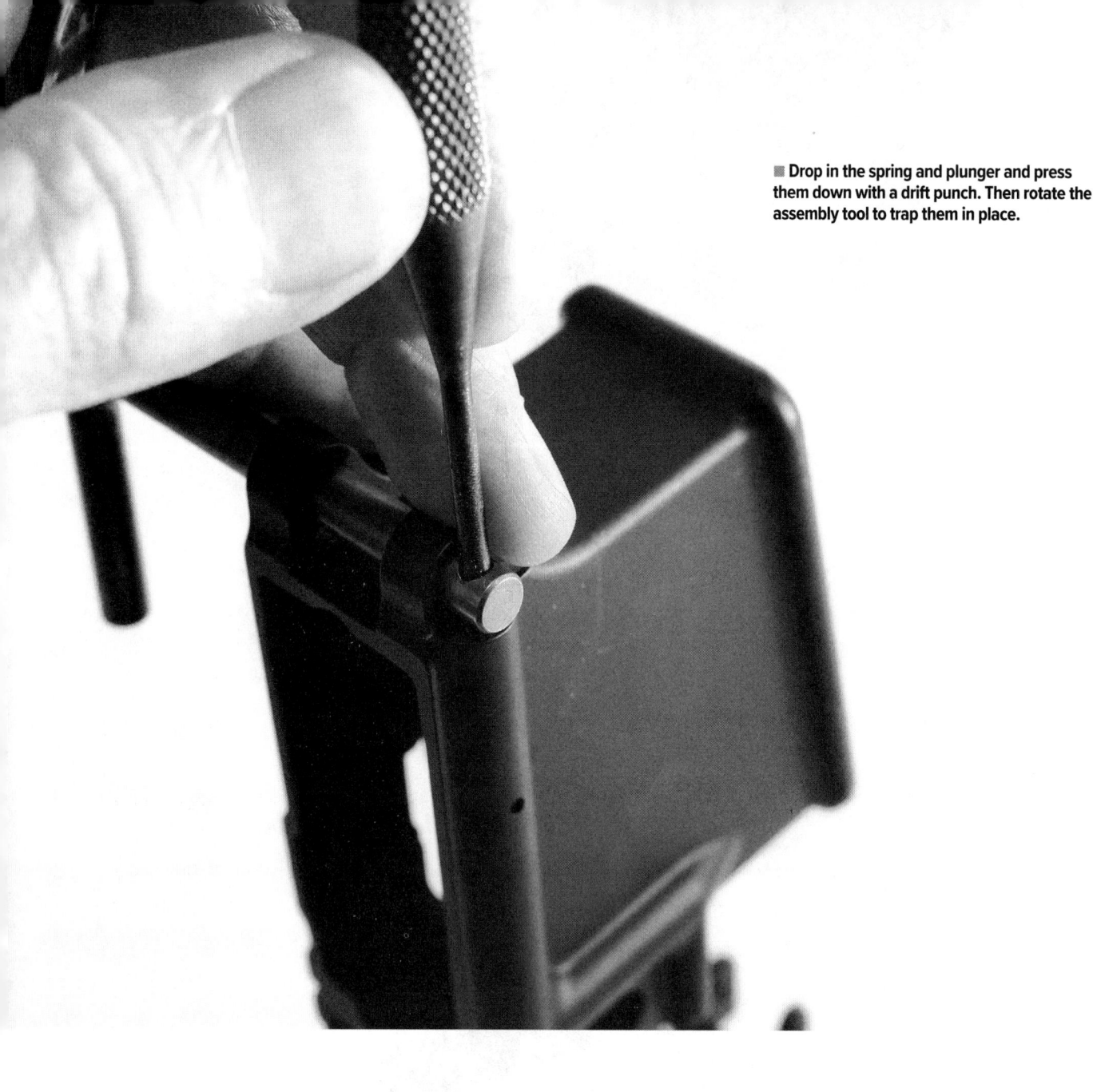

■ Drop in the spring and plunger and press them down with a drift punch. Then rotate the assembly tool to trap them in place.

Type III will only accept black dye. If you want a color anodized, you have to go with Type II. Does it matter? Not really, unless you are expecting the most arduous conditions, in which case you had better have eaten your Wheaties because the AR is going to do better than you regardless of which type of anodizing you have.

Most of what you will see will be Type III. It's what most shops are set up to do, and it's what most buyers expect to buy.

Retro builders will look for one detail: the earliest ARs didn't have a jet black finish. They were finished in (depending on era) medium or dark gray. Achieving that gray isn't always easy, as it has to come that way from the start. You can't "fade" a black finish.

Types

The more minor details vary across a wide range. You can have a mil-spec mag well opening, for instance, or you can have a wide flare for competition. The front of the magazine well can be checkered, grooved or otherwise machined for a non-slip grip. But the only real difference is between the "A1" and the "A2/M4" receivers. The one big difference they have is an extra amount of aluminum at the rear to reinforce the buffer loop. A1s don't have this; later ones do. Retro builders will argue that the radius on the front takedown pin boss is also a change, and it is, but it isn't much of one.

Some people building retro guns pay attention

to the "fence," the raised rib around the magazine release button and across the top of the lower, where the front takedown spring and plunger are installed. The very first AR-15s didn't have this fence. In a couple of rapid modifications, it gained a partial and then a complete fence. If you're building something historically accurate from Summer 1966, you need to know which fence configuration is correct. Otherwise, you'll be buying an A2/M4 lower.

There is one other consideration, courtesy of Colt. Back in the old days, when the idea of "gun control of assault weapons" was still not really a thing, Colt didn't want people putting stolen M16 uppers onto AR-15 lowers, so it changed the front takedown pin. Colt also changed the forging dies — instead of the .250-inch diameter captured pin, it made the front pin .312-inch diameter. The pin also had two screw heads, so you needed two screwdrivers to unscrew the threaded-together pin assembly. Yes, stupid. Colt stuck with that for a couple decades. If you run across one, you will find that there are few, if any, aftermarket uppers that will fit it. If someone offers you a Colt lower made this way (the hoops are larger, and there is no drilled hole for the plunger and spring in the fence), pass on it unless it comes with a matching Colt upper.

And if you have a complete rifle from Colt from this era, you can do pretty much anything else, but you can't swap uppers and lowers with others.

A rarity (not that these are collectibles) is a Colt transitional model. These used slot-headed screws, but they were .250-inch diameter, and the fence wasn't drilled for the plunger. If you could find some way to drill the plunger hole (not an easy task), you could rebuild one to a press-pin takedown. But if not, pass on it, too.

Only Colt did this. If we take as a first-guess estimate the number of AR-15 lowers ever made at ten million, there are less than a million Colt big-head receiver sets produced — probably closer to half a million. You will not run into one of these very often.

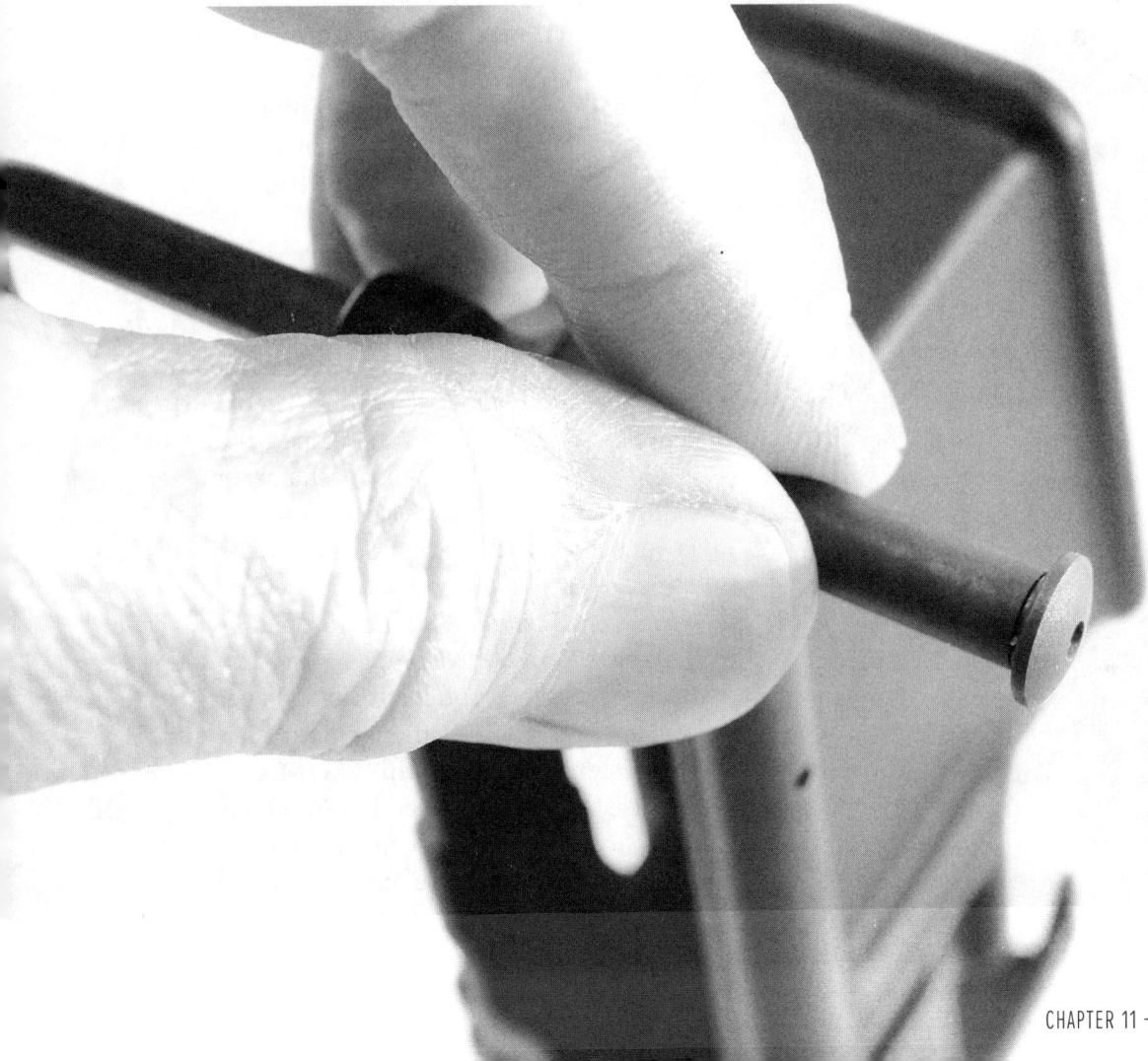

■ Now, pinch down with two fingers to keep things in place as you use the front takedown pin to push the assembly tool out of the way.

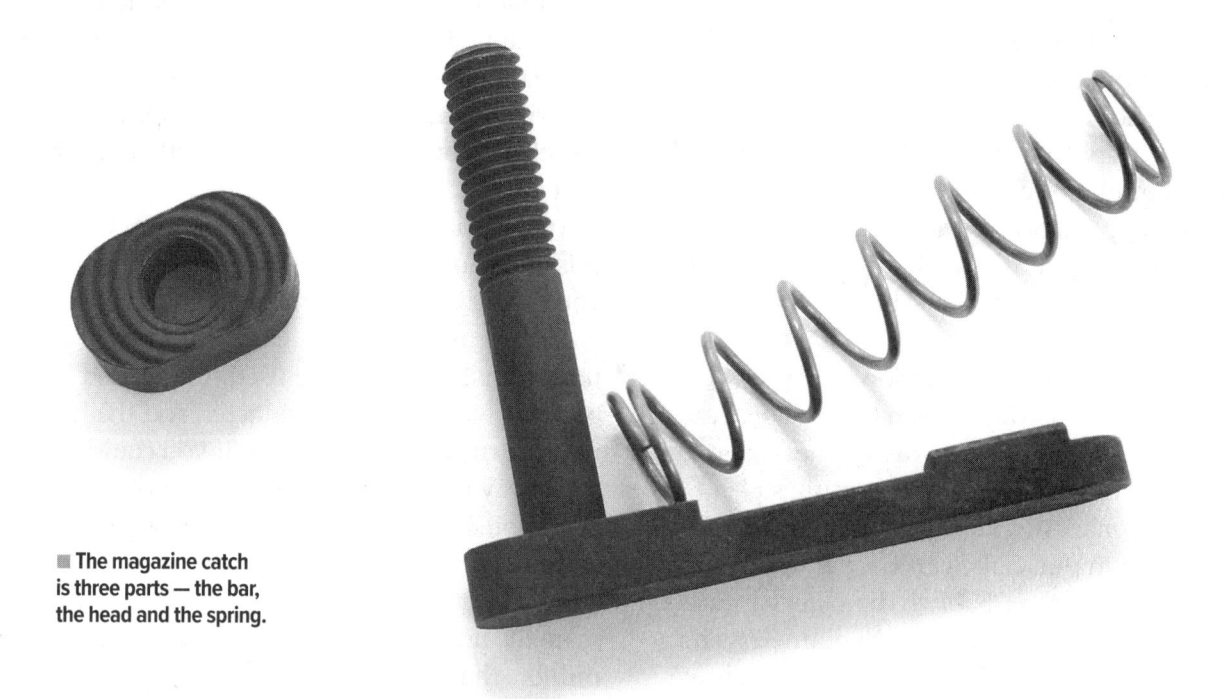

■ The magazine catch is three parts — the bar, the head and the spring.

■ Insert the bar from the left, threaded end first.

Another Acronym

You'll see parts kits listed as "LPK" or "lower parts kits." Do not be confused. These kits contain the parts needed to assemble the lower; they don't include the fire control parts (though they do include the safety) or the buffer tube, spring, buffer and stock. To fully assemble a lower, you need an LPK, a stock assembly kit and a trigger kit.

Lower Assembly

In covering assembly, I'll go over the lower-specific aspects. However, some steps, like the buffer tube and stock assembly, I'll cover in their own chapters, and here we'll assume you have done that part already. As I've mentioned before, the AR-15 is so interrelated that each part or assembly depends on something else. Let's start with a bare lower, just pulled out of the box as we did with the upper.

First, check the fit with your upper. If you have just the one and only complete parts kit, then "the upper" is the one you have. If you have a selection of them to work with, then you can check the fit and assign an upper to this lower that fits best. You can use the un-assembled takedown pins or install them and check fit. (Of course, if you install them and the upper doesn't fit, and you find out that the lower is the problem, you'll have to uninstall them to make a return. So, check first.)

Put the upper's front onto the lower to check fit, and press the takedown pin across. The front pin is flat on the edge, unlike the rear, which is a full-diameter circle. The pin should slide smoothly through the lower and upper hoops, and the upper should hinge smoothly on the pin once the pin is across. Now hinge the upper down to fit the lower and press the rear pin across. It, too, should slide smoothly across. The fit is incorrect if it requires force or the upper wobbles loosely once the pin is installed. A bit of friction is OK, especially since the parts will wear into each other once you use it a bit. But if it's so tight that it requires a hammer, that's bad. Wobbling like it will fall off is likewise not good.

Why the fit check? As mentioned in the upper chapter, Colt (and the government) owns the dimensions. Other manufacturers cannot simply "look at the blueprints" and ensure their parts are within tolerance. As a result, other makers of uppers and lowers have had to tweak their dimensions to make sure they are as compatible with Colt and everyone else as possible. If you have upper maker "A" and lower maker "Z," they might have settled on dimensional standards that are just different enough that they won't fit each other. But

> **"If your upper and lower don't fit, you can't make them fit. If the receivers came as a pair from the supplier, get on the phone or email them, let them know, and work out an exchange."**

both will fit with a Colt.

Welcome to the 21st century of the AR-15.

If your upper and lower don't fit, you can't make them fit. If the receivers came as a pair from the supplier, get on the phone or email them, let them know, and work out an exchange. If you bought them from different suppliers, all I can tell you is phone or email, and see what they can do. I repeat: *You can't make them fit.* Anything you do to remove

■ Drop the spring in from the right side.

■ Thread the head onto the bar with the grooved side of the head facing out.

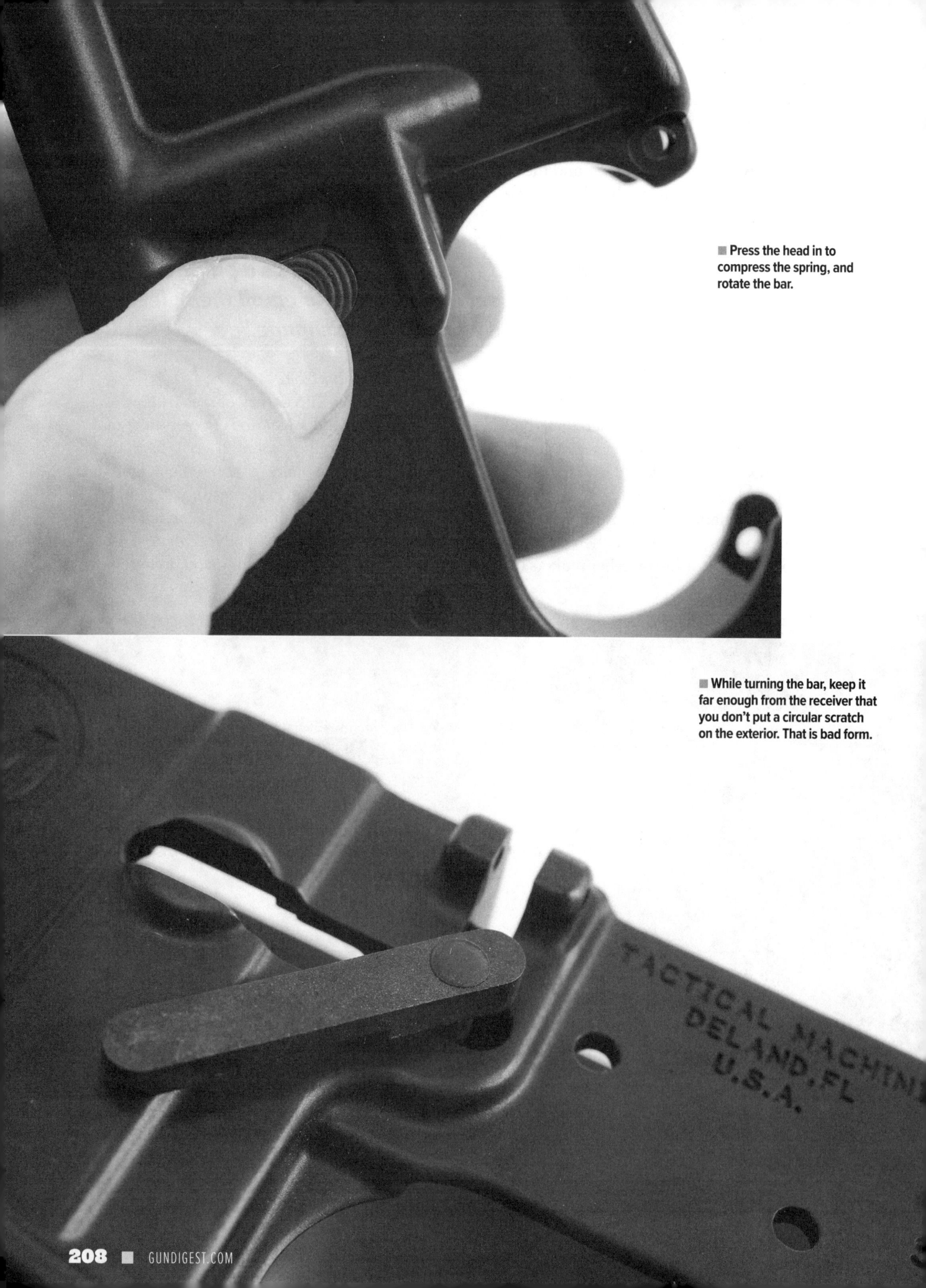

■ Press the head in to compress the spring, and rotate the bar.

■ While turning the bar, keep it far enough from the receiver that you don't put a circular scratch on the exterior. That is bad form.

metal removes anodizing, exposing soft aluminum. That is bad.

We'll assume things fit, or they fit now that you've made the calls and exchanged the parts.

Front Takedown Pin

The front takedown pin is flat on its head and has a thicker head than the rear pin. You'll need the assembly tool, which looks like a bent rod, a takedown pin spring and plunger, the takedown pin and a drift punch sized to fit the assembly pin.

You can do this to an otherwise bare lower, standing it on a bench, but it is easier if you clamp it in a padded vise. It's easier still if the buffer assembly is already installed, and you can clamp that part in a padded vise. All directions will be for a right-handed installer, with the receiver pointed straight up and the opening for the hammer and trigger facing toward the installer.

First, the installation tool. This tool is a simple bent steel rod with a hole drilled through it at one end. Take the tool in your left hand and insert the end with the hole from the left side. Press it through both hoops of the lower, until the hole in the tool lines up with the hole in the lower you see on the right-side "fence."

Push the spring through and into the hole in the fence using the installation tool. Follow that with the plunger. The plunger is none "ended," that is, it doesn't have an up or down, in or out. Either way works. Now, while holding the end of the installation tool with your left hand, use the drift punch. Press it down the hole to compress the plunger and spring until flush with the fence surface. Rotate the installation tool (and the drift punch) to trap the plunger and spring in the hole. Lift the drift punch out. You can shift the installation tool slightly so its hole will no longer align with the plunger and let go of things. If you don't, the tool's leg can swing back down, lining up the hole and popping the plunger out.

Note the takedown pin channel machined into the shaft. The plunger will ride in this channel, and it also retains the takedown pin when you take the rifle apart. You'll want to align this channel at the bottom with the plunger resting in the fence.

Most instructions (not mine) at this point all cheerfully tell you to use the takedown pin to push the tool out of the way and install the pin. They lie. If you try that, the spring-loaded plunger will push the pin out of alignment, you'll miss the hoop, and the now released plunger will hurl itself across the room, never to be seen again.

Instead, use the tips of your left thumb and forefinger to pinch and press down on the end of the

■ When the bar's top is flush with the grooved face of the button, or head, you are done.

installation tool where the plunger rides. As you push the pin across to move the tool out of the way, use your fingertips to keep the pin aligned with the tool. Resist the force of the plunger and spring to push things out of alignment. Also, if you grasp the takedown pin properly, you can use the pin as a lever to resist the escaping force of the plunger.

This all sounds terribly involved, delicate and maddening. But once you get a feel for things, it is a simple skill and one you'll retain for quite some time.

And in a "walked through the snow to school" historical point, before there were installation tools, we had to use the end of the takedown pin itself to compress the plunger into the fence. I must have launched half a dozen plungers while learning that skill. They are probably still in that building, someplace, even though I haven't been there for 20+ years, and it has since been several other things besides a gun shop.

Once installed, the takedown pin is retained by the plunger, which rides in the groove. It should slide in and out relatively easily and be held in place, open or closed, by small detents drilled into the endpoints of the groove.

The rear takedown pin is held in by the stock assembly retaining plate on the back end. This process is covered in detail in the stock installation chapter. Briefly, you do this one in reverse of the front installation: Put the takedown pin in the receiver, push the plunger into the hole from the receiver's back and follow with the spring. Then the retaining plate holds them in place.

Once installed, there is no need to remove the takedown pins or the plunger and spring from the receiver. They don't come out for cleaning, service or anything else except replacement should they become damaged. How do you damage a takedown pin? When I see one, I'll be able to tell you.

Magazine Catch

The magazine catch is perhaps the simplest parts set on the AR-15 and maybe any firearm. There's the L-shaped catch, the button and the spring. To install, you would be well-served to have a second button on hand. Not because you might lose one, but because it makes the leverage easier. You can do this with the receiver still clamped in place for the front takedown pin installation.

Place the catch spring into the tunnel on the right side of the receiver. Take the magazine button, and with the grooved side to the right, press it into the hole, compressing the spring. Now take the second one and do the same thing. You'll have to work to do this. Now, pick up the mag catch with your left hand and insert the threaded end

■ When installing the trigger-guard, pay attention to how fragile the tabs are when installing the roll pin. Give them plenty of support, with a backer board or fixture, because if you break them, there is no fixing them.

■ The roll pin goes into the rear of the triggerguard opening, and the locking plunger goes on the right side.

■ When properly installed, the triggerguard can be unclipped and folded down, so you can use mittens to shoot your AR-15 in the arctic cold.

CHAPTER 11 – LOWERS

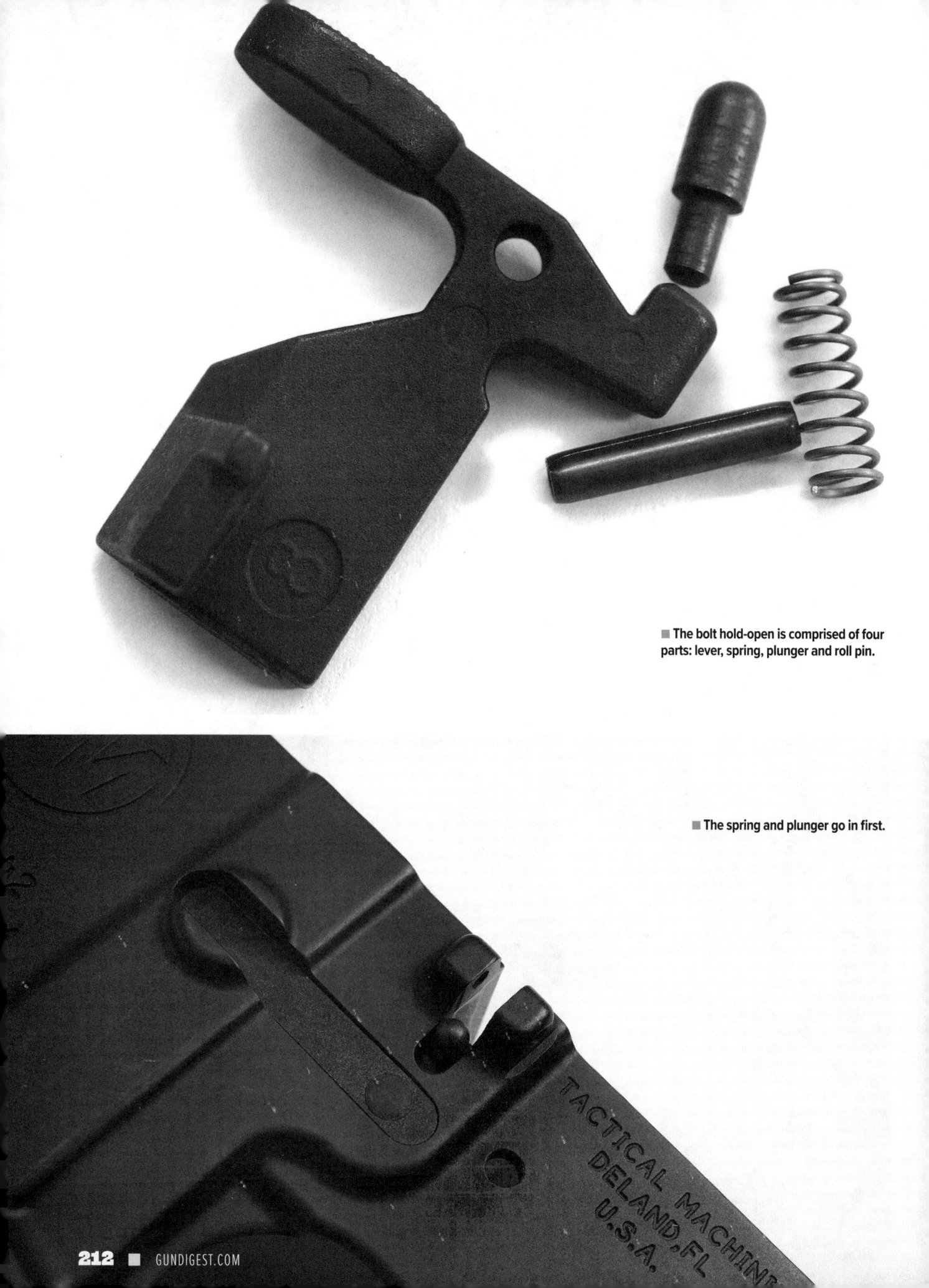

■ The bolt hold-open is comprised of four parts: lever, spring, plunger and roll pin.

■ The spring and plunger go in first.

into the left side of the receiver. You'll feel the end of it bump the mag button. Rotate the mag catch until it catches the button's threads. At this point, you can take a break. When you ease up on the button stack, the mag catch will pull to the receiver and bump against it. You'll have to press the stack again to continue rotating.

Now it's simply a "turn and check" process. Turn the mag catch bar until it aligns with the milled recess and ease the catch into place. Lift the extra button off the mag catch and look at the end of the mag catch's threaded shaft and the surface of the mag button. You want the end of the shaft to be flush or a turn below flush. If your fingertip is small enough, you can simply push the button in and turn the mag catch one way or the other to make it flush, checking on each turn. Once it's flush and the mag catch bar sits in the groove, you're done.

There are no magazine catch adjustments. Mag catch engagement to the magazine is determined by the catch shelf size and the receiver's machined groove. Rotating the mag catch until it's above flush doesn't increase spring tension (at least, not in any significant way) and just makes it uncomfortable to press the button to drop a mag.

So, let's say your rifle doesn't hold magazines in place. At odd moments, or when you really need them, a magazine will fall of its own accord. You likely have a badly machined or poorly stamped/blanked mag catch, and the only solution is to replace it. This means pressing the button (with the extra button) until the catch is high enough out of the far side to unscrew it and screwing in its replacement. That's it. There is no extra spring tension, no deeper seating, it is all built-in, and replacement is the only option.

Triggerguard

If you have a standard lower, then you need to install a triggerguard. The traditional one is hinged at the rear and has a plunger to keep it attached at the front. The idea was to use the tip of a bullet to press the plunger and hinge the triggerguard down so that you could wear mittens and still shoot the rifle in arctic-cold weather. This feature is not such a big deal for most of us, and it is not unusual to find shooters who have built theirs with a non-hinging triggerguard pinned at both ends.

Even so, we'll cover the traditional hinged style as it is the most difficult and delicate (the other styles are similar only with an extra pin).

The first thing to know: the tabs that the trigger-

■ Then press the bolt hold-open lever in place. You can use tape or a clamp to hold it while you get the roll pin started.

guard is pinned into are delicate. You can easily break them off if you aren't careful. Repairing them is nearly impossible. I suggest using a backing block or fixture to support the receiver and tabs when doing this. You'll need the triggerguard, the roll pin for the triggerguard, a hammer, punch and backing block. A pair of needle-nose pliers or the Real Avid pin holder is handy at this point.

Place the lower on the backing block or assembly fixture so the tabs are supported, and the lower is lying on the left side. Hold the pin in your pliers or Real Avid holder. Use a hammer to tap it into place on one side of the tab but stop before it begins to interfere with the triggerguard. The pin will now sit in place without having to be held. Slide the triggerguard into the tab, with the spring-loaded side of the guard to the front, spring-loaded up, or to the receiver's right. Gently tap the pin down, holding the triggerguard in place. You'll feel it when the pin bumps into the triggerguard. Now move the triggerguard until the hole in the guard lines up with the pin. You'll feel it loosen and align.

I should mention that, in a factory assembly process, the fixture for all this holds the lower and the triggerguard perfectly aligned, and the assembler simply whacks the pin into place. However, you won't have such a fixture and will have to do it by feel. The good news is, you aren't "on the clock" and don't have to get X number of lowers assembled during your shift or get words from the boss. If this takes a minute or two, no big deal.

Drive the pin flush with the tab. The triggerguard should pivot up and down. To lock it in place, hinge it up, press the spring-loaded button flush, and finish swinging the guard upward. To lower it, use some-

■ **The Roll Pin Wizard is like a third hand to keep your roll pin punch aligned while you drive the roll pin in place.**

thing to push the plunger down, and swing the guard down to the pistol grip.

If you're installing a non-hinged triggerguard, the process is similar: start the pin, insert the guard, tap to bind, find the alignment, set up and drive the pin flush. Finally, line up the other pin and drive it in as well.

Bolt Hold-Open

The bolt hold-open can be a real hassle. Unlike the triggerguard, where the pin goes in perpendicular to the receiver side, the bolt hold-open pin goes into its tabs parallel to the receiver side. You will also have the extra work of keeping the bolt hold-open in position while its spring and plunger try to push the lever out of alignment with the pin.

You have four parts here: the bolt catch, plunger, spring and pin that holds them all in the lower receiver. You'll need some special tools. It is possible

> "... the tabs that the triggerguard is pinned into are delicate. You can easily break them off if you aren't careful. Repairing them is nearly impossible."

to install the catch with an extra-long drift punch, hammer and needle-nose pliers, but having done this a bunch of times before special tools came along, I can't recommend it. You'll need an extra-long roll-pin starter punch. This tool is a punch with the end drilled open to the size of the roll pin. It holds the pin and is used to get things started.

You'll also need a way to hold the receiver while vertical with the buttstock up. This can be a set of magazine well blocks or a lot of padding in a vise and a mag well filler. I've done it in a pinch by standing the receiver on the bench with bags of shotgun shot. Fifty pounds of lead shot in a canvas bag works wonders, but that isn't something found under every workbench.

Set the receiver up in your holding system. Place the spring in the recess, followed by the plunger, and hold the bolt stop in place. A small piece of masking tape over the assembly will help keep them in place against the vagaries of gravity. While you're at it, place a strip of tape along the side of the receiver in line with the pin hole back to the buffer tube hoop. If everything works properly, you won't need it, but if there's an "oops," it can prevent marring the side of your receiver.

Push the roll pin into the end of the starter punch. Place the pin tip into the hole in the tab and tap it down until it stops. Not hard, just nudging. Wiggle the starter punch off the pin. The pin stopped because the hole in the bolt stop wasn't aligned. So, grab the bolt stop and move it around until you feel it come free of the binding from the pin and line up, just as you had with the triggerguard.

Some more tape can work wonders here, keeping the stop in place while you tap the pin into the hole. Once it passes through, drive the pin until just slightly higher than flush. It should be "proud" on both sides — sticking up a bit on each side. You may find that the pin and lower combine to be slightly more than proud or flush on both sides. Simply put, you want it equal on both sides.

Peel the tape off; you are done installing. To test it, push a magazine up into the receiver. If the magazine follower pushes the bolt stop up, great. If the stop pivots back down when you remove the magazine, you are done for now.

Pistol Grip

The pistol grip, besides being an inducement to evil behavior in California (other states don't see it as the Devil's Lure, I wonder what makes California residents so susceptible to the inducements of Beelzebub?), gives you a place to hold on while firing. The pistol grip also holds the selector lever detent and detent spring. When installing (or replacing) the pistol grip, installing the spring and detent properly is essential.

The pistol grip slides onto a machined tab on the lower. That tab is threaded for a standard machine screw. The screw is a standard thread, but it can be had in either a slotted head or two different Allen-head socket heads. (Yes, we see all three in classes, and it's annoying to have three tools for something as simple as a pistol grip screw.)

The screw has a "star" washer stamped with spikes or serrations on its edges to enhance friction. That's needed because the screw head, simply tightening up against the plastic of the pistol grip, can't be counted on to stay tight. The star washer keeps it in place.

When installing, the impulse for most people is to press the pistol grip all the way onto the lower and then spend an inordinate amount of time fishing around with the screw to find the hole, catch the threads, and not cross-thread the lower.

The lower is aluminum, the screw is steel, and the force you can generate is substantial. It's easy to get the screw at an angle and still force it in for a few threads, cross-threading and making a mess.

Instead, place the lower upside down on the bench. Put the selector in place with the lever in between the two stop bumpers on the exterior. Drop the selector detent into the hole. The selector detent differs from the other detents you have on the AR-15 in that it has a small rim or head. It looks like a short, fat nail. Wrap a small triangle of masking tape around one end of the detent spring.

You don't need much tape, just enough to keep the spring from falling out of the pistol grip. Insert the spring into the pistol grip, masking tape end first. Check to ensure it doesn't fall out.

Hold the pistol grip and slide the screw with its washer into the pistol grip opening, sliding it to the bottom. You can now use the screwdriver to guide the screw to the hole in the pistol grip and let gravity drop it into place. Now, start the pistol grip onto the edge of the lower tab, but only barely. Let the pistol grip act as a guide to hold the screw at the proper angle, and gently turn the screw until you feel it cleanly catch the receiver threads.

Here's a tip for starting the threads properly: Once you have the screw in position and at the correct angle, rotate it backward (counter-clockwise aka "lefty-loosey"). As the last thread of the screw and the first thread of the receiver bear against each other, the screw will turn normally. Once the ends of each thread reach each other, you will feel a little "click" as it drops from one thread edge down to the lower one. That means you now have the thread starts lined up. Turn the correct direction (clockwise aka "righty-tighty").

While making sure the detent spring lines up with and enters the detent hole in the receiver, press the pistol grip all the way to its seated position. Tighten the screw, and you are done. The selector has two detent stops and a groove between them, machined into the shaft. The way to check is to flip the selector between the Safe and Fire positions. It should move with some but not excessive force and click smartly into place at each position.

If you're swapping the standard pistol grip for some other design, unload, separate the two receivers, and stand the lower upside down on the bench. Unscrew the old pistol grip and repeat the above process with the new one. Yes, you can reuse the old screw and star washer or the new one. Same with the detent and spring. Depending on how hard you've used your rifle and how rough the bearing surfaces were on the selector, you may find the pointed end of the detent a bit worn. You can replace it if you wish. Slight wear is not a big deal if the selector clicks positively into place at each setting. If mushy or "soft," then you really must swap out the old for a new detent. If it hasn't taken much use to wear the detent to that point, the real solution is to replace the selector.

Trigger Removal and Installation

We'll go over the changing of triggers in the trigger chapter, here we'll cover the removal and installation of the standard trigger parts that came in your already assembled AR-15. To start with, unload the rifle and leave the bolt forward. Push the takedown pins out, and separate the upper and lower, setting the upper aside. Press the selector to the Fire position and put your hand or thumb in the hammer's path. Press the trigger and ease the hammer down. Be careful — if you let it fall of its own accord, it will eventually (sometimes quickly) damage the front inside face of the trigger assembly pocket in the lower. That is bad, as it will bind the bolt hold-open lever.

Set the lower aside on the bench and use a drift punch of the hammer and trigger pin diameter to give the hammer pin a quick jolt. I put the lower on its left side, creating enough clearance between the lower and the bench to permit the pin to move slightly.

The hammer pin is held in by a groove in the center of the pin, grabbed by a spring inside the hammer called the "J" spring. You can't just push the pin out; you'll have to give it a jolt to snap the spring out of the groove. Once free from the groove, hold the hammer with one hand (supporting the lower) while pushing the pin out with the punch in your other hand. Control the hammer. Once the pin is free, the hammer spring will launch the hammer out of the lower.

Set the hammer aside. We'll give it a once-over in a bit.

The trigger, on the other hand, is easy. It's held in place by the hammer spring legs, so you can push the trigger pin out of the lower receiver. When I went through the Colt Armorer's Course, the class guns we used were so shop-worn that, with the hammer out, I could "disassemble" the lower and remove the trigger just by shaking it. Indeed, the pin would fall out, followed by the rest of the part. I hope your AR isn't that worn and loose.

With the pin removed, lift the disconnector out. On most rifles, you should be able to fish the trigger out. The rear of the trigger is underneath the safety lever bar, so you'll have to move the trigger forward and tip and angle it out. Fair warning: sometimes you can't do this. The problem is that the clearance slot on the lower deck

■ Once installed, the bolt hold-open should look like this.

of the interior hasn't been machined far enough forward. This is not a brand-specific problem — we don't see it mostly on "Brand XYZ" lowers, for example. In each LE Patrol Rifle class of 20 to 30 officers, we'll see from zero to two or three that have this problem.

The temporary solution is to remove the pistol grip, next the selector lever, and finally the trigger. The long-term solution is to have the trigger slot opened to provide enough clearance. Few shooters opt for this, as it allows for more entry of gunk, cuts through the anodizing, and most can live with the trigger not coming out.

When taking the lower apart and removing the fire control parts, leave the selector in place. Unless it must come out to allow trigger removal, there is no need to remove the selector.

You now have five parts on the bench: hammer with its spring, hammer pin, trigger with its spring, trigger pin and disconnector. If the disconnector spring has been properly installed, it is held in the slot in the trigger. If it falls out, you'll have six parts and need to see what is up with the disconnector spring.

Parts Assessment

The hammer has the sear notch on the bottom of the circular boss and the "J" spring staked inside the hammer. You can see it and the staking holding it in the hole halfway up the hammer shaft. The "J" spring never comes out. If it does, the hammer is broken and needs to be replaced. The hammer spring rides on the two half-axles on the hammer, and it can be assembled four different ways, three of which are wrong. The correct way is this: the hooped connector of the spring rests against the back of the hammer shaft. Both hoops are around their respective axles. The open ends of the spring come off the axle at *the front* of the hammer. All other configurations are wrong.

The sear notch must be clean and unmodified. The hammer and trigger are casehardened parts. That is, they have a relatively softer core and hard skin. If you polish, grind or otherwise try to "improve the trigger pull," you risk breaking through the skin, exposing the softer core and accelerating wear.

A more significant concern is the shape. The hammer notch and trigger nose are angled such that if you pull partway through the trigger pull and then let go, the parts will cam themselves back to full engagement. The engagement surfaces are not large. It is all too easy to "polish" or "stone" the surfaces and inadvertently change the angles. Once changed, the angles may not allow a return to engagement. So, leave them alone.

The top of the hammer has a "bird's beak" shape. This geometry is where the mass to drive the firing pin is created. The top of the beak should be smooth or have a rectangular pad on it. This pad is where the auto-sear hook for the M16 would be, had it been an M16 part.

AR-15 and M16 hammers are the same except for this hook. The rectangular pad could have been a hook ground off or a plug put in the mold or the forge die to prevent the hook from existing in the first place. Can you take an M16 hammer, grind off the hook, and use it as an AR-15 hammer? Sure, just be sure you get it all ground off.

Why would you do this? The old way of doing a "trigger job."

You see, before there were aftermarket hammer/trigger sets available, the only way to improve a

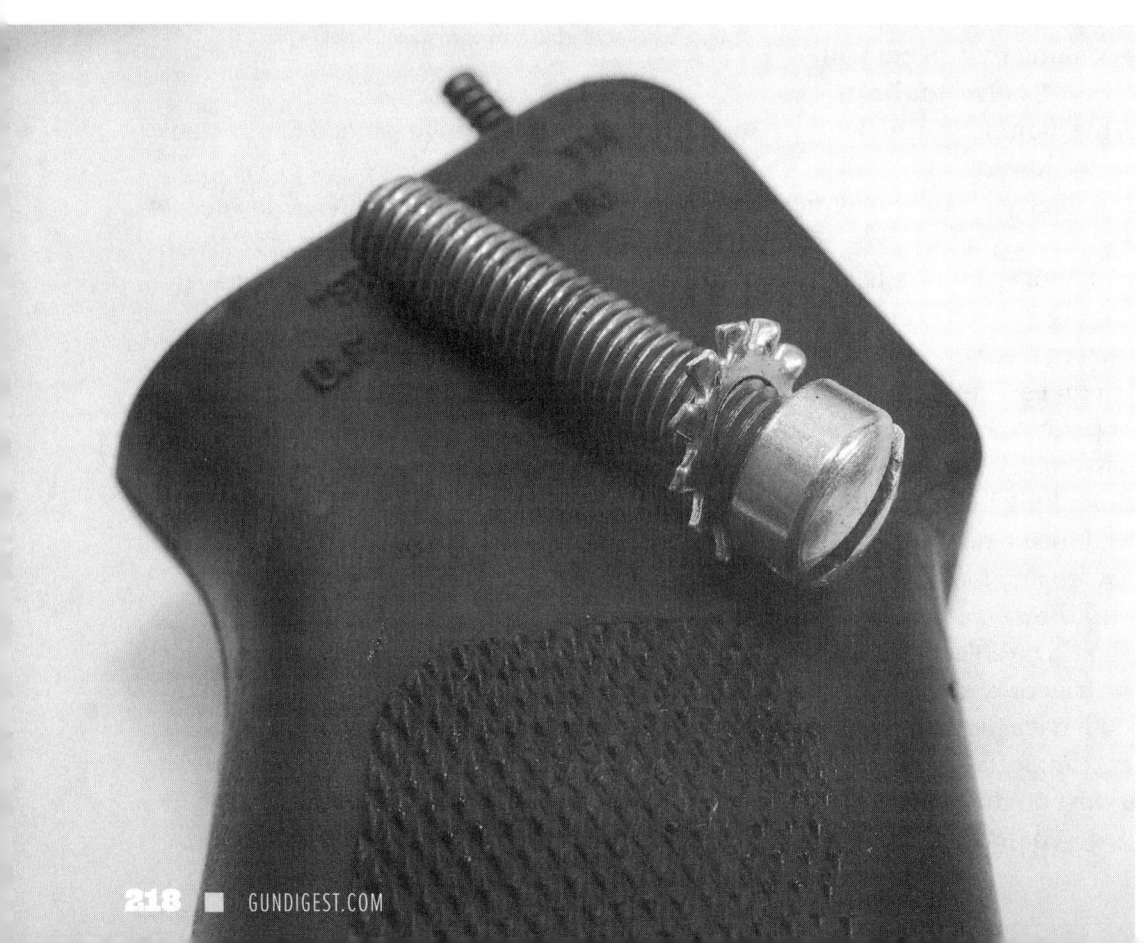

■ The pistol grip screw has a star washer to keep it tight. Use it.

■ Get the screw started with the pistol grip only partly on the receiver, so the pistol grip acts as a guide to keep the screw straight.

trigger pull was to swap parts. We'd have a couple bins — one with hammers, the other triggers. We'd mix and match (after marking the originals so we knew which was which) until we had the kind of trigger pull we wanted. If it just so happened that a surplus M16 hammer produced the best trigger pull in an AR-15 build, then that's what would get used once we ground the auto-sear lump off.

Last, on the hammer, we have the disconnector hook. This hook is the smaller one underneath the bird's beak. It's what the disconnector latches onto after you've fired and before you let go of the trigger and reset the mechanism. There is no service, tuning, adjusting or "improving" of this hook. Either it works as it is supposed to, or it doesn't. If it doesn't, the solution is in the disconnector itself (we'll go into that shortly) or replace the hammer.

Nowadays, aftermarket trigger/hammer sets are standard. You can even get USGI-like sets that are as good as any trigger pull, appearing to be plain-Jane AR-15 parts sets.

Now to the trigger.

The trigger has a trough down the center where the disconnector rides. The spring for the disconnector has a larger bottom loop, which wedges in the hole drilled for it in the trigger, and stays there. You can pull it out to scrub it clean, but when you reinstall it, place the wider end in first and seat it to the bottom. The front of the trigger has a sharp sear nose that engages the hammer notch. The spring for the trigger has a loop that rides under the main bar of the trigger. Both hoops are around the axles, and the two legs point straight forward, with the "ski" tips pointing up.

The trigger spring has one minor quirk that you should watch out for: when you install the spring on the trigger (if you take it off, it really doesn't need to come off, ever), you can put it back on and have the forward crossbar of the spring get caught lower than it should be. If you see the crossbar resting across the trigger bow not snugged up against the horizontal bar, it is wrong. Pry the spring off one of the axles so you can move the crossbar, work it up underneath the horizontal bar and put the hoop back over the axle.

The disconnector has one task: keep your AR-15

semi-automatic. When you fire a round, the hammer gets pushed back by the carrier, and the hammer hook catches the front nose of the disconnector. The spring in the trigger for the disconnector pushes the hook forward, so as the hammer comes back and cams the disconnector out of the way, the disconnector snaps back to catch the hammer. The disconnector holds onto the hammer as you release the trigger until the trigger nose has lifted high enough to engage the hammer. Then the disconnector lets go of the hammer, and the "click" you hear is the hammer notch snapping onto the trigger nose.

This process must happen within a narrow window, which we'll call the timing.

A late-timed disconnector will only release the hammer when the trigger lifts almost all the way up or entirely up. In a severe case, the disconnector might not let go of the hammer at all. Not letting go is bad, obviously, but a very late timing is also bad. If anything interferes with the trigger movement, such as powder residue, dirt, gunk, whatever, the trigger might not have enough range of movement to let the disconnector release.

Too early is even worse. A disconnector that releases the hammer too soon will fire when you let go of the trigger, as the trigger hasn't lifted far enough to catch the hammer notch. This problem usually happens when someone is trying to shoot slowly from the bench. The shooter will slowly pull the trigger until the rifle fires. Then, they carefully ease the trigger forward, and "BANG!" — the rifle goes off because the trigger hasn't lifted far enough. That doesn't happen when shooting fast because, by lifting their finger off the trigger quickly, the spring has enough power to push the trigger up, barely in time. They don't get the advantage of this momentum by slowly releasing the trigger and using their finger to slow the trigger's movement.

Does this make your AR-15 into a machine gun under the law? Well, yes and no. Yes, in that, you are getting more than one shot for each trigger pull. But, if you don't have any M16 internals in your rifle (with the allowed exception of the carrier), then what you have is obviously a defective rifle. Get it fixed, and all is good.

Fixing is easy, and adjusting the timing of the disconnector is a simple task.

However, if this happens with a new, out-of-the-box rifle, you may want the seller or manufacturer to fix it. Or you may prefer to fix it yourself (you are, after all, reading a book on AR-15 gunsmithing).

Fixing late timing isn't tricky, but it's also not obvious. Look at the front hook of the disconnector. It's probably holding onto the hammer hook for too long. The "obvious" place to stone or file is underneath the hook since you want it to have a smoother release. Nope. The disconnector, like the hammer and trigger, has a harder surface than its core. The disconnector hook catches and releases the hammer every time you dry fire or shoot the rifle. You don't want to be doing anything that makes the wear surfaces softer. Instead, you can shorten the hook. Use a file (one or two passes are usually all it takes) and keep it perpendicular to the axis of the bore. Do the trigger check and find yours releases late or not at all. Take the disconnector out, take a pass on it with the file and put the disconnector back in and check.

Take your time and sneak up on this because if you cut too much, there's no going back. You'll have to buy a replacement hook and check its timing.

■ Once the screw gets started, push the pistol grip all the way on, taking care to not pinch the spring in the process.

File a disconnector that releases early in the opposite way. The front spur on the disconnector controls it, so file the underside of that spur to tip the disconnector farther forward and delay the timing.

Now, disconnectors are all of five bucks each. If you want to learn how this is done, but your rifle works just fine, then buy a disconnector from Brownells. Install it and check the timing. The remove it and file one or the other. See how much it changes, and file to correct. Five bucks to learn a lot of useful information and build skills is not a high cost. In this day of high ammo prices, you'll spend more than that just making sure one magazine works properly.

Trigger Mechanism Check

OK, you're checking out an AR you want to buy, or you're checking the one you just bought, and you want to make sure the trigger works appropriately. Depending on the gun shop, you might not be allowed to do all this, as it seems somewhat harsh.

First, make sure the gun isn't loaded. I know we go over this many times, but it's always worth repeating: make sure it is empty. And ensure there are no loaded magazines, indeed, no ammo at all, nearby.

Open the bolt and look in the chamber. No round? Good. Use a light, or even stick a finger in there. Steel-cased ammo may disguise a round stuck in the chamber. You'll be pulling the trigger a lot; it is worth getting into the habit of chamber-checking regularly.

Press out the rear takedown pin and hinge the action open. Look at the trigger assembly. Check three things: that the hammer spring is correctly assembled on the hammer, that the hammer spring legs are on top of and outside the trigger spring hoops, and, finally, that the trigger spring crossbar is resting properly under the trigger bar. Close the action and push the takedown pin back. Check the chamber.

Close the bolt and check the selector. It needs to flip smoothly back and forth, click into place, and stay at each of the Safe and Fire settings. If it doesn't, refer back to the pistol grip installation section, remove the pistol grip and find out why the selector is recalcitrant.

Press the selector to Safe and pull the trigger

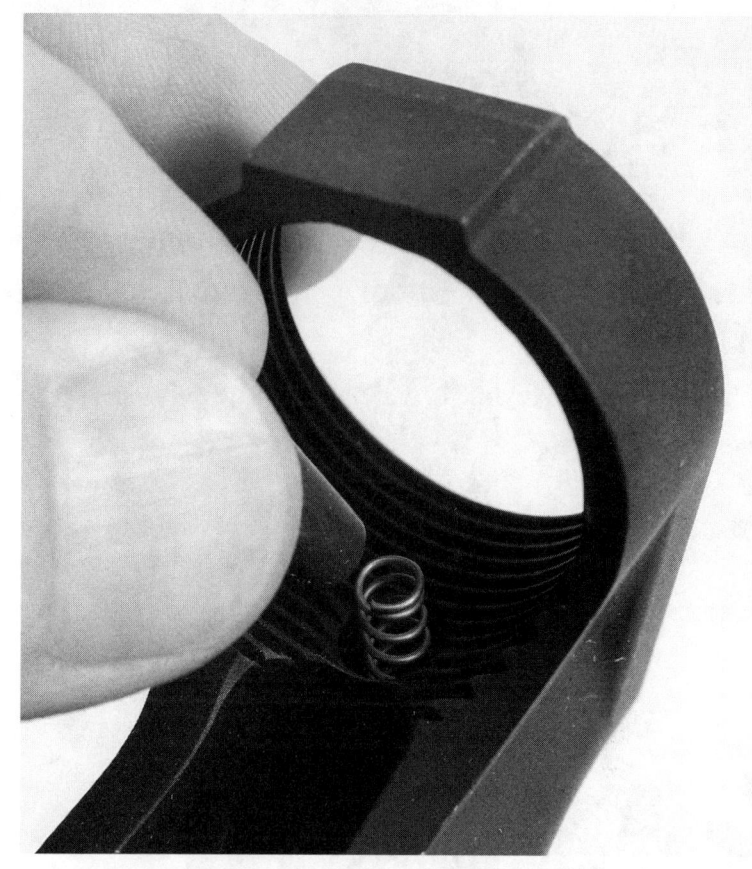

■ Here is where the rest of the lower parts kit goes: the buffer retainer and spring.

with about 10 pounds of force. Nothing should happen. Oh, the trigger might move a bit, but there should be no "click." If your AR releases the hammer at this point, you have serious problems, as there is something wrong with the trigger, selector or both. If this happens in the gun shop, hand it back.

If the rifle passes this test, press the selector to Fire while keeping your finger off the trigger. Again, the hammer must stay cocked. If it falls, hand it back. These steps test the selector and trigger engagement. Now, to timing.

With the selector on Fire, pull the trigger, hear the hammer fall and hold the trigger back. Now work the charging handle to cycle the bolt. You might feel the hammer press the disconnector out of the way, or you may not; it depends on how smoothly the various parts cycle. With the bolt fully forward, slowly ease the trigger forward. The slower, the better. Listen for one of two sounds, a "click" or a "whack." The click will be the hammer slipping off the disconnector and catching on the trigger nose. The whack is the hammer slipping from the disconnector, missing the trigger and

■ During assembly, use your thumb to hold the retainer in place. Yes, your thumb will object. That's life.

hitting the firing pin. (That's why you make double sure it's unloaded.)

A whack instead of a click means disconnector timing work. Ditto a very late or non-releasing disconnector.

The final test is to lock the bolt back and, with the selector on Fire, press the bolt stop to release the bolt and let it crash home with full force. Then rotate the selector to Safe. If it won't go, either the hammer didn't stay cocked, or you have a hammer/trigger sear engagement issue, which is corrected by replacing parts. No, you can't file, stone, machine or otherwise adjust the sear engagement — it's determined by the mechanical fit of the trigger and hammer. There is one instance where the hammer might fall that isn't caused by incorrect dimensions, and that is incorrect assembly. So, let's put the parts back and cover reassembly, pointing out the spots where you might have caused a problem.

Reassembly

When it comes to reassembling your lower, you might find a "slave pin" to be handy. The slave is a shorter-than-needed pin that holds various parts in one assembly before pushing the main pin through. In this case, a slave pin would allow the trigger and disconnector to fit but not so long to hold them in the receiver.

To reassemble using a slave pin, press the disconnector into the slot in the trigger, putting the disconnector spring into the slot in the disconnector, and when the holes line up, press the slave pin into place. The disconnector is now held in place in the trigger for the next step.

Lacking a slave pin, here's how you assemble the lower. Turn the elector to Fire.

Insert the trigger down into the lower, starting forward, and bringing it back to hook it underneath the selector bar while putting the trigger bow through the clearance slot. Pick up one of the lower pins and push one end into the receiver. It doesn't matter which. They're identical. Look down into the receiver and align the pin with the pivot hole through the trigger. Exercise care here, as the top of the trigger axle has been milled off to pro-

■ Once done, this is what your retainer will look like on your completed lower.

■ If you are going to keep spares, use containers. The springs and pins for many AR assemblies are small and easily lost in the jumble of a parts bin.

vide clearance for the hammer spring legs. There are sharp points on the axle, and if you mash the pin against one of these points, you can kick up a burr. That burr will complicate or resist assembly in the future. Push the pin into the trigger until you see it begin to protrude into the disconnector slot. Pull it back slightly. Place the disconnector into the trigger and press it down to compress the disconnector spring. You'll have to move the disconnector around a bit as you press gently on the trigger pin, until the holes line up. Once you have the disconnector captured, you can let go of it. Turn the receiver on its side, so you can see the side the trigger pin is coming to.

Looking through the hole, use the trigger bow as a lever to move the trigger around until you have the trigger pin and the trigger pin hole aligned, and press the pin flush. The trigger is done.

The hammer requires a bit more strength and dexterity. There are several methods. This is the one I use. I hold the receiver in my right hand while I grasp the hammer in my left. I hold the hammer with my index finger straight down on the front face of the hammer and my thumb clamping the hammer spring tight to the hammer from the back. I bring the hammer spring legs into the receiver first, making sure I run them on top of the trigger pin. I press the hammer down into the lower while sliding my index finger in the magazine well. Once the hammer gets to the hammer pin hole, I can hold the hammer and the lower as one unit in my left hand while picking up the hammer pin. I move the hammer and receiver around relative to each other until the hammer hole lines up. Press the hammer pin into place. It will only go as far as the J hook, no farther. But by then, the hammer will stay put against its spring, and I can use the butt end of

> *"Before you move on, check the hammer spring legs. It is vitally important they are on top of the trigger pins and outside the trigger spring hoops."*

a screwdriver to tap the hammer pin until it has nudged past the J spring.

Now, I turn the receiver over and, using the hammer as a lever, move the hammer around until the hammer pin hole on the side aligns with the receiver hole. I can then press the far side of the pin against the bench and push the pin into place in the receiver.

Before you move on, check the hammer spring legs. It is vitally important they are *on top* of the trigger pins and *outside* the trigger spring hoops.

Once the lower is assembled, do your trigger parts check. ■

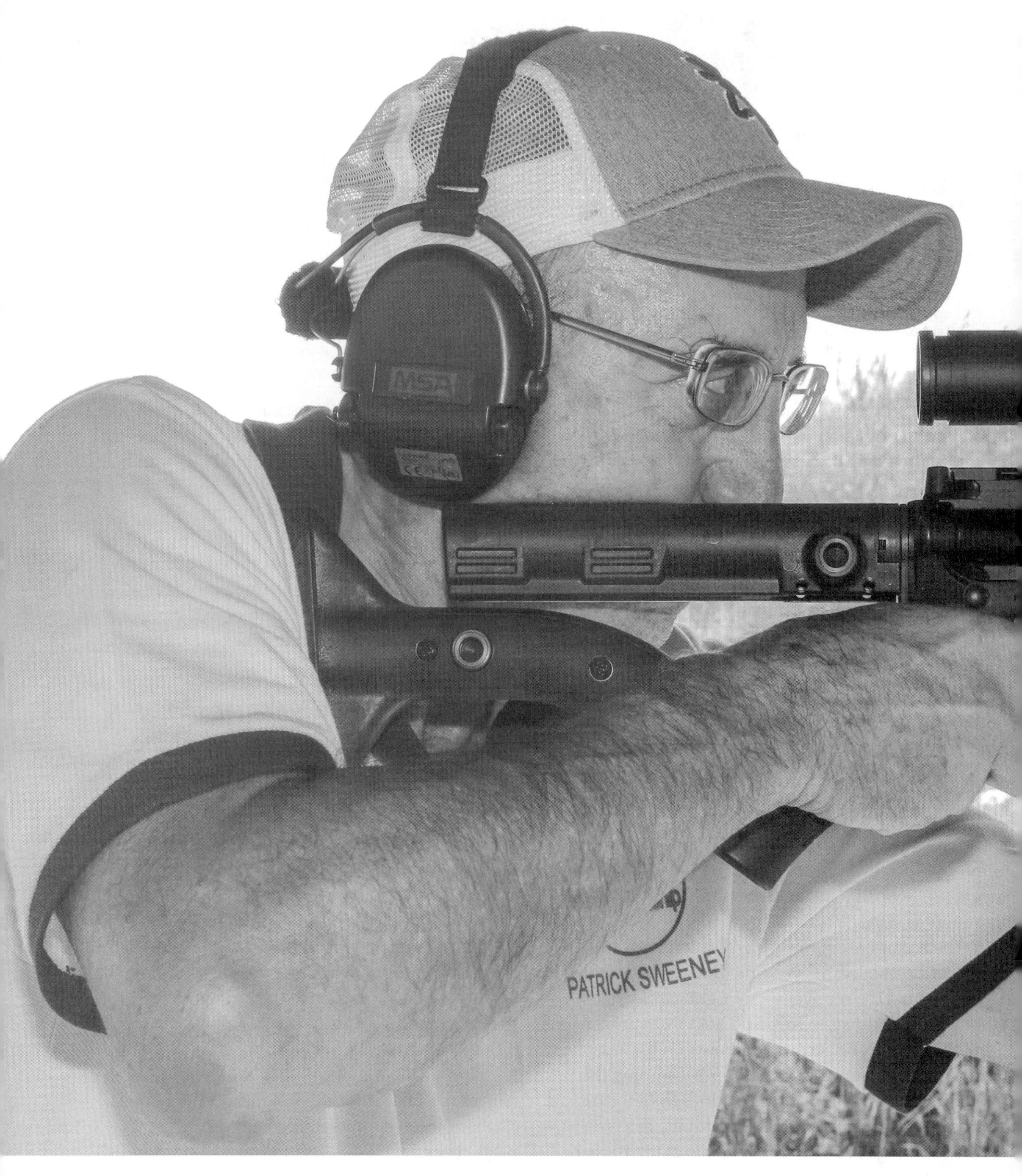
MSA
PATRICK SWEENEY

12

Stocks, Springs and Buffers

We'll cover AR-15 stocks in the order they historically appeared, with some adjustments, and start with a quick history. The first stocks were simply hollow plastic shells of two molded sheets sonic-welded together to fit over the receiver extension tube (hereafter known as the buffer tube).

It wasn't a remarkably durable design, so in R&D improvements, the shell got filled with plastic foam. When the government adopted the M16, it changed the stock to include a storage compartment, ostensibly for a cleaning kit. However, cleaning kits weren't available for those early M16s. The Army was set up for .30-caliber rifles and machine guns and had been since 1892. No cleaning kits meant no cleaning. The M16 was "self-cleaning" anyway, so not to worry.

In the 1980s, the M16 was showing its age, so it needed to be upgraded. The stock part of that upgrade (to the M16A2) was a lengthened stock made from a more durable composite. The longer stock went over the same-length buffer tube, and in a bizarre decision, the inside of the A2 stock was not made to fit the A1 buffer tube (which is the only buffer tube). As a result, the A2 stock required a cylindrical spacer to fill that interior gap. More on that mess in a bit.

■ The California-only stock from Thordsen Custom allows you to have an AR-15 in the Peoples' Republik.

Assembling a Fixed Stock to a Receiver

You'll need the lower, the buffer retainer and its spring, the rear takedown pin and its spring, the stock and buffer tube and the stock screw. If you're installing an A2 stock, you'll also need the spacer cylinder (which should be included in the stock parts kit) and note: the A2 stock screw is longer than the A1 stock screw, and *they are not interchangeable*.

Tube installation is the first step. The fixed-stock buffer tube is simply a cylinder, threaded on one end with a stop shoulder and drilled through the other end with a pair of flats on a small boss that is your torque point. First, the fit check. Hand-screw the buffer tube into the threaded hoop on the lower receiver. It should spin in with some friction, primarily due to the roughness of the anodized finish on each. It should turn all the way up, and its shoulder should tighten flush to the hoop. If not, something is wrong, most likely the buffer tube, and you need to get to the bottom of it.

If all is well, unscrew the buffer tube enough to clear the hole in the bottom of the lower receiver hoop (this is where the buffer retainer will go). Insert the buffer retainer spring and the buffer retainer, holding them down with your thumb. With your other hand, tighten the buffer tube. When the tube is tight, its front lip will trap the buffer retainer in the hole, but the top of the retainer will protrude enough to hold the buffer and spring in when you get to that point of assembly.

You can gently clamp your lower receiver in a padded vise (don't squeeze it too much, and clamp on the pistol grip web if you don't have padding) to torque it. A lot of people don't bother with torquing. You can simply wring it on hand-tight, as firmly as you can, and count on the stock to keep it from unscrewing. But, to do it right, you should torque it. The torque limit on the buffer tube is 35 to 39 ft-lbs.

Next, the stock itself. For both A1 and A2 types, you'll need the rear takedown pin, its spring and plunger, the stock and the stock screw. For A2 stocks, you'll also need the cylindrical spacer. Push the rear takedown pin into the receiver. Stand the lower receiver on its front face and insert the plunger. Press the spring in behind it. Pull the rear takedown pin partway out and rotate it until the plunger drops into the guide slot. When that happens, the takedown pin won't be able to rotate. This point is where you balance the A2 filler on top of the end of the buffer tube. (The A1 doesn't

■ In addition to a "featureless" stock, a California AR can't have a flash hider or threaded barrel. That, and the 10-round magazines, makes owning an AR on the West Coast a real drag.

■ Once you have the tele-stock buffer tube assembled, stake the retaining plate to the castle nut notch.

CHAPTER 12 – STOCKS, SPRINGS AND BUFFERS

■ A properly staked retaining plate. Note the castle nut with large slots to the rear, not to the front.

need it). Now, pick up the stock and slide it down the buffer tube. When you get near the receiver, carefully guide the stock and use it to compress the spring into its receiver tunnel. Once the stock is flush, note that there's a tab sticking out of the front of the stock. This tab fits into the recess in the rear of the receiver to keep the stock from rotating. Press the stock with the tab into the recess. Pick up the screw (the top screw, the bottom screw attaches the sling swivel) and drop it into the stock hole.

There are no special tools here. Just use a properly fitting screwdriver to tighten the stock screw. To torque it, it gets a "hard, hand-tight" limit. Yes, that's right, there is no government standard torque limit for the stock screw. It's a simple screw that can easily be checked. If it bothers you that there's no torque range, then use a dab of paint to indicate its location and visually check it when you feel the need.

Tele-Stocks

Tele-stocks for the AR-15 came about when the Army wanted something smaller and lighter than the M16. Having switched from a .30-caliber M14 rifle that was 44 inches long and weighed 10 pounds to a 35-inch M16 rifle weighing six pounds, the military found that end-users wanted less weight. One way to make the rifle more compact was to shorten the barrel. The other way was to shorten the buffer tube. But a shorter tube and stock made it difficult to shoot, so the stock was made to telescope over the tube so it could be contracted for storage and transport and extended for firing.

The first ones were made with sliders (the stock portion) composed of aluminum coated with glossy black vinyl. That design didn't save much weight, and the second version was simply molded out of durable plastic. The original tele-stocks had two settings — open or closed. Today, it's common to have five settings, with even six or seven possible.

The M4 telestock got some improvements — some added reinforcement ribs — but it was much the same: a plain cylinder for your face to rest on. It wasn't until the late 1990s that we got the "Sopmod" stock design, although the Choate company had been making something like it for a decade before. The Sopmod stock has a wedge shape on top and offers a much better cheek weld for aiming.

The tele-stock is more complicated in design and assembly. Along with the buffer tube (which is no longer a simple tube), the buffer and spring (which is not the same buffer as the rifle/fixed stock assembly buffer, ditto the spring), there is the retaining plate, castle nut and slider assembly.

Mil-Spec Vs. Commercial

The original tele-stock (aka carbine) buffer tube was made from a forging of 7075-T6 aluminum. It was bored out, the rib machined and the threads lathe-cut. Then, to lighten it more, the tube body was profiled to make it smaller in diameter. In the pre-CNC machine days, this was a complicated and expensive way to make the tube. It still is, and the mil-spec stock tubes continue to be produced this way.

When shooters wanted AR-15s that Colt would not build, commercial makers stepped in. The commercial tube was manufactured from a 6061 aluminum alloy extrusion, not a forging, and the threads were cut or rolled, but the tube was not thinly profiled. Extrusion is precisely what you are mentally picturing right now. The heated-soft alu-

■ If you don't correctly position the carbine buffer tube lip during assembly, the retainer and spring can come out. They will rattle around in the lower until they stop the rifle.

minum is squeezed out through a form that shapes the tube and the rib in one step. That saves a bunch of machine work, and while 6061 can be extruded, 7075 is not happy with the process. So, commercial tubes get 6061, also known as "aircraft aluminum." As a result of this process and the lack of post-threading profiling, the commercial tube was larger in diameter. That was not a problem because commercial tubes (back then) came with commercial-diameter sliders. Now, with everyone making tubes and sliders and custom stocks, knowing your tube diameter matters. You can eyeball it or measure it. The eyeball method is easy once you know what to look for: on commercial tubes, the threads don't protrude above the surface of the tube diameter behind the threads. Their thread tops are often flattened, and the overall thread diameter is the same as the tube. In mil-spec examples, the threads do protrude, and they have sharp edges on top. The last few threads might even be milled down as part of the tube-slimming process. Once you've had a chance to see one of each, it's easy to tell them apart. The diameters, at least nominally, are mil-spec, 1.140 inches; commercial, 1.170 inches. These dimensions are measured behind the threaded portion and not across the rib.

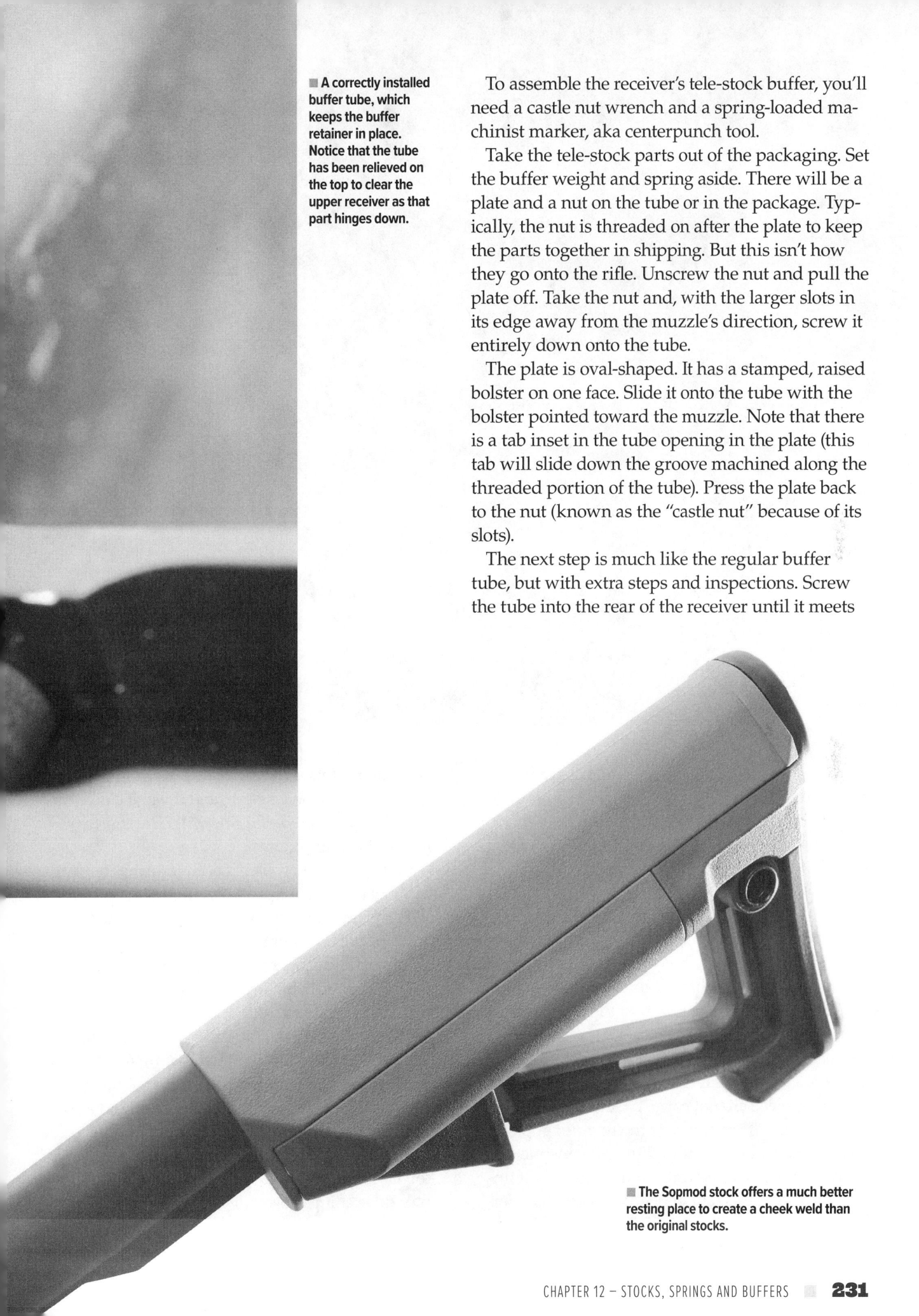

■ A correctly installed buffer tube, which keeps the buffer retainer in place. Notice that the tube has been relieved on the top to clear the upper receiver as that part hinges down.

To assemble the receiver's tele-stock buffer, you'll need a castle nut wrench and a spring-loaded machinist marker, aka centerpunch tool.

Take the tele-stock parts out of the packaging. Set the buffer weight and spring aside. There will be a plate and a nut on the tube or in the package. Typically, the nut is threaded on after the plate to keep the parts together in shipping. But this isn't how they go onto the rifle. Unscrew the nut and pull the plate off. Take the nut and, with the larger slots in its edge away from the muzzle's direction, screw it entirely down onto the tube.

The plate is oval-shaped. It has a stamped, raised bolster on one face. Slide it onto the tube with the bolster pointed toward the muzzle. Note that there is a tab inset in the tube opening in the plate (this tab will slide down the groove machined along the threaded portion of the tube). Press the plate back to the nut (known as the "castle nut" because of its slots).

The next step is much like the regular buffer tube, but with extra steps and inspections. Screw the tube into the rear of the receiver until it meets

■ The Sopmod stock offers a much better resting place to create a cheek weld than the original stocks.

CHAPTER 12 – STOCKS, SPRINGS AND BUFFERS

■ This Primary Arms buffer tube has a clearance hole for the retainer. The tube holds the retainer and provides a bottom surface to counter carrier tilt.

the back of the buffer retainer hole. Press the retainer and its spring into the hole, hold it there and turn the buffer tube another turn or two.

However, the tele-stock assembly is a bit more complicated because the buffer tube threaded process must stop when all the following occur:

- The buffer tube must be far enough forward on the bottom edge to trap the retainer but not bind it in place.
- The buffer tube must not be so far forward that its top edge is forward of the lower receiver loop's edge.
- The rib on the buffer tube must be at precisely six o'clock on the receiver.

If any of these are not correct, there will be function problems. If the tube lets the retainer pop out, the retainer will rattle around until it jams the operation. If it's too far forward and binds the retainer down, the buffer will pop loose when you open the receivers for cleaning, and the spring-driven buffer can be painful when it hits you. If the buffer tube is too far forward and protrudes from the loop, the upper won't clear it, and it won't close. And if the rib is tilted, the rifle will be at the very least awkward to shoot.

We'll solve those problems each in turn, after we finish the assembly of properly fitting parts.

With the buffer tube screwed in and aligned, and the buffer retainer in place, insert the rear takedown pin, plunger and spring. At this point, it will be easiest if you stand the lower up on the bench on its front face with the buffer tube vertical. Press the retaining plate down on the buffer tube and compress the rear takedown spring into the receiver. The plate must be flush, with the bolster nestled in the socket machined in the lower. Now hand-turn the castle nut down to the retaining plate until it holds it in position.

You can relax. No springs will pop loose if you've done things correctly to this point.

Inspect the fit of the parts. The rib should have remained at six o'clock. The plate should be flush and the castle nut tight to it. Does the rear takedown pin move in and out, and is its movement stopped by the plunger once open? If everything is correct, secure the castle nut. It's easier to do this if you already have the pistol grip installed, as the grip can act as a leverage enhancer.

First, place the receiver with the buffer tube on its side on the bench. Hold one hand flat against the receiver to keep it in place. Using your other hand, hook the castle nut wrench's teeth into the castle nut. Now lean onto the receiver to hold it in place and press the wrench to tighten the nut. As with all things proper, "lefty-loosey, righty-tighty" is the operative phrase. I do it with the muzzle end of the lower (if it had the upper on it) to my right, the pistol grip pointing toward me. I then lean onto the wrench to tighten the castle nut. The official specs call for 38 to 42 in-lbs. *Note that it is inch-pounds, not foot-pounds.*

The large slots on the castle nut are for the wrench; the smaller ones are for the staking. You can clamp the receiver in a fixture of some kind. That's easily done by hand with the receiver flat on the bench. Place the tip of the spring-loaded punch against the edge of the retaining plate by a fraction of an inch, back from the castle nut joint. Press and let the spring-snap of the punch kick up a divot. The edge of that divot is intended to push into the small notch of the castle nut. Do this several times on the exact same location until you have kicked up enough of the stake to keep the castle nut from turning. Then repeat on at least one other slot.

Torque is good, but physically locking the castle nut in place means it can't shimmy free if vibration attempts to loosen it. I will repeat here what I've said elsewhere: a non-staked castle nut is a sign of an incorrect assembly. If someone tries to sell you a rifle that lacks staking, be careful.

Now you are ready for the last steps. To install the slider, pull directly down on the latch handle — not leveraging but pulling it entirely free. Slide it onto the buffer tube, and once the plunger is forward of the back edge of the buffer tube, you can let go. Now, when you press the lever, you can slide the stock back and forth. If you ever want to remove the stock, pull the latch handle directly down and the stock off the back of the tube. Simply pressing the lever won't provide enough clearance for the stock to come off.

Press the spring into the buffer tube and use the buffer to finish pressing the spring in. Pressing the buffer tube in, you'll notice that the buffer lip's back edge is beveled. This beveling acts to compress the buffer retainer. Once it passes the retainer, the retainer pops back up and keeps the buffer in the tube when you separate the upper and lower for cleaning.

Installation Problems and Solutions

Retainer timing problems. Here, the buffer tube won't line up to hold the retainer in place, with the rib at six o'clock. One turn back, and it won't hold in the retainer. One turn forward, and it binds the retainer in place. This problem usually happens in conjunction with the top lip of the tube projecting past the loop and binding the upper. You have two choices; replace it with another buffer tube (hoping it was the buffer and not the receiver at fault) or lots of hand-fitting. Having several sets of parts on hand comes in handy in situations like this. You can also try another tube from a different parts kit.

If it was the tube, then a replacement would solve the problem. (Send the old tube back, if you can, for a replacement.) If it's the receiver, send it back for a replacement. If those options are not available to you, then there's work ahead.

And remember, do all the fitting with the rib at six o'clock.

> *"Torque is good, but physically locking the castle nut in place means it can't shimmy free if vibration attempts to loosen it. I will repeat here what I've said elsewhere: a non-staked castle nut is a sign of an incorrect assembly. If someone tries to sell you a rifle that lacks staking, be careful."*

If the bottom lip of the buffer tube is binding the retainer but isn't protruding enough to bind at the top when the lower hinges down, use a round needle file to make clearance for the retainer tip. Use a felt-tip marker to mark the spot, unscrew the buffer tube, clamp it in a padded vise and file. File lightly and then check the fit. You can always file more, but you can't put metal back. Once you've created enough clearance so the retainer moves properly, you can finish the installation of the stock assembly.

If the buffer tube binds the retainer and hinders upper movement, first fit the retainer, as above. You'll need to file the upper edge of the buffer tube enough to clear the upper in hinging. Again, mark it with a felt-tip marker, file lightly and check the fit as you go.

Receiver Plate Problems

You may run into a problem with the receiver plate where the plate is too hard to be staked. This issue usually happens with a non-standard plate with wings for sling attachment or other "additions." (Not a fan, can you guess?) Since the plate is too hard, you can't stake it. If you're determined to stick with the plate, the only solution (and again, not a fan of this, either) is to use Loctite to hold the castle nut in place. The hassle is that to get the Loctite to work correctly, you have to de-grease the threads. That means taking apart your assembled buffer tube. To do that, use the wrench to loosen and unscrew the castle nut. If you have enough dexterity, you can hold the retaining plate in position (so the rear takedown spring and plunger don't push it out of place) while spraying degreaser on the threads. Apply enough Loctite to hold it (blue would be best here) and screw the castle nut back down into place. Use the wrench to tighten it and wipe off any excess Loctite that has flowed out of the joint.

Takedown Pin and Spring Problems

If you don't pay close attention to the takedown pin's spring, you will not compress it into its tunnel but could bend it over and trap it under the plate or stock. The spring, lacking sufficient tension, may not retain the takedown pin. The solution is to watch the spring closely as you use the retaining plate (tele-stock) or stock to compress it and ensure it goes entirely into the tunnel. If you've mangled it, then replace it.

It's common in some circles to tap the back of the takedown pin hole and use a set screw to hold the shortened (you have to shorten it by the length of the set screw) spring in place. As a clever bit of workmanship, I had to give that trick a hat-tip. But a properly installed retaining plate will keep the spring in place and won't require receiver modification. Plus, this process adds another tool (and a tiny Allen wrench at that) to the ones you need to service your rifle.

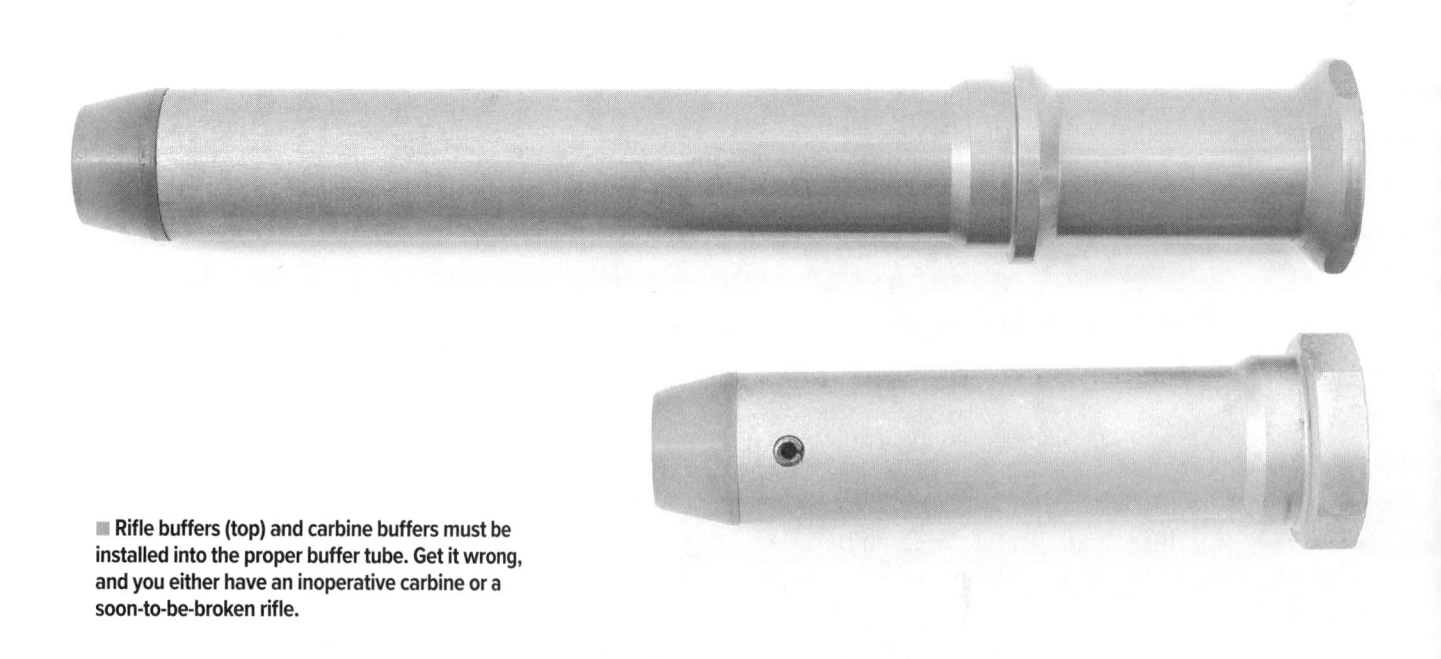

■ Rifle buffers (top) and carbine buffers must be installed into the proper buffer tube. Get it wrong, and you either have an inoperative carbine or a soon-to-be-broken rifle.

■ One of the worst buffers ever seen. This one had a single steel weight in it. It wasn't heavy enough, and it broke apart in use.

Mis-Aligned Buffer Tube

If the buffer tube is cocked on the receiver, the front lip can bind or fail to hold the buffer retainer. Even if it holds the pin, the stock's angled buttplate can make shooting uncomfortable or difficult. The only solution is to loosen the castle nut, turn the buffer tube vertical (this is easiest done by turning the rifle upside down and eyeballing alignment with the pistol grip) and then tightening the castle nut without changing the buffer tube alignment.

Buffer Springs

Rifle and carbine buffer springs are not the same. The rifle spring should have between 41 and 43 coils and be no shorter than 12 inches long. The carbine spring is 37 to 39 coils and no shorter than 10 inches. If your springs are tired and short, replace them. There is no benefit in replacing them with stronger springs than they were designed, which risks unreliable function.

Flat springs are the new coolness in the AR-verse, and they do offer benefits. A flat-wire spring is less likely to stack or increase resistance as it compresses. The recoil impulse is thus smoother and less "bouncy." Does this matter? As with most things, not much. If you're using a vanilla-plain M4gery and shooting whatever ammo is on sale, then you might not notice a difference. If you're running a competition-tuned rifle or carbine and are in the thick of the match-winner race at any level above your club's, you might find it beneficial. As with many such improvements, it might not be noticeable, but it can't hurt.

Buffer Weights

The buffer weight, or buffer, is an added mass to allow the system to cycle properly. It's also the spring face, which allows the spring to engage the rear of the carrier. All buffers (except for one bizarre military-moronic one) are built in the manner of a dead-blow hammer. The weights inside are free to slide back and forth a small amount. When the carrier crashes home, chambering a round, the front lip of the carrier contacts the rear of the barrel extension. Even if it doesn't, the carrier will bottom out on the bolt itself. The steel-on-steel impact is very elastic. We think of "elastic" in terms of stretchiness. But in the physics world, an "elastic" collision is one where the energy of the impact is not absorbed by the bodies impacting each other. As an example, dropping a rock into the mud is an inelastic collision.

So, the carrier bounces a fraction of an inch, with the spring and buffer continuing to push it forward. This effect can cause malfunctions in full-auto fire. (It is not a problem in semi-auto shooting.) When the spring hurls the buffer and carrier forward, the buffer weights slide to the rear of the buffer interior. When the system closes, the weights in the buffer slide forward and strike the inside interior of the buffer, dampening carrier bounce. Some carbines need more weight to dampen the bounce. I have seen carbines and SBRs fail to fire after the first shot in full-auto and carbines and SBRs that became more reliable with a heavier buffer.

> "Can your buffer be too heavy? Perhaps, but that would manifest as a failure to lock back when empty, which would most likely happen when the carbine is dry, dirty, or you're using underpowered ammo."

As with springs, the two weights are not the same. You shouldn't use a carbine buffer in a rifle (fixed stock) lower, and you probably cannot get a rifle buffer to even chamber a round installed in a carbine (tele-stock) lower. The rifle buffer is the longer of the two, with a pair of circular shoulders on it, and it weighs 5 ounces. Carbine buffers are the shorter ones, with a single circular shoulder. The originals had three steel weights inside of their aluminum tube, and they weighed 3 ounces. Short-barreled rifles and AR pistols have gas systems that can be more problematic and benefit from heavier buffers. These are marked H or H1, H2 and H3. The H/H1 has one of the steel weights replaced with one made of tungsten. H2 has two tungsten, and the H3 has all three weights made of tungsten. The weights are H/H1 3.8 ounces, H2 4.6 ounces and H3 5.2 ounces.

■ Carbine buffers come in various weights, as each steel piece inside is replaced with one made of tungsten.

■ Not all stocks have to be adjustable. If the length works for you (and most shooters can accommodate a range of stock lengths), the lightweight Wilson Combat stock is a bonus.

Avoid the plastic buffers. Colt made these for a while, and we see them from time to time in really *craptastic* parts kits. They are molded plastic tubes with lead or steel shot inside and, while they *should* weigh the same as mil-spec buffers, usually they don't. And even when they do, they don't provide reliable functioning. If your carbine has one (I do not recall ever seeing a rifle buffer made this way), replace it immediately.

Which buffer should you use? Many "commodity" carbines are over-gassed. That is, the gas port is a size too large to feed enough gas to the system and ensure reliable function with all ammo, even when the rifle hasn't been properly cleaned for a long time. The cost of this is that recoil can be harsh, and such carbines benefit from using a heavier buffer than standard. Also, short-barreled ARs can benefit. Can your buffer be too heavy? Perhaps, but that would manifest as a failure to lock back when empty, which would most likely happen when the carbine is dry, dirty, or you're using underpowered ammo.

Oh, and what happens if you mix up the buffers? A rifle buffer in a carbine lower won't permit the bolt to go back far enough to chamber a round. The carbine buffer in the rifle lower cycles too far back in the tube, and the gas key will crash into the receiver hoop. If you're lucky, the gas key screws break off first. If you're unlucky, the gas key cracks the hoop, and you'll need to replace the lower. Don't mix the buffers.

CHAPTER 12 – STOCKS, SPRINGS AND BUFFERS

Non-Standard Stock/Buffer Systems

There are two directions you can go when it comes to using a non-standard stock design and buffer system. You can go lighter, or you can go heavier. Lighter systems are primarily competition-oriented, and they can be a bit picky as far as reliability goes.

A lightweight competition system (often in conjunction with a lighter-than-normal carrier) reduces the bottoming-out impact of recoil. When the carrier and buffer move to the rear, driven by the gas system (or piston), they will cycle all the way back until the spring is completely compressed. When the cycling parts bottom out, that jolt is small. However, every minor negative is a problem when scoring points or shooting at max speed. To reduce the jolt, competition shooters reduce the mass. The problem with this approach is that you cannot do it as a stand-alone solution. Simply making the parts lighter means they bottom out at a higher velocity, not reducing the jolt. The higher cycling velocity can also induce reliability problems. If the bolt/carrier whips back and forth too quickly, it can arrive at the magazine before the magazine spring has had time to lift the cartridge stack. Also, the harsher bottoming-out impact can jolt the cartridge stack, misaligning the top round and preventing feeding.

Competition-built guns commonly use an adjustable gas block to combat this, which allows the shooter to tune the gas flow to cycle the rifle reliably but not hammer the parts bottoming out. Doing so requires that the shooter use one specific load, but this is not a problem since it's common to reload competition ammunition. However, such a rifle might be testy or even unreliable if fed standard off-the-shelf ammo, and the more varied the ammunition available, the less reliable it might be. It also can make the rifle more sensitive to lube and gunk. A finely tuned AR-15 competition rifle might be a joy to shoot, but if it has to be thoroughly scrubbed every few hundred rounds to ensure reliability, then that is a price you must take into account.

The other approach is to go heavier. With the H, H1, H2 buffers and a buffer system from VLtor called the A5, you can accomplish that. The A5 uses a rifle spring, a slightly longer buffer tube and

■ The armed services still have a *bazillion* M16A2s in their inventories with fixed stocks installed. These will be in use for decades to come.

a longer (and heavier) buffer. Not only that, but VLtor builds the buffer differently. It has internal weights, but the buffer has a spring inside it to push the weights forward. That way, there's no "slack" on firing, with the weights floating in the middle of the buffer, allowing the initial buffer movement to be just the aluminum housing. A rifle spring (which can only be done in the VLtor A5 buffer tube) gives more mass and a smoother spring cycle to the movement. The longer tube allows for the spring to have a longer cyclic space, smoothing things more. You cannot use the A5 buffer and spring in a regular carbine buffer tube. You must use A5 parts in an A5 buffer tube. The extra mass smoothens out the cycling of pistols, SBRs and suppressed carbines.

Another approach High Power shooters employ is to strip a rifle buffer and replace the steel weights with tungsten ones. This mod can bump the rifle buffer from 5 to 8 ounces or so. Those shooting at 600 or 1,000 yards commonly load 80- or even 90-grain bullets at the maximum velocity, and the heavier buffer slows unlocking just a bit more, keeping the brass from being worked harder than it otherwise would be. You won't need to do this change until you've worn out several barrels learning to shoot at those distances.

13
Triggers

■ The author marked this hammer and trigger with a silver Sharpie to illustrate where the springs go when properly installed. Anything else is wrong.

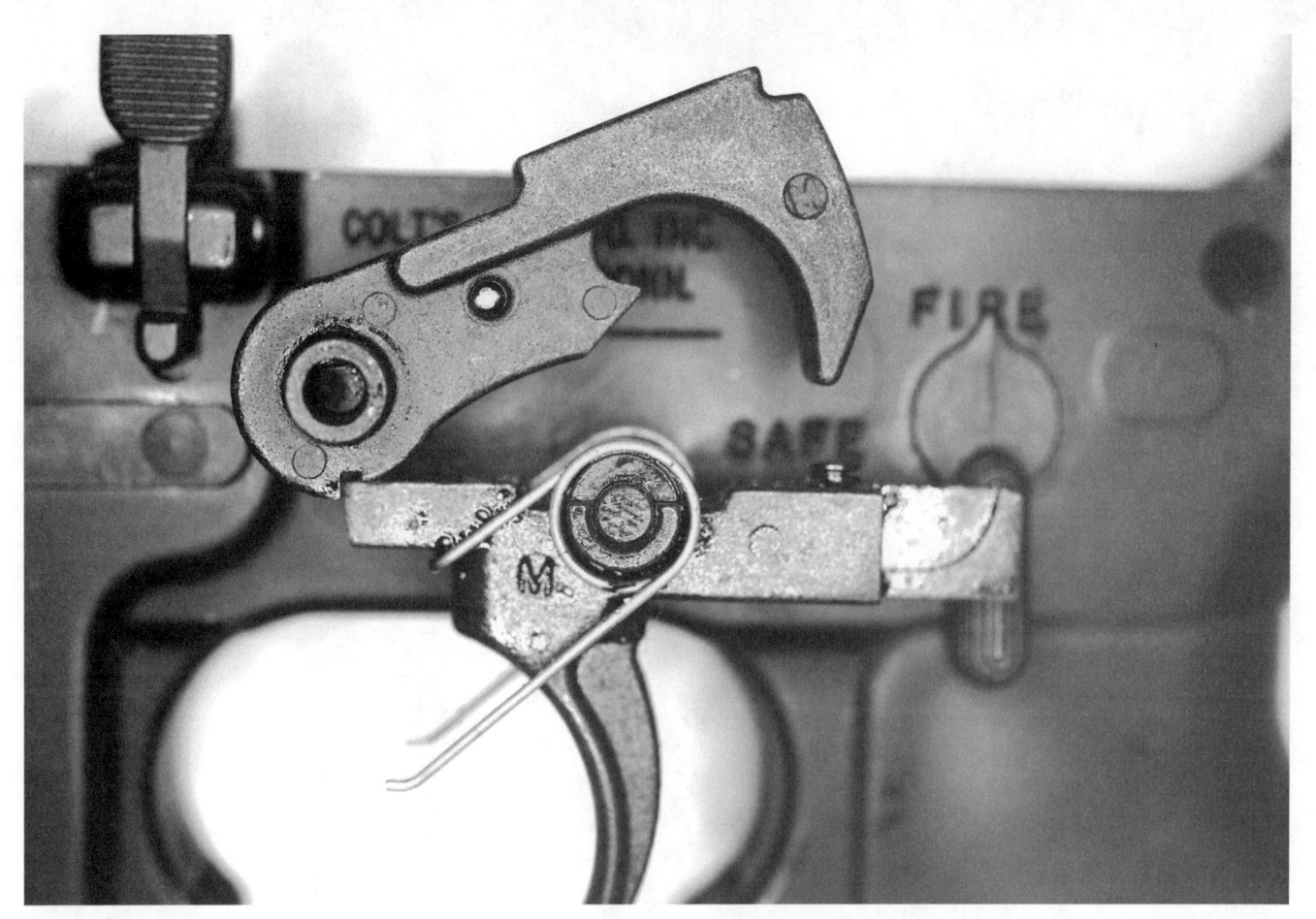

■ Note the single-stage trigger and how simple of a lever it is. Your finger press pulls the trigger down out of contact with the hammer notch.

As initially designed, the AR-15's trigger is a single-stage type. It is a simple lever. The hammer, forward of the trigger, has a hook machined into its lower edge. This hook, the hammer sear, engages the tip of the trigger, which is the surface known as the trigger sear. When you pull the trigger, you're pulling the trigger sear tip directly down out of the hammer sear notch, with no additional leverage to aid you.

As a result of this design decision, the mil-spec trigger pull is kept relatively high to ensure reliable function even during years of service and rugged use. Where a bolt-action hunting rifle might come from the factory with a trigger pull of 3.5 pounds, it will be a rare AR-15/M16/M4 with a mil-spec engagement and spring set that has a pull under 5.5 pounds. And the allowable trigger pulls in military use range from 5.5 to 9.5 pounds. "Nine and a half pounds?" Yep, the military doesn't want anyone to be shot accidentally, just shot on purpose. And they wear gloves a lot of the time.

Just to elaborate on the geometry, the trigger's engagement surfaces and hammer are slightly angled to the pivot point of the trigger. This angle works to pull the trigger back into full engagement if you pull it partway out and let go. That is a good thing. Any partial pull, jostling, bumping, or vibration that acts to partially disengage the sear surfaces, once stopped, allows the system to slide back to full engagement. This design does, however, make it difficult to safely lighten the trigger pull weight.

The AR-15's firing mechanism consists of four parts: three springs, two pins and a plunger.

Let's assume you have an assembled lower, one you bought as a lower or a complete rifle or carbine. Disassembly works this way:

Unload and make sure the rifle is clear. Close the bolt. Press both takedown pins across and remove the upper from the lower. Press the selector to Fire, and keeping a thumb on the hammer to control its movement, press the trigger. Ease the hammer forward. This step is important. The lower is made of aluminum. If you let the hammer crash forward, unrestrained, it can damage the front of the receiver pocket and bind the bolt hold-open lever. It can even crack the receiver or break the hammer. (No, I

■ The hammer springs must go on the top of the trigger pin, outside of the coils of the trigger spring.

have no idea how aluminum can break steel, but I saw it happen.)

Use your takedown punch and press the hammer pin from the receiver. Either side will do. The pins are not tapered, nor are they oriented one way or the other. Getting it started will take some effort, as there is a spring in the hammer that latches onto the pivot pin. Pull the punch out of the receiver. Lift the hammer out, with its spring attached. Now press and remove the trigger pin. When you ease the punch out from the trigger, go easy. First, the disconnector will come free. Then the trigger will pop loose, with its spring and the disconnector spring (if correctly assembled, we'll go into that) attached.

In some instances — in a predicament known as "dimensional stack" — the trigger can't be wiggled out under the selector while the selector is still in the receiver. If this is the case, you'll have to undo the pistol grip screw to allow the selector spring and plunger to move out of the groove in the selector. Once you do that, remove the selector from the lower. Most levers won't permit removal until you've relieved the plunger tension. You most likely won't have to remove the pistol grip. Just loosen the screw enough so that you can pull it down to ease the spring tension on the selector.

At this point, you can scrub the various parts, hose out the lower's interior and be ready to reassemble. While you're here, let's take a moment to get to know the various parts of the AR-15 trigger.

■ This is how the disconnector sits on the trigger. Adjust the trigger's nose bearing for early timing. Adjust the hook on top for late timing.

CHAPTER 13 – TRIGGERS ■ **243**

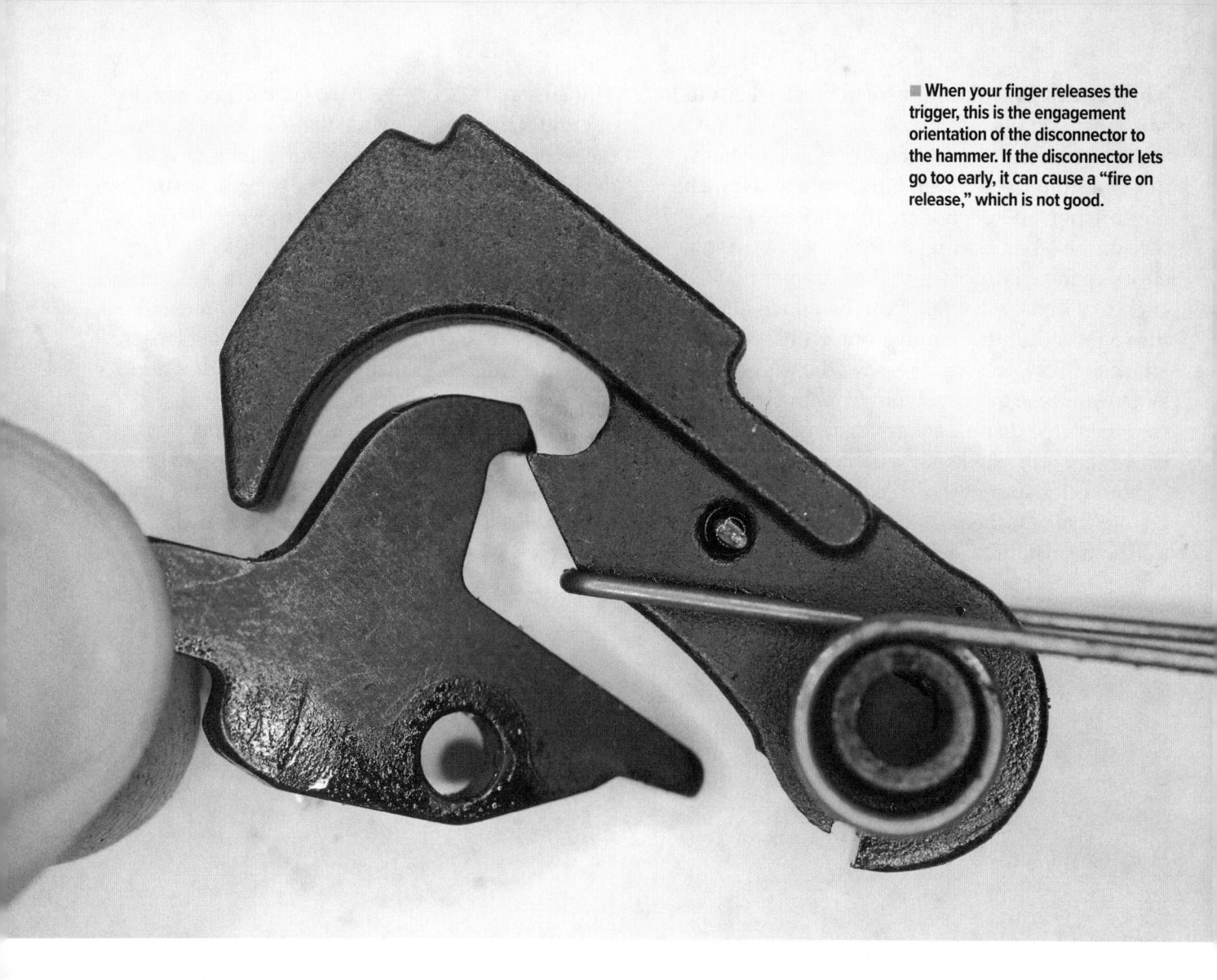

■ When your finger releases the trigger, this is the engagement orientation of the disconnector to the hammer. If the disconnector lets go too early, it can cause a "fire on release," which is not good.

Hammer

The hammer has an axle hub, with a small spring inside known as the "J" spring. This spring clips into the center groove of the hammer/trigger pin and locks the hammer to that pin. The bird's beak on the hammer provides mass in the spot where it best pounds the firing pin. It also provides a location for the auto-sear hook on M16 and M4 firearms. Your hammer's auto-sear block will be ground off in most cases before it is built into an AR-15. Some few older rifles won't, which is not usually a big deal.

On the bottom, the hammer's arc has had a slot ground through it to create the sear notch. The notch should be bright, even though the hammer has a black oxide finish.

■ If your disconnector is timed late or won't release at all, file here. File carefully, only a few strokes, then re-install and test. You can't put metal back.

Trigger

The trigger bow is the part your finger presses on. The front tip, which should be surface ground to a smooth and shiny finish, engages the hammer sear notch. Behind that is an open-topped slot with a circular hole drilled down into it. That slot is where the disconnector rides; the hole seats the disconnector spring. The back end of the trigger will be closed on an AR-15 trigger and open on an M16 trigger. Mechanically, there is no difference, but if you're going to do an "Armorer's trigger job," avoid using M16 triggers.

Some Colt triggers will have two holes drilled for the disconnector spring. The very earliest AR-15 mechanism had the entire rear portion of the disconnector chopped off and a hole for the spring drilled in a location different from the M16. This design was to preclude people from modifying the AR-15 to full auto. I have to think the engineers were disgusted with the "suits" on this. If someone wanted to break the law and make their AR-15 into an M16, they would use M16 parts, not modify the existing ones.

The two holes are there if someone needs to replace a trigger on an ancient Colt AR-15 and needs that second hole location for the also-ancient disconnector.

■ If your disconnector releases early, file here. Again, a few strokes and test.

■ Geissele makes the High Speed National Match Trigger. It provides a proper trigger pull that meets the requirement of Service Rifle competition but is much, much cleaner than a service trigger.

If you look inside enough Colt rifles, you'll see triggers with some or most of one side of the rear portion milled away. That machining was for clearance around the internal auto-sear block Colt installed in its rifles for a while. These triggers work fine in modern rifles, but today's AR-15 triggers won't fit into the old Colts with the auto-sear block. In such an instance, you would simply grind the new trigger to match the contour of the old one.

New owners, with new AR-15s: this is all historical info and a head's-up just in case you luck into an old Colt.

Disconnector

If your disconnector was made correctly and assembled, the disconnector spring should still be in place, even after taking the trigger out of the lower. The bottom coil of the disconnector spring is larger than its hole; spring tension and friction keep it in the hole. If it's in place, leave it alone. If it falls out, then you have a small problem. It was either assembled wrong (small end down, reverse and press into place) or the wrong spring. If it doesn't stay in, pressing either end in first, get the proper spring and replace it.

The disconnector is a flat piece of steel stamped out of a sheet of the proper steel alloy, hardened (or not), black oxide finished and assembled.

Hardness Note

The hammer and trigger are harder than a cheap file. These parts are not meant to be altered, polished, filed or otherwise modified. The disconnector is "hard enough" steel, which is good because sometimes it needs to be modified to correct timing problems, a subject we'll go into once we have the basics covered.

Selector

The selector is a round hub with a lever outside the receiver. You rotate that lever to switch between Safe or Fire. Inside, it has a milled shelf in the hub, and that slot provides clearance for the tail of the trigger when you pull the trigger. When on Safe, the un-milled portion of the hub blocks the trigger tail from lifting when you press the trigger.

A slot milled on one end of the hub controls the selector, and in this slot, the tip of the plunger rides, powered by the spring captured by the pistol grip. The slot is recessed into the hub, and you cannot simply press the selector out to disassemble it.

Ambidextrous safeties have a lever on both sides of the hub. The one on the left (usually) is an integral part of the selector, while the one on the right side of the lower is secured in place, usually with a small Allen screw.

Springs

The system works with four springs: hammer, trigger, disconnector and selector. The selector spring pushes the selector plunger and is installed from underneath and held in (both plunger and

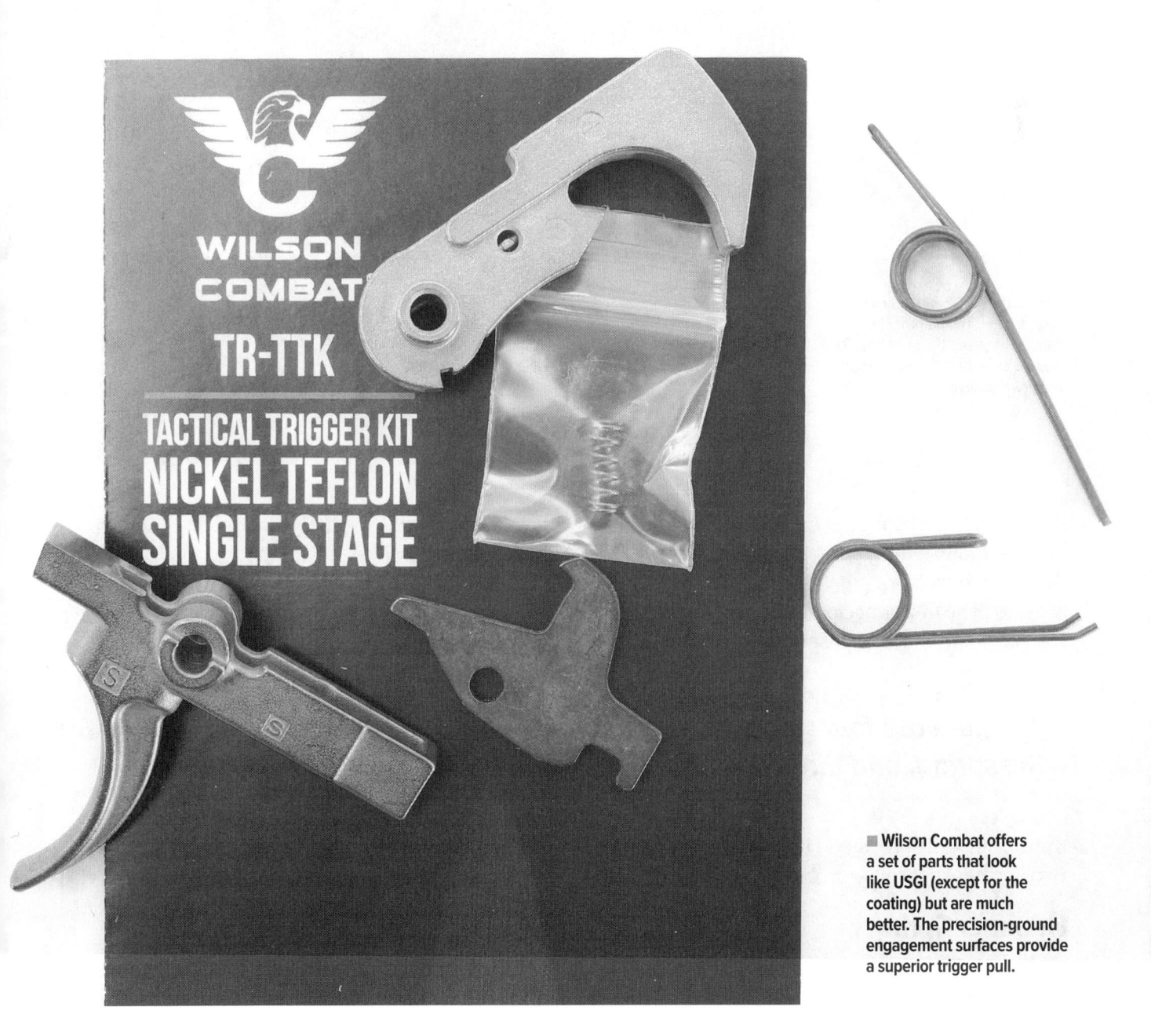

■ Wilson Combat offers a set of parts that look like USGI (except for the coating) but are much better. The precision-ground engagement surfaces provide a superior trigger pull.

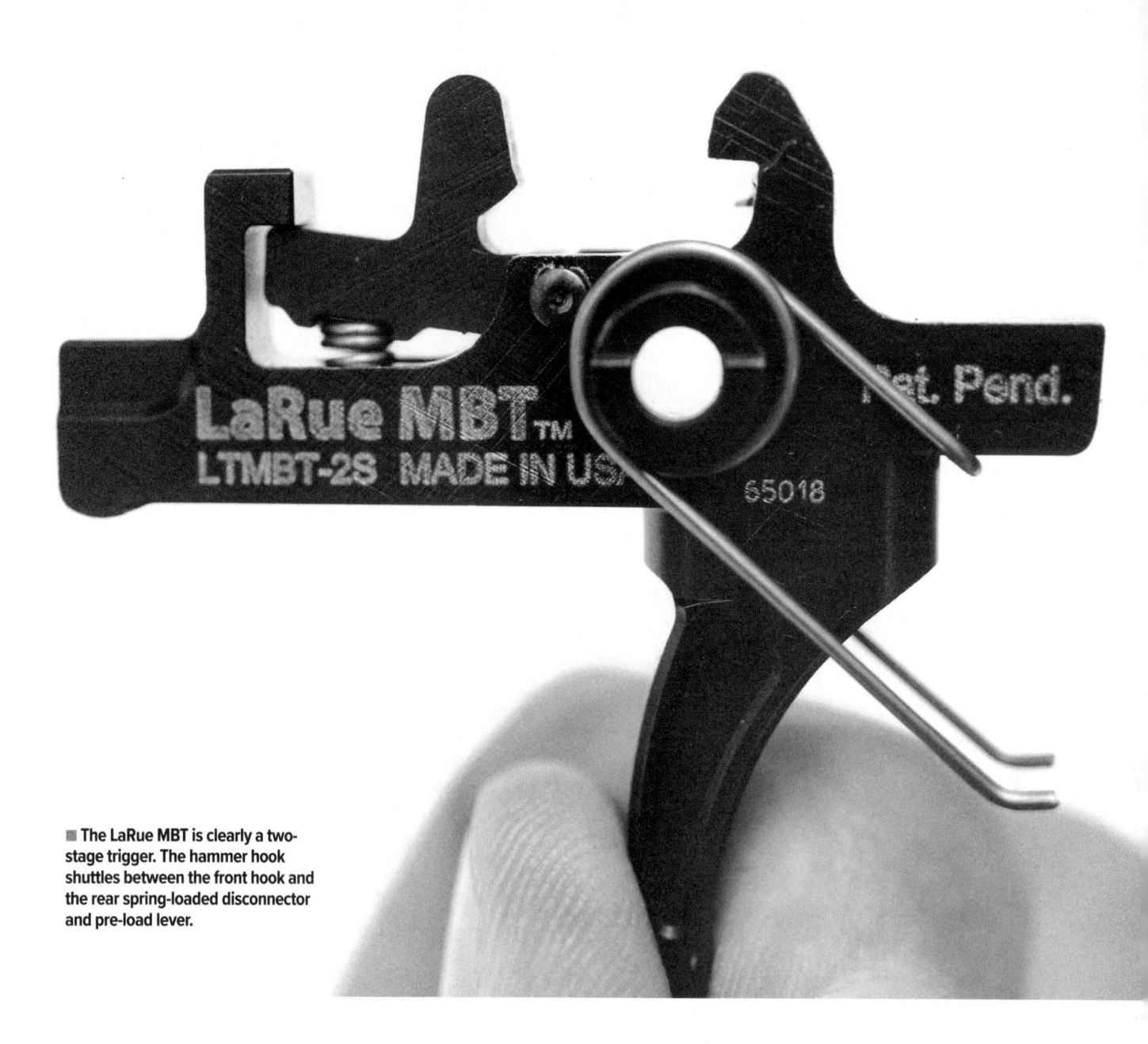

■ The LaRue MBT is clearly a two-stage trigger. The hammer hook shuttles between the front hook and the rear spring-loaded disconnector and pre-load lever.

spring) by the pistol grip. Installation is easy as long as you use the correct plunger and spring and don't pinch the spring between the pistol grip and receiver. The disconnector spring goes into the trigger slot in the hole. Insert the wide end first, so

> "... there are four ways you can install the spring, and three are wrong."

the spring will stay put on its own. It's the other two springs that cause problems.

Hammer Spring

The hammer spring's coil loops go around the two axle-like sections of the hammer hub. You can't easily break or distort that spring by flexing it enough to go over the hub/axles unless you are incredibly ham-handed. What you can do is install it in the wrong orientation, causing malfunctions.

As mentioned in the chapter on lowers, there are four ways you can install the spring, and three are wrong. The description of what is correct is as follows: the coil loops are around the hub axles. The closed end of the spring bears against the back of the hammer upright. The open end should point away from the bird's beak. And most important: the straight line formed by the legs of the closed and open-end are forward of the hub axle. That is, they are toward the muzzle.

The open-end legs will ride on top of the trigger pivot pin when the hammer goes into the lower.

Trigger Spring

The trigger spring also must be installed correctly, but it can't be installed incorrectly in as many ways as the hammer spring and still appear to be "correct." The coil loops go around the trigger axles, and like the hammer spring, you would be hard-pressed to flex the spring enough to cause damage. The spring's closed-loop fits underneath the trigger's sear nose, and the open ends project forward. It's possible to get the closed loop underneath the sear nose but too far down and bound against the trigger-curves body. (Why this dimensional problem wasn't corrected half a century ago is unknown.) If you install the spring this way, you can't just force it up into the correct location. Take it off and re-install it properly.

Install each spring on their respective part on both the hammer and the trigger before assembling the lower.

Assembly

I covered lower and trigger assembly in Chapter 11, Lowers, so refer there for step-by-step instructions.

How a Two-Stage Trigger Works

The disconnector is attached to the trigger in a two-stage design, but it serves a second purpose. When your trigger pull releases the hammer-sear engagement that holds the trigger to the hammer, the hammer's rear hook (two-stage triggers have two) or disconnector hook acts as a trigger-stop point. To illustrate, let's start at the point you have fired a shot but have not released the trigger.

When you let go of the trigger, the disconnector

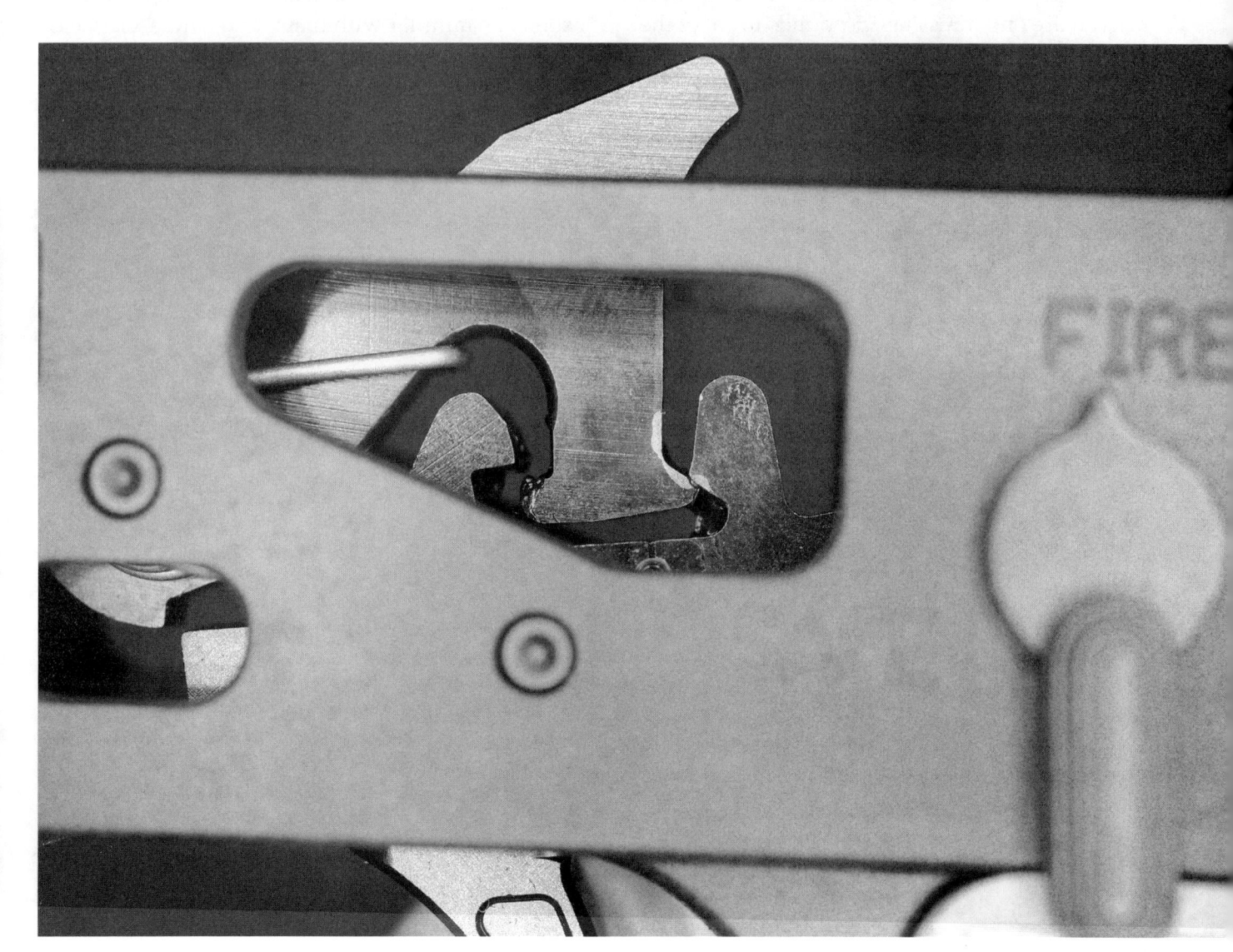

■ After you have fired, the rear hook and the disconnector hold the hammer before releasing the trigger.

hook slides off the hammer hook and releases it to be caught by the trigger hook. Now, when you pull the trigger, the trigger slides forward but is stopped temporarily by the disconnector, which bumps into the hammer hook. To continue the pull, you must force the disconnector post back against its spring. Then the rifle goes bang.

How does this design help?

Simple: since the two hooks and the sear and disconnector are permanently assembled to the trigger bar, their dimensions are more closely controlled. You can therefore have a low take-up weight since the trigger can't, of its own momentum when jostled, push the disconnector spring out of the way.

The take-up can thus be two pounds, and the disconnector requires another pound and a half, totaling 3.5 pounds. But the "slack," or take-up, is one pull, and the let-off is another. You feel as if you are only pressing 1.5 pounds to shoot the rifle.

Where this really matters is for the Service Rifle shooter. The 3-Gun or Multi-gun competitor is happy getting a 1.5 feel, but the Service Rifle shooter must lift a certain weight with their trigger pull. Let's just say that is 4.5 pounds (though there will likely be more). If you make the take-up three of those five pounds and the let-off the other two, it will lift 4.5 pounds in test all day long but feel like two pounds when shooting. That's a near-miracle when it comes to felt trigger-pull weight and worth a basketful of points.

But such precision is not inexpensive, and even the lowest-cost two-stage trigger will run you twice a selection of mil-spec single-stage trigger sets would cost — and sometimes a lot more.

There is no tuning, timing or adjustment of most two-stage triggers. Those that have adjustability should be installed and adjusted by someone familiar with them. The LaRue, Geissele and others just drop in.

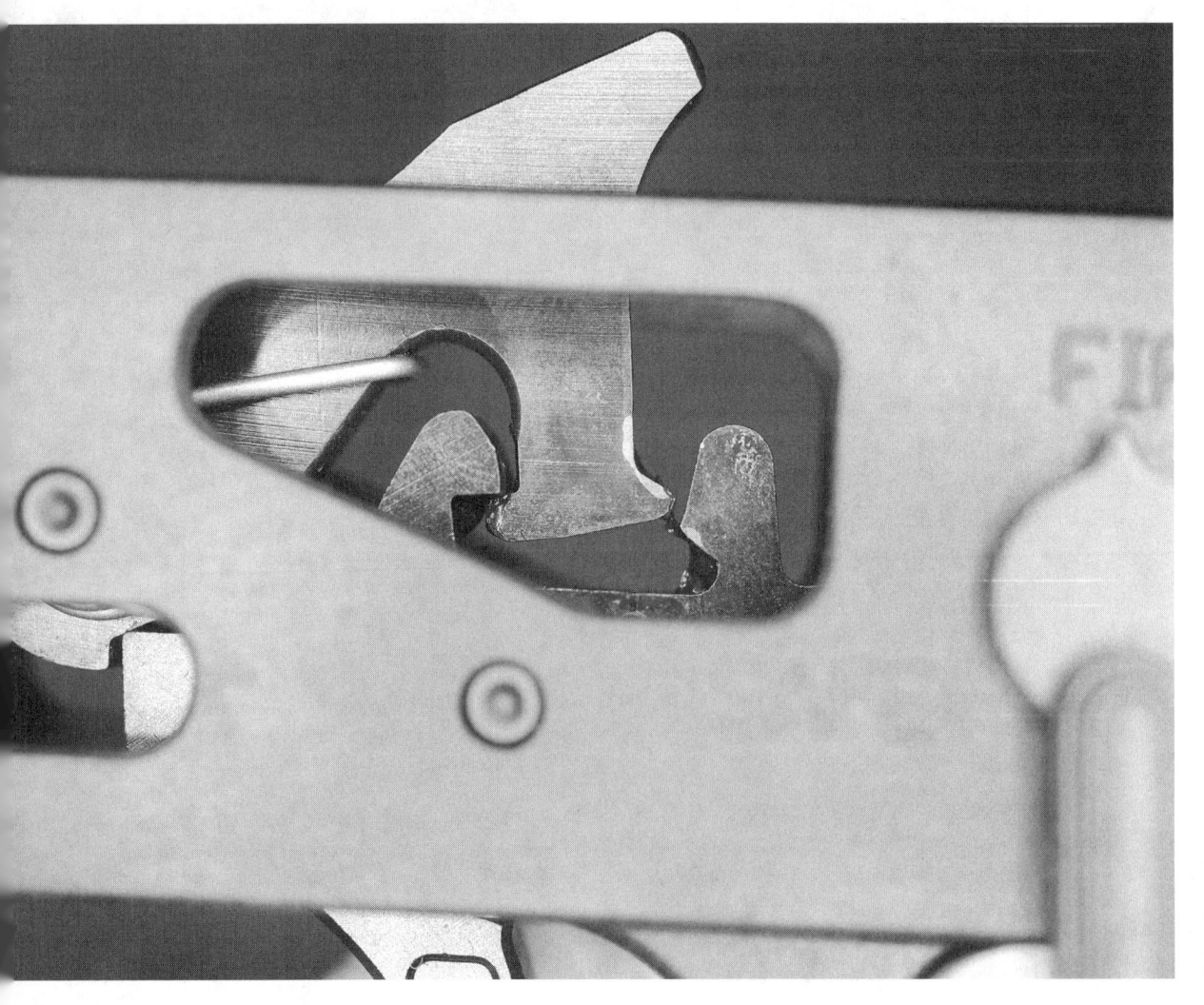

■ When you have released, the hammer is not caught on the sear hook.

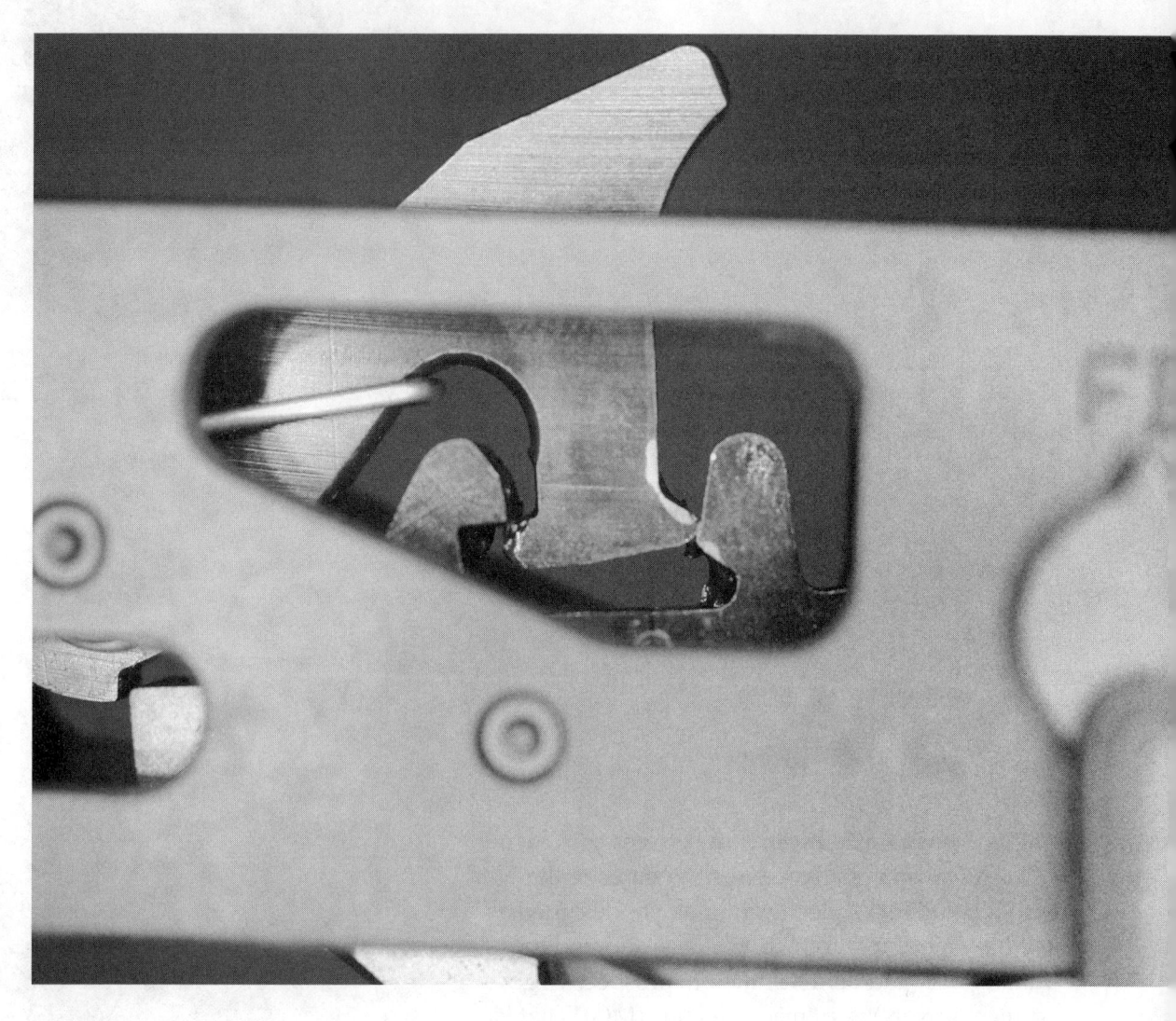

■ When you begin your pull, the take-up is the part that happens until the hammer hook contacts the disconnector nose. Then you must press the disconnector back and fire.

Packet Triggers

The packet trigger was first unveiled by the late Chip McCormick. Here, the trigger parts are made to the utmost precision and assembled in a packet that will never be disassembled. The packet, in its entirety, slides into the lower receiver. It uses the same hammer and trigger pins but doesn't care about pin hole location. If you can get the pins through (and if you can't, it is a terrible lower receiver), then the sear engagement built into the packet stays the same.

Installing a packet trigger is the easiest way to get a primo trigger pull in your AR-15.

When Chip first offered them, they were rare, but now everyone makes one or another version of the design. And why not? There are ten million (or more) AR-15s out there, and sooner or later, every owner will want a better trigger pull. ■

14

AR-15 or M16?

A point of contention between gun owners and gun banners is the status of the AR-15. While the original was designed as a lightweight, small-bore rifle, it was adopted for military use (and demonstrated to prospective government buyers) as a "machine gun" (MG). That is, it was made to be a select-fire firearm. "Select-fire" means the operator can determine that the firearm is on Safe, fires semi-automatically, or fires automatically with some lever or button.

Machine guns are not illegal under federal law. As a point of law, machine guns (which term of art covers both select-fire and solely automatic firearms) have been regulated since the National Firearms Act of 1934. NFA/34 mandated a $200 transfer tax on each purchaser of a machine gun and for suppressors/silencers as well. In 1934, $200 was a lot of money. A quick inflation calculation shows it to be equivalent to $4,000 in 2021 dollars. The government really wanted to discourage the ownership of machine guns. Those MGs that were

■ The A2 came about in the mid-1980s. Even before then, Colt reminded shooters — and the government prosecuted them — about building AR-15s with M16 parts. Except for the carrier, don't bother with M16 parts. You aren't saving any money. Clearly, the government is saving money, judging by the condition of this **M16A2**. It has been there and back several times.

CHAPTER 14 — AR-15 OR M16?

On top is an M16 disconnector. You can safely use this by cutting or grinding off the extra tail that projects past the other two disconnectors. The middle one is an AR-15 disconnector, the bottom one is a very early AR-15 disconnector, and the reason some triggers have two spring seat locations.

in existence at the time could be registered or have the tax paid on them, and for a brief period in the late 1960s, there was an "amnesty period" when existing ones that had not previously been registered could be put on "the list." Plus, during the decades from 1934 to 1986, it was possible to make a machine gun. Those registered and those made and registered during that time are known as "Transferables." That is, any law-abiding citizen in a state where they are not prohibited can undergo the background check, apply for the tax stamp and own a transferable machine gun. So, an MG made before 1934, registered in 1934, or registered during the 1968 amnesty period is a transferable. An MG built before 1986 on what was known as a "Form 1" is a transferable. All others are non-transferable. The non-transferable ones are either illegal (made without a Form 1 or not registered when the opportunity arose) or known as "Dealer's Samples" and can only be owned and sold between dealers or manufacturers.

I can hear you thinking right now: "Where do I get one of these Form 1 things you're talking about?"

You can't. You can blame the late Senator William J. Hughes (D) of New Jersey. (New Jersey will have a lot of explaining to do when the subject of gun control all gets settled sometime in the future.)

The Firearm Owners Protection Act of 1986 brought some good things. One was protection for those traveling. (Some states have been eroding that protection, but we expected that from some of them.) But the passage of FOPA/86 had a last-minute amendment tacked onto it by Senator Hughes: no more Form 1 approvals. No new transferable machine guns. The number of transferable MGs was frozen.

The fundamental law of economics took hold, and prices have risen since. In 1986, you could buy a machine gun — in the few states where it was legal — for perhaps $100 more than an AR-15, so call it maybe $600 to $700. The current prices of transferable M16s hover around $30,000. Machine guns have not stopped being made or imported. Howev-

■ The right-hand carrier has the M16-length bottom shelf. This shelf was a cause for worry in the old days, but today it is just another AR-15 part. Even Colt ships semi-auto rifles with these installed.

er, since 1986 they are all non-transferable and can only be made or brought in as Dealer's Samples or for the use of various governmental agencies and police forces.

It's fashionable in the movies to show every low-level drug dealer and corner drug crew member armed with various machine guns. I'm sure some have them, but they don't want the extra attention and prosecution for the most part. The corner operators don't have more firepower than what the boss allows them (shootings to settle arguments and territorial disputes are typically decided well above the corner guys' pay grade). And when they are, all the regular guns they have been able to buy, steal or accept in trade for drugs will do the job. If they did use a real-deal machine gun in a shootout, various federal agencies would be elbowing each other for the chance to make those headlines and nightly news video clips. So, the number of actual machine guns used in crimes is vanishingly small. The number of registered MGs used in crimes is almost non-existent.

However, since the AR-15 was first a select-fire rifle, and everything the military has purchased for rifles and parts have been select-fire, there are a lot of M16 internal parts out there. In the early days, most parts to be had were M16 parts. Colt was very controlling of its parts supply and charged full retail since it owned the market. Gun shows were awash in M16 parts, which we all dutifully denatured into AR-15 parts since Colt wouldn't sell them to us. (At least not unless we were willing to pay for them as if they were wrapped in gold foil.) The question always gets asked, "How many M16 parts can I have in my AR-15 and not get in trouble?" The answer is: the ATF won't say.

You can write to the ATF, but I will tell you right now what answer you will get back. Because many,

■ The M16 trigger is open at the rear. Yes, you could weld or silver-solder it closed, but that's more work than just getting an actual AR-15 trigger.

■ An AR-15 selector, as found in a typical parts kit. There are only two settings, and the machined flat is clearance for the end of the trigger.

many writers, asking for the last four decades or more have all received the same letter in reply. The format will be like this: the return letter will acknowledge receiving your letter and the question you asked. The letter will then quote the relevant laws on the subject, telling you the legal definition of a machine gun. And that a firearm that operates in a manner that would lead one to believe it is a machine gun will be subject to inspection, perhaps prosecution. They will not give you a firm answer.

Why? The cynics say the ATF wants to have all its options open if it wants to prosecute someone. True. But also, the law is the law. The meaning of a law is literally defined by the words used in it. So, the ATF is telling you what the law says. The agency cannot give you legal advice. Plus, and this is the practical answer: if it gave a number (pick one, any number from one to five) and said, "this is the most number of M16 parts you can have in your AR-15," it would unleash 100,000 experimenters all looking to fit that many M16 parts into an AR-15, and still be legal.

With that resolved, what do the M16 parts look like and can they be modified, so they are not M16 parts?

M16 Parts

The six parts unique in the M16 are the hammer, trigger, disconnector, selector, carrier and auto-sear. The first five are also present in the AR-15 but modified. Some in the manufacturing process start as M16 parts and are given some final work to make them AR-15 parts, and others are separate because of the way they're made. Let's take them in turn.

Hammer. The M16 hammer has a hook on top of the bird's beak of the upper portion. That hook engages the auto-sear in full-auto or burst-fire operation. By itself, it doesn't do anything. If you find you have a deal on M16 hammers, you can make them AR-15 hammers by the expedient process of grinding the hook off with a bench grinder. (If you do that, keep a bucket of water handy, they will get hot.) Once you've ground the hooks off, they are no longer M16 hammers.

■ The M16 selector has several cuts in it and a cam slot for the auto sear. Leave this one where you found it. It's not worth the hassle and can't be modified.

Trigger. The M16 trigger has the back end of the slot the disconnector rides in open to the receiver. On the AR-15, the back of the slot is closed. The trigger is usually made by casting, and the two parts are cast in different molds. A manufacturer could make M16 triggers out of AR-15 ones by setting up a milling machine and cutting the slot open in a pinch. That would be a very peculiar emergency, however. You cannot easily make an M16 trigger into an AR-15 one. You'd have to weld or high-temperature silver-solder the back end of the slot open and not interfere with the operation of the disconnector.

Disconnector. The M16 disconnector has a longer tail that needs the open back of the M16 trigger even to fit and function. Disconnectors are made by a process called fine-blanking, where a steel sheet has disconnectors punched out of it like cutting cookies from a sheet of dough. Manufacturers swap out the cutter and die to change from one part to the other, so there is no big hassle on the parts-making side of things. However, if, like the hammers, you luck into a bonanza of M16 disconnectors and want to make them AR-15 disconnectors, the easy way is to clamp each into a sturdy vice with just the extra tail sticking out. Using a big pair of pliers (over a foot long), grab the tail and work it back and forth until it breaks off. Or hit it from the side with a large hammer and break it off. Use a bench grinder to clean up the busted edge, and there you are. A bucket of M16 disconnectors will take you less than an hour to modify.

Selector. This one is radically different. The AR-15 selector has the rotating drum in the middle machined with one large flat in it. When on Safe, the drum blocks movement of the trigger. When on Fire, the flat is presented to the trigger, and the rear of the trigger can lift when you press the trigger, permitting the mechanism to fire. The M16 selector has slots machined in it to clear the open-ended trigger and engage the disconnector. There's also a cam slot to tip and engage the auto-sear. The difference is obvious. There is no easy way to make an M16 selector into an AR-15 selector, or vice-versa, so pass on even a smoking deal on M16 selectors. They are of no use to you.

Carrier. The carrier is a special case. The lower lip of the rear of the carrier engages the auto-sear in auto or burst fire. Colt, to discourage experimenters and (in a fruitless effort) forestall anti-gun legislation, machined the bottom lip of the carrier back so it could not engage the auto-sear. For a while, Colt even machined the entire rear lower part of the carrier off in this effort. The problem was that the AR-15 depends on a certain amount of mass in the moving parts to reliably function. Changing that mass caused problems. The ATF grudgingly allowed manufacturers to use M16 carriers in their builds. It's now common for AR-15 rifles and carbines to arrive at your local gun shop with an M16 carrier installed, so there is no need to worry about that. Even Colt does it these days.

Auto-sear. This is the big no-no. The auto-sear is the connecting part that permits the other M16 parts to work in select-fire mode. You might never see one simply because it won't fit into many AR-15 lower receivers, and even if it would physically fit, you'd need to drill the auto-sear pivot pin hole to install it. And let me be quite clear: *drilling that hole is a felony*. It is a clear indication that someone has tried or has made an M16 out of an AR-15. You could buy and wear an auto-sear as a tie-tack, and if your local ATF agent even noticed, they would think you were a smartass. But, if you have an AR-15 with the auto-sear hole drilled, *even if you do not have any M16 parts in your possession*, you would be in violation of the law, have committed a federal felony, and be subject to prosecution.

Remember, the law defines a machine gun as a set of parts that can be installed to create a firearm that fires more than one shot on each pull of the trigger or a receiver that has been modified to do so. If you modified the receiver, you did the crime. If you bought it that way, you own a machine gun, and the feds are going to want to know who you bought it from, or else you'll be the one they prosecute.

Now, let's talk about the rest of the M16 parts. Let's say you have an AR-15 that has been assembled by a hack. It has only AR-15 parts, but it's so poorly assembled that sometimes it shoots two or three rounds or dumps the whole magazine when you pull the trigger. Is it a machine gun? Not really. It is a poorly assembled rifle, and if none of the AR-15 parts have been modified or are M16, you simply need to get it fixed. Now, let's say your ham-handed assembler saved a few bucks and did the assembly job with M16 parts, except for the auto-sear because they had no means of machining the receiver to fit. Do you have a machine gun? It would be hard to argue that it is not. You have all the parts save one; it fires more than one shot, walks like a duck, and quacks like a duck. Well, you get the point.

What if it only has one M16 part in it? Really? Do you want to try and make that argument? Why run the risk? Why spend the time, money and angst because you could have saved a couple of bucks buying a surplus M16-whatever part in your build instead of an AR-15 part? I know of at least one person, a police officer (a Lieutenant in his department, if I remember correctly), who had used modified M16 parts by welding them to improve the trigger pull on his competition AR-15. When he was arrested on a different charge (politically motivated city rough-and-tumble politics), the "AR-15 with M16 parts" became a bigger headache than the other problems. Just Don't Go There. Leave M16 parts alone.

One last detail: there is no such thing as an "M16 receiver converted to AR-15." The bright, hard line the law established a long time ago is this: once a machine gun, always a machine gun. Yes, it is physically and entirely possible to take an M16 lower and weld the pin holes for the auto-sear. At that point, it will mechanically and dimensionally be the same as a made-as-an-AR-15 receiver. Your

> *"One last detail: there is no such thing as an "M16 receiver converted to AR-15." The bright, hard line the law established a long time ago is this: once a machine gun, always a machine gun."*

careful work won't matter. It was at one time made as an M16, and as far as the government is concerned, there's no going back. So, no to that question if it ever entered your mind.

Lastly, if you read some anti-gun screed or op-ed columnist claiming the AR-15 is an "easy to make machine gun," and that "you just have to file the sear" or "use a paperclip" to make it full-auto, know this: That person understands less about the AR-15 than your typical gender studies graduate knows about the orbital dynamics of space travel.

3M
POLICE
PROVOST MARSHAL OFFICE
MCAS BEAUFORT - MCRD PARRIS ISLAND

15
Finishes

"Today, black is boring. And, we have found, black is not the "disappears into the night" part of the color spectrum that works best."

The AR-15 started out with finishes in various shades of brown. However, the paint on the stock and handguards, and the light color of the gray anodized finish, were not entirely to the liking of the military buyers. In the 1960s, the hardest and most durable versions of aluminum and plastic were black. So black it was. Black was also easy to make and simple to match from one batch to the next.

Today, black is boring. And, we have found, black is not the "disappears into the night" part of the color spectrum that works best. However, it is what most ARs are made in. There are options, however.

■ If you see a pattern like this, then the coating was applied by dipping.

Color Anodizing

We've talked this one over already. While the Type II anodizing, the one that takes color, isn't as tough as the Type III, it isn't weak by any means. Also, if the handguards on your rifle are the aluminum free-floating type, they are probably Type II anyway, even if they are black. It is a complex mixture and calculation of the cost of anodizing and dying, the alloy used (handguards are usually a 6061 alloy), the desired durability, features desired or required, and end-results cost.

Competition shooters, who are sometimes as hard on gear as soldiers, often want bright colors. Next year, they won't be using the same handguard if they find something "better," so the "lesser" durability matters not one bit.

If the manufacturer has the specialized equipment, color-anodizing can be applied in patterns. Such patterns are not common, though, and cost more than hydro-dipping.

■ This FN AR-15 is finished in an FN Blue Cerakote. Basic black is no longer required.

Coatings

The finish you'll read about the most is Cerakote, a mixture of an epoxy-based carrier and ceramic slurry that is sprayed onto the surface and cured by baking. It adds perhaps a thousandth of an inch thickness to an object and works well with most parts.

You send your AR, or parts, off to be given a Cerakote coating. A finisher preps the surface, degreases it, applies the Cerakote, bakes it and then sends it back. Obviously, something like optics can't be coated.

Cerakote reduces friction, protects the surface, resists abrasion, precludes corrosion (at least until something scratches or abrades through the Cerakote) and provides the color.

In fact, it's such a durable product and in such demand that manufacturers are providing firearms, parts and accessories with out-of-the-box Cerakote finishes.

Dipped Finishes

Complex camouflage patterns are difficult to apply

with something like Cerakote. You need stencils, or an artist with an airbrush, to apply patterns. However, patterns can be applied by hydro-dipping. The process is also known as pattern transfer or immersion printing.

Dipping entails what amounts to a colossal inkjet printer, laying down a pattern on the surface of a film, and then the film is floated in a water tank. Through chemistry magic, the film dissolves, leaving the ink/paint/coating pattern floating on the surface. The object to be coated is lowered into the layer of coating, floating on the water. The transfer clings to the object, and when removed, can be cleaned, dried, and a protective spray

■ If the anodizer has the equipment, it can lay down an anodizing dye pattern that is camo, logos, or whatever. Such finishes do not come cheap, however.

applied. The result can be a glossy, semi-gloss or matte finish, but it is there to protect the delicate film, the transfer layer. Once coated, it is as durable as any other painted object.

If your AR-15's finish has a trademarked name, it was applied by hydro-dipping. The film is made by a special printer, and the operators can take sheets of film, float, activate, apply, clean, and then dry and coat in an efficient sequence that doesn't raise the cost of the firearm. The coating is applied over the anodizing because the film doesn't offer hardness or protection equal to anodizing.

■ This Wilson Combat Ranger is done up in the company's proprietary Armor-Tuff coating.

DuraCoat

DuraCoat is a sprayed-on finish that doesn't require baking to cure. It's more durable than plain old paint and can be had in a variety of colors. You can apply it yourself, or you can have a DuraCoat-authorized shop or the original company apply a camo pattern (or other, they offer a dizzying array of color options) to your AR.

Rattle-Can Camo

This is good old spray paint out of an aerosol can. You can start with (or disassemble to) an un-assembled rifle. You paint, then assemble. This method is favored by shooters requiring every detail who want the results to be like a factory finish. That is not most people.

To give an assembled rifle a paint job, you must be aware of a couple of things. First, you need to protect any optics or sights. Your front sight post will be less useful once you paint it FDE than it had been when it was flat black. Simple masking tape solves a multitude of problems here, as will any other paint-edging tape. The second thing to remember is that paint doesn't stick to oil. So, thoroughly degrease your rifle, at least the exterior, before you paint.

The process is pretty straightforward, but you do have to attend to some details. Have paint on hand and a backer of some kind. A big sheet of cardboard or a layer of newspapers on the ground at the gun club will do. (You do not want to be doing this in your backyard.)

Use an aerosol degreaser, and make sure the rifle is clean and dry.

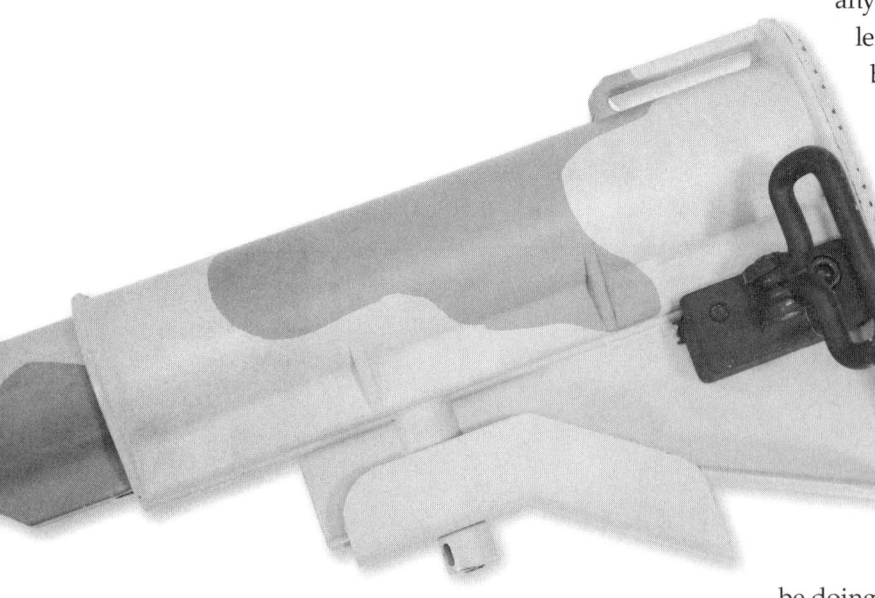

■ The beauty of coatings is that you can apply them to all surfaces: steel, aluminum and plastic.

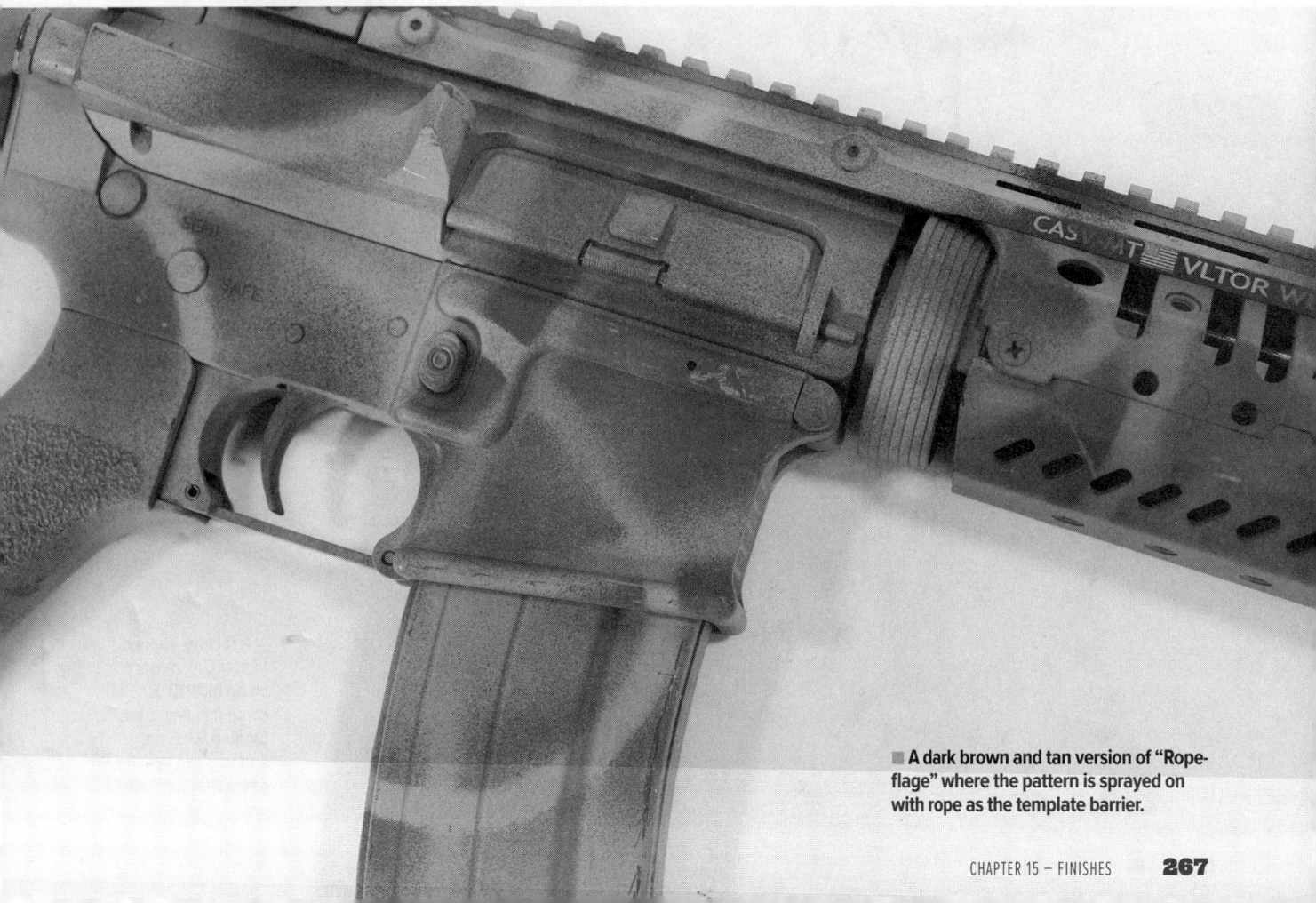

■ The world isn't black, and a lot of places are very sandy. So, a tan or desert sand color like this one will serve you well.

■ A dark brown and tan version of "Rope-flage" where the pattern is sprayed on with rope as the template barrier.

CHAPTER 15 – FINISHES **267**

■ A desert camo pattern from DuraCoat.

■ A factory-applied Mossy Oak pattern on an M&P15. It came this way from Smith & Wesson, and you can see the detail that dipping can deliver.

■ You can lay down a base coat of the primary color, like this one done in Foliage Green. Then put a net or mesh over it.

An important note here: the first color you lay down is the one that will predominate. So, if you want a green rifle with camo patterns of brown and such on it, paint green first. Ditto an FDE or desert tan rifle. Give the whole rifle an even and light green (or other base color) application. Give it time to dry, at least to the touch. Then lay down the blocking pattern, the stencil. Spray your next color. Let it dry. Lay on the third stencil/blocking pattern and spray the third color.

You can block with leaves, rope, mesh patterns, and you can apply the second and third colors overall or just in some areas. Use a sacrificial backer of some kind and do some experimenting with colors and patterns before you put paint on your rifle.

Another approach is to put down the base coat and then lay a net or mesh over the rifle. By applying broken patterns such as spots, ribbons or blobs sprayed through the net/mesh, you apply the added colors in a randomized pattern.

When you lift the blocking patterns from the rifle, you'll see the camo pattern the layers have created. If you really like it, you can apply a durable and matte clear overcoat to keep the paint from chipping as quickly as it otherwise would. Or you can just leave it, as the wear on the paint simply increases the camo-like appearance of the rifle. ■

■ And spot-paint a different color on top of the green. You end up with broken pattern spots on the base color.

CHAPTER 15 – FINISHES **269**

16
Torque and Tech Data

It's time for a bit of techno-speak, information and myth-busting. Torque is the measure of the rotational resistance in a system. (Or the output of an engine.) For us, it's a target region for securing parts meant to stay together.

Torque measurements define the force exerted over the length of the lever arm used. So, you have inch-pounds (in-lbs), foot-pounds (ft-lbs), you could have kilo-meters (not to be confused with kilometers, obviously), or you could make it anything you wanted. Tera-tons per Parsec? Sure, why not? The system is simple: take a lever (wrench, prybar, your arm) one foot long, and attach it to the object you're tightening. Exert one pound of force laterally on the end of that lever, and you have one foot-pound. (And at this point, the real techno-geeks are shouting, "It's pounds-feet." Yes, but I'm not going to be that pedantic.)

When it comes to figuring out AR-15 specs, it doesn't hurt to have access to the original blueprints. With these, the relevant Training Manuals ("TM" in the parlance), and diligent searching, you can find what you need.

CHAPTER 16 – TORQUE AND TECH DATA

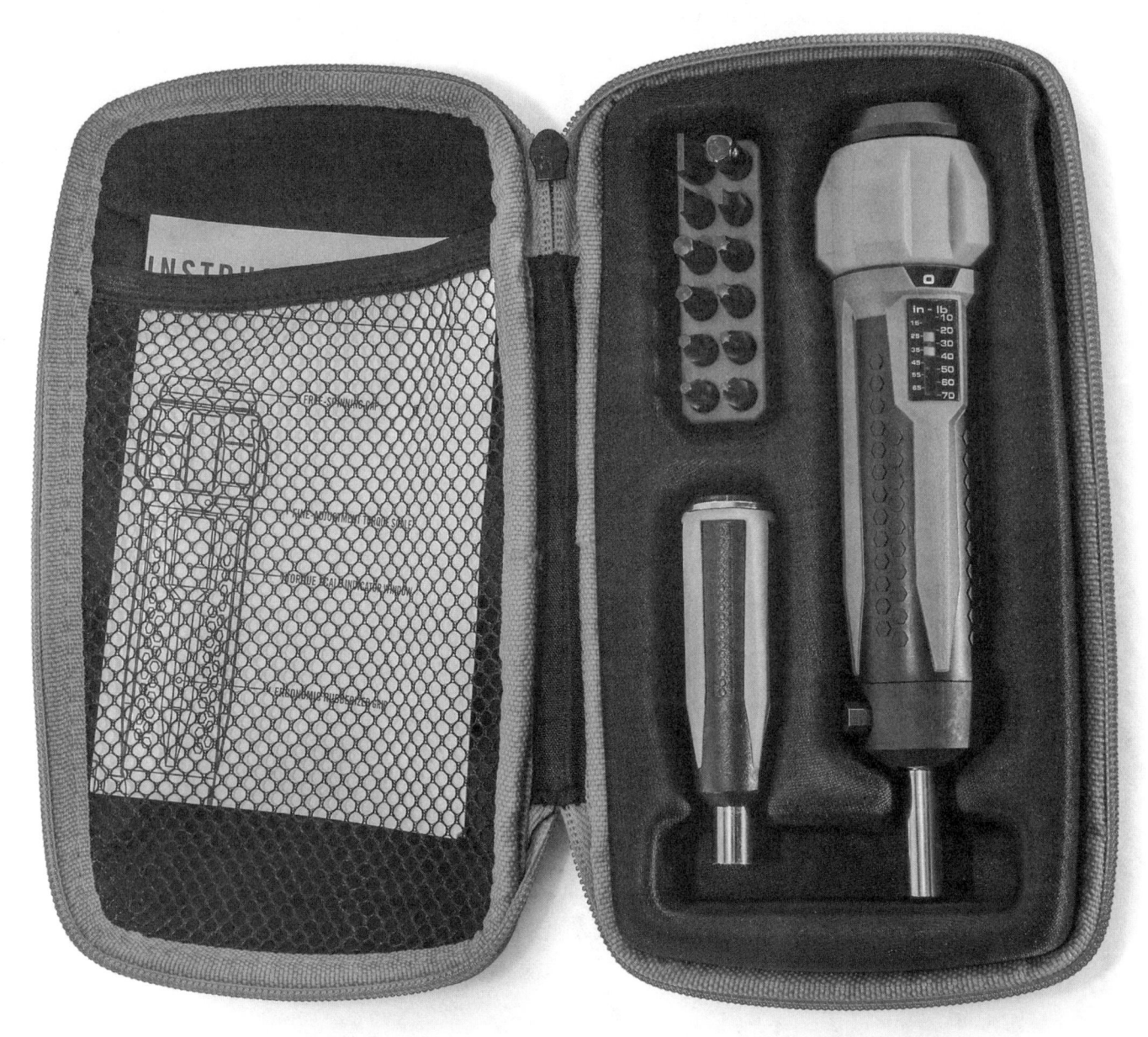

■ To be absolutely sure you have the torque right, use the Real Avid torque wrench for many details, just not the barrel nut.

Why does this matter? It matters because a threaded fastening system is actually a spring. When you spin a bolt or a screw into a nut, you're only overcoming the frictional forces involved. Once you've bottomed out the assembly, you begin flexing the threads of the bolt and nut. You bend them, as you would a spring. That's where the foot pounds comes in. We'll start with steel-on-steel. You can flex the threads in the system up to the failure load of the steel. When you exceed the failure load, you've bent the threads past their recovery point. (Or you broke the bolt head off.)

In many applications, the proper top-end of the torque range of a bolt is at 80 percent of its failure load. What we're looking for is not as precise and could be called the "load-to-hold" torque. That is, what torque level will keep the part from vibrating loose under the conditions we will be subjecting it to? If that is lower than the mechanical engineering desire of 80 percent, then life is good. If the "vibrating loose" environment the fastener is subjected to can overcome the 80 percent torque load, then you need something extra. In aircraft applications, that is known as a lock-nut. There, the nut has a notched flange on top, a castellation. A hole in the bolt allows the technician to run a wire through the bolt and across the gaps in the nut. The vibration must break the wire before the nut can loosen.

Thank goodness there are no firearms applications that need such a system, at least not in the AR-15.

The failure point — the tensile strength of the steel — depends on its alloying composition and its heat treatment. Bolts are grouped by class, with the typical scale being 1 to 8. A Grade 8 bolt has a much higher tensile strength than a Grade 1. The higher grades also cost more. Putting a Grade 8 bolt into a base whose threads are of an alloy only strong enough for a Grade 1 bolt will fail. If you torque it to the G8 torque load, the threads of the base will likely strip. If you only torque it to the G1 level's limit, the G8 bolt threads are not flexed and will slip. The bolt and base must match each other.

The failure load of a thread is also a function of its size. A larger thread will obviously have more strength than a smaller one. However, we don't have the luxury of changing the thread sizes on the parts we're installing. We must use what the specs call for.

Why do we care? Because as with the animals in George Orwell's dystopian novel *Animal Farm*, all bolts are equal, but some are more equal than others. The exemplars here are the screws holding the gas key onto the carrier. You want to be careful here because failing to sufficiently tighten them risks allowing them to work loose. But their failure load is not much higher than their working load.

In many applications, this doesn't matter much. Let's use as an example the bolts holding the top cover of an engine. Those bolts may have a working load of 60 to 70 ft-lbs. In such an application, a bolt may have a failure load of 100, 110 or even 120 ft-lbs. To exceed the failure load, you'd have to just about brace your foot against the firewall of the engine compartment, get both hands on the wrench and put all your weight into it. The gas key screws have an application torque of 55 in-lbs and a failure load of 80 in-lbs. It is well within the strength of many people, even without a wrench, to exceed 80 in-lbs, with just an ordinary Allen wrench, let alone a ratchet wrench with an Allen tip installed. Other applications aren't so critical. For example, you can install the castle nut "close enough" to the torque spec and be fine. It gets staked anyway (*it will be staked, won't it? Won't it?*), and thus can't move even if the torque is a little on the light side.

Years ago, torque wrenches were quite expensive and mainly found in automotive catalogs. With the increased attention to proper torque limits, especially optics mounting, torque wrenches are now standard in firearms and shooting catalogs.

The question then becomes, how much should you obsess about torque limits, and why? The quick answer is: where it matters.

You see, friction has a lot to say about things staying put, even within a broad range of torque limits. The flexed threads, loaded by torque, are also experiencing frictional forces. Without torque, vibration can loosen even a tight friction fit. But once there's at least some torque involved, friction plays a more significant part. At a high enough load, friction can cause the thread surfaces to micro-fracture, known as galling. That's why some people insist on using an anti-galling compound when installing a barrel nut, for example, when you torque that steel barrel nut to the aluminum receiver.

And that leads us to the curious engineering of cross-metal fastenings, such as the steel barrel nut screwing onto the aluminum threads of the upper. Or the steel pistol grip screw going into the threads of the aluminum lower receiver. The two threads, steel and aluminum, do not have the same failure point. You could, theoretically, put enough torque into the nut that you cause the upper threads to fail, stripping the extension. Or the low-

> **"Without torque, vibration can loosen even a tight friction fit. But once there's at least some torque involved, friction plays a more significant part."**

er receiver to be cross-threaded or stripped. Having seen uppers fail, I can tell you this is unlikely because the receiver walls will break or shear before the threads expire. (A classic demonstration of breaking a chain at the weakest link.) The real problem is that the load-to-hold level for an aluminum-to-steel assembly might be higher than the tensile strength of the aluminum. You can't tighten a steel bolt in an aluminum hole enough to keep it tight without stripping the aluminum threads. In the case of the barrel nut, the Armalite engineering staff (i.e., Jim Sullivan) made the threads large enough that this isn't a problem. On the pistol grip,

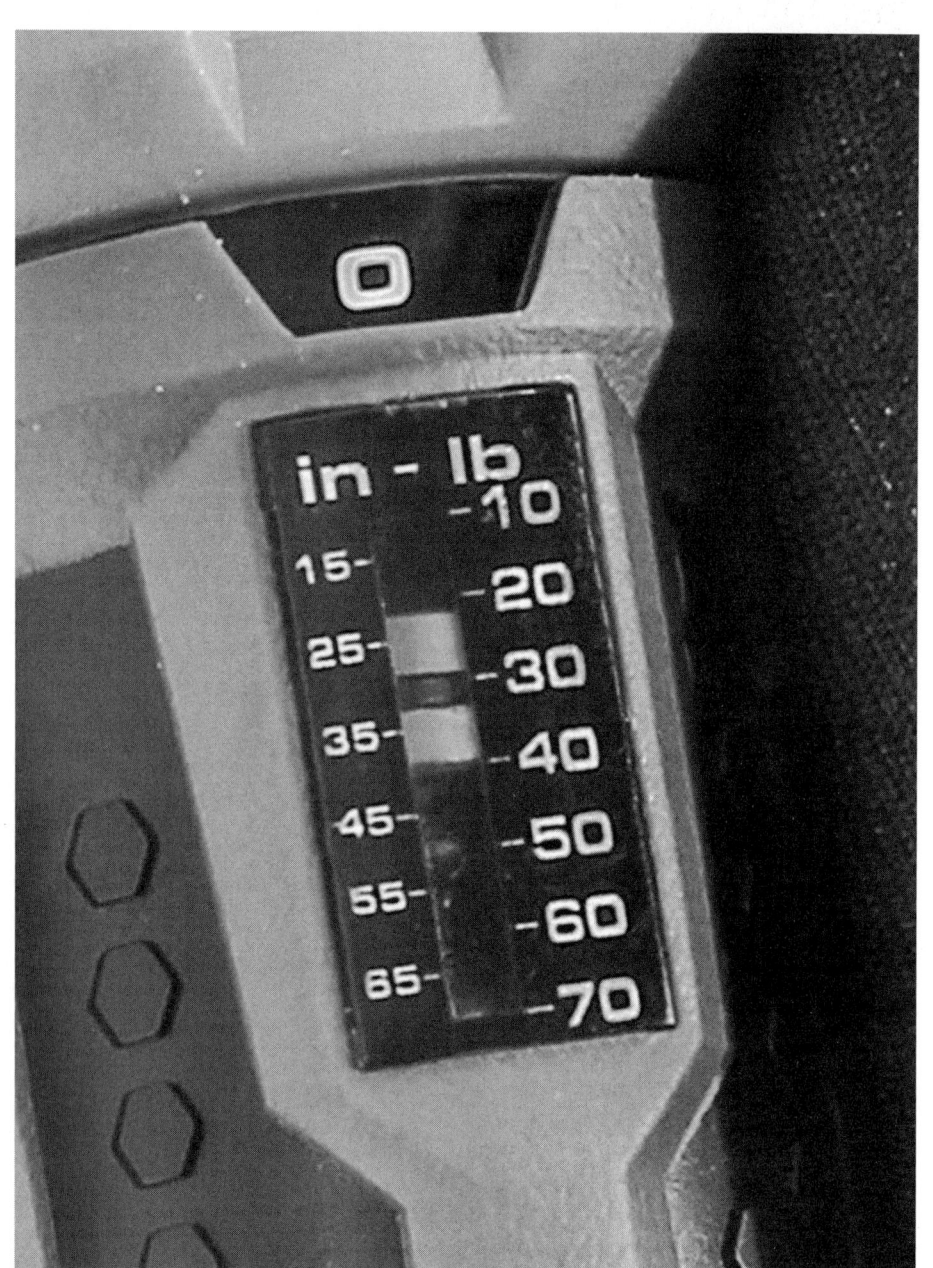

■ The Real Avid wrench adjusts to the torque setting you desire.

that's why there is a star washer in the assembly and why you should use it.

However, be careful with free-float handguards. Those that use a steel cross-bolt through the aluminum handguard to tighten the assembly risk stripping the aluminum thread if subjected to ham-handed assembly.

Thread Lockers

The thread locker brand under discussion here is Loctite, primarily because it's the one everyone will recognize, and in some circles, it has the same kind of reputation as the power tool known as Dremel. The AR-15 is designed to not need any thread-locking compounds in its assembly. However, as you veer further and further from the original mil-spec design, you may find that Loctite is not just useful but necessary. That said, Loctite, being a fluid, can go places you might not expect. Use only as much as you need, clean up the excess (there's always excess) right away, and when the task is done, inspect again for the excess you might have missed.

I'm not a fan of Loctite use in the AR-15, but I will use it when needed. Two situations come to mind. One is the castle nut. When using some designs and/or brands of receiver plates, you may find that the plate is too hard to stake to the castle nut. In that case, use Loctite. The flash hider is another special case. Service Rifle competitors must use a flash hider (I believe the regs allow for some to not have them, to follow state laws forbidding muzzle threads.) Builders of top-end Service Rifle competition guns have found that too much torque on the flash hider can constrict the bore at the muzzle by a few ten-thousandths of an inch, enough to take the gilt-edge off of accuracy. Shooters so affected will hand-fit a flash hider to be correctly "timed" in place, then Loctite or epoxy it, with no torquing. The flash hider experiences no torque forces in use, simply vibration, so that is plenty to keep it in place.

Loctite comes in a variety of strengths and flows, denoted by color. Blue is the low end and, if the fastener is up to it, you can disassemble a blue Loctite part by hand. Red is the next step up, which you can't un-wrench. Green is the strong stuff. If you need to remove a part affixed with red or green Loctite, it'll have to be heat-broken. You basically heat the parts up above 450 degrees or so until you see the white smoke and smell the burning Loctite. Once the Loctite has all been burned, you can loosen the part. It'll still resist, as the ashes of the Loctite remain in the threads, but at least you'll be able to remove it.

Applying Loctite

Before applying Loctite, clean and dry the parts. Clean the threads with a tap (or die) and degrease them, especially for the smaller threads and the threaded holes. Larger parts, like the castle nut and tube, will be good enough if degreased. Hand-assemble the parts to make sure they fit. Apply Loctite, tighten the parts, wipe out the excess and check again in a few minutes for any excess. Loctite is not a replacement for proper torque in assembly, except for the flash hider when called for.

Tech Data

As you'll see in the parts list below, there isn't just one "mil-spec," but each part has its own military specification list, description and definition. Also, a maker may call its rifle "mil-spec" or "fully mil-spec," but it isn't necessarily so. That's because the final military specifications are that it is select-fire or burst-fire and sold to the government. Lacking those last ones, a rifle could be made of mil-spec parts, but not be fully mil-spec. That's the Catch 22 of AR-15 manufacturing.

Roll Pins

You should never use a standard pin punch on a roll pin. Because of the hollow, thin wall construction of a roll pin, a standard pin punch will often collapse, mar or distort the end of the pin or be

List of Roll Pins

- Forward Assist Pawl Retaining Roll Pin (old teardrop) . . . 1/16 x 5/16 in.
- Charging Handle Latch Retaining Roll Pin . . . . 5/64 x 5/16 in.
- A1 Rear Sight Wheel Retaining Roll Pin . . . . 1/16 x 1/4 in.
- Bolt Catch Retaining Roll Pin . . . . 3/32 x 1/2 in.
- Triggerguard Retaining Roll Pin . . . . 1/8 x 5/8 in.
- Triggerguard Detent Retaining Roll Pin . . . . 1/16 x 1/4 in.
- Forward Assist Pawl Retaining Roll Pin . . . . 3/32 x 1/2 in.
- Forward Assist Pawl Retaining Roll Pin (new round) . . . . . 1/16 x 1/4 in.
- Forward Assist Retaining Roll Pin . . . . 3/32 x 5/8 in.
- Gas Tube Retaining Roll Pin . . . . 5/64 x 5/16 in.
- Ejector Retaining Roll Pin . . . . 1/16 x 7/16 in.

driven into, and jammed inside, its hollow core. A proper roll pin punch stays aligned with the roll pin, reducing the chance of the punch slipping off when you strike it. A punch slipping off can mar the part — or injure your hand.

The roll pin punch has a small dimple on the tip, which nestles inside the roll pin's hollow. Use the roll pin starter pin punch to align and start the pin, which prevents damage caused by accidental slippage while starting the pin.

Use a roll pin punch that is no larger than the compressed diameter of the pin. An oversized pin's dimple expands the end of the roll pin when you strike it. An undersized pin risks sliding into the roll pin, and that's even worse.

If the end of a roll pin punch is damaged or deformed, toss it. Start with a new one. Repairing the tip of the roll pin punch and shaping the center projection is a fool's quest.

Torque and Tech Data

Torque Limits

Buffer tube, A1 & A2:	35–39 ft-lbs
Castle nut, tele stock:	38–42 in-lbs
USGI barrel nut:	30 ft-lbs minimum, up to 80 ft-lbs to align collar notch to the gas tube
Gas key screws:	50–55 in-lbs (the old spec was 10 in-lbs lower, this proved inadequate)
Flash hider:	15–20 ft-lbs

Buffer Springs

Rifle	41–43 coils, replace if shorter than 11.75 in.
Carbine	37–39 coils, replace if shorter than 10.065 in.

Headspace Comparisons

	Go	No-Go
Commercial .223	1.4640 in.	1.4670 in.
Military 5.56	1.4646 in.	1.4704 in.
USGI Field*	1.4730 in.	
Colt Field II*		1.4736 in.
M249	1.497 in.	1.4982 in.
M249 Field*		1.5020 in.

Note: There is no Go/No-Go for a Field gauge. It simply is a pass-fail proposition.

Chamber/Leade Dimensions

Chamber part	.223 Rem.	5.56x45	.223 Wylde
Neck diameter	.2510 in.	.2550 in.	.2550 in.
Freebore diameter	.2242 in.	.2265 in.	.2240 in.
Throat angle	1.5–3 deg.	1.2–2.5 deg.	1.25 deg.
Neck length	.2034 in.	.2200 in.	.2220 in.
Freebore length	.0250 in.	.0500 in.	.0620 in.

Steel Alloys

CARPENTER 158 ALLOY QUALITATIVE TEST				
Carbon	Manganese	Silicon	Chromium	Nickel
0.10	0.50	0.30	1.50	3.5

Alloy	Carbon	Manganese	Sulfur	Silicon	Chromium	Molybdenum	Vanadium
4140	.40	.85	.040	.3	.95	.2	
4150	.50	.85	.040	.3	.95	.2	
CMV	.45	.75	.040	.28	.35	.25	-2.1
416	.15	1.25	.15	1.0	13	.060	-3.6
17-4	.07	1.0	.03	1.0	16		-9.6

Carrier Steel

Alloy	Carbon	Nickel	Chromium	Molybdenum
8620	.20	.30	.50	.20

The remainder in all instances is iron. All alloying constituents are permitted a small spread, such as carbon in 4150 allowed to be between .48 and .55 percent. Stainless alloys will sometimes have a small percentage of phosphorous and other trace elements, at the tenth of a percent level.

Mil-Spec Standards

Below are the mil-spec standards, which some but not all manufacturers stick to. Some makers use superior steels, better heat treatments and improved surface coatings.

Bolt	Carpenter Technology No. 158 alloy. Shot peened per ASTM B851/SAE AMS2430S. Individual high-pressure/proof (HP) test-fired in a fixture. Individual magnetic particle inspection ASTM E1444/E1444M and marked: (SP) Shot Peened, (HP) High Pressure Tested, (MP) Magnetic Particle Inspection.) or roll-marked before hardening. (Obviously, if they fail, they are destroyed if marked beforehand.)
Cam Pin	4340 Chromoly steel alloy per SAE AMS6415T/AMS6484D
Firing Pin	Machined 8640 steel alloy. Heat-treated. Hard chrome plate
Extractor Retaining Pin	Machined (the best are ground) S7 Tool Steel. Heat-treated per ASTM A681-08
Extractor Spring	5 coil, ASTM Grade A401 Chrome Silicon wire stock. Heat-treated. Stress relieved. Mil-spec black insert/synthetic elastomer extractor buffer (nitrile-butadiene, 80+/-5 durometer per MIL-PRF-6855)
Ejector	S7 Tool Steel. Heat-treated per ASTM A681-08
Extractor	Machined from 4340 tool steel alloy per SAE AMS6415T/AMS6484D (vs. 4140). Heat-treated. Shot peen per ASTM B851/SAE AMS2430S.
Gas Rings	Stainless steel per mil-spec
Carrier	Machined from AISI 8620 aircraft quality alloy per ASTM A108/A322-1. Heat-treated. Carburized/strain relieved, hard chromed bore. Surface ground gas key slot.
Gas Key	4130 steel alloy per ASTM A108/A322-13. Hard chrome internal. Hex screws torqued and (should be) staked all per mil-spec

Sight Adjustments

Rifle:	A2 rear sight 0.5 in.	front sight 1.25 in.
	A1 rear sight 0.4 in.	front sight 1.0 in.
Carbine:	A2 rear sight 0.75 in.	front sight 1.5 in.
	A1 rear sight 0.6 in.	front sight 1.2 in.

Trajectory Table (inches), 55 FMJ, 3,200 fps, 20-in. barrel

Zero distance (yards)	25	50	100	150	200	250	300
25	0.0	+2.4	+6.4	+9.3	+10.9	11.1	+9.5
50	-1.2	0.0	+1.6	+2.2	+1.4	-0.8	-4.7
100	-1.6	-0.8	0.0	-0.3	-1.8	-4.9	-9.6

■ The whole point of a self-loading rifle is that you have a ready supply of loading systems, aka magazines.

17

Magazines

Why a chapter on magazines in a book on AR-15 setup? Simple.
The whole point of a self-loading rifle is to have a feeding system that allows it to self-load. If that part or process fails, you have a clumsy single-shot rifle. So, magazines.

There used to be fewer choices when it came to AR-15 magazines. There were 20- and 30-round mags, and they were made from aluminum. The 20s were bulletproof. (As in reliability, they couldn't stop bullets.) The 30s were all over the map, mainly because they were either brand new and expensive or pre-owned and who knew what they had been through? The marginal reliability of the basic rifle (we're talking the early 1980s) made magazines a roll of the dice.

So, it was obligatory and routine to test your magazines, keep the ones that worked reliably, trade and sell the others, and never loan the good ones. Never. As explained elsewhere, many of the "unreliable magazine" problems we were having back then were due to other shortcomings in the rifle itself.

Today? Magazines are reliable like us old-timers never saw. We're living in what is truly the golden age of the AR mag. It's easy to find reliable ones, you simply order the big brand names, and you're

■ The military uses stripper clips to jam 10 rounds at a time into a magazine. If your ammo comes this way, then you can too. Otherwise, simply thumb them in one at a time.

set to go. Magpul, Lancer, Brownells, Surefeed, E-Lander, ASC, Hera, MFT, D&H, TangoDown and Daniel Defense are all magazines I've tested and found to be utterly reliable. Pick a brand, buy what is on sale and test them in your rifle (yes, you still need to test them, that is the nature of life on this planet).

Background on magazines, however, depends on a host of variables. Here's the basic info you'll need to choose, test and be happy.

What Magazines Do

In an AR-15, the magazine holds rounds in a double stack, staggered side-to-side, not in a vertical column. The mag supports the stack for feeding and presents the lifted stack (after the bolt/carrier has moved to the rear) in time for the bolt — during its return trip forward — to strip a cartridge off and feed it. The stack needs to be lifted high enough, soon enough and be aligned. We like to think the rounds are smoothly fed, but they sometimes wiggle, jump and stumble when viewed in high-speed video. But they feed.

The magazine spring must be strong enough to push the rounds up in time. It takes a lot of shooting to wear a spring down, and I suspect that you'll have gone through multiple barrels on a rifle before the magazine springs wear from feeding. What kills mags is dropping them, stepping on them or "tuning" them. Don't let anyone "tune" your magazines. The feed lip dimensions are not user-serviceable. You can't "refresh" the spring by pulling it out and stretching it past its regular length (in fact, that can worsen spring-strength problems). Disassembly and cleaning after you've doused it in murky water or doing it once a year is fine. Don't oil the inside. It doesn't need it, and that too can cause problems.

If you dent the shell, don't try to lift the dent; I'd be surprised if a dent prevents it from working. Magazine repair is usually a fruitless effort, and except for the entertainment value of trying to fix it, you're better off replacing a damaged magazine.

■ If you find you have a collection of magazines and they serve different rifles and calibers, you really need a marking system to keep them straight.

CHAPTER 17 – MAGAZINES   281

Mag Fit

Your magazines must slide into the mag well without resistance and fall of their own weight when you depress the mag release button. Any that do not fall must be sold off or traded, period, end of story. If too many are failing to drop, then your lower may be the problem. I'd like to tell you that there is an easy fix, but there isn't. If the dimension of your magazine well was made too far out of spec, you can't get in there and "polish things up" or "knock off the burrs" to correct it. It should be sent back (if you haven't used it much, and if the seller will take it back), or it becomes a "range queen" — a rifle used for practice and training but not competition or defense.

Aluminum mags have one failing: they're made

> *"We're living in what is truly the golden age of the AR mag. It's easy to find reliable ones, you simply order the big brand names, and you're set to go."*

Even the Marines accepted the idea of polymer magazines once they got over the shock of it.

These two magazines feed 7.62x39 (left) and 5.56. If these are the only calibers you have, then you can keep mags straight. But they are not all so obvious.

of aluminum. Heavily used and abused magazines can be dented out of square or have the lips spread and cause feeding and dropping-out problems. There is no fixing them. If the feed lips spread, ditch it. We all used to save the followers and springs "just in case," but I don't know of anyone who does that anymore, except for a few OCD competition shooters who just must have spares.

Background Info

There are various specs on magazine construction. First, while polymer mags are all the rage and are plenty tough, they're not so superior to aluminum ones that you need to abandon the originals. If they work, just use them. The oldest aluminum magazines are probably collector's items now. The newest ones are as good as anything. In polymer, Magpul is the original and makes excellent mags. Lance uses polymer with steel feed lips, also a great combo.

You'll read about music spring wire and silicon stainless wire. Both of these work. And both will rust — though neither will rust under the conditions you will use them in nor will they rust so

■ If you don't mark your mags, and you're in a class where everyone is loading and dropping theirs, how will you know the ones you get back are yours? Mark them, that's how.

badly that they'll fail to function.

You will also hear of "anti-tilt" followers. Strictly speaking, there is no such thing. Followers must tilt to smoothly feed the stack up. In a 30-round mag, they tilt to follow the curve of the magazine. In a straight 20-round magazine, they adjust to the stack's changing angle. What an "anti-tilt" magazine follower doesn't do is tilt so much that it binds in the tube or fails to support the cartridge stack. And every new mag is made with an "anti-tilt" follower. You'd have to go back in time and use an unmodified magazine produced before the early 1990s to find such a one. If you're buying new, and it isn't a no-name magazine company, it is anti-tilt.

Caliber

You'll most likely be feeding .223/5.56

■ Mark your mags to track which ones are working correctly and sort out those that aren't. If you only owned these three magazines, that would be easy. What if you own a dozen identical ones?

ammunition through your AR-15. In the old days, that was all there was. Today, the .300 Blackout is a hot contender for the "most often seen at the range" caliber. There are other contenders, however, if not for "most popular." The 6.5 Grendel is a high-performance cartridge that is based on a heavily modified 7.62x39 case. The 6.8 Remington SPC is another. It's based on the .30 Remington case, shortened, necked down and using bullets in much the same weight range. The newest is the 6mm ARC, also derived from the 7.62x39 and shows much promise as an accurate hunting and defensive cartridge.

Here's the thing. While the .300 Blackout (and the almost-identical and earlier-designed .300 Whisper) were intended to feed through unmodified AR-15 magazines, the non-.223 cartridges need caliber-specific mags to properly feed.

.223 and .300 Blackout Feeding

The .300 Blackout is supposed to feed just fine in unmodified .223 magazines, but that isn't always the case. There's a rib on the inside of the .223 mag that is meant to be a shoulder bump. That shoulder stops the case from shifting forward, bumping on the case shoulder, so the bullet tips can't impact the inside of the magazine tube. Full metal jacket (FMJ) ammo could dent the magazine. Soft points could "rivet" the soft lead bullet tips. Moreover, .300 BLK bullets of the subsonic and heavy type are so wide at the mag's rib that they can become angled toward the center. The lighter bullets of .300 BLK, like the 115-grain supersonics, are less problematic.

As a result, there are .300 Blackout-specific magazines on the market for those who feel the need or have a rifle that is a bit picky about feeding subsonic heavies out of .223/5.56 mags.

Magazine Marking and the Imperative

If you own both 5.56 and .300 Blackout, you must mark your magazines. The problem isn't so much inadvertently feeding 5.56 into a .300 chamber. It will feed, close, and even fire if the extractor holds the case rim. (The rims are the same diameter.) The .224-inch bullet, looking for guidance while rattling down a .308-inch barrel, won't generate enough pressure to cycle the action. You'll hear a "pop," and that's that. The problem is putting a .300 in a 5.56.

The .300 Blackout cartridge is designed so that any factory bullet will be too far forward to let the bolt close on a .300 in a 5.56 chamber. That's the good news. The bad news is that this safeguard isn't foolproof. If the neck tension is weak, the bullet might be set back in the case. And if you hammer on the forward assist or drop the round into the chamber and let the bolt crash home without feeding from a magazine, the bolt could close.

That will be bad.

The .308-inch bullet will not have a happy life trying to fit down a .224-inch bore. The bullet will get a few inches up the bore before the chamber pressure mounts to the point where it breaks the case, the bolt, the upper, the magazine, the carrier, the charging handle, sometimes the handguard, and occasionally bends the lower. The lower might be salvageable, but everything else is toast. Sometimes even the optics get busted if the upper breakage isn't contained by the scope mount.

The surprising thing about this is that the shooter, while startled, is *usually* unharmed. Many take the ride without so much as a scratch, although they do have a noticeable flinch for some time afterward.

The secret is: never mix the ammunition and rifles. Marking magazines goes a long way toward preventing that. Not taking both to the range at the same time is a good policy. And definitely don't take new shooters to the range with both cartridges and rifles for each.

■ A special magazine for an LWRCI 6.8. It fits only an LWRCI 6.8 rifle, and it is on loan. So, the author marked it temporarily with blue tape.

Markings

Marking your mags can be simple or complex. The simplest way is to dedicate one brand to one and another brand to the other. For example, Magpuls for 5.56 and Lancer for .300. Or vice-versa. Or whatever worked in your rifle for each and kept apart. Or dedicate .300-specific magazines for your .300 rifle or carbine. There are such mags now, and it would be wise to get them if you have a .300 BLK and mark them, also.

You can paint them. Use a band of color for one or the other. Even add the caliber in the band. For example, green for 5.56, blue for .300. You can write the caliber on the mag. Use a stencil and spray paint, and put a "556" on one set and "300" on another. (After you test them to make sure they work 100 percent with that caliber, of course.)

You can put your initials on them all and number them in sequence. That way, you'll know, "Hey, number four is getting a bit picky in feeding, I'll have to take a look." If you're attending a rifle class, having mags with your initials ensures that you get yours back and not someone else's. If a spray can isn't your thing, then a paint pen works.

By this point, you really don't have to put a camo pattern on your magazines; they will have enough swathes of paint on them that they will be camo'd just with markings.

Magazine Care

Dropping mags on the ground is part of life and what hurts them the most. A grassy surface is fine; a concrete surface is worst. If you drop them in mud, simply unload, hose, dry and keep using them. Once a year, remove the baseplate, ease the magazine follower out, wipe off everything and reassemble.

Magazine Testing

There are four tests to check a magazine: Fit, lock, low feed and high feed.

First, insert the magazine into the lower. Does it slide in smoothly? Does it drop out of its own weight when you press the mag button? If yes, you're done. If not, then it could be the magazine or the lower. If your lower has worked fine with every other magazine so far, replace it. You only want to own mags that work in your rifle. If your lower is picky, this will be a chore. If your buying habits lean towards cheap, then you'll be in for some disappointment.

With the magazine back in place, work the charging handle. Does the bolt lock open? Done. If not, the problem can be the magazine — worn follower, misassembled, tired spring — or the bolt hold-open lever. Check to make sure that neither is binding. If the magazine is so used it fails to lock open, replace it. If new, try a different one. If the

> **"There are four tests to check a magazine: Fit, lock, low feed and high feed."**

hold-open is binding, then tend to it.

To test low feed, load five rounds in the magazine and fire them. If the magazine's feed lips are worn, bent or "adjusted," then low spring tension near the end of its travel will allow the cartridges to rattle around in feeding and cause problems. Feed lip issues are typically easy to spot with a close look. Aluminum feed lips aren't worth bending or adjusting. Polymer ones can't be bent. And the steel lips on the Lancers can't be bent.

For high feed, load to capacity. If that is 20, then 20. If 30, then 30. Yes, yes, we all know that you're supposed to "load down" by two rounds to make reloading easier. In the famous words of the late-night TV announcers, "this is a test." Load up and with the bolt forward, see if you can seat the magazine. If you can, how difficult is it? If you can't hammer the magazine in place, you know yours is a 28-round-magazine rifle. If you can, but it's difficult, then be aware. And if they go in place without a problem, then you're set.

Now, fire one round. Pull the magazine, replace the fired round with a new one, re-insert the mag and try again. Here you're checking to see if the spring has enough power to lift the whole stack and that the rifle can work against the upward pressure of the loaded magazine. Do this for a few rounds, then fire five rounds to finish.

If the mag passes all these tests, you can start marking it as ready to go.

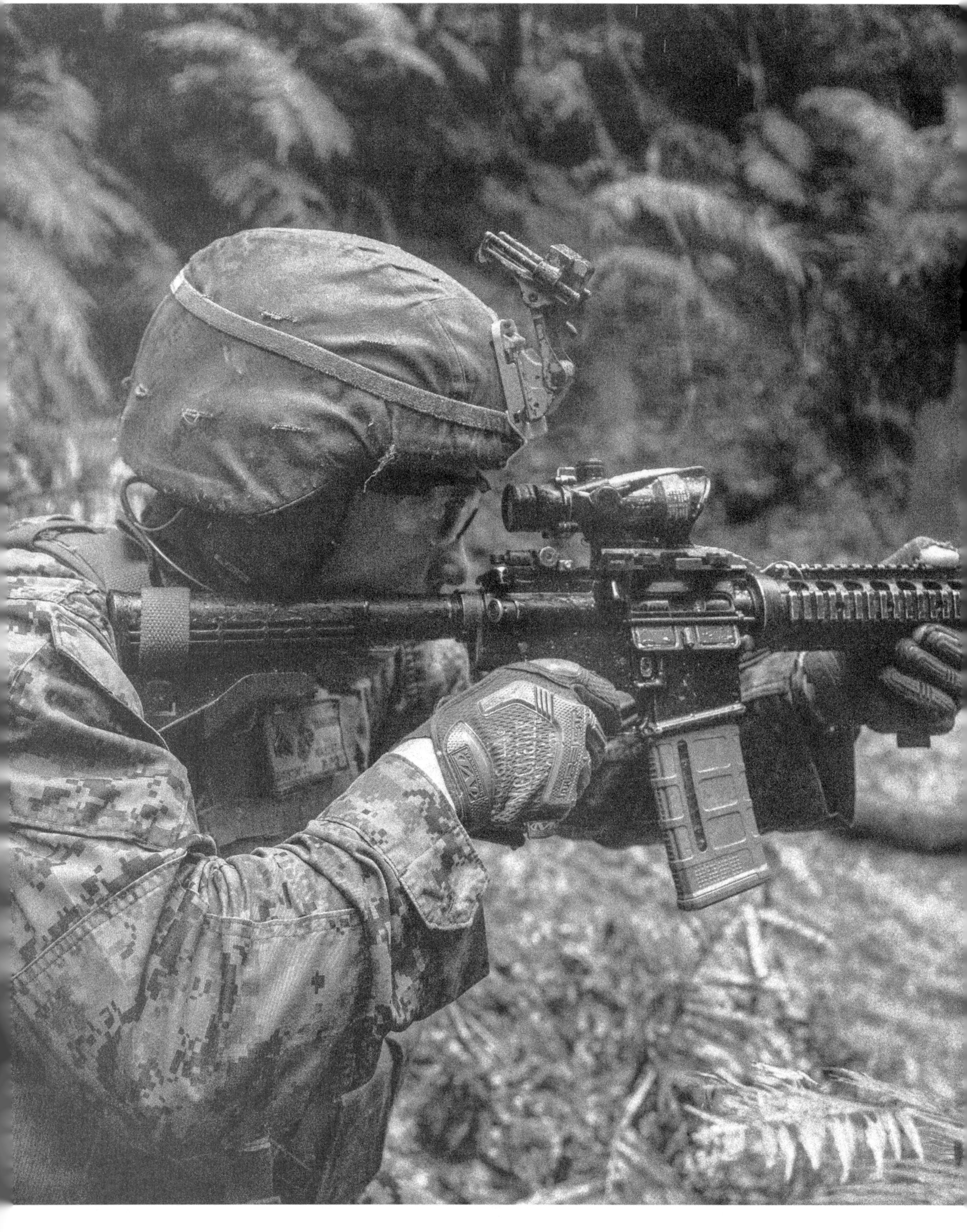

18
Handguards

■ In the transition to quad rails, the military bought large quantities of railed handguards, which fit into the regular handguard Delta ring and front plate.

As soon as "gonnes" could be held and fired, something to protect the shooters' hands came about. Rifles create heat when you fire them, and that heat goes into the barrel. (Much heat is carried out by the fired brass, and that is good. When HK was developing a rifle using caseless ammunition, the overheating problem was never really solved. All the heat must go *somewhere*.)

The original AR-15 handguards were paired and triangular-shaped. They were simply plastic shells with vent holes, and your hand was protected by being far enough away from the barrel. The next upgrade was interior stainless "heat shields." These were simply reflectors that kept the heat from going directly into the handguard. The originals and their copies are left-right pairs. If you break one, you'll need to replace that side.

When the A2 came about, the handguards were changed to fit top and bottom, cylindrical-shaped and interchangeable. They retained the interior metal heat shields.

■ The front of the A2 handguards fit onto the triangular front cap of an A1 upper. So, if you want to put A2 handguards on your A1 upper, you can, as the author did on this one.

For the M4, Colt wanted more heat protection. So, it made the handguards oval-shaped, taller top and bottom, and installed two layers of the heat shield with a space between the shields. This design makes the M4 handguard fatter, so some people prefer the older carbine design, which uses A2-size handguards.

The original AR handguard protected your hands, but it had other problems. Let's start by removing the handguards from a new rifle.

Unload the rifle. Stand it on the buttplate, muzzle up with the magazine well facing to the left. With one hand (usually the left, for right-handed shooters), grab the Delta ring and push it down toward the benchtop. This step usually works better if you tip the edge down, so the Delta ring tilts slightly. Now hinge the bottom end of the handguard from the barrel into the space created by the moved Delta ring. You're compressing the "waffle" spring that pushes the Delta ring forward. Once the handguard pivots far enough, you can remove the front edge from the front cap, which is directly behind the front sight assembly.

Set it aside. Tilting the Delta ring the other way, repeat with the other handguard.

If you successfully removed the handguards using this method, consider yourself lucky. The dimensional fit of the handguards is "close enough for government work." Some rifles are relatively straightforward, others complex, and the rest nearly impossible. How common are difficult removals? Well, the illustration in the training manuals issued with M16s shows two people taking the handguards off. One uses all his strength to compress the Delta ring against the waffle spring, while the other pivots the handguard out of the way.

There is an easier way. Real Avid includes a handguard removal tool in its Master Armorers Kit. (Other manufacturers produce similar tools.) Using it is easy. It's

■ The M4 marking on the front of the receiver means it has M4 feed ramps. Not that it needs some special M4 handguards.

■ Above: Note the gas tube clearance hole in the Delta ring.

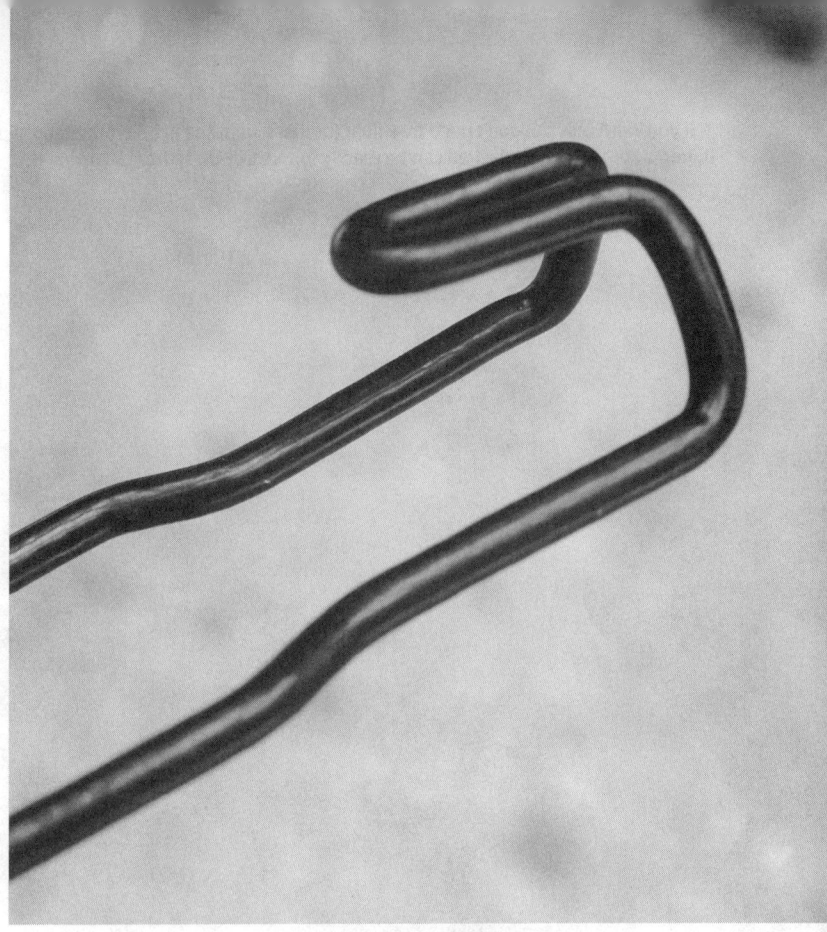

■ Right: The Real Avid handguard removal tool. If your handguards are on tight, there is no better way to remove them.

a bent section of steel rod with a folded tab in the middle of the handles. With the rifle muzzle pointed up, slide the long handles over the Delta ring and hook the middle tab into the front edge of the magazine well. Once the center tab is hooked into the well, compress the two handles enough to get a good grip on them and keep them in firm contact with the Delta ring. Then push the handle down. This method will give you plenty of leverage to compress the waffle spring. Once the waffle spring is entirely compressed, you'll have enough clearance to pivot out and remove the handguards.

If your rifle or carbine has enough slack in the assembly that you can remove the handguards by hand, then you're in fine shape. If not, then get the tool, whether from Real Avid or someone else, because trying to use a screwdriver to pry the Delta ring risks marring the rifle or stabbing yourself, and other potential methods are even worse.

■ The triangular front cap keeps the handguards from rotating. The A2 handguard on the left has punched tabs (the firing pin is pointing at one) that keep the handguard from rotating.

CHAPTER 18 — HANDGUARDS   291

■ If you want rails but don't need free-float (or don't want the extra work), then slip-in handguards with rails attached can be readily found, like these from Blackhawk.

■ Quad rail handguards can be portly. Some are less so. The Primary Arms handguard (right) is slimmer than the traditional size.

> "The original AR-15 handguards are a real hassle to install. Also, they can put force on the barrel, causing accuracy problems."

Installing Handguards

It would be unfair to simply say, "reverse the disassembly instructions." The front-end cap that holds the handguards in place comes in two styles — A1 and A2. A1 handguards will only fit into an A1 cap. A2 handguards can fit into both A1 and A2 caps (someone was clever, there).

However, the front cap's gas tube clearance hole should be on the top, and the cap cup must point backward to allow gas tube installation and hold the handguards in place.

There is one other detail you must be aware of when assembling: the barrel nut tabs. The front cap has a stamped section pressed into the handguard area to index the handguards correctly. The handguards also have clearances for the points of the barrel nut tabs. These act to keep the handguards from spinning around the barrel. However, if the barrel nut isn't timed correctly, the handguards can bind against the front cap tabs, and installing or removing them becomes even more hassle. It can be so bad that they simply won't fit into place. So, you must have the barrel nut correctly timed, not just for gas tube clearance but also handguard installation.

Also, the handguard assembly keeps the barrel nut from loosening. The gas tube is part of that, but the handguards keep things reasonably tight since they can't rotate and are locked to the barrel nut. Even if the barrel nut tries to loosen (not assigning it powers of intent, mind you), the nut will bind on the gas tube or be restricted from turning by the handguards.

To install, insert the front end of the handguard into the front cap at as close an angle as will clear the carry handle or Delta ring. Then compress the Delta ring on that side to get the handguard to clear it. In difficult cases, I've had luck compressing the Delta ring just enough to clear one corner of the handguard, getting it over the edge, then letting it prop the Delta ring open and compressing the other edge. Once both edges are caught, you can force the handguard into place, using it to lever the Delta ring the rest of the way. If this happens, the second handguard will be even more difficult, so start with the top handguard first, as you'll need the clearance the lower affords for the extra pressing, cursing and whacking.

This becomes easier if you have the Real Avid tool, but it still won't be easy.

Original Handguard Shortcomings

The original AR-15 handguards are a real hassle to install. Also, they can put force on the barrel, causing accuracy problems. Most shooters will never see these problems. As we've discussed before, if an accuracy-robbing issue takes 1/4 MOA from your potential accuracy, and you, the rifle, the scope and the ammo combined are shooting 3 to 4 MOA (a real-world condition), you'll never notice the difference.

But shooters who depend on MOA or even sub-MOA accuracy will notice.

The originals handguards also don't allow much in the way of accessory addition. Putting a light, laser, or other extras on a regular handguard isn't possible. Free-float handguards allow that by way of one or another attachment method.

Transitional Handguards

There wasn't sufficient room to mount extra gear such as lights, laser, night vision or thermals to rifles. To make room, the military adopted handguards that replaced the originals but had rails on them. This

■ Note the holes in the handguard for mounting accessories. You can see why they were named "Keymod" from the shape.

■ The various Geissele handguards all attach with steel screws into steel anchors.

■ Geissele uses not just anti-rotation tabs but ones with micro-adjustment screws built into them.

■ A reverse pliers is essential for removing the C-clip from the Delta ring assembly. Without it, you risk stabbing yourself in one hand or the other. (You know how the old-timers know this, right?)

■ The reverse pliers open the C-clip when you squeeze the grips.

change involved making the handguards out of curved aluminum pieces and attaching rails to them. The rails slipped into the handguard seats in the Delta ring and front cap.

It was a fast and easy way to have rails, and it's still popular because such a setup can cost less than a full-machined free-float handguard. They also don't require you to strip your upper. You simply remove the old handguards and install these in their place. There are a couple of drawbacks. They are heavier than the plastic ones, as heavy as a free-float, but they don't free float. Not only that, but they also lack heat shields and can get hot. But if you want rails and aren't looking to disassemble and rebuild your rifle, these will get the job done.

An early transitional handguard was one of the first free-float designs. These came as aluminum tubes, with a kinda-sorta barrel nut welded in the back (or pinned, epoxied, whatever). Since there was no reaching down the tube to turn the nut, it featured drilled holes for the gas tube, and you used the holes to turn and tighten the handguard.

The aluminum was heavy, and when it got hot (and it did), it stayed hot for a while. Avoid these if you can, and if you buy an AR as a bargain that has one, be prepared to disassemble it and remove the tube, replacing it with something else. The next step came from competition circles, and that was to bond a carbon-fiber tube to a steel barrel nut of the same design. This innovation was much lighter and didn't get hot. They were very popular, and I've seen photos of SpecOps operators using these handguards. For 3-Gun competition, they were great. But the bearded guys needed to mount lights, lasers, etc., and their armorers had to drill and tap the carbon-fiber tube to bolt things on. This method got old fast, and they asked the people who make custom gear to produce railed handguards, which is how we got the aluminum quad-rail handguards.

The Accessories War

In the beginning, there was nothing. The first step to modern civilization was the quad-rail handguard. It was either a slip-in (using the same attachment system as regular handguards, explained above) or a free-float. The quad-rail handguard has four equally spaced "Picatinny" rails along its length. ("Picatinny" because the Picatinny Arsenal did not invent it. It merely approved it.) You used a clamp to bolt the rail and the light or laser to your rifle. That worked but had problems. The quad rail was big. Without extra-large hands, it was a

■ If reusing the old barrel nut, remove the C-clip so you can remove the waffle spring and Delta ring from the barrel nut. If not reusing it, toss the whole assembly in your parts bin.

handful, could be clumsy, and wasn't ergonomic. It also was a mass of sharp edges. And finally, as if it wasn't bulky enough, the adapters and accessories added more bulk until you had a really portly rifle.

Now, not all quad-rail handguards are fat. Some are slimmer. The LaRue, for instance, is just under two and a half inches across. The Primary Arms quad rail is just over two inches. Half an inch might not seem like much, but you can tell just by picking them up, without even looking, and know which is which.

And then there is Keymod. Keymod machined the base tube of the free-float handguard, so you clamped the accessories into the slots. This meant the accessories had to have the Keymod parts built-in, but that wasn't a real problem. The problem with Keymod is that it didn't work all that well with polymer handguards. So MLok was invented, which did work well with polymer. For a while, the two duked it out, but it looks like MLok has won so far. There may well be another, even better system invented, but MLok seems to be it now.

Upgrading Handguards

If you're going to change from a traditional handguard setup to the new and improved free-float type, you'll have to remove the old handguard. That's the easy part. Then you need to remove the old handguard hardware, the Delta ring assembly. That's not so easy. Here's the process:

Unload the rifle. Install the upper in the Reaction Rod and the vise and remove the flash hider. Take the upper off and put it on the bench. With the Brownells Bench Block, drive out the old front sight pins (I'm assuming you're coming to this from an M4gery or A2/A3/A4 build) and pull the sight off the barrel. If installing a new gas block, remove the old gas tube pin, wrestle the tube out and re-install it in the new block.

Put the upper back on the Reaction Rod in your vise. Unscrew the barrel nut. Now take the barrel out of the upper receiver.

At this point, you have a decision. (Well, if you have a new handguard, the decision has already been made). Should you reuse the old barrel nut or install a new

■ The Midwest Industries free-float handguard uses screws that pass through a tab below the handguard tube.

one? You should install a new one only if the new handguard uses its own. Some free-float handguards before the current generation used the old barrel nut, and for them, you simply remove the C-clip on the back with a pair of reverse pliers. Pull out the waffle spring and the Delta ring, torque the nut back on, time it properly and proceed with the rest of the installation.

If it uses a proprietary nut, toss the old one in the parts bin without taking it apart.

Specialty Handguards

If the specialty handguards all use the same new system to be held in place, and almost all do then use the same method to install them. Free-float handguards for a while used the regular barrel nut, but the latest shift has been to proprietary barrel nuts with proprietary handguards. Why? Weight and bulk. Quad-rail handguards tend to be large. With the shift to Keymod and MLok, handguards can be slimmer, but they can't be made slimmer with the USGI barrel nut.

Like Giessele, Sig, Bravo Company or Midwest Industries, a proprietary handguard includes a proprietary barrel nut. They also have a special wrench that fits that

■ Note the "tuning fork" that Midwest uses to provide an anti-rotation anchor.

■ Note the steel clip just below the rail, the anti-rotation clip on a Bravo handguard.

nut and no other, so don't lose the wrench if you ever want to take the handguard off.

All the current systems work in a similar mechanical fashion.

They all have a barrel nut that does *not* have the collar or notches of the USGI nut. As a result, you don't have to worry about timing the barrel nut to clear the gas tube. (It also makes it easier to install a piston system.)

Various designs present two ways of locking the handguard: cross bolts into steel or cross bolts into aluminum. They use two methods to arrest rotation: handguard tabs or a steel insert that locks onto the upper.

First, we'll install the barrel nut, as they are all the same, and then we'll look at the differences between handguard installation.

Barrel Nut Installation

We'll start with a bare upper receiver. If you have an assembled upper that you're rebuilding, strip it down to the bare receiver, but leave the forward assist and

> *"Like the regular barrel nut, tighten to just short of the torque limit, then loosen, then tighten again to just shy of the final torque, and loosen, then on the third turn, bring it up all the way to the maximum torque value listed. Every maker will have a different limit, so go with their instructions. Don't wing it on this."*

■ The two clamping screws on the BCM KMR handguard screw into the steel anchors on either side of the handguard.

ejection port door installed. Obviously, install those on a bare receiver before installing the handguard.

First, secure the Reaction Rod in the vise and slide the receiver on. Insert the barrel into the receiver, and hand-tighten the barrel nut in place. Once you've checked fit and alignment, tighten the barrel nut. This is one of the few places on an AR that I think Loctite is beneficial. I'd use a small amount of the blue stuff, which can be hand-loosened (well, wrench-loosened, but no heat is needed) when you take it apart. It's essential to read the instructions and tighten the barrel nut to the manufacturer's top torque listing. Since there won't be any restriction on the nut loosening by the gas tube, you want to get the maximum benefit of torque.

Like the regular barrel nut, tighten to just short of the torque limit, then loosen, then tighten again to just shy of the final torque, and loosen, then on the third turn, bring it up all the way to the maximum torque value listed. Every maker will have a different limit, so go with their instructions. Don't wing it on this. "Close enough" isn't good enough in this case.

Handguards by Maker

For handguards with tabs, slide the handguard onto the barrel and receiver (you'll already have installed the gas block and gas tube and made sure they are correctly aligned) and fit the tabs over the receiver. Press the screws through the handguard and tighten to the manufacturer's torque limit. Pay attention here. Handguards like the Geissele that go into a steel anchor have one limit. Steel-on-steel allows for more torque. The ones that go steel-into-aluminum do not. Once they're in place, use paint to mark the ends of the screws as witness marks.

Geissele handguards have an additional locking method. Their tabs have small set screws that fine-tune the alignment of the top rail on the handguard with the top rail of the receiver. Once aligned (a straightedge is the tool here), tighten and paint the set screws.

The Bravo KMR uses a steel slip that fits over the top front face of the upper receiver, underneath the rail. So, as you slide the handguard over the barrel nut, insert the steel clip into the handguard and nestle it over the receiver. The KMR uses a pair of anchors. The screws insert from opposite directions and bear on the anchor of the other.

Midwest Industries takes a slightly different approach, which keeps its handguards a bit slimmer. MI uses a tab on the bottom of the handguard as the screw location and clamping point. This clamp holds — and the screws pass through — a tuning-fork-shaped steel insert. The "tuning fork" legs ride on either side of the upper, and the screws clamp the rear of the handguard tight to the barrel nut.

Handguard Security

If these free-float handguard systems don't have the notched flange of the original barrel nut, how do they keep the handguard from turning? In addition to handguard clamping force on the proprietary barrel nut, those screws also pass through grooves machined into the nut. The grooves prevent the forward movement of the handguard. The clamping compresses the barrel nut onto the receiver threads. The anti-rotation tabs or inserts prevent rotation, and the assemblage is self-reinforcing to resist rotation.

Modern Retro

Is "modern retro" even a thing? OK, let's call it a modern clone. If you want to be handling the same M16A3 that you see used overseas by USMC riflemen, then you need to be tracking down a Knight's handguard. (If you're a movie buff, this is the same thing carried in *Battle Los Angeles*.) The Knight's doesn't free-float, which is OK with the USMC. It also provides tension on the receiver and handguard, preventing rattle, and probably providing slightly more stiffness to the setup for added accuracy.

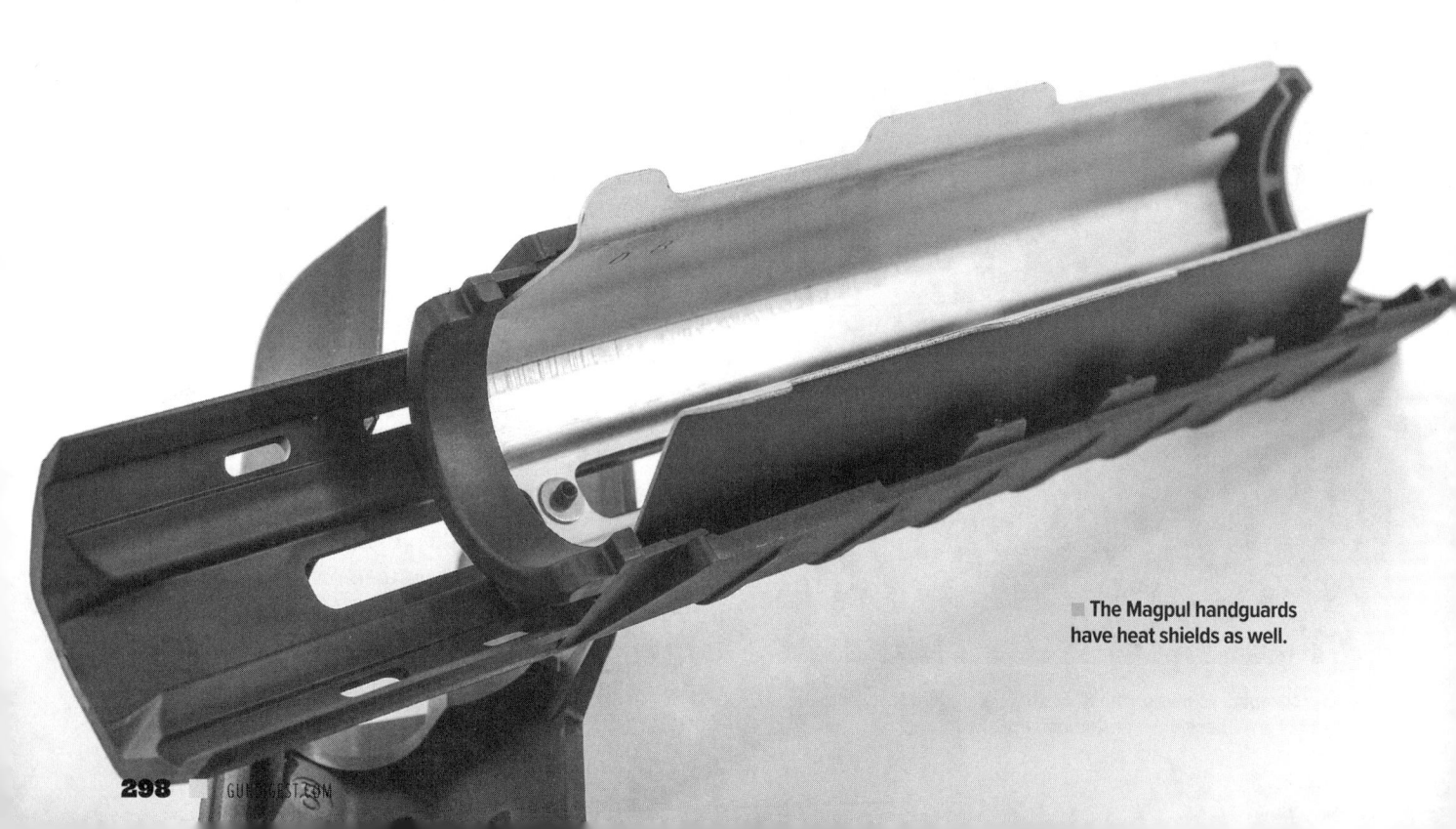

■ The Magpul handguards have heat shields as well.

■ If you want to build a modern retro-clone (is that even a thing?) like the USMC M16A3/4, then you need to be using a Knight's handguard.

■ With all the talk of free-float handguards, some people just want something better than USGI. This Magpul MOE serves the purpose, is easy to install and is more comfortable too.

Modern Non-Free-float

And if you want something better, but not the expense of a free-float handguard, track down something Magpul. The MOE, for instance, provides a plastic feel and cool heat shields, MLok slots, and drops right in, in place of your original USGI handguards.

They come in all sizes and colors and are so common that no one will notice except to say "Nice Magpuls." ■

■ One advantage of the SBR is that it's handy in close quarters. You give up some velocity, however.

19
Pistols, Braces and SBRs

■ A rifle or carbine with a stock and a barrel shorter than 16 inches is an SBR or short-barreled rifle. It requires special paperwork for you to own it.

What's an SBR, how do you legally own one, and why would you want one? An SBR is a creation of the National Firearms Act of 1934, where short-barreled rifles (SBRs) — includes short shotguns — were defined and taxed. Simply put, if it has a barrel shorter than 16 inches, it's an SBR, and it needs to have the proper paperwork to be lawfully possessed.

That is unless it's a handgun, lacking a stock, in which case it's covered by federal and local laws concerning handguns. (Some states don't see it that way and don't allow AR-15 pistols. We should not be surprised.)

So, let's go over the process paperwork because, as far as building is concerned, an SBR is the same as a carbine or rifle, and a pistol is just like an SBR.

SBR

The SBR starts with Form 1 (Form 4 is the one you fill out to buy an existing SBR from an FFL). Form 1 is the "mother may I" document you must complete to get approval. The form requires fingerprints (the ATF will only accept an FBI print card). You'll need to fill out the form, get the fingerprints, write a check for $200 (the tax) and send it off. A few tips: the ATF will cash your check the moment it hits someone's desk. That doesn't mean you have been approved. If it turns out there is some reason you're turned down, the ATF will issue a refund.

Do not call the ATF to "See how your application is doing." Applications get stacked on the desk of the examiners, who grind through the stacks in the order they arrive. If you call, someone must stop what they're doing, figure out which examiner has your form, walk over, paw through the stack to see how far down it is, return and answer your question. While that is going on, other work doesn't get done.

Every time you or someone else calls, every application gets delayed by another five minutes.

Your SBR receiver must be engraved with the maker's name, city and state. If that is you, then your name gets engraved. If you're buying one (sitting on the shelf in your local gun shop, you can't even shoot it until you get approved), the maker already marked it, so you get to skip that part. Engraving is fast and straightforward, but don't do it until you have approval. Once approved, fill out the engraver's form, enclose a check, ship it off, and a week later, it's engraved.

Be patient. You've sent your application in, but that doesn't mean you can start building it. In fact, you shouldn't even have all the parts on hand to build until you get approval. Oh, you can have most of the parts, and you'll need the lower because you'll have to provide the serial number. But don't have the barrel on hand. Yes, you've applied,

■ SBRs can be accurate. It depends on barrel quality, the ammunition and the shooter's skill level.

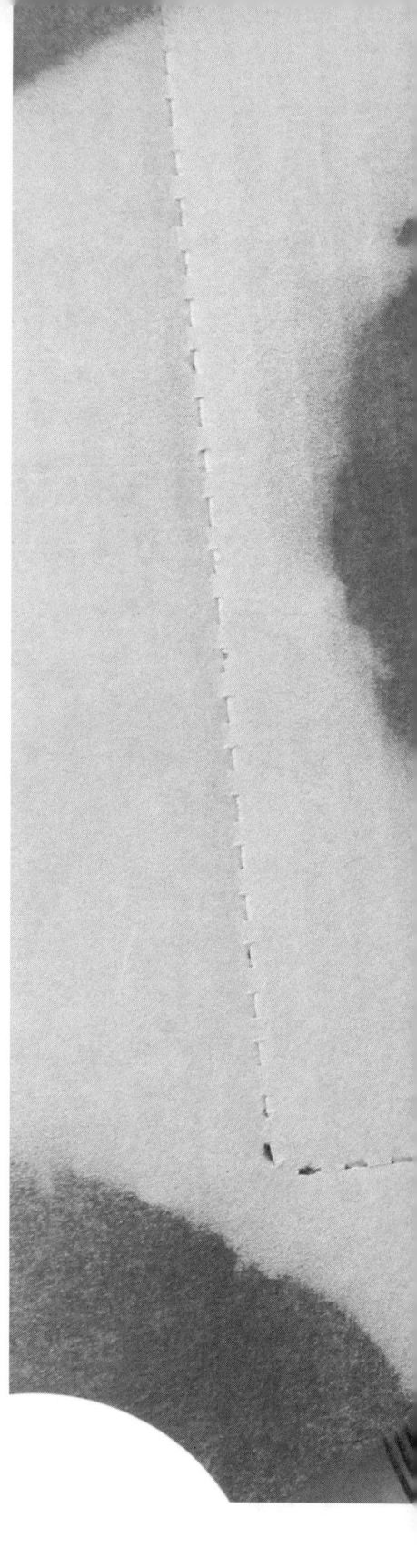

> "Your SBR receiver must be engraved with the maker's name, city and state. If that is you, then your name gets engraved. If you're buying one (sitting on the shelf in your local gun shop, you can't even shoot it until you get approved), the maker already marked it, so you get to skip that part."

but you don't have approval, and having all the parts on hand to build an SBR means that you have an SBR on hand without approval. The whole process takes months, so waiting a few more days for the barrel to arrive isn't going to kill you.

Once the ATF approves your form (that's the tax stamp applied to your application that everyone talks about), you can build your SBR from a box of parts. Or you can take an existing rifle or carbine and change the barrel. But remember, the SBR is *the serial numbered lower* listed on the form, and no other. This situation requires some explaining to police departments, curiously enough. Just because you have the approval to make an SBR doesn't

CHAPTER 19 – PISTOLS, BRACES AND SBRS   **303**

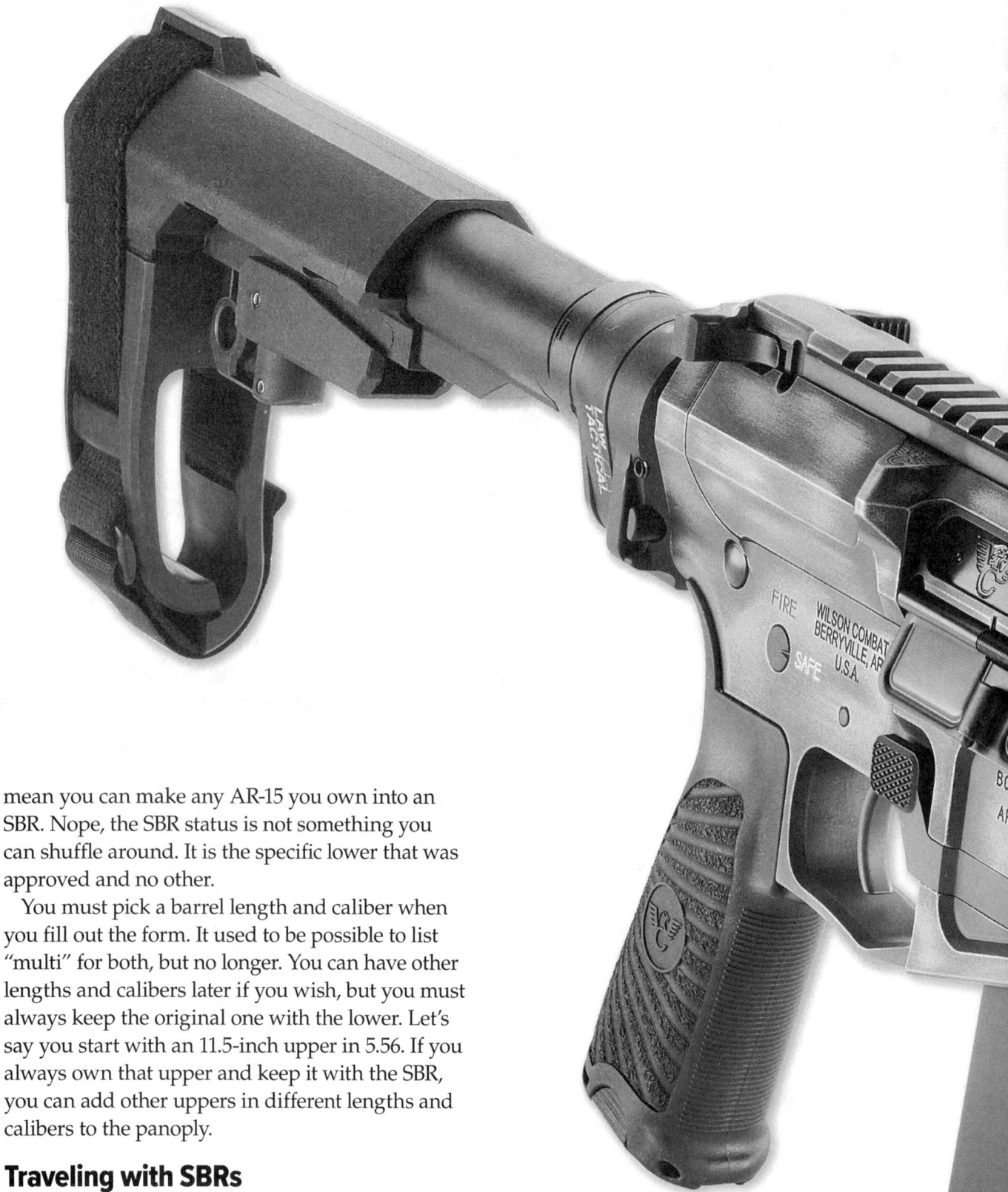

mean you can make any AR-15 you own into an SBR. Nope, the SBR status is not something you can shuffle around. It is the specific lower that was approved and no other.

You must pick a barrel length and caliber when you fill out the form. It used to be possible to list "multi" for both, but no longer. You can have other lengths and calibers later if you wish, but you must always keep the original one with the lower. Let's say you start with an 11.5-inch upper in 5.56. If you always own that upper and keep it with the SBR, you can add other uppers in different lengths and calibers to the panoply.

Traveling with SBRs

Since the SBR is special, it stands to reason that traveling with one would also be … "special." Within your home state, assuming an SBR is legal, you don't have any extra paperwork. Oh, I'd personally avoid big cities not so much for the danger but the possible local restrictions that they might have enacted. Going across state lines is another matter. You must fill out an ATF Form 5320.20 to cross state lines. As long as where you are going allows SBRs, you may travel to that state. Again, personally, I'd try to avoid states with state law restrictions on SBRs. Yes, your travel is protected by FOPA/86, but that hasn't stopped some jurisdictions from prosecuting stranded airline passengers or others under state law — people who found themselves there with a "prohibited" firearm.

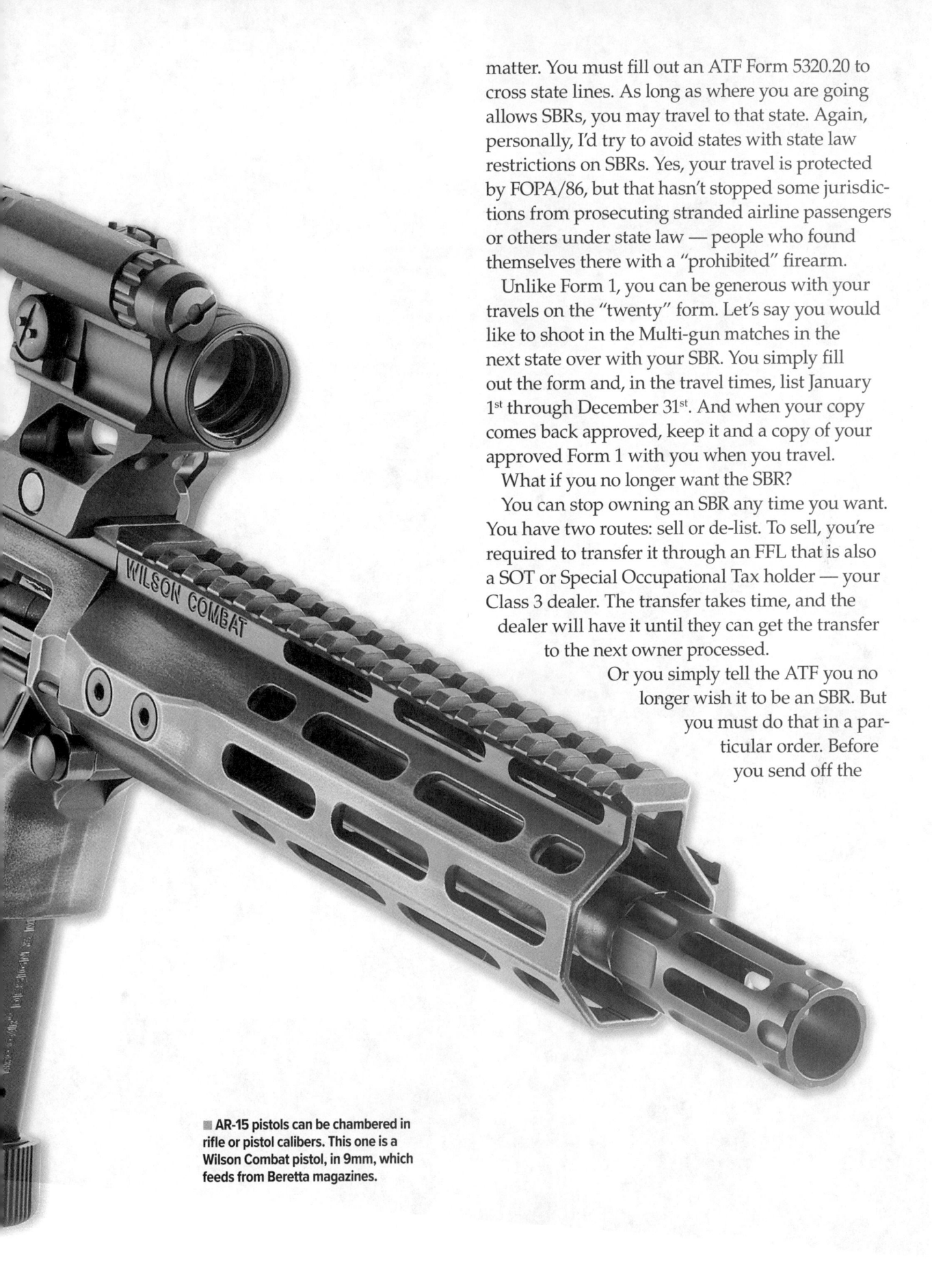

Unlike Form 1, you can be generous with your travels on the "twenty" form. Let's say you would like to shoot in the Multi-gun matches in the next state over with your SBR. You simply fill out the form and, in the travel times, list January 1st through December 31st. And when your copy comes back approved, keep it and a copy of your approved Form 1 with you when you travel.

What if you no longer want the SBR?

You can stop owning an SBR any time you want. You have two routes: sell or de-list. To sell, you're required to transfer it through an FFL that is also a SOT or Special Occupational Tax holder — your Class 3 dealer. The transfer takes time, and the dealer will have it until they can get the transfer to the next owner processed.

Or you simply tell the ATF you no longer wish it to be an SBR. But you must do that in a particular order. Before you send off the

■ AR-15 pistols can be chambered in rifle or pistol calibers. This one is a Wilson Combat pistol, in 9mm, which feeds from Beretta magazines.

letter, remove the upper and sell it, or sell the barrel and re-barrel the rifle to at least 16 inches long. Then send the letter. Why? As soon as the ATF receives the letter, you no longer have the approval to own an SBR, and the agency won't send you a letter saying they got it. So, you could possess an SBR but have lost approval, thus violating the law.

Oh, and at no time in any of this will you get a refund of your $200 transfer tax payment.

AR-15 Pistols

Like the SBR, building a pistol is simply doing all the other steps but making sure your shorter-barrel AR, which will be picky, is reliable.

Pistols are primarily covered under state law. If it isn't an SBR or a rifle, and you satisfy the federal requirements for purchasing a handgun; the ATF doesn't' care much about your AR-15 pistol. But the state and maybe even the city you live in might.

To build an AR-15 pistol, start with a bare lower. That is, one that has not had a stock on it. Lacking a stock, it is an "other" or an unspecified firearm. When it gets a stock, then it becomes a rifle or SBR, not a pistol. At the present time, Arm braces are not considered stocks, and as such, don't make a pistol into an SBR. That may change, even days or weeks after I've sent in this book before it reaches your hands. So, if the law has changed, the law has changed.

Travel with AR-15 pistols

Like SBRs, AR-15 pistols must be legal where you're traveling to. It would be good for it to be legal in the states in-between, but FOPA/86 should protect you there. Unlike the SBR, there is no 5320.20 form to fill out, so the feds don't care: to them, it is (at the present time) just like you were driving from Kansas to Arizona with your .38 Special revolver in the trunk.

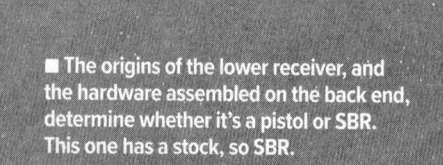

■ The origins of the lower receiver, and the hardware assembled on the back end, determine whether it's a pistol or SBR. This one has a stock, so SBR.

Mix' n Match

OK, you're a serious AR-15 assembler for fun, competition, hunting and defense — all the aspects. You own an AR-15 rifle, carbine, SBR and pistol and have spare parts for them — or some combination of those. Be careful. Let's say you own a rifle and a pistol. Don't let the pistol upper get assembled on the rifle lower because that's an SBR.

The messy part comes when you start accumulating spares and parts. For example, let's say there was a great deal at the gun show on an upper for your pistol. You bought a box of stuff at an estate sale, and there was an AR-15 stock assembly in there. The local ye olde *gonne shoppe* had a sale, and you picked up a bare AR-15 lower for half-price. You realize that you now have all the parts for an SBR, no Form 1, and the parts are "unassigned."

When you bought the pistol upper, it should have gone into the dedicated gun case for your pistol and stayed there. You "assigned" it to the pistol. And similarly with the other parts. When you got the other parts, you should have assigned them to a project. Box them up. Label the box. Keep like with like. Don't be in the position of letting someone else put you in a sticky spot. "That bare receiver? That's a project for an M4gery build; that's why it has the 16-inch barrel in the box with it." And so on with the other parts.

Why SBRs and Pistols?

The shorter barrel makes the firearm handier, lighter and more manageable. There are also legal aspects. In many jurisdictions, a "carry permit," or a license to carry a concealed weapon, is a "pistol" permit. Except for knives or pepper spray in some states, you can't carry anything else if you have a CCW/CPL. Not a rifle, not a shotgun. So, traveling with a rifle in the car under your CCW/CPL isn't kosher. It might even be expressly against the law. A pistol, however, even if it's an AR-15 pistol, is a pistol.

In many jurisdictions, the DNR has more arrest purview than do the local police. And if you're in the woods with a CPL in your wallet but are carrying a rifle, the DNR is going to view that with suspicion. An AR-15 pistol is, as I've said, a pistol.

The DNR might still be suspicious, but it isn't a slam-dunk.

There is a cost, however. The shorter barrel means more muzzle blast and less velocity. But that is a cost a lot of shooters are willing to pay.

■ **This Daniel Defense PDW (Personal Defense Weapon)** has an arm brace on the back, making it a pistol. The suppressor is also a Daniel Defense model.

20
Ammunition and Muzzle Devices

As mentioned earlier, there is a difference between .223 and 5.56 ammunition. The difference doesn't matter if your rifle has a confirmed 5.56 leade or was reamed with the M-guns reamer. If you haven't checked or seen loose primers when shooting, then get it checked. And corrected.

What does matter? Bullet weight, bullet material, case material, caliber, pressure and the magazines you feed rounds from.

We've covered bullet weight in the twist section, but a quick reminder: all-copper bullets are longer for any given weight and thus need a faster twist. Magazines we've also covered, so let's jump into

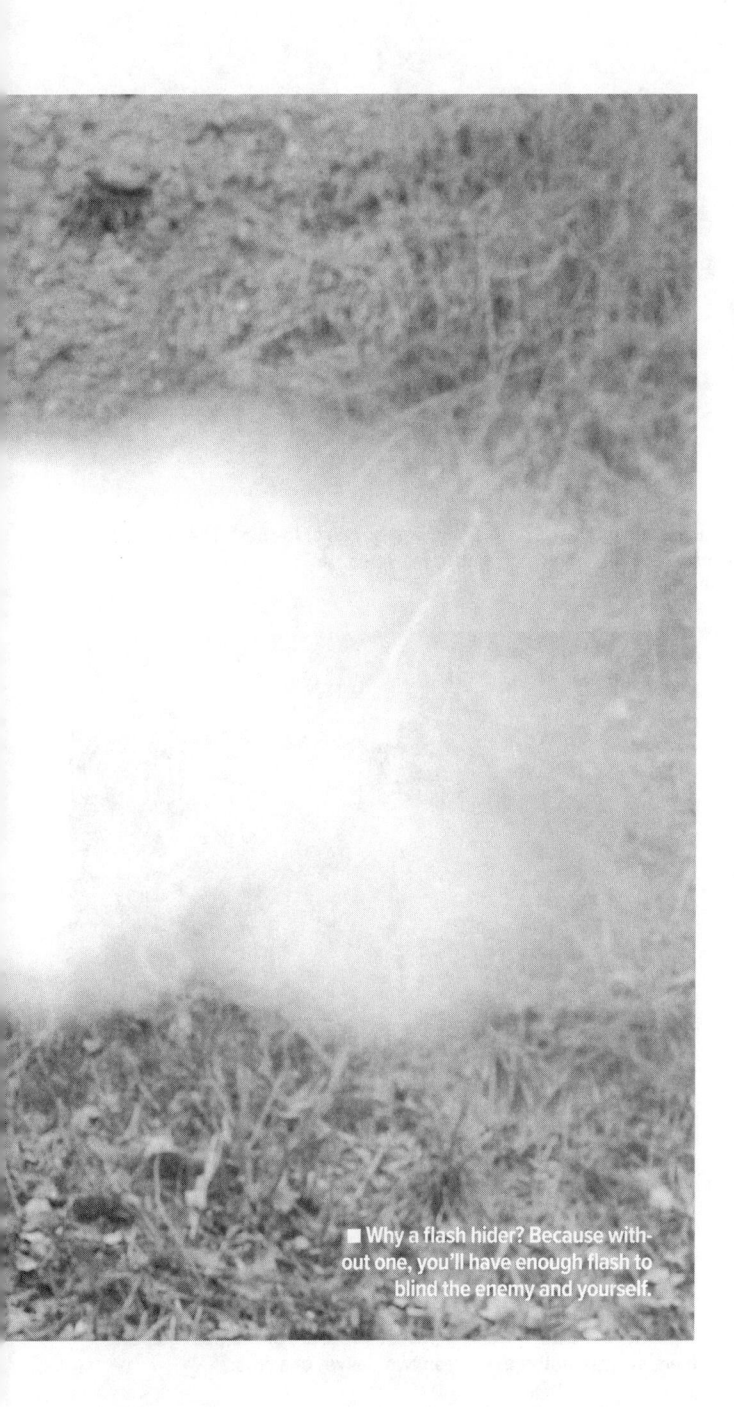

■ Why a flash hider? Because without one, you'll have enough flash to blind the enemy and yourself.

caliber and case material. Case material first.

Is Steel Safe?

In the old days, we worried a lot about steel-cased ammo. After all, there's a reason we only made steel-cased ammo during WWII, when there was a world war on. The Soviets produced ammunition

■ It's your AR-15, so inspect the ammunition that goes into it. At first glance, the round on the right might seem OK, but it's clearly bent. It will jam in the chamber, require a clearance drill and cause you headaches.

■ The variety of flash hiders and brakes is immense. On the right is an A2, which is very good. Next is a Smith Vortex, one of the best. The first comp is the author's design, very effective, if simple. Next are various multi-port brakes, some with angled venting or top vents.

with steel cases for two reasons: their rifles were designed for it, and they had more steel than copper. Basically, steel cases have less flexibility than copper. When they expand, they don't spring back as much. They also drag more coming out. So, the Soviets used lacquer on cases or just galvanized them.

That ammo came over here to the U.S., and people worry. Today, the process has been updated, and now you can see polymer-coated cases. Basically, plastic is sprayed on and allowed to cure.

The worry is twofold: the lacquer or polymer will build up in the chamber, the extractor will be stressed, and perhaps break.

I can tell you that lacquer can be a problem. However, you'd have to shoot in a week-long class with a full day of shooting each day and get the gun really hot. Then let a chambered round back in the hot barrel. It will weld itself to the chamber and not come out. If you're going to run your gun that hot, lacquer isn't for you. From what I've heard, the polymer does better, but there are still limits, I suspect.

As far as the steel cases stressing extractors, I haven't heard any good, solid testing or reports on that happening. AR-15 extractors break, and sometimes for no apparent reason. I don't know of anyone who has put enough rounds through enough guns, with both brass and steel, to be able to report on the subject. Basically, I don't worry about it.

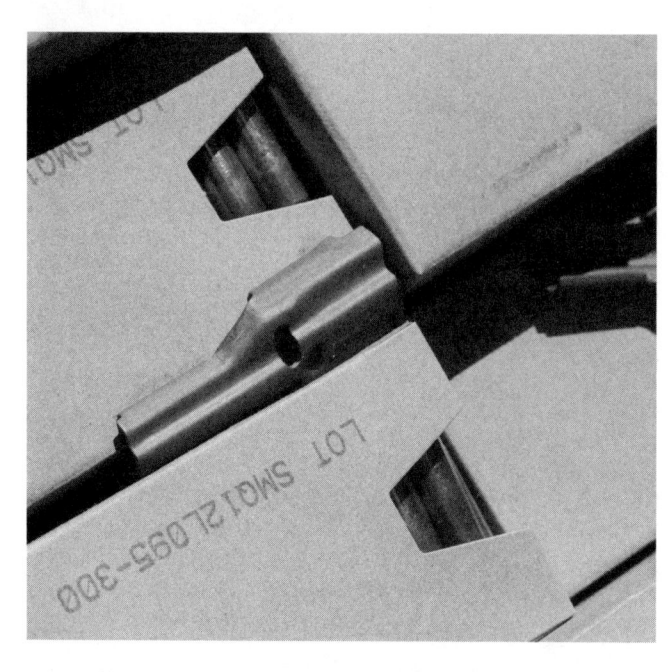

■ The military doesn't care about flashy packaging or bright colors on ammo boxes. Plain cardboard, pasteboard, and ammo on strippers with "spoons" are what it wants. Spoons? Those are the stripper guides; there's one right there between two sleeves of ammo.

Calibers

Mixing up ammo is a bad thing. Not the 223/5.56 one, but mixing .300 Blackout with 5.56, for example. A 6.8 Remington SPC cartridge looks enough like a 223/5.56 round that you could pick one up and stuff it in a magazine, but it will wedge in a 5.56 chamber before it gets halfway in.

5.56x45mm Versus .223 Rem.

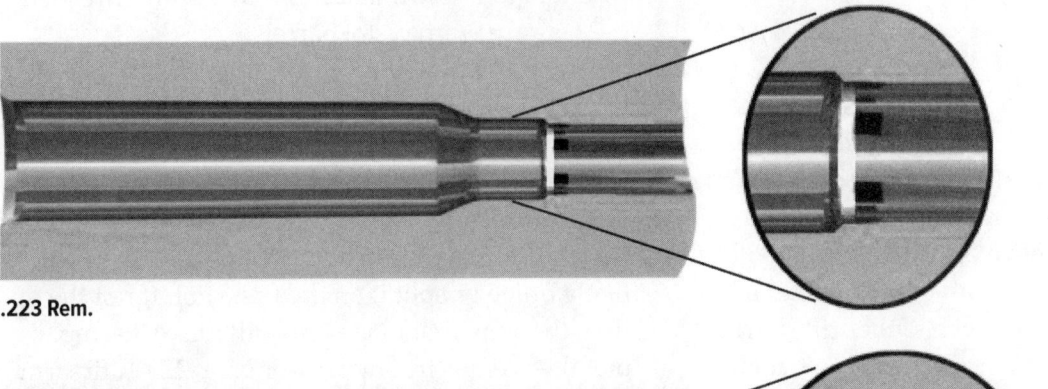

.223 Rem.

Freebore .224 Dia.
Freebore Length
.025 Inches

Throat Angle
3 Degrees 10 Minutes
36 Seconds

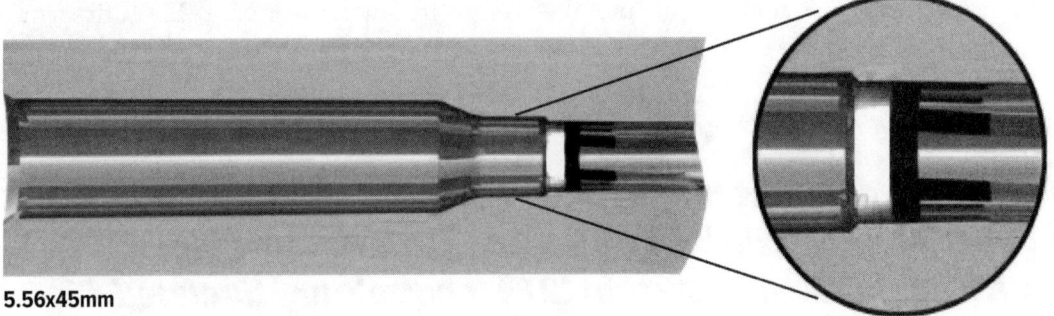

5.56x45mm

Freebore .226 Dia.
Freebore Length
.059 Inches

Throat Angle
1 Degree 13 Minutes
20 Seconds

■ Both of these popular calibers feature a .224-inch-diameter bullet and an identical overall length. However, the throat length for 5.56x45mm is longer than that of .223 Rem. As a result, you can safely shoot .223 ammunition in a 5.56 chamber, but not 5.56 in a .223 platform, as it can result in excessive pressures upon ignition.

■ There is a difference between .223 and 5.56 ammunition, and there is a difference between the chambers for them. Make sure of what you have.

Chamber Pressures

Pressure is part of the "popped primer" problem, and while that is mostly a leade problem, pressure does play a role. The pressure ceilings for various loadings to be found in the .223/5.56 universe are:
- .223 Remington . . . . .55,000 PSI
- M193 5.56x45 . . . . .55,000 PSI
- Mk 262 Mod 1 . . . . .58,000 PSI
- M855 "green tip" . . . . .58,000 PSI
- M855A1 . . . . 64,000 PSI

The bump up in pressure from .223/M193 to Mk 262/M855 ammo is only five percent. And that is the allowed ceiling. I have had various factory ammunition lots pressure-tested, and I've encountered some that posted pressure only in the mid-to-upper-40,000 PSI range. Yes, they made the required velocity but did so at 46,000 PSI to 49,000 PSI. If you're an ammo maker and meet the specified velocity while still below the pressure ceiling, you stop. You don't get paid more for ammo that goes faster, and you're saving money on powder. Do you think it doesn't matter? A million rounds of 5.56 are going to use something like 13,000 pounds of powder. If powder costs you $12 a pound, that's $162,000 in powder. A one-percent savings nets you $1,620, which is not

CHAPTER 20 – AMMUNITION AND MUZZLE DEVICES ■ **313**

nothing. Keep that in mind when loading your own ammo.

Flash Hiders and Brakes

Barrels are threaded for flash hiders and other devices. The thread pitch for each caliber/bore diameter is different, and for a good reason. Well, mostly different. An A1 or A2 flash hider, and anything else that goes onto a .223/5.56 barrel, will be threaded ½-28. That is half an inch diameter and 28 threads to the running inch. Other rifle barrels have different thread pitches, so you can't, for example, fit your 5.56 suppressor or muzzle brake on a 6mm, 6.5 or .30-caliber barrel. However, it's essential to know that .22 LR barrels are threaded ½-28, as are 9mm pistol barrels.

You must know this.

You must pay attention to this.

Because if you don't, you can have an expensive bad day.

A rimfire suppressor will, then, fit onto a 5.56 barrel. It will not be at all up to the task. You will likely bulge or split it on the first shot. If not the first, then the first magazine will make it scrap metal. A centerfire suppressor on a .22 LR firearm will quickly get clogged with lead and powder,

"Other rifle barrels have different thread pitches, so you can't, for example, fit your 5.56 suppressor or muzzle brake on a 6mm, 6.5 or .30-caliber barrel. However, it's essential to know that .22 LR barrels are threaded ½-28, as are 9mm pistol barrels. You must know this. You must pay attention to this. Because if you don't, you can have an expensive bad day."

■ The Surefire suppressor mount is also a flash hider. Surefire makes a Warcomp, which adds ports on top to decrease muzzle rise, one of the few that does an excellent job of both flash and recoil reduction.

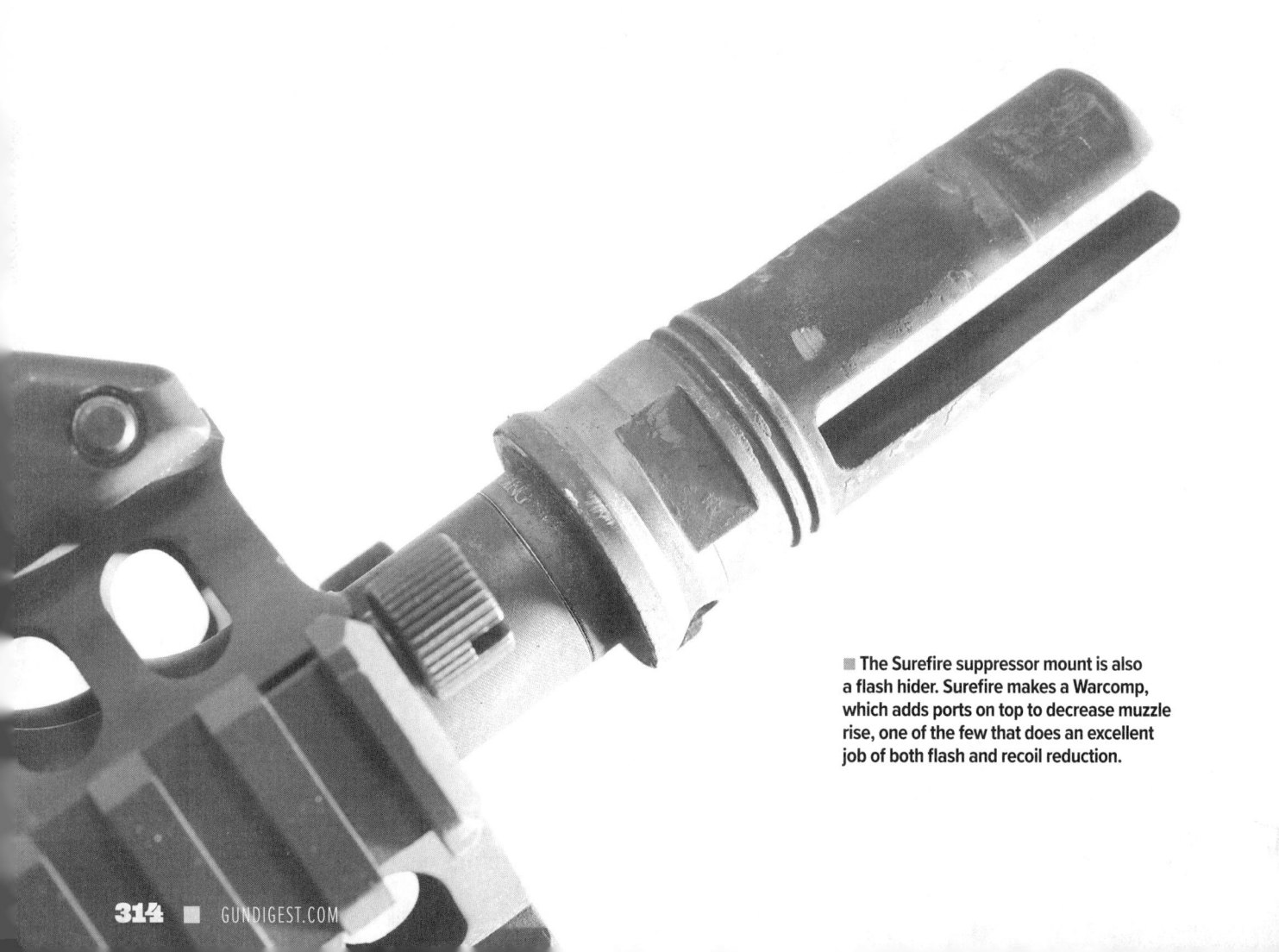

■ When installing a suppressor, it's vitally important to install it straight. You can check this with an alignment gauge, which is a straight steel rod. Emphasis on "straight" and "steel."

■ The Noveske KX3 dampens flash and diverts muzzle blast downrange. It's not a suppressor, but it does ease the hit on your ears. Not hearing-safe, but still more comfortable to shoot.

and you will not be able to clean it out. The 9mm? A 9mm suppressor on a 5.56 rifle might survive longer than the rimfire one did, but it will suffer. And if you happen to put a 5.56 suppressor onto a 9mm, then expensive repairs will await you.

All this goes for muzzle brakes as well. Make sure the thread pitch of the device you're installing is not just "it fits" but also "It is proper." ■

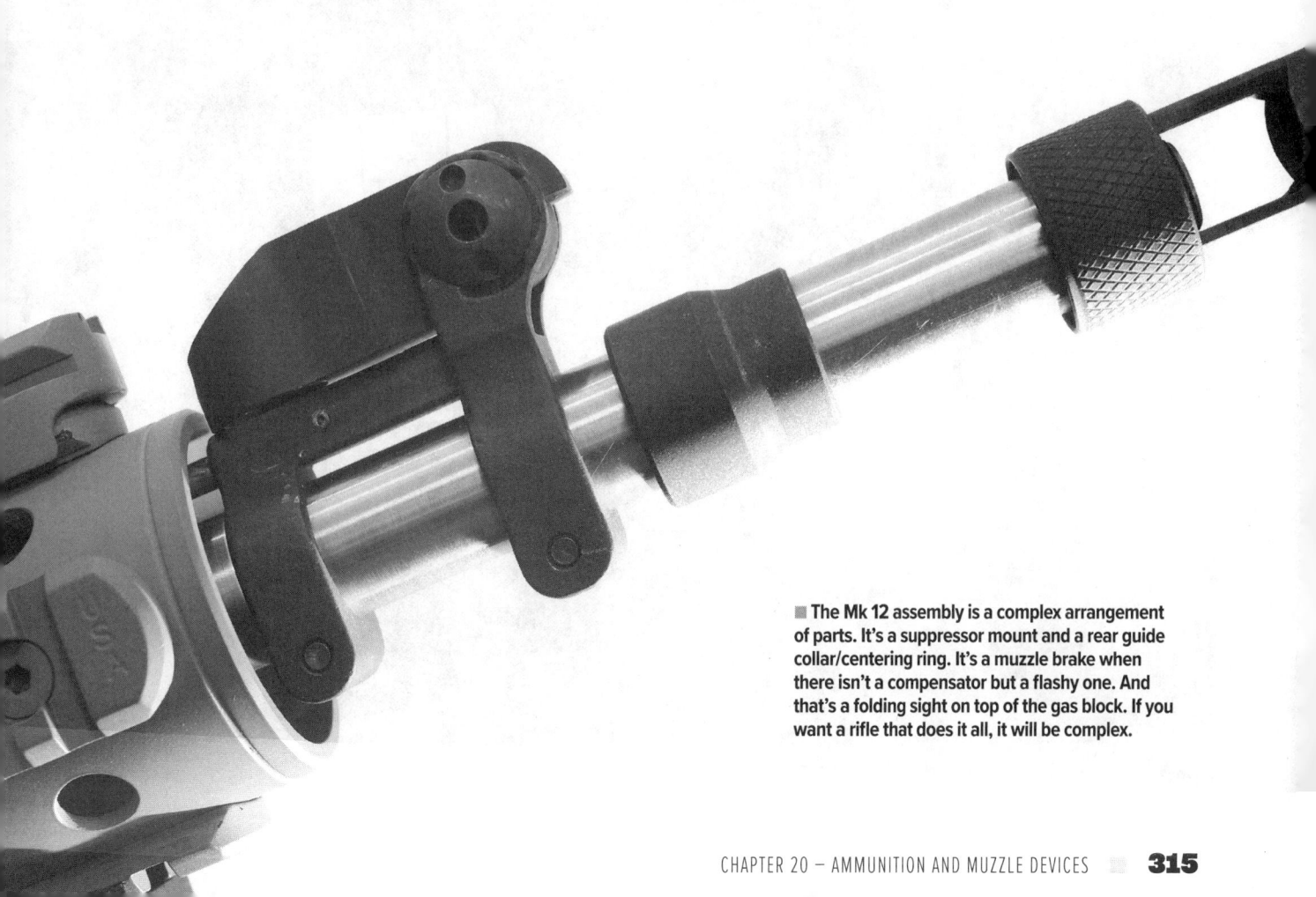

■ The Mk 12 assembly is a complex arrangement of parts. It's a suppressor mount and a rear guide collar/centering ring. It's a muzzle brake when there isn't a compensator but a flashy one. And that's a folding sight on top of the gas block. If you want a rifle that does it all, it will be complex.

CHAPTER 20 – AMMUNITION AND MUZZLE DEVICES

21

Build Sequence

■ Once you've built or bought your AR-15, test it and check to make sure everything is tight, correct and that it's zeroed. Then you can do the painting and have it ready for the next match.

Many new AR-15 owners will be rebuilding an existing rifle. They will want to change this or that or upgrade something. But there is a subset of AR-15 owners with a box of parts and the burning desire to assemble a rifle. They might already own an AR-15, but they want a different one. (As I've said before, this is America. You have that right.) What to do? Well, the various steps have been detailed before, but now that you know how those steps go, we'll put them in sequence.

Parts Check

This should be obvious, but even the best of us sometimes get caught unawares. Inspect all the parts and count them out. If they are all there, great. If something is missing, contact whoever shipped it. Once you know the parts are all accounted for, you can proceed. If something is missing later, you know it was there when you started.

The Sequence

Start with the lower. Why? Because you need to start someplace, and a finished lower is a home for an already finished upper if you happen to have one. And the lower is the firearm, so most people who build will have already completed uppers on hand, as those are "just parts" and can be assembled any time.

Install the selector and pistol grip.

The pistol grip is like a blocking lever. You'll find it handy when installing and tightening the castle nut. It's also a valuable handle to have when juggling the lower into position for the next installation step. The selector is held in by the pistol grip, so that must also be done now.

Install the rear takedown pin, spring and plunger, buffer tube and stock. Why? You'll find that having the stock on makes the following steps easier. Install the buffer spring and buffer because it'll need it sooner or later, and you might as well do it now. What buffer weight? It doesn't matter. For a rifle, use the one-and-only rifle buffer. If a carbine or pistol, then whatever buffer you have — you'll be testing and maybe replacing it later anyway.

Next, install the front takedown pin, magazine catch and bolt stop. These three can be done in any order in this step, but I like to install the bolt hold-open last simply because it's a bit trickier to do, and by the time I've done the other steps, I'm back in the groove of putting things into or onto an AR-15.

Next up, install the fire control system. This system is the hammer, trigger, disconnector, and these parts have to be checked and the disconnector timed if need be. If you must remove the selector to weasel the trigger into place, then do that.

The upper is next.

If unassembled, assemble the bolt and carrier. Check the gas ring count and conduct the "stand on its head" test.

First, if the bolt and carrier are already assembled, install the forward assist and then the ejection port door. From there, things become slightly complicated.

If you're using a standard barrel with USGI handguards and sight system, use your clamshell or Reaction Rod, install the barrel and time the barrel nut. Thread the gas tube into the upper, rotate it to align it, push it into the front sight A-frame, and pin it in place. Check the gas tube fit to the carrier, and bend to fit if needed. Once fit, install the handguards, charging handle and bolt/carrier assembly, and do the non-firing checklist and function test.

If your barrel is not a USGI type, then install the barrel in the upper. Install and align the gas block and secure it in place. Install the gas tube. (The gas tube can be installed in the gas block first, but some prefer to do these as separate operations.) Check the gas tube fit on the carrier.

Install your free-float handguard.

Now, if the barrel came without a flash hider, install it or a muzzle brake or suppressor mount. If it has something installed and you're happy with it, then you're done. If it has one and you want something else, take the old one off and install the new one.

In the case of a muzzle brake or suppressor, check the alignment with an alignment rod.

Install the sights, be they irons, red-dot or magnifying optics.

Do the non-firing function test.

Plan your range trip.

Attaching slings or other goodies and painting-in parts and trajectory markings come after you've completed a test-fire session at the range to your satisfaction. Once all that is done, put it in the rack, safe or other storage location, and plan on the next one.

YOUR GUIDE TO LONG RANGE RIFLE SHOOTING
EXCELLENCE!

GunDigest PRESENTS

Precision Rifle Marksmanship: The Fundamentals

A Marine Sniper's Guide to Long Range Shooting

by Frank Galli — SNIPER'S HIDE

From the first steps to the finer points of long range rifle shooting, author and retired Marine Scout Sniper Frank Galli covers all the details in *Precision Rifle Marksmanship: The Fundamentals.*

Galli, a full-time shooting instructor, breaks down the pursuit of accuracy in simple terms, following a logical order of discipline from shooter to target, the same way he teaches students on the firing line. Learn about these points from a true professional!

- Understanding the Basics of Marksmanship
- Preparing a New Precision Rifle for the Range
- Expert Advice on Buying the Right Scope
- Detailed Tips for Reading the Wind
- Internal and External Ballistics, Explained
- And Much, Much More!

Order online at **GunDigestStore.com** or call **920.471.4522**
Product No. R8086

The Book That Can Save Your Life!

One of firearms trainer Massad Ayoob's most popular books delivers a lifetime of expertise in how to defend yourself and loved ones in life-threatening situations. This revised and expanded 7th edition of *Combat Handgunnery* arms you with knowledge to:

- Choose the right handgun
- Pick the best holster for concealed carry
- Assess the many self-defense ammo choices
- Improve your shooting skills
- Understand CQB fighting techniques

The best defense is being prepared!

$29.99

PRODUCT NO. R8096

Order online at GunDigestStore.com or call 920.471.4522

The NEW Bible on Rimfire Rifles!

Gun Digest PRESENTS

RIMFIRE REVOLUTION
A COMPLETE GUIDE TO MODERN .22 RIFLES

MICHAEL R. SHEA

Author and rimfire rifle expert Mike Shea takes you on a deep dive into the world of rifles from Anshütz, Bergara, CZ, Ruger, Sako, Tikka, Savage, Volquartsen, Vudoo, RimX, and more!

Inside this full-color, 272-page must-have book:
- Keys to maximum rifle accuracy
- How ammo from CCI, Lapua, and ELEY is made
- Matching the right ammo to your rifle

You'll get further insights from Q&As with Mike Bush of Vudoo, 22Plinkster, Olympic gold medalists, Anschütz USA, the inventor of 17HMR and other industry icons!

$34.99
Product No. R8113

Order online at **GunDigestStore.com/rimfire/**
Or call **920.471.4522**   **FREE SHIPPING** On Orders over $59!